teacher's edition

EXPLORING MUSIC 6

Eunice Boardman • Beth Landis

Consultants:

Milton Babbitt • Bjornar Bergethon •
Robert W. Buggert • Chou Wen-chung •
Harry Coopersmith • Lucrecia R. Kasilag •
Egon Kraus • Alan Lomax •
Kurt Miller • Juan Orrego-Salas •
Virginia Stroh Red • Henrietta Yurchenco

HOLT, RINEHART AND WINSTON, INC., New York

CONTENTS

ii

ACKNOWLEDGMENTS

Grateful acknowledgment is given to the following authors and publishers:

J. Curwen & Sons Limited for "Alleluia," English translation by W. H. Draper from *School Worship*, and "The Purple Bamboo" from *Folksongs of China*. Used by permission of J. Curwen & Sons Limited, London, England.

Doubleday & Company, Inc. for "Little Gray Cuckoo," from *An Introduction to Haiku* by Harold G. Henderson. Copyright © by Harold G. Henderson. Reprinted by permission of Doubleday & Company, Inc.

Carl Gehrmans Musikförlag for "All Hail, Fridolin" by Jean Sibelius, published by Carl Gehrmans Musikförlag, Stockholm, Sweden. Used by permission.

Hallmark Cards for haiku poetry, "Snow" and "Waterfowl." Reproduced through the courtesy of Hallmark Cards, Incorporated, and Hokuseido Press.

Wilhelm Hansen Musik-Forlag for "My Little Bird, Where Do You Fly?" Copyright © 1917 and 1944 by Wilhelm Hansen Musik-Forlag, Copenhagen, Denmark. Used by permission of the publishers.

Hughes A'I Fab for the melody to "Migildi Magildi," copyright by Hughes A'I Fab, Wrexham, North Wales. Used by permission.

Irmãos Vitale S/A., Sao Paulo, Brazil for the musical quotes from the piano score of "Dansa" from *Bachianas Brasileiras, No. 4* by H. Villa-Lobos. Copyright 1941 by H. Villa-Lobos.

Oak Publications for "Le premier mois d'l'année," traditional French folk song, English words by Alan Mills, copyright 1963 by Oak Publications. Reprinted from the book *Favorite French Folk Songs* by Alan Mills.

Oxford University Press for the English words by Jack Dobbs to "Migildi, Magildi," and the English words by Elizabeth Fiske to "The Trout," both from *The Oxford School Music Books*, copyright by Oxford University Press, London, England. Used by permission.

Oxford University Press for "Ev'ry Night When the Sun Goes In" from *Folk Songs from the Southern Appalachians*, copyright 1917 by Oxford University Press, London, England. Used by permission.

C. F. Peters Corporation for the musical quote from "Peasant Dance for Norwegian Fiddle" (*Slatter*, No. 4) transcribed by John Halvorsen, reprinted by permission of C. F. Peters Corporation, 373 Park Avenue South, New York, New York 10016, publishers of the complete work.

Random House, Inc., Alfred A. Knopf, Inc. for "Skylark." Reprinted by permission of the publisher from *A Pepper Pod* by Kenneth Yasuda. Copyright, 1946 by Alfred A. Knopf, Inc.

M. Ring, 4 Sharnolds, Boughton Lane, Kent, England for "Hungarian Round" by Betty Askwith from the *Kent County Song Book*.

G. Schirmer for "I Wonder As I Wander" by John Jacob Niles, copyright 1934 and 1962 by G. Schirmer, Inc. Used by permission.

G. Schirmer for "The Home Road" by John Alden Carpenter, copyright by G. Schirmer, Inc. Used by permission.

G. Schirmer for the musical quotes from the *Fourth String Quartet, Opus 37*, by Arnold Schoenberg. Copyright, 1939, by G. Schirmer, Inc. International copyright secured.

Schocken Books for "Tum Balalyka," reprinted by permission of Schocken Books, Inc. from *A Treasury of Jewish Folksong* by Ruth Rubin, copyright 1950 by Schocken Books, Inc., New York.

Silliman Music Foundation, Inc. for "Si Pilemon" from *Folksongs of the Visayas, Volume I*, copyright 1957 by the Silliman Music Foundation, Inc., Dumaguete City, Philippines. Used by permission.

Silver Burdett Company for "Infant Jesus, King of Glory" from *Music from Shore to Shore*, © 1956, Silver Burdett Company. Used by permission.

Janet E. Tobitt for "Peace of the River" from *The Ditty Bag*. Used by permission.

EXPLORING MUSIC: A CHALLENGE TO THE TEACHER

TO HELP THE CHILD DISCOVER THAT

music is part of his heritage

The history of man can be found in his music. Woven into the musical fabric of the centuries is the tale of man's striving toward a richer life. As children in the classroom learn the simple, direct songs of the people and the music of the artist, they will become aware of the place of music in the past and present life of man.

music is a vital part of life

Many of the significant events of life have an accompanying musical expression. As the child explores music, he will realize that music has been an important part of rituals of primitive and sophisticated cultures. As he learns music from many countries and periods in history, he will discover that music reflects the culture from which it springs. The child will come to know and value the musical life of his own society. Through involvement in a variety of musical activities, he will find ways to participate in that life.

music is a means of personal expression

Music provides an avenue for personal expression in a way that language does not. Music is not bound, as words are, by specific meanings. Through music, each individual can communicate his own musical ideas or reflect the ideas of others. The child will discover his own potential for musical expression as he is given the opportunity to explore many different areas of musical performance and response.

TO HELP THE CHILD DEVELOP

a knowledge of the literature of music

As children discover their musical heritage, they should have an opportunity to explore many kinds of literature: folk songs and dances, music composed for solo voices or instruments, choruses, orchestras, or other instrumental ensembles. As children study music literature, they will become aware of the infinite variety of musical expression and of the many different media through which it may be communicated. The teacher will help children realize that the exploration of music can be a lifetime pursuit.

understanding of the structure of music

Although anyone may enjoy music on a limited level without knowledge of its structure, musical independence is contingent upon an understanding of musical organization. The teacher will move beyond the obvious and help children become aware of the principles which govern rhythm, melody, and harmony. He will guide them in the comprehension of musical form, style, and expression. Such understanding results in musical maturity, deeper musical enjoyment, and more complete participation.

skills of musical performance and response

Every child should have the opportunity to explore the activities through which music can be an expressive medium for him: singing, playing, listening, dancing, creating. Each skill contributes in a different way to the total musical development of the child. The child should also learn to perceive musical ideas visually through the written symbol. As the child develops skills of performance and response, he will find greater satisfaction in expressing his feelings and ideas through music.

EXPLORING MUSIC: PROCEDURES

EXPLORING MUSIC THROUGH SINGING

Singing should be the most important musical activity in the class-room. Whether or not the experience is satisfying depends upon the interpretation of the song and the quality of the singing. A song that is intended to inspire noble feelings and thoughts cannot do so if it is sung in the wrong tempo or out of tune. Singing can provide important musical learnings only when possibilities for development are pursued: pupil's accompaniments; the study of rhythm, melody, and harmony; and the study of the culture from which the song came. Songs of high quality, good vocal production, and the development of related learnings will justify the important place of singing in the classroom.

Expressive singing

Songs are poetry first and poetry is composed of words. The meaning of the text is the basis for almost every skill needed in good singing. Children begin to study a song by understanding the text, discussing it, pronouncing the words correctly, and putting the text in the proper historic period and geographic locale. When children thoroughly understand the text, it will be easy to teach the tempo, interpretation, phrasing of the melody line, and other aspects as intrinsic elements of the song itself. A composer does not write the "forte" or "piano" above a measure as something to be added. Rather, such markings are indications of changes that will take place naturally in good expression of the text and the music. Tempo markings and other expression markings are also the composer's indication of the appropriate expression of text. Many songs, especially folk songs, are unmarked; and appropriate expression is derived directly from the text.

The study of musical expression through artistic vocal production is emphasized in this textbook. One important aspect is expression in performance as derived from the song itself.

Such expression in singing will have meaning for children. They will soon develop the ability to set an appropriate tempo, sing with good phrasing, good tone quality, proper dynamics, and in the style that the song requires.

Teaching a new song

At this grade level, many songs will be learned in part or entirely by reading the music. See "Exploring Music Through Reading," page vii.

The recording of the song may often be used as the model from which children work in learning a new song. When learning in this way, children should hear the song for the first time with books closed in order to concentrate on the aural experience. A discussion of all that is heard should take place at this point. Study the music page and hear the recording again with books open. The class should then be ready to begin singing the song and developing the various activities and skills that are outlined in the teaching suggestions.

Part singing

Singing in harmony is an important part of the course as planned in this textbook. At this grade level, it is likely that the children have had extensive experience in playing and singing harmony. This is not always true, however. If children have had little opportunity to develop this skill, you can prepare them for experiences in harmony as they study this book.

The approach to part singing is important. Harmony should first be experienced aurally. Various other experiences should also precede singing in harmony from notation. Here are some of the procedures for teaching children to sing in parts:

. . . Combining instruments with voices. Many of the descants and harmony parts can be played on the bells or other melody instruments as most of the class sings the melody of the song. Children who play orchestral instruments might play such parts.
. . . Hearing an autoharp accompaniment is excellent preparation for part singing.
. . . Hearing the part songs on the recordings will be very helpful.
. . . The teacher may sing the harmony part as the class sings the melody. A few of the most capable children might first join

the teacher in singing the harmony part. The group will grow as class members become more secure and as their ability to "hear" and "think" harmony improves.

. . . Improvisation is an important approach to part singing. A child may "make up" a part on bells which will harmonize with a familiar song. A child who has a good ear can sing an original harmony part or harmonize as other children sing the melody.

. . . The fundamental chords (I, IV, V) which children learn most easily through the autoharp are useful in teaching children to harmonize. Class members may sing one or more tones of the fundamental chords as they are played on the autoharp while the melody is sung by other members of the class.

. . . Resonator bells are also excellent for chording. They offer the advantage of sounding individual tones within a chord. Children may find it easier to sing chord tones when they are asked to sing with a particular resonator bell. Chord names or numbers which aid in this work appear with many of the songs.

With the experiences in harmonizing outlined here, children will develop an "ear" for harmony and will soon learn it easily from the recordings and by reading the music. It is a mistake to think of part singing as some highly technical aspect of music. The kind of harmonizing by ear which children do at camp, or the kind they hear in the "barbershop quartet," is basic to any development of the skill. Fifth and sixth grade boys who have learned to sing fundamental chord tones with a melody are well prepared for the parts they will later sing when their voices change.

Tone production and diction

The principles of good singing observed by accomplished singers and choirs are important in the classroom if children are to experience the beauty of vocal music. Beauty of tone should often be discussed as children listen to the recordings. The teacher should also call attention to beauty of tone quality as the children sing. Through such discussion they should become aware of tone which is clear (not "breathy"), of tone which has vitality, and of tone color as another expressive element in singing. (Some songs require "dark" tone; others require a "light" tone; some require full voice, while others may require restrained tone.)

It is not necessary to go into all the principles of breath support in the classroom; however, the teacher should call attention to good posture. Well-supported tones will result from children's awareness of the sound of good tone and from an understanding of good phrasing. Children will probably be able to breathe properly and give natural support to tones when the phrases of a song have been analyzed and discussed; that is, where the phrases begin and end, which phrases are sung as the climax of the song, which phrases are building toward the climax, and which phrases recede from it.

Possibly the most important factor in good tone production is the way in which vowels and consonants are enunciated and produced. Singing pure vowel sounds will greatly help the children attain clarity of tone and good diction. Children will enjoy "vocalizing" (singing scales or other patterns on such syllables as "ah," "oh," "ee," and listening for proper vowel sounds as they sing). The sounds practiced in vocalizing should then be transferred to words in the class singing of songs. Crisp consonants before and after vowel sounds produce clear enunciation.

Children should often be encouraged to practice the artistry of starting and ending words and phrases in a choral manner; that is, altogether as one voice rather than as separate singers. To help children attack and release tones together, the teacher may find it necessary to conduct.

Sitting posture is important. Children should sit erect. Books should be held so that the children do not have to bend their heads down to see the music. Children should often stand to sing. They should frequently sing without books so that they can concentrate on good tone production and expressive singing.

EXPLORING MUSIC THROUGH LISTENING

The time in which we live gives the classroom special responsibility for teaching the literature of music. Electronic media which bring music into the lives of people everywhere also make it accessible to the classroom. Discrimination and broad musical interests are important goals of study through listening. As children learn to analyze and understand what they hear in music, these goals will be more easily accomplished. A great teacher, Lilla Belle Pitts, once said, "Listening to music is an extremely difficult skill. It requires a background of appreciation that takes a lifetime to develop. Our purpose in study is to hear more and more of the beautiful details."

This book includes the study of various styles and forms, both folk and composed, both Western and Asian, with emphasis on contemporary developments in the music of recognized composers. It also includes a study of American jazz and the American musical theater. Many compositions are presented in the listening lessons of the book. The teacher may wish to add others which have a particular purpose in the classroom. Children should be encouraged to develop home record collections and to add the compositions studied in this book to their collections. Encourage children to listen to music at home and in concert and to discuss it in class, comparing it with music studied in the classroom and using the analytical and discriminatory principles learned there.

Although the procedure for teaching the listening lessons is given with each lesson, some general guidelines will be helpful.

. . . Occasionally, begin with the question WHAT DO WE THINK ABOUT WHEN WE LISTEN TO MUSIC? Through the search for answers to such a question, the true nature of music can be revealed to children. They can be guided away from answering, "We try to make up a story or imagine a scene," as they learn to observe the musical elements of the composition—its melody, rhythm, harmony, form—and to recognize that its greatest charm may lie in one or more of these elements.

. . . After the children have listened to a composition, help them verbalize their reactions. In order to avoid too much lecturing about the music, use discussion and question methods that will draw from the children many of the observations and ideas needed in the study. Assist children to expand their vocabulary so that they can express ideas about music with more and more precision.

. . . Help children realize that design in music is the order in which things happen. The study depends upon recognition of repeated melodies and sections of the composition and upon observation of the various musical devices used by the composer. Children in this grade level should identify the most common designs in the music they study. Gradually, they should be able to apply the principles of analysis to music they are hearing or performing for the first time. Every effort should be made to follow the complete plan for the study of each listening lesson.

. . . This book gives considerable emphasis to the elements of music and to design as they are related to the composer's style. The time lines and commentary are also meant to help children understand musical style. Children should become sufficiently aware of characteristics of historical periods, of national characteristics, and of compositional processes so that they are able to identify and discuss various aspects of style in music.

. . . Whenever possible, help children study music through genuine participation: class discussion, interpretation through movement, playing themes on melody instruments, or playing the rhythm of themes on percussion instruments.

. . . When a composition is too long to study in one lesson, use the principle of presenting the whole—the part—the whole. In the first lesson, hear the whole composition or enough of it to grasp the general character of the piece. In subsequent lessons, study sections of the composition in detail. Make any digressions which are pertinent, such as a study of a specific instrument. Finally play the entire composition.

. . . Give opportunities for children to hear the compositions many times so that more of the details will be observed. Completion of the initial study should be considered as preparation for enjoyment of the music on many occasions.

. . . In order that children hear the music as perfectly as possible, pay attention to the tone quality and volume of the record player. The volume should be set to make the reproduction as much as possible like a real performance. Even small record players usually have tone controls which will improve the sound when properly adjusted.

EXPLORING MUSIC THROUGH READING

The ability to interpret the music page is an essential skill. This skill makes it possible for a person to expand his musical repertoire and to gain increased satisfaction from his own musical performance. Before one can interpret music notation, however, he must be able to identify musical patterns he hears. For example, he must be able to discriminate between steps and skips in a melody, between longer and shorter tones in a rhythm pattern. If children have not yet gained this ability, help them by emphasizing aural activities which involve listening, moving, playing, and singing. Encourage these children to develop a vocabulary which describes what they hear. Children must be able to identify musical patterns they hear before they can relate notation of patterns to the sound.

Keep in mind that music symbols can only have meaning in terms of the sounds they represent. Understanding of the relationship between sound and symbol will come only as children observe these relationships in actual music making: playing a melody on bells, clapping a rhythm pattern, singing a melody, and studying the symbols which represent these patterns.

Begin the study of a new song with an examination of its expressive purpose. Study the words. What kind of melody and rhythm will give musical expression to the poetry? What tempo and performing style will be appropriate to the meaning of the text? What is the national origin of the song, its period, its composer? What musical characteristics do these clues lead us to expect? Examine the rhythm. How does the natural stress of the words govern the meter and the rhythm of the melody? Notice how the expression of the words is reflected in the melody through the general range, the contour, and movement by steps or skips.

As children explore the relationships between text and musical sound, help them apply their discoveries to the notation. As they listen to a recording of a new song, guide them to associate with increasing specificity the sounds they hear with the symbols they see.

Complete musical independence implies the ability to reproduce music from a score without first hearing it. Although few elementary children will achieve this goal completely, the learning of each new song should help them move closer to this goal. The ability to complete the following steps is one measure of such independence:

. . . Study the symbols pertaining to rhythm. What is the meter? How does the rhythm of the melody move in relation to the meter?

. . . Establish the meter by tapping the basic beat in a tempo appropriate to the mood of the song. Isolate difficult patterns for practice.

. . . Study the symbols pertaining to melody. Determine the key and home tone by studying the key signature and the pitches found in the melody. Identify common scale passages and chord patterns. Isolate difficult intervals or patterns for practice.

. . . Establish tonality by singing or playing the tones of the I chord or the complete scale. Sing the song in rhythm, using numbers, letters, or a neutral syllable.

. . . Study the design of the song. Where does each phrase begin and end? Which phrases are repeated exactly, which are similar, which are new?

. . . Encourage children to move toward the goal of expressive performance as quickly as possible. For example, challenge children to sing passages of songs made up of familiar rhythm and melody patterns immediately with the words, thus helping them realize that some steps can be omitted as they improve in reading skill. Follow a similar procedure when learning to play new songs on melody instruments. Also, use instruments to practice difficult passages in songs which children are learning to sing.

. . . Skill in music reading will develop most readily if each child has the opportunity to practice the skill individually. Encourage children to learn new songs by themselves or in small groups and to play or sing them for the class. Help children realize that interpreting the music score is a useful and satisfying musical skill.

EXPLORING MUSIC THROUGH PLAYING MELODY AND HARMONY INSTRUMENTS

Children in the intermediate grades should be given many opportunities to play melodic and harmonic instruments. Understanding the relationship between musical sound and the printed page will be developed more quickly if the child has an opportunity to play an instrument. Each child should be encouraged to develop proficiency on at least one classroom instrument, such as bells, autoharp, piano, recorder, or song flute. Provide time for the child to practice by himself. Children may wish to purchase one or more of these instruments for use at home.

Playing the bells

Resonator bells will be invaluable in helping children relate the symbols on the staff to pitched sounds as they learn to play descants and melodies in their book. The bells will also help children develop their own musical ideas through improvisation and composition. Here are several other suggestions for using resonator bells:

    . . . Use bells to teach letter names of notes.

    . . . Help children learn scale structure as they play the bells. Guide them to choose bells for a specific scale (major or minor) by ear. Then help them determine the sequence of whole and half steps within the scale.

    . . . Ask individual children to play the bells to establish tonality and starting pitch of a song. When a song has a definite key center, the tonality may be established by playing the complete scale or the tones of the I chord (1-3-5).

    . . . Teach children to play chordal accompaniments on the bells by arranging the bells in groups, one group for each chord (I, IV, V7). Strike the bells lightly and rapidly to produce sustained tones. Bell accompaniments sound best with songs where each chord is sustained for several beats (as in "Silent Night" or "Down in the Valley").

Playing the piano

If a piano is available, it should be used regularly in classroom activities. The suggestions for resonator bells can also be used with the piano. Help children associate letter names with lines and spaces of the staff and with the keyboard. First show children how to locate middle C on the piano, the first white key to the left of two black keys near the center of the piano. In notation, middle C is in the middle of the grand staff, the first added line below the treble staff. Locate other pitches on the piano in relation to middle C.

Assign simple melodies to children who do not study piano privately. Help them learn to play from notation as well as by ear. Children with piano experience might be assigned as "student teachers."

Teach children simple piano chording. Help them transfer their knowledge of chording learned at the autoharp to the piano keyboard. At first, ask them to play the root of the chord with the left hand. To do this, follow the autoharp markings given above a song and play the note indicated by the name of the chord.

Later, help children play a complete chord pattern. Children can soon chord in several keys if they memorize the relationships between the notes; the sequence of this pattern remains the same in all major keys.

When children know the chord patterns in a specific key, they may play an accompaniment as the class sings familiar songs which can be harmonized with I, IV, and V7 chords.

Encourage children who are studying piano to develop their own accompaniments. For example, they may play the melody with the right hand and improvise an accompaniment with the left hand. Suggest that they experiment with variations on the basic chord pattern, playing the notes in different rhythms or as arpeggios.

Playing the autoharp

Children will enjoy accompanying class songs on the autoharp. Give individuals time to practice by themselves before accompanying the class. Help children follow these directions:

. . . Place the autoharp on a flat surface with the low strings closest to the player.

. . . Press the chord buttons down firmly with the fingers of the left hand. Usually the index, middle, and third fingers are used. Suggest that children locate the chord buttons they will need and keep their fingertips over these buttons.

. . . Strum the strings with the right hand. Use a pick or fingertips. The strings may be strummed on either side of the bars, although a better tone is obtained by strumming to the left of the fingerboard, right hand crossed over left. Strum away from the body with a sweeping motion, moving from lowest to highest strings.

Discover the chords which are to be used in a song. When appropriate, the chords are indicated above the notation of the songs in the pupil's book. Occasionally encourage children to keep their books closed and discover the chord sequence by ear. Practice moving from one chord to another; establish tonality by playing I, IV, V7, I.

Play the appropriate chords in rhythm as the class sings the melody.

For special effects with appropriate songs, experiment with various picks, such as erasers, pencils, or paper clips. Discuss the difference in quality of sound. An excellent pick for regular use may be made from vinyl flooring. Cut a piece about the size of a quarter in an oblong shape.

Experiment with rhythm patterns characteristic of the style of various songs. For example, accompany a waltz by playing the lowest strings on beat one, the higher strings on beats two and three.

A Latin-American melody might be accompanied with this rhythm pattern:

A descant which uses only a few tones and does not move rapidly may be plucked on the autoharp for a special effect.

Transposition for the autoharp is explained on the next page.

Playing recorder-type instruments

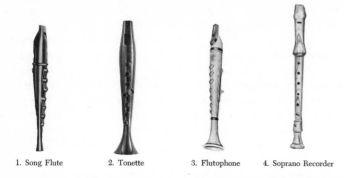

1. Song Flute   2. Tonette   3. Flutophone   4. Soprano Recorder

Easy-to-play instruments such as the song flute, tonette, and recorder offer children additional opportunities for performance. However, these instruments (except for the recorder) have a limited range of a ninth.

Method books are usually sold with each of these instruments.

Recorders are available in several sizes: sopranina, soprano, alto, tenor, and bass. Although recorders are more expensive than other instruments of this kind, they are also the most musically rewarding. There is a large repertoire of literature written for recorder ensembles.

Recorders and song flutes can be used to strengthen understanding of musical concepts previously discussed. Many of the descant parts in the pupil's book may be played on these instruments. Assign the descant to certain children and give them an opportunity to practice before performing with the class.

Harmony parts to songs are often within the range of these instruments. This is a good way to introduce part singing. Help children to play the part on an instrument. Later, encourage them to sing the part independently.

Encourage children to form small ensembles and rehearse compositions especially written for these instruments. Children may also play many of the rounds and part songs in their books as instrumental compositions.

Playing orchestral instruments

Invite children who are studying orchestral and band instruments to share their abilities with the class.

Plan concert days when these children may perform for the class. Assign children who play orchestral instruments to learn the instrumental descants included in their book. Instrumental folios for band and orchestra instruments are available from the publisher.

Provide opportunities for the children to work in small groups. Children who play piano or an orchestral instrument may join with others who are learning to play the bells or autoharp. The group may learn to play some of the songs in their book.

Invite the instrumental music teacher in your school to visit the class. Ask him to demonstrate various instruments and to explain the instrumental music program to the class. Cooperate with him in identifying children who would profit from such instruction. Ask him to assist members of the class as they prepare music for performance.

Transposition for orchestral instruments

When children play harmonizing parts to the songs in their books on certain orchestral instruments, the music must be transposed, that is, written in another key. The trumpet and clarinet always sound one whole step lower than notated on the staff. Therefore, the notation must be written a step higher if these instruments are to play with the piano, bells, autoharp, or with non-transposing orchestral instruments, such as the violin or flute. Write the part for the clarinet or trumpet one full step higher than the original music.

Transposition for the autoharp

The twelve-bar autoharp can accompany only those songs written in the keys of C, G, and F major and in A and D minor. Songs written in other keys must be transposed to one of these keys. When you transpose songs for the autoharp, choose the key which is closest to the original key of the song: songs in B or D, play in C; songs in Eb or E, play in F; songs in A or Gb, play in G: songs in B minor, play A minor; songs in C minor or E minor, play in D minor.

EXPLORING MUSIC THROUGH PLAYING PERCUSSION INSTRUMENTS

With improved muscular coordination, children in the upper grades will be able to experiment with many kinds of percussion accompaniments and instrumental compositions that they were unable to handle in lower grades. Many concepts relating to rhythm, form, tone quality, and style may be expanded as children play various percussion instruments.

Percussion instruments may be used in many ways: to establish the beat; to play distinctive patterns as children learn the rhythm of a new song; to accompany folk songs using instruments characteristic of the country; to play rounds as a percussion exercise; to play original percussion compositions.

Encourage children to work in small groups to develop their own percussion compositions. Choose instruments of contrasting tone quality and pitch levels. Remind children that their compositions will be more interesting if the rhythm patterns are varied instead of repeated over and over. Suggest that one child begin the composition by playing a basic pattern. The other children may join in, one at a time, each one improvising a variation on the original pattern.

Experiment with various classroom instruments to discover different qualities of sound. Try striking each instrument in different places. Experiment with mallets of various sizes, weights, and textures to discover their effect on tone quality. Children may locate various objects around their homes which will make interesting sounds: pans, pot lids, automobile brake drums, railroad spikes, and pieces of hard wood. Incorporate these sounds into the children's percussion compositions. Some children may be interested in making their own instruments, discovering the effect of different kinds of shapes and sizes of materials on the sound of the completed instrument.

When buying percussion instruments, tone quality should be the primary consideration. It is impossible for children to perform musically or to grow in musical taste when they are encouraged to use instruments of inferior musical quality. A listing of the standard classroom instruments with directions for playing them may be found in the teacher's books for *Exploring Music 1, 2,* or *3.* In addition to these instruments, the classroom may include others which are more complex and those typical of various countries.

Many Latin-American songs are included in *Exploring Music.* The following instruments are typically used with Latin-American music:

Claves (clah′-vehs): To hold, cup the left hand with thumb extended and balance one clave in this cup. Do not grip the clave tightly; leave it free to vibrate. Hold the other clave loosely in the right hand. Use the clave in the right hand to strike the one in the left hand. The claves usually play the same basic rhythm:

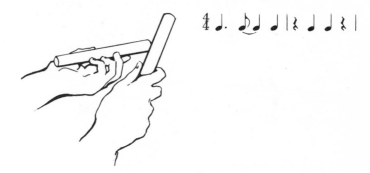

Cowbell: Hold the cowbell flat in the palm of the left hand with the open end facing away from the body. Strike with a stick or wire. For variations, strike the top or edge of the cowbell with different parts of the stick. The cowbell is often used to control the basic tempo in Latin-American music. The basic pattern of the cowbell is:

The cowbell may be struck in different places to create contrasting tones and placement of accents. Variations in the basic pattern may be improvised.

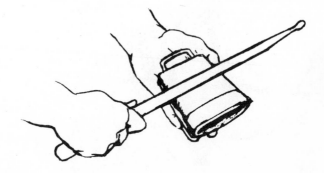

Maracas (mah-rah'-kahs): Shake the maracas with a circular wrist motion. To create variation and accent, move the maracas up and down in front of the body while continuing the circular wrist motion. The maracas usually play a steady eighth note pattern. Interest is created by the variation in accent.

Guiro (gwee'-roh): Hold the guiro in the left hand and scrape the corrugated surface with a small stick (chopsticks are a good size and weight). Scrape down with short motions, up with one long stroke. Do not lift the stick from the guiro. A basic guiro rhythm is:

D D D up   D D D up

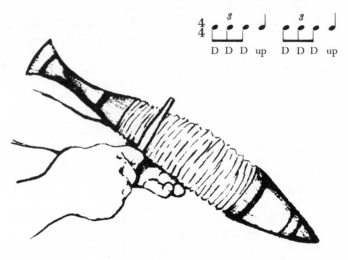

Conga Drum: If a conga drum is not available, use a tom-tom with a low, deep sound. Play with palms of hands. To get variation in sound, strike the edge with the left palm for short muffled sounds; strike the center with the right palm for booming sounds.

R L L R

Bongo Drums: Hold bongo drums between knees with the larger bongo to the right. The bongo is struck with the fingertips. The fingers must strike the bongo with a snap of the wrist to make the sound short and crisp. The pattern of playing is:

Tambourines: Hold by the rim with one hand. To get different effects, strike the center of the tambourine with the knuckles; tap with fingers in the center or at the edge; press heel of hand in center and tap with fingers. Play with various mallets; turn over and tap the rim; place on a cushion and tap rim. To obtain a sustained tone, shake the tambourine while moving the arm in a circular motion.

Wood Block: Strike over the hollowed-out section. Experiment with various beaters. Create variations in sound by striking in different places on the wood block.

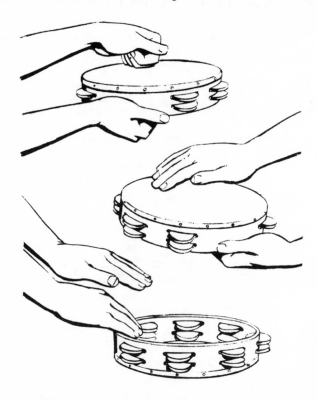

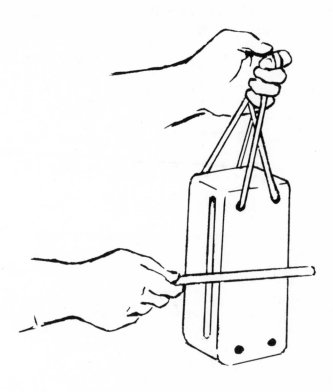

Castanets: Use the type of castanet that is made on a handle. Strike in the air with a whiplike action or strike against palm of hand or leg. Castanets may also be played by tapping the handle with the fingers.

ELEMENTS OF MUSIC THEORY : RHYTHM

Rhythmic notation. The following chart gives the names of the various notes and rests. It also indicates the relative duration of each. All basic note values are based on a 2–1 relationship.

Note values based on the 3–1 relationships are shown by triplets or by dotted notes.

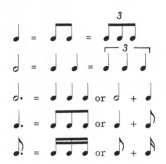

Meter and rhythm.

Beat: The underlying pulse of the music.

Meter: The systematic grouping of beats resulting from the **accenting** of certain beats.

Bar Line: Vertical lines across the staff which indicate metric groupings.

Measure: A single metric grouping marked off by two bar lines.

Meter Signature: The symbol which indicates the meter of the composition and the note which will be the beat note. The meter signatures found in this book follow:

$\frac{4}{4}$ The song moves in fours and the quarter note is the beat note.

$\frac{2}{4}$ The song moves in twos and the quarter note is the beat note.

$\frac{3}{4}$ The song moves in threes and the quarter note is the beat note.

$\frac{2}{2}$ The song moves in twos and the half note is the beat note.

$\frac{3}{8}$ The song moves in threes and the eighth note is the beat note.

$\frac{6}{8}$ There are six beats in the measure with accents on beats 1 and 4. The eighth note is the beat note. In quick tempo the song seems to move in twos, and the dotted quarter acts as the beat note.

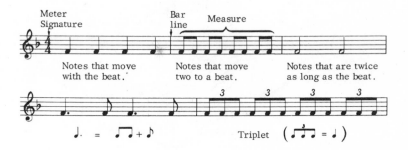

ELEMENTS OF MUSIC THEORY : MELODY

Pitch notation. Pitches are indicated by **notes** on a **grand staff**. The grand staff consists of two staves, treble and bass. Each staff consists of five lines and four spaces. Ledger lines may be added above or below each staff for additional pitches. The treble staff is indicated by the G clef establishing the second line of this staff as G. The bass staff is indicated by the F clef establishing the fourth line of this staff as F.

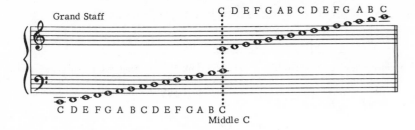

Grand Staff

Middle C

Scales. A scale is a group of tones arranged in a particular sequence of whole or half steps or a combination of both. Scale steps may be named by letters, indicating their pitch; by numbers, indicating their position in the scale; or by syllables. (Numbers and letters are used in the pupil's book. For those teachers who wish to use syllables, the syllable names are included here for the major and minor scales.)

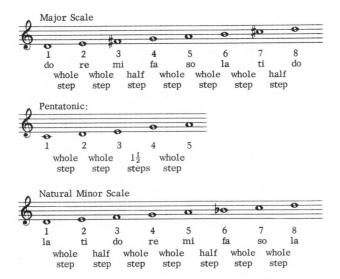

Major Scale

1	2	3	4	5	6	7	8
do	re	mi	fa	so	la	ti	do
whole step	whole step	half step	whole step	whole step	whole step	half step	

Pentatonic:

1	2	3	4	5
whole step	whole step	1½ steps	whole step	

Natural Minor Scale

1	2	3	4	5	6	7	8
la	ti	do	re	mi	fa	so	la
whole step	half step	whole step	whole step	half step	whole step	whole step	

The lowered third is characteristic of all minor scales. The harmonic minor scale is the same as the natural minor scale except that the seventh step is raised, which creates a step and a half between the sixth and seventh steps.

In the melodic minor scale the sixth and seventh steps are raised a half step when ascending and are unaltered when descending.

Keys. The key of a composition, which indicates the scale on which the composition is based, is symbolized by the key signature, which appears at the beginning of the first staff of a song. The key signatures found in this book are listed following the discussion of chords.

Chords. A chord is the simultaneous sounding of several tones. The most common chords are called triads, made up of three tones each a third apart. Occasionally, a fourth tone is added to a chord; these chords are called seventh chords because the fourth tone is seven tones above the first tone of the chord. The most common chords are those based on the first, fourth, and fifth steps of the scale. Following are the I, IV, and V7 chords for the keys found in this book. The largest note is the home tone of the key.

Key of C	Key of G	Key of D	Key of A
I IV V7	I IV V7	I IV V7	I IV V7
C F G7	G C D7	D G A7	A D E7

Key of E	Key of F	Key of B♭	Key of E♭
I IV V7	I IV V7	I IV V7	I IV V7
E A B7	F B♭ C7	B♭ E♭ F7	E♭ A♭ B♭7

Key of A♭	Key of G♭	Key of C♭
I IV V7	I IV V7	I IV V7
A♭ D♭ E♭7	G♭ C♭ D♭7	C♭ F♭ G♭7

Key of A minor	Key of D minor	Key of G minor	Key of F minor
I IV V7	I IV V7	I IV V7	I IV V7
A D E7	D G A7	G C D7	F B♭ C7

Musical Growth in the Sixth Grade

	LISTENING	SINGING	PLAYING
SKILL	Listens with discrimination to a wide variety of music.	Sings accurately and independently with expressive tone and good diction. Is aware that boys' voices approaching voice change may have a temporary limitation of range.	Plays classroom percussion instruments, including the Latin-American types, with facility. Exhibits increasing skill in chording on autoharp or piano. Demonstrates skill in playing some melodic instrument: bells, recorder, song flute.
LITERATURE	Is acquainted with musical literature representative of various media of music and musical forms.	Knows a repertoire of many types of songs: folk songs of many countries, art songs, and songs from opera and oratorio.	Knows a repertoire of songs of which he can play the melody and/or accompaniment.
CONCEPTS **Melody**	Perceives the difference in structure of the major, minor, pentatonic scales, and other kinds of melodic organization such as twelve-tone row, modes. Recognizes patterns in melody as moving by scale-line, chord-line, sequence. Identifies common melodic intervals.	Sings many melodies independently, revealing understanding of tonality and melodic movement.	Plays simple melodies in a variety of keys on some melodic instrument, by ear, as well as from notation.
Rhythm	Distinguishes common metric groupings; is aware of mixed and asymmetric meters. Understands the varying contributions of beat, accent, and pattern to rhythmic movement. Perceives 2-1 and 3-1 relationships of tones to the beat.	Sings songs in a variety of rhythms accurately without assistance.	Exhibits understanding of meter and rhythmic relationships and maintains complex rhythmic patterns independently when playing on melody or percussion instruments. Exhibits understanding of meter and rhythmic relationships when playing rhythm patterns by ear or from notation.
Harmony	Identifies the tonality of a composition as major or minor. Is aware of other kinds of tonal organization, such as atonality, polytonality. Identifies major and minor chord sounds. Realizes the possibilities of chords based on intervals other than the third.	Shows awareness of harmonic relationships by singing two- and three-part homophonic or polyphonic songs, understanding the harmonic relationship of tones.	Establishes tonality for songs in major or minor by playing chords on autoharp, bells, or piano. Exhibits knowledge of chord progressions when playing accompaniments.
Form	Indicates understanding of various forms: two- and three-part song form, rondo, theme and variations, fugue, sonata allegro. Is sensitive to the contribution of repetition and contrast to musical design.	Sings songs in a manner which reveals understanding of phrase, repetition, and contrast.	Demonstrates understanding of the importance of repetition, contrast, and variation when planning accompaniments.
Expression	Responds to subtle changes in rhythm, melody, harmony, tempo, dynamics, and tone quality. Is sensitive to the contributions made to musical expression by climax, unity, and variety.	Indicates understanding of expressive purposes of melodic contour and rhythmic pattern. Uses increasingly subtle variations of tone color, tempo, dynamics, in own performance.	Demonstrates increasing sensitivity to expressive purposes of melodic contour, rhythmic movement, and harmonic organization in own performance. Plays expressively with appropriate tempo, dynamics, and tone quality.
Style	Identifies a particular historical period by its distinctive musical characteristics. Distinguishes music of various cultures by musical characteristics. Identifies some musical devices as belonging to the style of a certain composer.	Indicates understanding of songs of various periods and cultures by singing with appropriate tone quality, tempo, and dynamics.	Shows consideration of cultural and period characteristics when selecting instruments and planning accompaniments.

MOVING	CREATING	READING
Is developing poise and originality in free movement with concentration on the music and increasing ability to interpret rhythm, melodic contour, phrasing, style, instrumentation, and design. Is developing a vocabulary of formalized steps for dances of various periods and countries.	Uses voice and/or instruments to develop original compositions.	Is gaining independence in using notation as an aid to listening, performing, and creating. Possesses a functional knowledge of notational symbols.
Is acquiring a repertoire of folk dances from various countries.		
Reflects sensitivity to melodic contour in body movement.	Demonstrates increasing awareness of possibilities for melodic variety in creating own compositions. Experiments with various kinds of tonal organizations, including twelve-tone row and whole tone, and electronic music.	Can sing or play simple melodies from notation. Reveals understanding of scale structure by using numbers to sing new melodies. Interprets key signature and establishes tonality. Is able to analyze melody in terms of scale or chord pattern, repetition, contrast, and sequence.
Demonstrates recognition of meter and rhythm patterns by clapping, stepping, and dancing. Exhibits knowledge of rhythmic structure when executing formalized dance steps.	Uses simple and complex rhythm patterns and various meters (including mixed and asymmetric) in improvising rhythms. Reveals understanding of meter and rhythmic pattern in planning accompaniments.	Plays, sings, or claps rhythm patterns from notation. Interprets meter and relationship of note values within a composition by studying the meter signature and tempo indication.
Demonstrates awareness of cadence and countermelody when planning dances.	Improvises a harmonizing part to familiar songs vocally and/or instrumentally, showing understanding of chord progression and structure. Experiments with secondary chords or chords built on intervals other than the third when creating original compositions.	Performs accompaniments on autoharp and/or piano by reading chord symbols. Analyzes part songs in terms of chord structure and harmonic intervals. Recognizes music as being primarily homophonic or polyphonic by studying notation.
Indicates recognition of musical form when planning dances.	Exhibits knowledge of musical form when planning own compositions.	Recognizes the form of a song by studying the notation. Uses notation as an aid when studying the form of compositions: theme and variations, rondo, sonata allegro, two- and three-part songs.
Expresses mood and musical content of music through increasingly precise physical response.	Displays interest in expressive possibilities of tone color, tempo, and dynamics when creating compositions and accompaniments. Considers importance of unity and variety when planning original compositions.	Observes all pertinent expression marks in the score when listening or performing.
Displays understanding of period and cultural characteristics when executing folk dances or when composing original dances.	Illustrates recognition of period and cultural characteristics in planning accompaniments, dances, or original compositions. Explores the possibilities of various contemporary musical styles in own compositions, including electronic music.	Studies the musical score for clues as to musical style.

EXPLORING MUSIC: PAGE BY PAGE

The section that follows contains specific and practical aids for the teacher. In it, each page of the pupil's book is reproduced, slightly smaller in size and in black and white only. Next to that page are aids for the teacher—essential information about the song, suggestions for handling the lesson, recording information, and occasional supplementary material. These notes carefully coordinate all parts of the program. They follow a regular pattern. The teacher's edition page, combining the reduced pupil's page and the teacher's aids, carries the same page number as the regular pupil's page. These features make this section particularly easy to use.

Song Information: At the very top of the teacher's edition page, the key and the starting tone are noted. In parentheses after the letter name of the starting tone is the number of the scale step for that one.

Then the meter is indicated in two ways: (1) the meter signature as it appears in the song, and (2) in parentheses an interpretation of that signature. For example, if a song is in $\frac{3}{4}$ and should be felt three beats to a measure, the interpretation will be $\frac{3}{\quarternote}$. If the song is in $\frac{3}{4}$ and should be felt one beat to a measure, the interpretation will be $\frac{3}{\dottedhalf}$.

Finally, if a piano accompaniment for the song appears on a page in the back of this book, there is a statement to that effect. The piano accompaniment section, pages 210-328, is set off by the gray bands along the edge of each page. Songs in it are keyed to songs in the pupil's book by a number that appears in front of each song title. That number tells the page on which the song is found in the pupil's book. As a further convenience, a symbol above the staff of the piano accompaniments shows where each line of music begins in the pupil's book. For instance, $\overset{2}{\blacktriangledown}$ means that the second line of the song in the pupil's book begins at this point.

Teaching Suggestions: Most of the space on the teacher's edition page is devoted to specific suggestions. More are often included than can be used during one lesson. In the first session, use the suggestions from the pupil's page and the ones marked by an asterisk in the teacher's edition. Another time, use some of the other ideas. The comments and questions printed in small capital letters can be addressed directly to the children.

Recordings: Under the reduced pupil's page is a reference to the recording made for the lesson. The record number, side, band, and information about the performance are given. All listening lessons and songs in the pupil's book are recorded. Use these recordings regularly. They can help the children learn new songs, study expressive performance, and become acquainted with various compositions, instruments, voices, ensembles, and accompaniments.

For teaching convenience, the recordings are banded. The songs are simply separated by locked grooves. The appreciation records, however, have three types of bands: (1) locked grooves to separate major compositions or complete listening lessons; (2) standard five-second bands to separate movements of a larger work or arias of an opera; and (3) bands of a continuous sound to isolate particular sections of a composition for concentrated study. These visible intermediate bands are marked either on the reduced pupil's page or in the teaching suggestions by the symbol ◉ . The recordings come in a boxed set of eleven 12-inch long-playing records and are available from Holt, Rinehart and Winston, Inc., 385 Madison Avenue, New York, N. Y. 10017.

Supplementary Material: On a number of pages in the Teacher's edition you will find special articles included as an aid to better teaching. Some treat the musical status, ability, and expected growth of children at each grade level. Others provide historical or musical background of composers and musical styles. Of significance, too, are the articles on the orchestra (pages 62, 104, 118, 142 and 183). They discuss the history and make-up of the orchestra and all the major orchestral instruments and tell how the sound is produced, the range, the quality of timbre, and the relationship of instruments within a family. The articles are listed in the Classified Index of Music and Poetry under "Supplementary Material."

Organization: This book is organized in eight sections, six of which emphasize the study of music from different areas of the world. The book is planned to be studied sequentially. The teacher may, however, wish to introduce some sections in a different order so that the children may study the music of a country at the same time the country is being discussed in social studies class. Each section of the book contains musical materials and related content organized around the topic of the section. Building strong relationships into units of music study helps the children organize ideas and experience music in depth.

The music in this book has been selected to introduce folk songs and dances from different lands and periods. Composed songs and instrumental works of composers are also included to represent different countries and eras. There is considerable emphasis on contemporary developments in music. In choosing the material for class study, it is strongly recommended that all sections of the book be included in the year's work. Deletions should be made by omitting some folk songs in each section. Study all listening lessons in the book.

Full page painting in pupil's book.
See page 209 for explanation of art.

Let's Explore Music

Music can be a lifetime exploration! As you explore the many paths that lead to the enjoyment of music, you will discover that each path has some interesting branches to follow. Music is a form of personal expression, and each of us can express our thoughts and feelings in music.

Music is an important part of daily life. You can find many kinds of music and people who are engaged in musical activities everywhere, even in the place where you live. You can find music for entertainment, music for dancing, concert music, and music on records, radio, and television. Some people enjoy music as a hobby and make music at home with the family or with folk-singing groups. For other people music is an occupation. These people use musical skills in their work just as some people use other skills in factories, offices, and fields. Your explorations will help you find a place in this musical world and will help you develop some special interests of your own.

Music is the sound we hear, play, or sing; but the symbols which represent musical sound are also very important to us. Through these symbols we can produce music written by composers or music which has been passed down to us from the folk of other times and places. Through written music we can communicate our own musical ideas to others. Some paths of exploration will help you understand musical notation and how to make use of it.

Music, like language, has a literature which we can explore. In language literature we have poetry, drama, and novels. In music literature we have an unending number of compositions. Rather than the names "poetry" and "drama," musical forms have names such as "symphony," "tone poem," "concerto," "cantata," and "madrigal." What a great number of interesting roads we can follow as we explore the literature of music!

The exploration of music will help you understand the peoples of the world because their interests, longings, and hopes are found in their music. Even the geography and history of nations can sometimes be discovered in music. As you sing and play music, and as you dance and listen to music, you will find that the explorations become more interesting with each path you follow.

The pupil's page provides a general outline of the musical explorations contained in the book. Read it aloud to the class or have one of the children read it aloud so that all class members can concentrate on the ideas as they follow the words. After reading the page with the class, reread each paragraph (or ask a class member to do so) and discuss each idea separately. Encourage the children to express their personal insights and describe any experiences they may have had that relate to these ideas.

Paragraph 1—NAME A SONG IN WHICH YOU HAVE EXPRESSED YOUR THOUGHTS AND FEELINGS. (Possibly " Sing Your Way Home " or "Battle Hymn of the Republic.") DESCRIBE A MUSICAL ACTIVITY IN WHICH YOU HAVE EXPRESSED SOME ORIGINAL IDEAS OF YOUR OWN. (An original verse, a new descant, or a harmony part might have been added to a song.)

Paragraph 2—Make a class list of occupations that have to do with music. (Concert performer, entertainer, music teacher, composer, disc jockey, publisher, orchestra member, opera singer, conductor, instrument manufacturer, piano tuner.) TELL WHAT YOU KNOW ABOUT THE WORK OF ANY OF THESE PEOPLE.

As children examine their new book to discover songs, names of composers, and titles of sections, they might relate the new music, ideas, and activities to the various paths of exploration outlined in the opening page. You might ask them specifically to find an example of each during the initial examination of their book.

The pupil's page should be reviewed and reread occasionally through the year as various studies and activities proceed.

The Home Road

Key: E♭   Starting Tone: G (3)
Meter: 4/4 (♩)
Piano accompaniment on page 210

* EXPRESSION: Read the words of the song together and discuss their meaning. Tipperary is a county in Ireland. American soldiers of World War I sang the popular British song "It's a Long Way to Tipperary" as they sailed overseas. It is this song to which Carpenter refers in the refrain. Suggest to the children that they ask their grandfathers whether they know these songs.

* MELODY: Study the melody carefully and observe its interesting design. Ask the children to listen for the melodic contour as they hear the recording. Notice how the verse gradually builds to a **climax** in the third phrase as each two-measure phrase echoes the opening **motive** (short musical idea) at a higher pitch. This rising melodic line is balanced by the downward movement of the melody at the end of the fourth phrase. Notice the **sequential** pattern in the refrain. Starting with the words "O'er hills and plains," the contour of each four-note motive is repeated five times. The sequence is not exact but the contour remains the same:

Ask the children to make a chart of the melodic contour.

COMPOSER'S STYLE: John Alden Carpenter was born in 1876 and died in 1951. He was one of the major American composers during the first part of the 1900's. He was especially famous for his songs, including this one which was written during World War I. Two well-known orchestral compositions by Carpenter include "Adventures in a Perambulator" and "Skyscrapers." Carpenter was influenced by Debussy, and his music is sometimes described as **impressionistic.** (See the discussion of Debussy and Impressionism on page 93.) However, Carpenter is truly an American composer and much of his music reflects American life.

The Home Road

Words and Music by
John Alden Carpenter

This song was composed during World War I. The words express feelings that are as meaningful today as when they were first written. As you sing this "song of freedom," communicate its spirit through the sound of your voices.

1. Sing a hymn of free-dom, Fling the ban-ner high!
2. In the qui-et hours ___ Of the star-ry night,

Sing the songs of Lib-er-ty, Songs that shall not die,
Dream the dreams of far-a-way, Home fires burn-ing bright,

Refrain

For the long, long road to Tip-pe-ra-ry Is the

road that leads me home, O'er hills and plains, By lakes and lanes, My

wood-lands! My corn-fields! My coun-try! My home!

Record 1   Side A   Band 1.   VOICES: mixed choir.
ACCOMPANIMENT: brass quartet, percussion.
FORM: Introduction, *4 meas.;* Vocal, *vv. 1-2.*

Scored for instruments.
See "Exploring Music Instrumental Supplement."

2

Listen carefully to the recording. The mellow tone of the **alto flute** enhances the plaintive mood of this song.

Johnny Has Gone for a Soldier

American Folk Song

Key: A minor   Starting Tone: C (3)
Meter: 4/4 (♩)
Piano accompaniment on page 211

Johnny Has Gone
for a Soldier

Although peoples of the world are different in some ways, they also hold many things in common. They often share the same interests, longings, and hopes. Sometimes they use the same melodies to express their common feelings. This song is an example. The melody was first sung by the people of Ireland. The original Irish song appears on page 34 of your book under the title "Shule Aroon." When the Irish came to the New World, they brought this song with them. Gradually it was altered to express the feelings of the Americans as their soldiers left home to fight in the American Revolution.

1. There   I   sat   on   But - ter- milk   Hill.
2. Me   oh   my,   I   loved — him   so;

Who   could   blame   me,   cry   my   fill?   And
Broke   my   heart   to   see   him   go,   And

ev - ery   tear   would — turn   a   mill;
on - ly   time   will — heal   my   woe;

John - ny   has   gone   for   a   sol - dier.

Record 1   Side A   Band 2.   VOICE: soprano.
ACCOMPANIMENT: alto flute, guitar.
FORM: Introduction, *2 meas.;* Vocal, *v. 1;* Instrumental; Vocal, *v. 2.*

* EXPRESSION: Discuss the ideas presented in the pupil's book. Stress the constantly changing character of folk music and the fact that folk music always reflects the interests, needs, and concerns of the people. This ballad is derived from an Irish folk song that was known as "Shule Agrah" or "Shule Aroon." The meaning is "Come with me, my love." The song comes from the period around 1691 when many young Irish patriots fled to France to serve in the French army. There are many variants on the song, but all of the words have centered around the thoughts of the young girl who was left behind while her absent Johnny served in battle. This ballad became popular during the American Revolutionary War. Many colonists were descendants of people who sang this ballad in Ireland.

Play the recordings of the two songs "Johnny Has Gone for a Soldier" and "Shule Aroon." Compare the ideas expressed in each. After "Shule Aroon" has been learned, sing the refrain of this song as a refrain to "Johnny Has Gone for a Soldier."

* HARMONY: The autoharp accompaniment for this song is easily learned and is especially appropriate for this song. For suggestions on the playing of the autoharp, see page ix.

Children will be able to develop a vocal accompaniment for this song after they have gained skill in vocal harmonizations as presented on pages 16-17. The accompaniment will sound best if the chords are sung as shown. Boys, whose voices are changing, will find it easier to sing in this range. However, the chords may be sung an octave higher if some of the tones are too low.

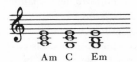

Am   C   Em

This song may be accompanied in two ways. The A minor and C major chords may be used throughout, or an E minor chord may be used on beats three and four of measures one and seven. Try it both ways; decide which the class prefers.

Roll On, Columbia

Key: F   Starting Tone: F (1)
Meter: $\frac{3}{4}$ ($\frac{3}{\downarrow}$)
Piano accompaniment on page 212

FOLK STYLE: Woody Guthrie wrote this song in 1941 to commemorate the completion of the Bonneville Dam located on the Columbia River in the northwestern United States. Even though he is the composer, "Roll On, Columbia" is considered a folk song. The term "folk song" refers primarily to a song's intent, use, and style. Folk songs tell of ideas and events that are of immediate concern to the people. Help children to realize that all folk songs originated at some time with a "composer" who first made up the music and the words. Folk songs were not written down but have been passed on orally to become part of a country's musical tradition. The composer's name is long forgotten although his work lives on. Over the years, the people continued to sing these songs, changing and adapting them to fit their own musical and expressive tastes. American folk music usually has a simple style with easily remembered melodies and rhythms that fit the rhythm of the words. Guthrie's "composed folk songs" fit this definition. Some people have compared his songs to those of Stephen Foster. The songs of both composers reflect the spirit of the time in which they lived in America. Some of Guthrie's songs, such as "This Land Is Your Land," have become as much a part of the American musical tradition as "Oh! Susanna" and "Old Folks at Home."

* **MELODY:** Encourage children to sing the verse at sight while you play the chords on the autoharp to provide a key feeling. The melody moves primarily stepwise. Review page vii, "Exploring Music through Reading." Children should be able to sing it with a minimum of assistance. The melody of the refrain is an adaptation of another popular American folk song "Good Night, Irene." When this similarity was pointed out to Guthrie, he exclaimed, "Why sure 'nough!" Borrowing melodic ideas from other songs is a common practice among folk singers. Sometimes it is deliberate; in other cases, as with Guthrie, the adaptation is unconscious. Listen to the recording to learn how to match the words to the rhythm in verses two through five.

* **HARMONY:** After the song has been enjoyed for several days as a unison melody, proceed to the discussion on page 5. When the children have completed the study of intervals, return to "Roll On, Columbia" and examine the refrain to discover the intervals between

Roll On, Columbia

Words and Music by Woody Guthrie

1. Green Doug - las fir where the wa - ters cut through,
2. Oth - er great riv - ers add pow - er to you,
3. Tom Jef - fer - son's vi - sion would not let him rest;

Down her wild moun - tains and can - yons she flew,
Ya - ki - ma, Snake, and the Klick - i - tat, too,
An em - pire he saw in the Pa - cif - ic North - west;

Ca - na - dian North - west to the o - cean so blue;
Sand - y Wil - la - mette and Hood Riv - er, too;
Sent Lew - is and Clark and they did the rest;

Roll on, Co - lum - bia, roll on!

Refrain
Roll on, roll on,
(Melody)
Roll on, Co - lum - bia, roll on!

Roll on, roll on,
Roll on, Co - lum - bia, roll on, Your

Record 1   Side A   Band 3. VOICES: baritone, children's choir.
ACCOMPANIMENT: oboe, guitar, double bass.
FORM: Introduction, *4 meas.;* Vocal, *vv. 1-5.*

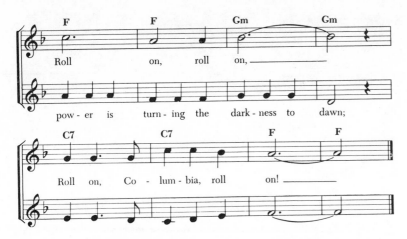

4. At Bonneville now there are ships in the locks;
   The waters have risen and cleared all the rocks.
   Shiploads of plenty will steam past the docks;
   Roll on, Columbia, roll on!
   Refrain

5. And on up the river is Grand Coulee Dam,
   The mightiest thing ever built by a man,
   To run the great fact'ries and water the land;
   Roll on, Columbia, roll on!
   Refrain

After you have learned the melody of the verse and refrain, study the **descant.** Notice that it usually moves with the same rhythm as the main melody. Look at the first phrase of the descant melody. It is nearly the same as the main melody except that it is higher. We say that the two parts are an **interval** of a **third** apart. An interval is the distance between two tones.

Divide the class into two groups. Practice singing these intervals. Discover the intervals between the descant and the melody in the last phrase of the refrain. Sing the descant and the melody of the refrain together. Listen carefully as you sing to be sure you are keeping the intervals "in tune."

the descant and the melody. Divide the class into two groups. Ask one group to sing the melody while the second group learns the descant. Remind the children to listen carefully to be sure each interval is sung accurately.

STUDY OF INTERVALS: The ability to hear and sing **intervals** is important for good part singing. Study the explanation in the pupil's book carefully and refer to it often. Help children to realize that intervals are named in accordance with the number of steps between the two notes. To determine the name of an interval, call the lower note "1" (regardless of its position in the scale). Count each line and space; the number of the top note is the name of the interval.

Most of the intervals shown on page 5 of the pupil's book appear at least once in the refrain of this song. The voices are a **third** apart most of the time. A **second** appears at the beginning of measure seven. There is a **fifth** in measures three and four. A **sixth** may be found in measure twelve. An **octave** and a **seventh** appear in measure fourteen.

As the children sing the two parts, suggest that they hold a particular interval. THIS TIME, AS YOU REACH THE POINT IN THE SONG WHERE THE VOICES ARE A SECOND APART, HOLD YOUR TONE UNTIL I GIVE YOU A SIGNAL TO CONTINUE. LISTEN CAREFULLY TO THE TWO PARTS TO BE SURE YOU ARE IN TUNE.

Help the children practice identifying intervals by their sound. One child may play an interval on the piano or bells while the class tries to name it. On another day, play a pitch on the piano or bells and ask the class to sing the top pitch of a given interval. For example, play F and ask the class to sing a third above. (A)

Peace of the River

Key: E♭ Starting Tone: E♭ (1)
Meter: $\frac{4}{4}$ ($\frac{4}{\text{♩}}$)
Piano accompaniment on page 214

* EXPRESSION: Listen to the recording of this song. Give children an opportunity to verbalize their reactions to the mood created by the words and music. Some children may wish to share their experiences in response to the question in their book.

Chart the **dynamic contour** to help children understand the relationship between melodic contour, rhythmic movement, phrasing, and dynamics. During the first, second, and third phrases, voices should gradually grow louder throughout the entire phrase. Discuss the importance of singing each phrase as a complete musical thought even though it is divided into two two-measure motives.

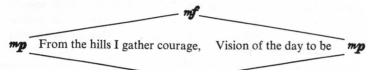

pp — Peace I ask of thee, O river, Peace, peace, peace. *mp*

Phrases three and four must crescendo to a climax, then decrescendo to the end of the phrase. The crescendo for phrase four should be somewhat stronger than that of phrase three.

mf
mp From the hills I gather courage,   Vision of the day to be *mp*

MELODY: Notice that the melody in the first and last sections uses only three tones and moves by steps, adding to the serene mood of the song. Draw attention to the contrasting character of the melody in the middle section. Discuss how this helps emphasize the important thoughts in this section.

HARMONY: Refer to the discussion on page 5 regarding intervals. Scan the song and discover that the voices move in **unison, thirds,** or **sixths.** Notice that the two voices usually move in **parallel motion;** that is, both voices move in the same direction. Find places where the two voice parts move in opposite directions or **contrary motion.** Becoming aware of these relationships between voices will help children as they learn to sing a song in harmony.

Peace of the River

Music by Viola Wood
Words by Glendora Gosling

Have you experienced the serenity and inspiration described in this song as you enjoyed the beauty of the woods, the hills, and the streams? Sing the song expressively.

Peace I ask of thee, O riv-er, Peace, peace, peace.

When I learn to live se-rene-ly, Cares will cease.

From the hills I gath-er cour-age, Vi-sion of the day to

be, Strength to lead and faith to fol-low,

All are giv-en un-to me. Peace I ask of thee, O

riv-er, Peace, peace, peace.

Record 1   Side A   Band 4.   VOICES: children's choir.
ACCOMPANIMENT: harp.
FORM: Introduction, *4 meas.;* Vocal; Interlude, *4 meas.;* Vocal.

6

William Tell Overture

by Gioacchino Rossini

Many people are familiar with the dramatic and thrilling story of William Tell, the Swiss hero who was such a skillful archer that he was able to shoot an apple off his son's head. Review the story in a class discussion or read it together from a book. The story has had meaning for lovers of freedom since the fourteenth century when William Tell was a courageous leader of a group of Swiss patriots.

Although the "William Tell Overture" was written for an opera of the same name, it is most often heard separately as a concert piece. It has been called one of the most beautiful pieces of "nature music." The overture is in four parts.

At Dawn
The first section suggests sunrise in the Swiss Alps. It begins with a beautiful, quiet passage in which only the cellos are playing. Why do you think the composer chose the cellos to play this passage? What in the music causes us to imagine the peacefulness of the scene?

◉ The Storm
The strings and woodwinds give warning that the scene is changing, and the storm breaks quickly and furiously through the orchestra. What happens in the music to build the excitement of the storm?

◉ The Calm
This section is a **pastorale** which suggests the peacefulness of the land and of the shepherd's life. It begins with an Alpine shepherd song. Which orchestral instruments imitate the sound of the Alpine horn and its echo through the mountains?

◉ Finale
The tranquil scene is interrupted by the fanfare of trumpets which begins a stirring march. This familiar march moves so fast that it is more like a gallop. Then the overture closes brilliantly with a **coda**.

When you know the music, listen to each section separately and discuss the questions. What musical devices does the composer use to paint each picture? Which of the elements of music—rhythm, melody, harmony—seems to you to be most important in each section of the overture? How are the contrasting moods of the four sections created by the composer? Using this piece as an example, what do you think is meant by **program music**?

Record 8   Side A   Band 1.
New York Philharmonic,
Leonard Bernstein, conductor.
Symbol (◉) for visible intermediate bands appears on reduced pupil's page.

William Tell Overture

BY GIOACCHINO ROSSINI
BORN 1792   DIED 1868

Because of the length of the composition, it would be well to play only parts of it in the introductory lesson. Many children are familiar with the Finale section, which might be played first. The Storm is also an interesting section to play in the first lesson. With only the title as a clue, the class might discuss descriptive music and the musical devices the composer employed in building the tonal description. Having captured the interest of the class, announce the two sections as part of the "William Tell Overture" and review the story on which the opera is based.

On another day read the page in the pupil's book with the children. You might then play the entire overture, and ask them to follow the page again and discover answers to the questions.

The tone color of the cello is rich and expressive. Possibly Rossini thought this tone color could best represent the quiet scene and the rosy hues of dawn. The soft roll of the timpani is heard in the first section to suggest thunder in the distance.

The approaching storm is announced by the strings and woodwinds. The storm is expressed vividly: syncopated rhythms give a feeling of unrest; the entire orchestra joins in at full volume; descending scale passages are played by the strings against the ascending passages of the trombones as the music builds to a climax. This is followed by "question and answer" phrases in which both strings and trombones play descending melody patterns. The volume lessens quickly, and strings and woodwinds are again heard.

The third section of the overture—the serene calm after the storm— is based on the best known of all Swiss melodies, *"Ranz des Vaches"* (rahn-deh-vash), the song of the cowherdsmen. In this overture the Swiss melody is first played by the English horn echoed by the flute as the plucked strings furnish the accompaniment. Then the English horn continues the melody as the flute plays a countermelody.

A fanfare of trumpets ushers in the quick march of the last section. The strings and other instruments take turns playing the march.

The contrasting moods of the four sections depend upon changes from melodic to rhythmic material, changes in tempo and dynamics, and changes in instrumental tone color. Program music is descriptive of scenes or a story, the "program" being the composer's plan for the description or story.

God of Our Fathers

Key: Eb   Starting Tone: Eb (1)
Meter: 4/4 (♩)
Piano accompaniment on page 215

EXPRESSION: Listen to the recording; draw attention to the accompaniment. Discuss how the brasses and timpani add to the nobility of the martial air. Ask children to follow the notation of the interludes as they listen to the voices sing the hymn. These interludes are notated in small notes in their books. Children who are studying trumpet may practice these interludes and perform them with the class. The trumpet part must be transposed to the key of F if it is to be played with the piano accompaniment. (See page x for instructions on transposition.) Notice that the choir often sings in parts in the style of an anthem.

On the recording, the first trumpet plays a descant on the last stanza. The descant is notated below with words. It may be sung by a few high voices or played by the trumpet, clarinet, flute, oboe, or violin. Like the trumpet interludes above, the descant must be transposed to the key of F for the trumpet or clarinet.

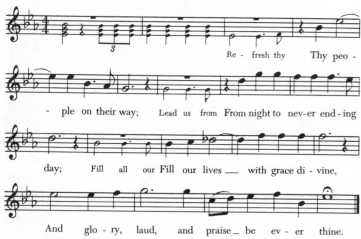

* MELODY: Discuss the function of the symbols which appear in measures seven and eleven (counting from the beginning of the melody). Play the second and third phrases, omitting the A natural and the D flat. Compare the sound with the original melody. Discuss how these two tones strengthen the melodic line. WHEN A COMPOSER MAKES USE OF TONES WHICH ARE NOT PART OF THE SCALE OF A SONG, HE MUST INDICATE THE CHANGED PITCH. THESE SYMBOLS ARE CALLED ACCIDENTALS.

Scored for instruments.
See "Exploring Music Instrumental Supplement."

God of Our Fathers

Music by George W. Warren
Words by Daniel C. Roberts

1. God of our fa - thers,
2. Thy love di - vine hath
3. Re - fresh thy peo - ple

whose al - might - y hand   Leads forth in
led us in the past;   In this free
on their toil - some way;   Lead us from

beau - ty all the star - ry band
land by thee our lot is cast;
night to nev - er end - ing day;

Of shin - ing worlds in splen - dor through the skies,
Be thou our rul - er, guard - ian, guide, and stay,
Fill all our lives with love and grace di - vine,

Our grate - ful songs be - fore thy throne a - rise.
Thy word our law, thy paths our cho - sen way.
And glo - ry, laud, and praise be ev - er thine.

Record 1 Side A Band 5. VOICES: mixed choir.
ACCOMPANIMENT: brass quintet, percussion. FORM: Introduction, 2 meas.; Vocal, v. 1; Interlude, 2 meas.; Vocal, v. 2; Interlude (modulates to Bb major); Instrumental; Interlude (modulates to Eb major); Vocal, v. 3.

Listen to your recording of "God of Our Fathers." It has been arranged for choir, brass ensemble, and timpani. Listen closely to the section in which the instruments alone play the song. The **interlude** before this section is a variation on the opening trumpet statement. The music **modulates** from the key of E flat to the key of B flat during this interlude. Can you hear that there is now a different **home tone**? Listen for the **modulation** back to E flat just before the third verse begins.

Reading the Rhythm

How many of these steps can you complete independently as you study "You're a Grand Old Flag" on page 10?

1. Determine how the song will move by looking at the **upper number** of the **meter signature**.

2. Discover which note will move with the beat by looking at the **lower number** of the **meter signature**.

3. Scan the notation.

 Look for notes that move with the beat.
 Look for notes that are held for two beats.
 Look for notes that sound two to a beat.
 Look for rhythm patterns that appear more than once in this song.
 Look for distinctive rhythm patterns that include dotted notes, syncopation, or other rhythmic variations.

4. Establish the meter by clapping lightly or by playing a percussion instrument on the beat.

5. Practice tapping the various rhythm patterns of the song or chant the words in rhythm.

6. When you know individual patterns, put them together, first tapping, then chanting the whole song.

This page and page 13 ("Reading the Melody") have been included to help children synthesize the various music reading skills they have previously learned. Help children realize as they study these pages that they are making progress toward musical independence. Emphasize that they are capable of using these skills on their own—at home as well as in music class—and that they will enjoy using these skills all of their lives.

Refer to the pupil's page regularly as new songs are learned. Gradually encourage children to recall the steps without returning to this discussion. Work for independence on the part of each child. Suggest that steps five and six can sometimes be omitted and that they can sing some new songs at sight without practicing the rhythm separately if they study the notation carefully.

Review the fact that the rhythm of a song will move according to the number of beats in a measure. Emphasize the fact that most songs move in twos, in threes, or in some combination of these two. For example, a song with four beats per measure usually has two accents per measure and sounds in twos: ♩♩♩♩ 1 2 3 4 A song with six beats per measure may also sound in twos: ♩♩♩♩♩♩ 1 2 3 4 5 6

Encourage children to look for patterns, rather than individual notes, as they scan the notation. Notice the overall character of the rhythm of the song. HOW DOES THE RHYTHM MOVE MOST OF THE TIME? DOES IT MOVE PRIMARILY WITH NOTES THAT ARE THE SAME AS THE BEAT, SHORTER THAN THE BEAT, OR LONGER THAN THE BEAT? DOES THE OVERALL MOVEMENT SEEM TO BE PRIMARILY EVEN OR UNEVEN? DOES THE RHYTHM SEEM TO MOVE IN ONE LONG FLOWING LINE PER PHRASE OR IS EACH PHRASE MADE UP OF SHORT RHYTHMIC PATTERNS?

Choose individual children to determine the meter and establish the tempo for various songs. This is a difficult skill and children will need frequent opportunities for practice before they can establish a meter which moves steadily and in the appropriate tempo.

After a steady beat has been established at an appropriate tempo, ask individuals to tap specific rhythm patterns or clap them together as a class. When chanting words, emphasize the importance of chanting lightly and crisply with accents on the important beats.

You're a Grand Old Flag

Key: F   Starting Tone: C (5)
Meter: $\frac{2}{4}$ (♩)
Piano accompaniment on page 216

* **EXPRESSION:** Discuss the fact that every war has had its own songs. All have much in common: the pride in country, assurance of victory, longing to return home. The songs of each war, however, are tailored to fit the events and mood of the particular time. The songs of World War I are different from the songs of almost any other American war. Many of them are light, full of the spirit of adventure, and are often very funny. The mood of the songs shows the patriotic spirit of the American soldiers as they left home for the battle front. As the soldiers fought in the war, they discovered that singing kept their morale high and helped to sustain their courage.

RHYTHM: After the children have read and discussed the words, challenge them to study the rhythm of the song as suggested on page 9. Notice the repetition of the syncopated pattern (♪ ♩ ♪ | ♩).

Practice tapping this pattern while one child keeps a steady beat. Discuss the fact that syncopation is dependent for its effectiveness on a strong steady beat under the shifted accent of the syncopated pattern.

After children have tapped and chanted the rhythm of the song, listen to the recording. Ask the children to make sure that they have read the rhythm correctly.

* **HARMONY:** As the children listen to the recording, draw attention to the piccolo descant. Suggest that they follow the notation at the top of pupil's page 11 as they listen. Later, assign the descant to a few children to sing. They can sing it on the syllable "ta" to imitate the sound of the piccolo. Some children may be able to play this descant on a flute, clarinet, or trumpet. Remember that, in writing for the B♭ clarinet and B♭ trumpet, the part must be transposed one step higher. (See page x.)

You're a Grand Old Flag

Words and Music by
George M. Cohan

This song, like "The Home Road," was popular during World War I. It was written by George M. Cohan, one of our best-known composers of popular music.

You're a grand old flag, you're a high- fly - ing flag;
And for - ev - er in peace may you wave; _____
You're the em - blem of the land I love,
The home of the free and the brave. _____
Ev - ery heart beats true un - der red, white, and blue,
Where there's nev - er a boast or brag; _____
But should auld ac - quaint - ance be for - got,
Keep your eye on the grand old flag. _____

Record 1   Side A   Band 6.   VOICES: mixed choir.
ACCOMPANIMENT: piccolo, trumpet, French horn, trombone, percussion.
FORM: Introduction, *8 meas.;* Vocal; Vocal.

Scored for instruments.
See "Exploring Music Instrumental Supplement."

As you listen to the recording of "You're a Grand Old Flag," notice the descant played by the piccolo. It is written here so that you can follow the notation as you listen. When the class knows the melody very well, choose a few singers to learn the descant. Sing it on the syllable "ta."

COMPOSER'S STYLE: The composer of this song, George M. Cohan (1878-1942), was one of the leading popular song writers in the early twentieth century. His best-known song is "Over There," one of the most widely sung songs of World War I. He was given a Congressional Medal for this song by the President. Cohan's songs are representative of the popular music of that era. They are melodious, influenced by jazz syncopation, and based on the old ballad design A A B A.

Review "The Star-Spangled Banner." Encourage the children to sing all of the verses.

The Star-Spangled Banner

Composer Unknown
Words by Francis Scott Key

1. Oh, say, can you see by the dawn's early light,
   What so proudly we hailed at the twilight's last gleaming?
   Whose broad stripes and bright stars, through the perilous fight,
   O'er the ramparts we watched were so gallantly streaming?
   And the rockets' red glare, the bombs bursting in air,
   Gave proof through the night that our flag was still there.
   Oh, say, does that star-spangled banner yet wave
   O'er the land of the free and the home of the brave?

2. On the shore, dimly seen thro' the mists of the deep,
   Where the foe's haughty host in dread silence reposes,
   What is that which the breeze, o'er the towering steep,
   As it fitfully blows, half conceals, half discloses?
   Now it catches the gleam of the morning's first beam,
   In full glory reflected now shines on the stream;
   'Tis the star-spangled banner, Oh, long may it wave
   O'er the land of the free and the home of the brave!

3. Oh, thus be it ever when free men shall stand
   Between their loved homes and the war's desolation!
   Blest with vict'ry and peace, may the heav'n-rescued land
   Praise the Pow'r that hath made and preserved us a nation.
   Then conquer we must, for our cause it is just,
   And this be our motto: "In God is our trust."
   And the star-spangled banner in triumph shall wave
   O'er the land of the free and the home of the brave!

Swinging Along

Key: F   Starting Tone: C (5)
Meter: $\frac{4}{4}$ ($\frac{4}{4}$)
Piano accompaniment on page 218

* EXPRESSION: Children will enjoy adding this vigorous hiking song to their repertoire. Suggest that they share it with their scout troops and plan to sing it as they go on field trips.

* MELODY: Learn the main melody by following the steps on page 13. Notice that the first six measures of the melody are based on a two-measure pattern. Study the patterns and discover that each uses tones from a familiar chord: the first pattern (measures one and two) is based on the I chord, the second pattern is based on the V7 chord, and the third pattern uses tones from the II chord.

RHYTHM: Draw attention to the rhythmic notation in measure nine. Compare the rhythms of the descant and the main melody. The main melody moves evenly with quarter and eighth notes. WHAT IS THE RELATIONSHIP OF THE EIGHTH NOTE TO THE BEAT NOTE IN THIS SONG? (Two eighth notes to a beat.) Point out the symbol in the descant part: ♫. WE CALL THIS SYMBOL A TRIPLET. THIS SYMBOL TELLS US TO CHANGE THE RELATIONSHIP FROM TWO EIGHTH NOTES TO A BEAT TO THREE EIGHTH NOTES TO A BEAT; THAT IS, FROM 2-1 TO 3-1. To further children's understanding and feeling for triplets, practice clapping the following rhythm patterns while one class member taps a steady beat on the drum or wood block. Stress that the three notes of a triplet are **evenly** divided into one beat.

Clap the beat and chant the words of the melody and the descant separately. As soon as the children can do each accurately, divide the class into two groups and chant the words of the two parts simultaneously; listen carefully to the rhythmic relationship of the two parts.

* HARMONY: This song is a good example of how an arranger can create an interesting **descant** for a melody. A descant must be interesting as an independent melody, yet harmonize with the main melody. Compare the descant and melody of this song. Notice that both melodies use tones from the same chords. The descant provides melodic and rhythmic contrast with the main melody.

Swinging Along

Girl Scout Song

Swing-ing a-long the o-pen road.
(Melody) Swing a-long ___ the o-pen road un-der
Swing-ing a-long un-der sky that's clear. Swing-ing a-long the
sky that's clear. Swing a-long ___ the o-pen
o-pen road, All in the fall, in the fall of the year. ___
road in the fall of the year. Swing a-
Swing-ing a-long, swing-ing a-long the o-pen road, ___
long, swing a-long, swing a-long the o-pen road, ___
All in the fall of the year.

Record 1   Side A   Band 7. VOICES: children's choir.
ACCOMPANIMENT: woodwind quintet.
FORM: Introduction, *2 meas.;* Vocal (voices on melody; instruments on descant); Interlude; Vocal (voices on descant; instruments on melody); Interlude; Vocal (voices on melody and descant); Coda, *2 meas.*

12

How many of these steps can you complete independently as you study "Streets of Laredo"?

1. Study the words, notice the meter, and tap the rhythm. Then read the melody.

2. Determine the **home tone** by studying the **key signature**. Remember that when a song is based on a **major** scale:

   The last **sharp** to the right is the **seventh** step of the scale.
   The last **flat** to the right is the **fourth** step of the scale.
   Count up or down from the appropriate line or space
   to locate the home tone.

3. Scan the notation.

   Look for melody patterns that include **scale steps.**
   Look for patterns that include **skips** which use tones
   from the **I chord.**
   Look for patterns that use tones from some other common
   chord, such as 5-7-2 of the V chord and 4-6-8 of the IV chord..
   Look for wide skips which form unusual intervals.

4. Establish key feeling by playing 1-3-5-8 on the bells or the piano, or I-IV-V7-I on the autoharp.

5. Sing 1-3-5-8-5-3-1.

6. Practice singing any unusual intervals.

7. Sing the melody with numbers, a syllable such as "loo," or with words.

Review this important page regularly as the children learn new songs throughout the year. Discuss the fact that learning a song involves studying three different problems: studying the words, studying the rhythm, and studying the melody.

Review the function of the key signature. Help children realize that a song is based on a particular **scale** (or some other kind of tonal organization). A scale is made up of specific pitches designated by letter names. The **key signature** indicates the scale on which the song is based. When we name the **key** of a song, we are naming the **scale** as well. If we say a song is in the **key of F major,** we mean that the melody uses tones from the F major scale and that the harmony is based on chords built on steps of the F major scale.

Review the pattern for the major scale. Ask individual children to play the F major scale by ear on bells or piano. Help them see that, in order for it to sound right, the scale must include B flat. After the children have found the correct pitches, determine the sequence of whole and half steps: whole-whole-half-whole-whole-whole-half. All major scales follow this sequence. The key signature tells us which pitches need to be made sharp or flat in order to create this sequence.

After the scale of a song has been determined, follow the directions in step two on the pupil's page. During early reading experiences, put the I, IV, and V7 chords of the appropriate key on the chalkboard so that the children can review the notes of these chords on the staff.

Encourage children to look for patterns of melody as well as individual intervals. Remind them to look for **repetitions** and **sequences.**

A strong feeling for the **home tone** is essential to good melodic reading. Ask individual children to establish the key. Be sure that each child understands the relationship between the symbol of the key signature and the actual pitched sound. WE NEED TO KNOW THE NAME OF THE HOME TONE SO THAT WE CAN FIND THAT PITCH ON THE PIANO OR BELLS. ONCE WE KNOW THE PITCH OF THIS TONE, WE CAN LOCATE ALL THE OTHER PITCHES IN A SONG BECAUSE WE WILL KNOW WHERE THEY BELONG IN THE SCALE.

After a strong key feeling has been established, sing the complete song with numbers or on a neutral syllable. If the melody is simple, invite children to sing the song immediately with words.

Streets of Laredo

Key: F   Starting Tone: C (5)
Meter: 3/4 (♩.)
Piano accompaniment on page 220

* FOLK STYLE: This song is another example, like "Johnny Has Gone for a Soldier," of the changing character of folk music. There are numerous versions of "Streets of Laredo," including the famous Negro blues "St. James Infirmary." All originated with an old Irish melody "The Unfortunate Rake." In each version the story remains essentially the same: the misfortune of an individual and his desire for an appropriate funeral. The occupation of the person changes from song to song; originally it was that of a soldier. An interesting point is that, although the occupation changes, the request for the type of funeral remains the same. A military funeral is always described.

* RHYTHM: Suggest that the children follow the steps on page 9 as they learn the rhythm of the song. Notice that the song has four phrases with each phrase composed of one rhythmic idea. The four phrases are similar rhythmically. Guide the children's attention to the fact that the main difference is in the third measure of each phrase. In phrases one and three this measure includes a dotted pattern; in phrases two and four the notes are all even. Children will tend to repeat the dotted pattern each time unless they are made aware of the difference.

* MELODY: Follow the directions on page 13 to learn the melody. Notice that the melody moves primarily by steps. The skip in measure four uses tones from the V7 chord. Notice repetitions between phrases one and three, two and four.

* HARMONY: Add a vocal harmonization to this song after the melody is familiar. Follow the directions on pages 16-17. Measure fourteen may be harmonized with either a II chord (G minor) or a V7 (C7). Try harmonizing it both ways; ask children to decide which they prefer.

Scored for instruments.
See "Exploring Music Instrumental Supplement."

Streets of Laredo

Cowboy Song

This cowboy ballad has been traced back to Ireland by folk song collectors. It originally told of the misfortunes of a soldier. In the gradual change from soldier to cowboy, the final verse of the ballad was evidently never brought up to date.

1. As I walked out in the streets of La-re-do,
2. "I see by your out-fit that you are a cow-boy,"
3. "Get six jol-ly cow-boys to car-ry my cof-fin,
4. "Oh, beat the drum slow-ly and play the fife low-ly,

As I walked out in La-re-do one day,
These words he did say as I bold-ly walked by;
Get six pur-ty maid-ens to sing me a song;
Play the dead march as you car-ry me a-long;

I spied a young cow-boy all wrapped in white lin-en,
"Come sit down be-side me and hear my sad sto-ry,
Take me to the val-ley and lay the sod o'er me,
Put bunch-es of ros-es all o-ver my cof-fin,

All wrapped in white lin-en and cold as the clay.
I'm shot in the breast and I know I must die."
For I'm a young cow-boy and know I've done wrong."
Ros-es to dead-en the clods as they fall."

When you know the melody well, harmonize vocally as suggested on pages 16-17.

Record 1   Side A   Band 8.   VOICE: tenor.
ACCOMPANIMENT: accordion, guitar, double bass.
FORM: Instrumental; Vocal, v. 1; Interlude, 4 meas.; Vocal, v. 2; Interlude, 4 meas.; Vocal, v. 3; Interlude, 4 meas.; Vocal, v. 4; Coda, 4 meas.

14

This hymn reflects the hopes and aspirations of all peace-loving people. Put the meaning and strength of its resolution into your voices.

These Things Shall Be

Music by Thomas Williams
Words by John A. Symonds

Key: D   Starting Tone: D (1)
Meter: $\frac{2}{2}$ $\left(\frac{2}{}\right)$
Piano accompaniment on page 222

These Things Shall Be

Majestically

2. New arts of loft - ier mold,

(Melody)

1. These things shall be: a loft - ier race Than
2. New arts shall bloom   of loft - ier mold, And

And mu - sic   thrill — the   skies. Ev - ery

e'er   the   world — hath — known   shall   rise   With
might - ier   mu - sic — thrill   the   skies,   And

life _____ shall be a   song,   a — song, _____

flame   of   free - dom   in — their — souls,   And
ev - ery   life   shall   be — a — song,   When

When   all   earth   is   par - a - dise.

light   of   knowl - edge — in   their   eyes.
all   the   earth — is — par - a - dise.

* EXPRESSION: Read together the words of this inspiring hymn. Discuss any difficult words, such as "loftier," "fraternity," etc. The poem, written by John Addington Symonds in 1880, is part of a longer poem entitled "A Vista." For many years this hymn has been popular at festivals and patriotic meetings. The hymn was published by the League of Nations and often used at gatherings of that organization during the 1920's.

Discuss how the song should be sung to reflect the meaning of the words. It should be sung with strong accents in a stately tempo.

MELODY: Follow the steps on page 13 to learn the melody. This song is in the key of D; therefore, D is the home tone. Decide that the song moves primarily by **steps.** Look at the melody of the first two measures. Discuss the fact that, although there is a G included in this two-measure pattern, the overall melody outlines the I chord (D-F♯-A). The G is a short note which passes by quickly. It is called a **passing tone.**

After the notation has been carefully studied, ask one child to establish tonality by playing the home tone on bells or piano. Ask the class to sing 1-3-5-8-5-3-1. Practice the difficult intervals in measures thirteen and fourteen. Sing the melody with numbers or on the syllable "loo" before singing it with words.

* HARMONY: The descant may be learned by the entire class or assigned to a few voices. Ask everyone in the class to study the notation of the descant and to observe its relationship to the melody. Locate the places where the descant moves in **parallel motion** with the melody (first phrase, beginning of third phrase) and in **contrary motion** (beginning of second phrase, end of song).

Record 1   Side B   Band 1. VOICES: children's choir.
ACCOMPANIMENT: organ.
FORM: Instrumental; Vocal, v. 1 (melody only); Vocal, v. 2 (melody and descant).

Scored for instruments.
See "Exploring Music Instrumental Supplement."

Understanding Harmony

The concepts which are introduced on this page are very important to the children's progress toward musical independence. Refer to this discussion many times as the children study other songs based on the common chords. Understanding harmony is essential to good part singing; it will also help children in their melodic reading.

Sixth grade children will probably have been introduced to the common chords (I, IV, V7) in fourth and fifth grade music classes. The first steps suggested in their book may be considered review. However, study each statement carefully to be sure children understand the construction and naming of chords.

After children have constructed chords in the key of F, check their understanding by asking them to construct chords in the keys of C and G. Here are the chords for these two keys:

Some familiar folk songs that are suitable for autoharp chording (as suggested in steps three and four) are "Animal Fair" in the key of C, "Sandy Land" in the key of G, and "Down in the Valley" in the key of F. These songs may be found in other textbooks of the *Exploring Music* series.

When the children can harmonize their chosen song by singing the letter name of the root, suggest that they sing the words of the song on these root notes. They may also create a chant by making up a pattern to sing over and over, using harmonizing tones. For example, the children might repeat the words "Streets of Laredo" over and over as a chant:

streets of La - re - do streets of La - re - do

Understanding Harmony

Many folk songs of the Western World are harmonized with chords built on steps 1, 4, and 5 of the scale. By using these chords, you can add your own harmonizing part to many songs. Follow these steps.

1. Discover the tones that will make up the I, IV, and V chords. Remember that a chord is named for the step of the scale on which it begins. We call that tone the **root** of the chord. The roots of the I, IV, and V chords in the key of F are F, B♭, and C.

2. Complete the chords by adding the tones above the root. Each tone is a third above its neighbor. The I, IV, and V chords are each made up of three tones. Often a fourth tone is added to the V chord. The chord is then called the V7 chord because the fourth tone is seven steps above the root.

3. Play the four chords on the autoharp. Start with the I chord. Now sing the melody of the song you want to harmonize as you strum the autoharp. Let your ear help you decide when to play a different chord.

4. Harmonize the song by singing the root of the chord as some people sing the melody and one person plays the autoharp. Sing the name of the harmonizing chord—I, IV, or V.

5. Later, accompany the song by singing the full chord. Divide the class into four groups. One group will sing the melody; the other three groups will sing the chordal accompaniment. Practice this pattern.

6. Sing the chords on the syllable "loo" while one group sings the melody of the song. Change chords with the autoharp.

7. Notice that these chords use the same letter names that you found when you were building the chords. The notes have been rearranged so that you can sing them more easily. Study the pattern of each voice part.

Group 3:   5 ——→ 6 ——→ 5 ——→ 5

Group 2:   3 ——→ 4 ——→ 4 ——→ 3

Group 1:   1 ——→ 1 ——→ 2 ——→ 1

             I   IV   V7   I

8. Try singing this pattern in other keys.

9. Sing a chord accompaniment to "A Hundred Years Ago." Many songs, including "Roll On, Columbia" and "Streets of Laredo," can be harmonized in this way.

A Hundred Years Ago

American Windlass Song

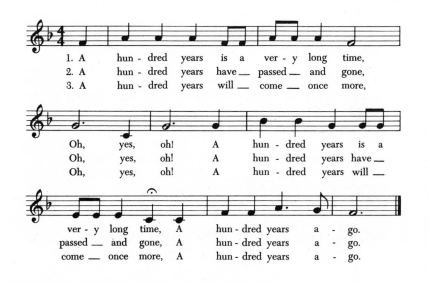

1. A hun - dred years is a ver - y long time,
2. A hun - dred years have — passed — and gone,
3. A hun - dred years will — come — once more,

Oh, yes, oh! A hun - dred years is a
Oh, yes, oh! A hun - dred years have —
Oh, yes, oh! A hun - dred years will —

ver - y long time, A hun - dred years a - go.
passed — and gone, A hun - dred years a - go.
come — once more, A hun - dred years a - go.

Record 1   Side B   Band 2. VOICES: men's ensemble.
ACCOMPANIMENT: percussion.
FORM: Introduction, *2 meas.;* Vocal, *vv. 1-3.*

Key: F   Starting Tone: F (1)
Meter: $\frac{4}{4}$ ($\frac{4}{\text{♩}}$)
Piano accompaniment on page 223

A Hundred Years Ago

MELODY: Analyze the melody of this song before the children sing it. Review the chords for the key of F and write them on the chalkboard. Ask children to study the notation of each measure. Discover that the melody in measures one and two is made up of tones from the I chord. Measures three, four, five, and six use tones from the V7 chord. Measures seven and eight use tones from the I chord (plus one tone, G, from the V chord).

Practice singing tones from these chords in **arpeggio** form. Sing the numbers of the scale to help children become more familiar with the relationship of scale steps to chord tones.

1 3 5 3 1 7 2 4 5 4 2 7 1 3 5 3 1
I   V7   I

Challenge children to sing the melody of "A Hundred Years Ago" on the syllable "loo" without assistance.

* HARMONY: When the song is familiar, sing chord patterns as suggested in the book. Follow each step: determine the autoharp chords; sing the root of each chord as an accompaniment; then sing the complete chord. Emphasize the fact that, in harmonizing a given melody, the harmony is determined by the movement of that melody. Both are based on the same pitches.

EXPRESSION: This song was originally a "windlass" song, sung as the sailors hoisted the sails. It should be sung freely, without strict rhythm, almost as a meditation.

The Swan

Key: C   Starting Tone: C (1)
Meter: $\frac{4}{4}$ $\left(\frac{4}{\downarrow}\right)$
No piano accompaniment

* HARMONY: Give children ample opportunity to experiment with the activities suggested on pages 16-17 before proceeding to the discussion on this page. Read the information concerning the structure of chords. Emphasize the idea that a chord may be built on any step of the scale.

Play chords on the piano; alternate between chords which are **major** and those which are **minor.** In a **major** chord there are two whole steps between the lower and middle tones; there are one and one-half steps between the middle and upper tones of the chord. In a **minor** chord the intervals are reversed; there are one and one-half steps between the lower and middle tones and two whole steps between the middle and upper tones.

Ask children to decide which chord they hear. Encourage them to think of additional words besides "bright" and "somber" which describe the difference in quality of sound between the two chords.

Use the chord pattern given in the pupil's book as a "warm-up" and sing it at the beginning of the class period. Sing the same chord sequence in different keys.

Learn the melody of "The Swan" thoroughly before singing it as a round. Remind the class to listen carefully as they sing. Then ask the children to sing the song as a round very slowly and to hold each note for a given number of beats. Listen to each chord and decide that the chords which are heard above the repeated C are: major (IV chord), minor (III chord), minor (II chord), and major (I chord).

Stress the fact that melodies may be harmonized in more than one way. The children have harmonized "A Hundred Years Ago" with only two chords. Play the chord sequence given in the pupil's book on the autoharp as the children sing the melody of "A Hundred Years Ago" very softly. Ask them to decide where the differences occur between this accompaniment and the one they had developed. Practice singing the chord sequence several times before using it as a vocal harmonization for "A Hundred Years Ago."

The Swan

Traditional Round

Sweet-ly the swan sings Do - de-ah-do,   do-de-ah-do,   do-de-ah-do.

A chord can be built on any step of the scale. The I, IV, and V7 chords are the most common and are called **major.** Major chords have a bright quality of sound. Chords built on the second, third, and sixth steps of the scale are called **minor.** They have a somber quality of sound.

Sing the following pattern that includes chords built on the second and sixth steps of the scale. Notice that only one voice moves at a time as you change chords. Notice the difference in the quality of the sound of each chord.

Sing "The Swan" as a four-part round very slowly. Listen to the chords. Decide which chords are major and which are minor.

A more interesting accompaniment can often be created by using the II and VI chords in addition to the more familiar ones. Try singing this pattern as an accompaniment for "A Hundred Years Ago."

Record 1   Side B   Band 3.   VOICES: boy choir.
ACCOMPANIMENT: celesta.
FORM: Introduction, *2 meas.;* Vocal (unison); Interlude, *2 meas.;*
Vocal (3 times as 4-part round).

He's Got the Whole World in His Hands

Spiritual

1. He's got the whole world — in his hands, — He's got the
2. He's got the wind and rain — in his hands, — He's got the
3. He's got both you and me — in his hands, — He's got both

whole world — in his hands, He's got the whole world —
wind and rain — in his hands, — He's got the wind and rain —
you and me — in his hands, — He's got both you and me

in his hands, — He's got the whole world in his hands. —
in his hands, — He's got the whole world in his hands. —
in his hands, — He's got the whole world in his hands. —

One group may sing this chant while another group sings the melody. Listen to the interesting harmony created by the two voices.

He's got the whole wide world — in his hands, He's got the
whole wide world in his hands, He's got the whole wide world —
in his hands, He's got the whole world in his hands. —

Record 1 Side B Band 4. **VOICES**: baritone, children's choir.
ACCOMPANIMENT: piano.
FORM: Introduction (child on chant); Vocal, v. 1 (baritone); Vocal, v. 2 (choir); Vocal, v. 3 (baritone on melody, choir on chant).

⑲

Key: F   Starting Tone: C (5)
Meter: 4/4 (4/♩)
Piano accompaniment on page 224

He's Got the Whole World in His Hands

FOLK STYLE: Children may have heard different versions of "He's Got the Whole World in His Hands" because many professional singers have recorded it. Have the children discover that this song may be performed as a quiet, meditative song or as a "rocking" rhythmic melody. After they have learned the song, let them sing it slowly and quietly. Then have the children sing it as a "shout" with a quick tempo and a hand-clapping accompaniment.

Discuss the characteristics of this song which make it representative of the spiritual: the religious text is reassuring of a safe and happy future; the melody uses tones from the I and V7 chords; the rhythms are syncopated.

Listen to the recording and discuss any discrepancies which the children notice between this version and other versions they may have heard. Relate these differences to previous discussions about how folk music develops and changes.

MELODY: Study the notation as suggested on page 13. Discover that most of the melody moves with tones from either the I or the V7 chord. The D in measure four is an "extra" note which is not part of either chord. It adds an interesting color to the sound of the V7 chord.

HARMONY: Learn the chant at the bottom of the page and notice that a similar pattern is repeated three times. The last phrase is slightly altered to make the ending sound final. The song may also be harmonized vocally. Refer to pages 16-17.

On other days motivate the children to improvise their own harmonizing part by ear. Remind them that the tones they sing should usually come from the harmonizing chord although they may use passing tones, as in the chant, to add interest and color.

* **RHYTHM:** Scan the notation and discover the syncopated patterns. Review the fact that syncopation usually occurs when a short note precedes a long one at the beginning of a measure, as in measures two, four, and six of this song. This causes the accent to be shifted from the beginning of the beat to the **offbeat**.

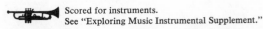
Scored for instruments.
See "Exploring Music Instrumental Supplement."

The Peddler

Key: E minor   Starting Tone: B (5)
Autoharp Key: D minor   Starting Tone: A (5)
Meter: $\frac{4}{4}$ $\left(\frac{4}{\text{♩}}\right)$
Piano accompaniment on page 225

* FOLK STYLE: Listen to the recording. Discuss the characteristics which make this music typically Russian. (The Ukraine is that part of Russia on the northern coast of the Black Sea.) In addition to those mentioned in the pupil's book, the following might also be discussed: melodies in Russian folk songs often use intervals of the fourth and fifth; descending melodic patterns are common; harmonizing voices usually move as a countermelody or descant. Typical folk instruments include the balalaika (a triangular-shaped string instrument of the guitar family), bagpipe, hunting horn, flute, tambourine, drums, and bells.

MELODY: After the minor scale has been studied on page 23, study the notation of this song. Notice that the melody constantly returns to E, G, and B (the I chord of the E minor scale).

* HARMONY: The autoharp chords for this song are shown in Roman numerals instead of letters. The reason for this change is that the song must be transposed in order to play the accompaniment on the autoharp. See page x for directions for autoharp transposition. Ask children to determine the I, IV, and V7 chords for E minor. (I = E minor, IV = A minor, V7 = B7 major.) WHAT MINOR CHORDS CAN YOU PLAY ON THE AUTOHARP? (A, D, and G minor.) WHICH OF THESE IS CLOSEST TO THE I CHORD OF "THE PEDDLER"? (D minor.) IF WE USE D MINOR AS THE I CHORD, WHAT WILL WE USE FOR THE IV AND V7 CHORDS? (G minor and A7.)

WHEN WE PLAY A SONG IN A DIFFERENT KEY FROM THE ONE IN WHICH IT IS WRITTEN, WE SAY THAT WE ARE TRANSPOSING THE SONG. WE HAVE TRANSPOSED THIS SONG FROM E MINOR DOWN ONE WHOLE STEP TO D MINOR. ON WHAT NOTE WILL THE MELODY NOW BEGIN? (A.) ON WHAT NOTE WILL IT END? (D.)

The Peddler

Ukrainian Folk Song
Words by Margaret Lowrey

The minor quality of this Russian folk song and its strong rhythmic character are typical of music from this part of the world. Listen to the recording; notice the accompaniment played on the **balalaika** and the **tambourine**, two typical Russian instruments.

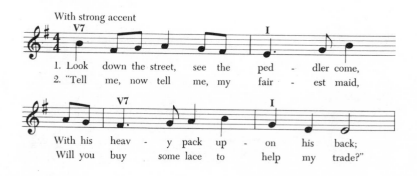

With strong accent

1. Look   down the street,   see the   ped - dler come,
2. "Tell   me, now tell   me, my   fair - est maid,

With his   heav - y pack up - on   his   back;
Will you   buy   some lace to   help   my   trade?"

Record 1   Side B   Band 5.   VOICES: soprano and tenor.
ACCOMPANIMENT: clarinet, accordion, banjo, double bass, percussion.
FORM: Introduction, *4 meas.*; Vocal, *vv. 1-2.*

He is tired and his shoul - ders ache,
"Please, good man, you need not in - sist,

But he must move on for mon - ey's sake.
For such love - ly lace I can't re - sist."

Refrain

Hai - da, hai - da, hai - da, hai - da, —

Hai - da, hai - da, hai - da, da.

Play your own accompaniment; use the autoharp to imitate the balalaika. Improvise an interesting rhythm pattern on the tambourine.

Sing the following descant on the syllable "loo" or play it on the bells.

Refrain

Follow the directions in the book and imitate the sound of the bala- laika as one child plays the autoharp accompaniment. A typical

rhythm pattern would be:  Add a second pattern

for the tambourine such as:

tap   tap shake

The descant pattern written in the pupil's book must also be trans- posed if it is to be played on the bells with the autoharp accompani- ment. Ask children to determine the key signature for **D** minor (B flat) and help them to write the bell pattern in the key of **D** minor. It will start on **E.**

Refrain

Tum Balalyka

Key: D minor   Starting Tone: A (5)
Meter: $\frac{3}{4}$ ($\frac{3}{\text{♩}}$)
Piano accompaniment on page 226

* FOLK STYLE: Read the introductory paragraph in the pupil's book. Listen to the recording. Notice that this song is in minor, each phrase ends with a descending melodic pattern, the harmony is a countermelody moving in contrast to the main melody, and an instrumental accompaniment similar to that of "The Peddler" is used in this song. Many Jewish people originally lived in Russia and Eastern Europe. It is only natural that some Jewish and Russian music should reflect similar characteristics.

* MELODY: Introduce the discussion given in the pupil's book following the song. AFTER LISTENING TO THE RECORDING, WE HAVE AGREED THAT THIS SONG IS IN MINOR. IF YOU HAD NOT HEARD THE SONG, HOW WOULD YOU KNOW THAT IT IS IN MINOR? To help them answer the question, read the paragraph on page 23 together. Discuss each step and each question thoroughly. The last note of the song is D. One would expect to find F at the end of this song since the key signature has one flat. In answer to the second question, the melody seems to move around D, F, and A. One would expect it to move around F, A, and C if the song were in F major.

Help children arrange the bells in the correct order: first for the F major scale (F G A B♭ C D E F), and then for the D natural minor scale (D E F G A B♭ C D).

Discuss thoroughly the fact that the reason the two scales have the same key signature is because both scales use exactly the same pitches. WHEN A MAJOR AND MINOR SCALE USE THE SAME KEY SIGNATURE, WE SAY THAT THEY ARE "RELATIVES." D MINOR IS THE RELATIVE MINOR OF F MAJOR.

Be sure the children can distinguish between the sound of whole and half steps before determining the scale sequence. Play from F to G, then F to F♯, and notice the difference. Practice singing whole and half steps from a given pitch. When children indicate they can hear the difference, determine the sequence of whole and half steps for the F major scale.

Tum Balalyka

Jewish Folk Song
Words by Ruth Robbins

The same musical characteristics may sometimes be found in the folk music of distant countries. Notice the similarities between this Jewish folk song and "The Peddler." The people who first sang "Tum Balalyka" may have migrated from Russia.

Record 1   Side B   Band 6.   VOICES: soprano, baritone, children's choir.
ACCOMPANIMENT: 2 violins, mandolin, double bass, tambourine.
FORM: Instrumental; Vocal, *vv. 1-2.*

22

Tum - ba - la, Tum - ba - la, Tum - ba - la - ly - ka,

Tum - ba - la, Tum - ba - la, Tum - ba - la - ly - ka,

Tum - ba - la - ly - ka, Tum - ba - la - ly - ka,

Tum - ba - la - tum, Tum - ba - la -

Tum - ba - la - ly - ka, Tum - ba - la - ly.

tum, Tum - ba - la, Tum - ba - la - ly.

How many of the steps found on page 13 can you complete as you learn this song? Remember that sometimes you need to look at other clues besides the key signature to determine the **home tone**. To discover whether a song is based on a **minor scale**:

> Look at the last note of the song. Is it the note that you expected when you looked at the key signature? Study the notation. Find the tones around which the melody seems to move. Are they the tones of the I chord?

Compare the F major and D minor scales. Play them on the bells. You will need these bells: C D E F G A B♭. Notice that the two scales include exactly the same tones. For this reason, they have the same key signature. They sound different because the eight tones are played in a different order, which causes the whole and half steps to occur in a different order.

Show children on a piano keyboard that half steps occur between one note and the note closest to it, between B and C or C and C♯.

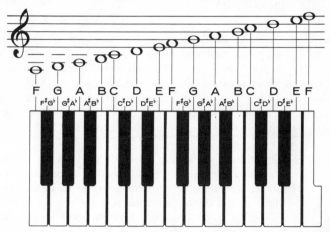

Play the D minor scale. Determine the sequence of steps: whole-half-whole-whole-half-whole-whole. This is called the **natural minor scale.** Discover that the differences between the major and natural minor scales occur at the third, sixth, and seventh steps.

There is an additional clue, not discussed in the pupil's book, which one may look for when studying minor songs. In a natural minor scale there is a whole step between 7 and 8. To give added strength to the minor home tone, composers sometimes raise the seventh step and make a half step between 7 and 8. The presence of accidentals in a song may sometimes be a clue that the song is in minor.

Discover the C♯ accidental in the harmonizing part of the refrain. C is the seventh step of the D minor scale. In this song it has been raised one half step, making a half step between C and D, the seventh and eighth steps. Play the melody, replacing the C♯'s with C♮'s. Compare this sound with the sound when C♯ is played. Notice how the C♯ moves toward D, reinforcing the feeling of home tone, or D. When the seventh step is raised in a minor scale, we call this scale the **harmonic minor scale.** The sequence of whole and half steps is as follows:

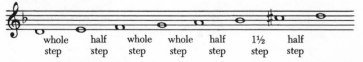

| whole step | half step | whole step | whole step | half step | 1½ step | half step |

Refer to the "Elements of Music Theory" in the front of the teacher's book on page xiv.

Kalvelis
(Little Blacksmith)

The figure section of the dance is played seven times on the recording with the chorus section following all but the last section. The accordion player improvises on the folk tune by playing it in the higher and lower registers of the instrument, by decorating it with added notes, or by playing a countermelody against it. The music changes key in the fourth playing of the chorus (one step higher) and again in the sixth playing of the chorus (one step higher).

After the children have studied the music, they should practice each part of the dance as suggested in their book until they can dance it freely. The dance directions for the chorus are given in the pupil's book. The three figures danced with the polka step are as follows:

Figure 1—Circle right (starting with right foot) 7 polka steps ending with 3 stamps on the 7th step.
Circle left in the same way.

Figure 2—Girls, holding out skirts, dance 3 polka steps forward toward center, turn around and dance back 3 polka steps finishing with 3 stamps on the last step. Repeat.

Figure 3—Boys, with hands on hips, do the same figure as the girls, but more vigorously. Repeat.

From the circle position the dance patterns are done in this order: Figure 1, Chorus, Figure 2, Chorus, Figure 3, Chorus, Figure 1, Chorus, Figure 2, Chorus, Figure 3, Chorus, Figure 1.

The dance can be made more interesting by replacing some of the repeated figures with new ones:

A weaving pattern can be used as one figure. Boys stand still as girls polka around the circle in 16 steps, weaving in and out in front of one boy, in back of the next.

The figure might be repeated again with girls standing still and boys weaving in and out of the circle.

A figure might be done with partners in ballroom position, dancing 16 polka steps around the circle.

The dance should be done in a merry style with light steps and knees lifted. Clapping should be crisp, and partners should look at each other with smiles of enjoyment.

Kalvelis (Little Blacksmith)
Lithuanian Folk Dance

This dance from the north of Europe is popular in many countries of the world, including our own. It is danced by adults and by children.

The dance tune is in two parts: the A section and the B or "chorus" section. Listen to the music and discover how many times each section is played. The music is interesting because the musicians **improvise** on the folk tune. Listen for the variations. Listen for the changes in **key**.

The A section is called the "figure" section because you dance different patterns or figures with this section. The figure section is done with a polka step. The polka is basically a two-step: step-together-step. In this dance the feet must stay close to the floor and the steps must be short and "bouncy." When you have mastered the step, try it with the A section of the music and stamp three times in the eighth measure.

The chorus of the dance is a clapping dance and is the same each time you do it. Face your partner and pretend you are hammering an anvil. Clap your hands four times with the accent of the music. Now, hook right elbows with your partner and turn in four skipping steps. Repeat the clapping and turn with the left elbow. Then repeat the whole chorus. When you can do this without music, try doing it with the six choruses of the record. To do the dance, form a circle of partners, hands joined.

Record 8   Side A   Band 2.

Dance and Its Music

Expression in music and expression in dance have always been closely related. Folk dances have developed side by side with folk songs. Primitive societies, such as those of the American Indians and the African tribal peoples, developed elaborate dance ceremonies. In Greece, dance was a part of education. Athletes and soldiers danced to develop control of mind and muscle.

Dances were exchanged as people traveled from the Old World to the New World. Dances of the Mexican Aztec Indians were taken to Spain. African rhythms were mingled with Spanish melodies. Traveling gypsies spread dance ideas from Spain to the rest of Europe. The country dances of Europe were adapted to become American square dances.

Popular dances of the sixteenth century in England and Europe developed into the seventeenth century dance forms such as the minuet and gavotte. The nineteenth century was the century of the waltz, polka, and barn dance. The twentieth century ballroom dance is often related to jazz forms. After two centuries of chiefly importing dances and dance music, the United States and South America have become leaders in dance music and dances for recreation.

Acrobatic dance is seen in many countries and has been popular for centuries. Today the performers are seen on television and stage. Decades ago they gave spectacular shows in village squares or at the banquets of noblemen.

Classical ballet grew up in the French courts where it was planned and danced by courtiers. Soon it became a principal art with composers writing ballet music and choreographers planning the movement. The classical style is based on definite positions and steps developed in the seventeenth century. Nowadays the style is often more free, and new movements of expression are created.

Many types of dances are well known to people of today. Folk dances are danced as vigorously as ever. Dance entertainment is part of American musical shows. Ballet performances are well attended. Dancing continues to be a chief form of entertainment and recreation. The dance continues to develop as an art.

Ask the children to discuss their own interests in dance. (Some take ballet lessons; some like to do square dancing, etc.) Ask them to describe any dance music they have heard and dances they have seen.

Read aloud the pupil's page with the class. As each paragraph is re-read, discuss each idea separately. Children may be able to cite examples of dances mentioned and pertinent experiences they have had. Ask piano students in the class whether they have studied compositions for the piano titled "minuet," "gavotte" (guh-vaht′), "bourrée" (boo-ray), or "gigue" (jeeg). They may be able to describe the music and play the compositions for the class at a later time. Ask class members to discuss the ballroom dances their parents or older brothers and sisters know and to discover, if they can, the origin of the dance (the waltz from Europe, the samba from Latin America, the jitterbug from the United States, etc.).

Ask the children to recall classroom dances they know which are examples of the type mentioned on the pupil's page. (They might remember the acrobatic dance interpretation of Smetana's "Dance of the Comedians" in the third grade, the interpretation of Moussorgsky's "Pictures at an Exhibition" in fourth grade, American folk dances in the fifth grade, and other dance interpretations.)

Review the pupil's page or reread portions of it as various dances and dance forms in orchestral music are studied throughout the book.

Farandole
from *L'Arlésienne Suite No. 2*

BY GEORGES BIZET (bee-zay)
BORN 1838   DIED 1875

"Farandole" by Bizet is a part of a suite written for the play *L'Arlésienne (The Woman of Arles)*. A march is played first by full orchestra. The second time, the march is played as a round. After two notes are played, the second part of the round begins. The dance theme is a French folk melody in two sections. The march is in minor, the dance in major until they are both played together in major. The form of the composition is determined by the repetition of the two melodies rather than by division into sections. The form can, therefore, be written by designating the appearance of the A and B themes: A-A (round), B (B_1-B_1, B_2-B_2, B_1-B_1, B_2-B_2, B_1-B_1), A-B_1, A-B_1, with bridge to A and B_1 together, A and B_2 together, Coda.

The children will probably be able to identify the following sounds: the full orchestra playing the A theme first, the strings predominant in the round, the bridge of drum beats which leads to the B theme; the flute predominant in the B theme with offbeat "swoops" of the violins, and finally the whole orchestra playing the B theme; the buildup by combining the two themes with increasingly faster tempo, increasingly louder dynamics, and addition of the cymbals.

When children play percussion instruments, they will discover that by playing two drums, they can play the rhythm of the A theme in the round, and maracas or sand blocks might play the "swoops" of the B^2 theme. Other instruments can be added as the composition grows to the final climax.

The children may engage in various other activities as they study the composition at different times: sing the march theme in minor (on the syllable "ta"); sing it as a round; sing it in major; sing the B theme on the syllable "ta"; sing the two themes together.

The French sometimes call the dance *"L'Escargot"* (The Snail). The nickname might suggest the formation for your farandole. A simple dance can be done by having two circles (one inside the other or side by side), the A circle marching each time the theme is heard, the B circle running in quick, light steps with each playing of the theme, and the two circles moving together with the last part of the farandole. The dance can be more expressive of the music if there are two A circles which perform together and in a round, and if the B dancers divide into B′ and B^2 circles, with B^2 dancers developing a knee-bend or arm movement with the "swoops."

Farandole
from *L'Arlésienne Suite No. 2*
by Georges Bizet

Composers have often written orchestral pieces using ideas taken from dances. The French composer Bizet must have been very familiar with the farandole, a spirited street dance from Provence in southern France. The dancers form a procession and, joining hands, dance through the village imitating the leader. The tempo gradually increases until the dance comes to a rollicking climax.

Listen to the entire orchestral composition and enjoy the melodies, the rhythms, and the design. Discuss all that you noticed in the first hearing. Listen again and discover all that happens to the two themes—the first or march theme, and the second or dance theme.

March Theme A (key D minor)

Dance Theme B (B_1 and B_2) (key D major)

Compose a class dance which expresses the spirit and form of the music. Explore ideas for movements to be done with the March Theme. Experiment until you find a good dance idea for the second theme. Combine your dance ideas in one grand farandole.

Record 8   Side A   Band 3.
Philadelphia Orchestra,
Eugene Ormandy, conductor.
Symbol (◉) for visible intermediate bands appears on reduced pupil's page.

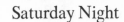

Key: D   Starting Tone: D (1)
Meter: $\frac{2}{4}$ ($\frac{2}{\downarrow}$)
No piano accompaniment

Saturday Night

Nigerian Folk Song

1. Ev-ery-bod-y   loves   Sat-ur-day   night.

2. Ev-ery-bod-y   loves   Sat-ur-day   night.

3. Ev-ery-bod-y,   ev-ery-bod-y,   ev-ery-bod-y,   ev-ery-bod-y,

4. Ev-ery-bod-y,   loves   Sat-ur-day   night.

Add a rhythmic accompaniment to this African round. Choose several different rhythm patterns from the notation.

Begin with a pattern of notes that move with the beat. Play it on a low-pitched drum.

Add other patterns, one at a time, on drums of different sizes. Begin to sing the round after all the drum patterns have been established.

Record 1   Side B   Band 7.   VOICES: children's choir.
ACCOMPANIMENT: piccolo, oboe, clarinet, bass clarinet.
FORM: Vocal (unison); Vocal (4-part round);
Instrumental (4-part round).

* RHYTHM: Children will enjoy the syncopated rhythm of this song from Africa. Follow the steps on page 9 to learn the rhythm.

Ask children to locate measures using this rhythm: ♪ ♫ ♪ Discuss the fact that it begins on the last half of the beat, or the offbeat. Review the relationship of an eighth note to a sixteenth note (twice as long, or ♪ = ♬). Notice the triplet (♫). Review the function of this symbol. (See page 12.) Practice tapping this pattern to help children understand the difference between two tones to a beat and three tones to a beat.

Pattern / Beat

Choose individual measures from the song and use these as a basis for a percussion accompaniment. Begin with the pattern which contains four eighth notes (♫ ♫). Add other patterns, one at a time:

Choose drums with different pitches for each pattern. If drums are not available, invite the children to experiment with different ways of clapping in order to produce a different sound for each pattern.

On another day, suggest that the children improvise an accompaniment as the class sings. Instead of repeating the same patterns, encourage the children to experiment with different patterns and to improvise variations as they play. Remind them that the accompaniment will be more interesting if it moves in a rhythm that is different from the rhythm of the melody.

* HARMONY: Sing the song as a four-part round; remind children that it is important to keep a steady beat when singing a round.

Ghost of Tom

Key: E minor   Starting Tone: E (1)
Meter: $\frac{4}{4}$ $\left(\frac{4}{4}\right)$
No piano accompaniment

* **RHYTHM:** Complete the steps on page 9 to determine the rhythm. This song is in two sections. Compare the rhythm of the first section with that of the second section. Read and discuss the information in the pupil's book regarding **augmentation.** Help children realize that each note in the lower voice is now **twice as long** as the corresponding note in the upper voice. Quarter notes are replaced with half notes, eighth notes are replaced with quarter notes, etc. Chant the rhythm of the lower part; then divide the class into two groups and chant both parts at the same time.

* **MELODY:** Follow the directions on page 13 to learn the melody of the round. Discover that the song is in E minor. Be sure that the D in measures one, two, and eight is sung as D natural with a whole step between D and E. The D natural indicates that this song is written in the **natural minor scale.**

* **HARMONY:** When children are familiar with the melody of the round and the rhythm of section two, teach them to sing the harmonizing part of the second section. Although the rhythm is altered, the melody of the lower part remains the same as the upper voice for the first eight measures. Review the study of intervals found on page 5. Analyze the last five measures of the song and determine the intervals between the two voices (octave, sixth, fourth, third, unison).

Ghost of Tom

Traditional Round
Arranged by Kurt Miller

The first section of this song is to be sung as a four-part round. When the last group finishes singing the round, the class sings the second section in two parts. Notice that the low part begins with the same melody as the high part with one difference—each note is twice as long as before. This interesting rhythmic device is called **augmentation.** The rhythm has been "augmented"; that is, lengthened or stretched out.

The "spooky" mood of this song can be emphasized by playing the melody on a xylophone. Choose one or two percussion instruments with unusual tone quality and add some special sound effects. One instrument might be played on the final beat of each phrase. Plan a pattern for the **introduction** and the **coda,** using several instruments. The same pattern might also be played as an **interlude** between the round and the second section.

1. Have you seen the ghost of Tom?

2. Long white bones with the flesh all gone. _____ Oh,

3.

4. _____ Would-n't it be chill-y with no skin on?

Record 1   Side B   Band 8.   VOICES: children's choir.
ACCOMPANIMENT: string quartet, harp.
FORM: Instrumental (melody); Vocal (as written in book).

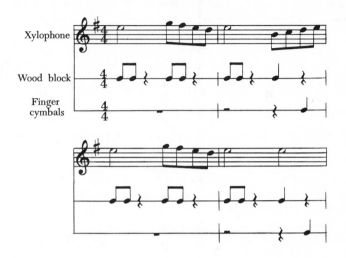

* FORM: Encourage children to develop a "spooky" introduction, interlude, and coda for this song. The same pattern can be used each time, or a different pattern can be developed for each section. Continue the patterns throughout the song as an accompaniment. The following pattern may be used, or children may plan their own, using a variety of "spooky-sounding" instruments.

Let Us Break Bread Together

Key: F   Starting Tone: C (5)
Meter: 4/4 (♩)
Piano accompaniment on page 228

* FOLK STYLE: After reading the discussion in the pupil's book, decide that this song is a quiet, plaintive spiritual. Ask children to recall spirituals they know that belong to the different groups described in the book. For example, "Lonesome Valley" is a quiet spiritual. "Somebody's Knockin' at Your Door" is a "shoutin' spiritual." (These songs can be found in *Exploring Music 5.*) Recall the experiment with "He's Got the Whole World in His Hands."

* EXPRESSION: IN EVERY SONG THERE IS ONE POINT, OR SECTION, WHICH IS THE MOST IMPORTANT PART OF THAT SONG. IT IS CALLED THE CLIMAX. WHERE DOES THE CLIMAX OCCUR IN THIS SONG? Help children decide that it occurs in the third phrase. It is the most important phrase of the song and is different from the other phrases: the words change at this point; the rhythm contrasts with the rhythm of the first two phrases; the strong harmonic progressions created by the three voices contrast with the unison singing of the first two phrases. The descending melodic line in the fourth phrase also lends importance to the climatic third phrase. Read page iv for other ideas on expressive singing.

* HARMONY: Study the notation of the third and fourth phrases carefully and notice how each part moves in relation to the others. Play the chord sequence on the piano. Encourage children to sing as much as possible of these two phrases on a neutral syllable. Listen to the recording to help correct errors. Return to the beginning of the song and learn the first and second phrases. Study the notation at the ends of these phrases to discover the relationship of the harmonizing parts to the main melody.

Let Us Break Bread Together

Spiritual
Arranged by
William S. Haynie

The songs of the American Negro are among the most beautiful folk songs of our country. They have a quality which is different from folk songs found anywhere else in the world. There are at least two types of spirituals: the quiet, plaintive type and the joyous, rhythmic type known as "shouts."

This devout spiritual should be sung in fervent spirit and in an easy, swinging tempo. Is this a quiet spiritual or a "shout"?

Record 2   Side A   Band 1.   VOICES: children's choir.
ACCOMPANIMENT: piano.
FORM: Introduction, *4 meas.;* Vocal, *vv. 1-2.*

30

When I fall on my knees with my face to the ris-ing sun,

When I fall on my knees with my face to the ris-ing sun,

Oh Lord, have mer-cy on me.

Oh Lord, have mer-cy on me, on me.

Talkin' Blues

The American Negroes sometimes sang "blues" as they worked in the fields or rested in front of their cabins in the evening. Most blues are slow, melancholy jazz songs; but this is a "talkin' blues." The words are chanted in a rhythmic "sing-song" while chords are strummed on a guitar or banjo.

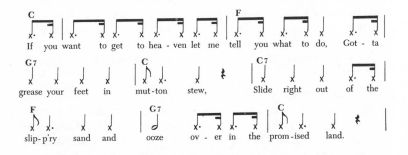

If you want to get to hea-ven let me tell you what to do, Got-ta
grease your feet in mut-ton stew, Slide right out of the
slip-p'ry sand and ooze ov-er in the prom-ised land.

Discuss the information about blues before learning the chant. Further information on the blues song style may be found on page 171.

To learn the rhythm, ask one group of children to tap a steady beat while the rest of the class taps the rhythm of the words. To make sure the dotted patterns are chanted correctly, practice clapping a pattern of four sixteenth notes (♫). Without breaking the rhythm, clap only the first and fourth sixteenth notes in each group (♫ = ♪. ♪). Suggest to the children that they think of each sixteenth note as belonging to the note which follows it (♪. ♪ ♪. ♪). This will help to keep the sixteenth notes short and the rhythm crisp.

When the children can chant the words correctly, add the autoharp accompaniment. Experiment: stroke on every beat, on every other beat, or on the first beat of each measure. Decide which pattern seems to be most appropriate.

Encourage the children to make up new "Talkin' Blues" either individually or in small groups. Ask them to teach their "blues" to the rest of the class.

Record 2 Side A Band 2. VOICES: children's choir.
ACCOMPANIMENT: banjo.
FORM: Vocal (children on chant with banjo); Instrumental (children in class may chant with banjo); Vocal (children on chant with banjo).

Dance in the Study of Music

Because dance is closely related to the development of the art of music and because it is an excellent classroom activity, this book gives considerable emphasis to the relationship of music to dance. Original ideas in free movement will be used to interpret several songs and orchestral compositions. Teachers may wish to add other favorite folk dances to the list for the year.

At this grade level especially, the activities of the child must be taken into account if the dances are to succeed. Children of this age cannot be asked to move "daintily" or in the small movements used by younger children. Boys should not be asked to dance in the same way as girls. Stylized movement, often based on dances the children have seen, is usually of interest to them. When asked to improvise an original Spanish dance, they will use ideas they have seen in Spanish dances, adapting them for their own purposes and the music they study. Vigorous movements not requiring great coordination are appropriate at this age level. Such movements will be truly expressive of the child and will not cause him to reject the activity because it seems too feminine or too childish. Because of different stature, coordination, and interests, boys and girls often enjoy dancing in separate groups. In many countries, some folk dances are danced only by men, just as some dances are only done by women. Such a plan is educationally sound and can result in more expressive dances and more wholehearted participation.

The four folk dances included in the book and the music on the records are typical of the countries from which they come. Children must understand the design of the music on which the dance is based. Foot patterns and other movements should often be practiced without music until physical coordination is achieved. The different dance figures should usually be mastered and danced separately before the complete dance is performed. When the children know the dance, they should incorporate attractive style into their movements. The style of folk dancers of the country in which the music originated should be imitated as closely as possible. Style most often depends upon such things as accent in movement; lifting the feet high or keeping them close to the floor, depending upon the dance; moving with lightness as momentum of the movement carries the dancer along; turning or bending the body or moving the arms in a way which prepares the dancer for change of direction and lets the dance move along smoothly; dancing with smiles, freedom, and enjoyment that are a natural part of folk dance. Adult folk dance groups of the community should be invited to dance for the class, and some people from such a group might help the children with class dances.

Originally, folk songs were often danced as well as sung. The dance ideas of class members and those found in the words of the song will usually be sufficient for composing a simple dance. The class may experiment with dancing in lines, in sets, in a circle, or in several circles; dancing separately or with partners; playing an instrument such as the tambourine as they dance or having an accompanying group play percussion instruments as others dance; wearing a sash or arm ribbon or whirling scarves as they dance. The meter, accent, phrasing, and design of the song should be followed in the dance. In composing original dances with orchestral music, children will need two kinds of preparation: analysis of the music they are to dance and sufficient experience with dance ideas and movement patterns to feel freedom and confidence; a continuing activity that takes place through the year and helps children explore movement and overcome self-consciousness. All members of the class sometimes work at the same time but more often will take turns in groups so that there is space for freedom of movement. Children will be encouraged to "look like the music sounds"; that is, to interpret accent and rhythm patterns in foot movements, melody line in body movements, to turn with phrase endings, to enact repetitions in the music with identical dance movement.

Such interpretation is taught, not by teacher demonstration or verbal planning, but by pointing out the appropriate and interesting movements of class members. Large movements—stamping, leaping, turning—should be encouraged when appropriate, as well as small foot patterns and body movements. Free interpretation will often follow instrumentation as some children notice the part of one instrument or group of instruments in the composition, and other children follow another instrument or group. Boys and girls will often work in separate groups with music of special interest for each. Children who are not in the dance group will be asked to comment on dance ideas of class members, especially the ways in which the ideas match the music.

This free work will prepare children for patterning their movement with the design, style, and musical elements of specific compositions. Before they begin to develop the dance, they should know the music, or section of the music, they are to interpret. Interpretation in movement is an excellent way of listening to music. It requires concentration. It allows for true expression and originality, for physical freedom which is genuine, yet acceptable in the classroom, and for development of self-discipline and cooperation in ensemble work.

Full page painting in pupil's book.
See page 209 for explanation of art.

Music of the British Isles

The British Isles, which include England, Scotland, Ireland, and Wales, have made many musical contributions to the world. They are sometimes known as the "Singing Islands," because singing has been an important part of the lives of the British people since early times. Bards and minstrels once wandered over the countryside singing their ballads and airs.

Although small in area, the British Isles contain several distinct groups of people. The people of each country are loyal to their homeland and possess a strong individual spirit which is reflected in their music.

We find in the songs of the Irish their love of storytelling, their affection for the beautiful "Emerald Isle," and their unique sense of humor. Harp music is so important to the Irish that they use the harp as an emblem on their flag.

The Scottish people, dressed in plaid kilts as they play the bagpipes and dance the Highland Fling, have produced a unique folk song literature. It reflects their rugged life, their famous battles, their heroes, and their royal families. This rocky, mountainous country of lakes and windswept marshes has produced songs and dances with unusual melodies and rhythms which are easily identified as Scottish.

The people of Wales are well known for their great song festivals and for the choruses in which many participate. From the earliest times Welshmen have sung "in parts" in contrast to the unison singing of the people of many other countries. Among their songs are many strong hymns. These hymn tunes often appear in the hymnals of churches in our country.

The song of the cuckoo, the shepherd with his sheep, and the serene lakes of England have inspired the great poets. These pastoral scenes are also woven into English songs. A country with so long a coast line must develop a great love of the sea. In England this love is reflected in the many sea songs of the sailors and fishermen.

The pupil's page presents a brief overview of the various characteristics of music of the British Isles, which will be studied in this section of the book. As preparation for the study of this section, conduct a class discussion about these islands. Ask children who have been there to relate their experiences. Encourage children to review what they know about the geography and history of the British Isles. Help them recall the role the islands have played in the history of the United States and our relationship with this "mother country" throughout our history.

The music of the British people is of special interest to us, because so much of our American folk music is derived from the music of these islands. Even the melody for one of our favorite patriotic songs, "America," is the same as the English national anthem. Singing societies known as "glee clubs" have come to us from England.

Read the page aloud with the class. Discuss the paragraphs dealing with each country separately. Encourage children to make comments and ask questions having to do with national characteristics expressed in the music of a country. Ask the class to look through the pages of this section of the book in order to study the pictures and titles and to gather general impressions about the music of the British Isles.

As the music of each country is studied, ask the class to reread the appropriate paragraph from this page. From their knowledge of the music they have learned, ask class members to make other general statements that might be added to the paragraph on this page. This might be a written assignment. For example, after the songs and related activities have been studied in the section dealing with Scotland, class members might be asked to reread the paragraph on this page which deals with Scotland and then to write two additional statements. These statements might be compiled into the class description of Scottish music.

Shule Aroon

Key: A minor   Starting Tone: G (7)
Meter: 4/4 (♩)
Piano accompaniment on page 230

* FOLK STYLE: Listen to the recording. Look for characteristics of Irish folk music which are apparent in "Shule Aroon." Its free-flowing melody moves over a wide range. It is a love song. Love is a common topic of Irish songs. The combination of Gaelic and English words reminds us of the effect of English rule over Ireland. The changing rhythms in the song are also typical of Irish folk music.

EXPRESSION: Although the melody and rhythm have been altered, the mood of the two songs remains the same. The feeling of longing and concern for loved ones is common to all.

The title "Shule Aroon" may be translated as "Come with me, my love." The words "Iss guh day thoo avoorneen slawn" mean "Go thee now, good-bye my love."

MELODY: To help children learn to sing this version of the melody, listen to the recording. Compare this melody with the melody of "Johnny Has Gone for a Soldier," page 3. The overall contour of the two melodies remains the same, although the melody for "Johnny Has Gone for a Soldier" has been simplified. Many of the turns and embellishments have been omitted. This kind of "smoothing out" of a melody often happens as a folk song is passed on "by ear." Practice measures five, six, and seven, where the melody moves with eighth notes. Sing the melody with numbers; be sure that the children sing each note correctly.

FORM: Study the design of the song. There is a verse and refrain, each of which is made up of short, two-measure phrases. Each phrase is a new melodic idea. The lack of repetition adds to the rhapsodic nature of the lovely melody.

Shule Aroon

Irish Folk Song

The title of this song is in Gaelic, the ancient tongue of Ireland. "Shule Aroon" was first sung during the early eighteenth century. After defeat by the English, many Irish soldiers fled to France. They hoped to return eventually, drive the English out of Ireland, and regain their freedom.

1. I would I were on yon-der hill,
2. I'll sell my rock, I'll sell my reel,

'Tis there I'd sit and cry my fill,
I'll sell my on-ly spin-ning wheel,

And ev-ery tear would turn a mill,
To buy for my love a sword of steel,

Iss guh day thoo a-voor-neen slawn.

Refrain

Shule, shule, shule a-roon! On-ly death can ease my woe,

Record 2   Side A   Band 3.   VOICE: soprano.
ACCOMPANIMENT: harp.
FORM: Introduction, *2 meas.;* Vocal, *v. 1;* Interlude, *2 meas.;* Vocal, *v. 2;* Interlude, *2 meas.;* Vocal, *v. 3;* Interlude, *2 meas.;* Vocal, *v. 4.*

34

Since the lad of my heart from me did go,

Iss guh day _____ thoo a - voor - neen slawn.

3. I wish, I wish, I wish in vain,
   I wish I had my heart again,
   And vainly think I'd not complain,
   Iss guh day thoo avoorneen slawn.
   Refrain

4. But now my love has gone to France,
   To try his fortune to advance;
   If he e'er comes back 'tis but a chance,
   Iss guh day thoo avoorneen slawn.
   Refrain

Music of Ireland

The two songs "Shule Aroon" and "The Minstrel Boy" are examples of airs for storytelling that are particularly Irish. Their free-flowing melodies move over a wide range.

The importance of music in the lives of the Irish is revealed in every line of "The Minstrel Boy." The harp was the most prized possession of young men in Ireland and was often buried with them. In this "land of song," music helped to tell the history of a proud people. Many of the ballads tell of the struggle for independence from England. The "foeman's chains" in "The Minstrel Boy" undoubtedly refer to the unwanted control of Ireland by the English. Other songs, such as "Shule Aroon," tell of the loneliness of those left behind.

The Irish music which we know comes primarily from the seventeenth century after English had become the official language of the country. The songs are usually of love or patriotism. Few lullabies or work songs are found among Irish folk songs.

Read the description of Irish music aloud; relate it to the Irish songs found in the pupil's book. Some students may wish to look for other Irish songs which contain these characteristics.

Most Irish folk songs are polished and musically sophisticated. They are carefully structured—usually sixteen bars long with phrases of equal length. The complexity and the careful design suggest that the music may have been influenced by composed music. The harpists of ancient Ireland were trained musicians. The more elaborate Irish folk melodies may have been originally composed by these men.

The influence of England and Scotland can be observed in many Irish songs. The texts refer to the almost constant warfare between the countries. Musical characteristics of the songs found in each of the countries are common to all. English and Scottish soldiers were encamped in Ireland off and on for centuries. Often the families of these men migrated to Ireland. As a result, Irish, English, and Scottish folk songs mingled until their origins were sometimes lost and forgotten. One of the most famous of Irish songs, "The Wearing of the Green," can be traced back to a Scottish air.

The Minstrel Boy

Key: E♭   Starting Tone: B♭ (5)
Meter: 4/4 (♩)
Piano accompaniment on page 231

* MELODY: After the children have enjoyed the recording, conduct a discussion about the words and the folk characteristics. Read the words of the song aloud to the children. Help them define difficult words, such as "girded," "sully," and "asunder." "Bard" is another word for "minstrel." The minstrel boy was probably one of the wandering harpists who originally gave Ireland its beautiful airs.

Ask children to follow the notation as they listen to the recording a second time. WHERE MAY YOU HAVE PROBLEMS WITH THE MELODY? (Phrase three.) Practice singing this phrase on a neutral syllable until children feel comfortable with the changing tonality created by the B♮ accidental. LISTEN TO THE PHRASE. WHAT TONE SEEMS TO BE THE "HOME TONE"? (C) THAT IS BECAUSE OF THE B♮ WHICH MOVES TOWARD C, GIVING IT A STRONG FEELING OF COMING TO REST. With the beginning of the fourth phrase, E♭ is reestablished as the tonal center.

* RHYTHM: The song should be sung with spirit, strong accents, and clearly defined rhythm patterns. Review the relationship of the dotted quarter to the eighth and the dotted eighth to the sixteenth. (See page 31.) Be sure that the long note of each pattern is held three times as long as the short one:

Listen to the recording to learn how to match the words of the second verse to the rhythm of the melody.

FORM: Discover the design of the song. There are four four-measure phrases: A A B A. This pattern is found in folk music throughout the Western world. Show children that studying the design of a song will help them learn and recall the melody more easily. IN THIS SONG, THERE ARE ONLY TWO DIFFERENT PHRASES TO LEARN. WHEN WE HAVE LEARNED THE FIRST PHRASE OF THE SONG, WE HAVE ACTUALLY LEARNED THREE OF THE FOUR PHRASES OF THE SONG!

The Minstrel Boy

Irish Air
Words by Thomas Moore

The words for this song were written by Thomas Moore, an Irish poet who adapted many of the ancient Irish legends to the folk melodies of the people. Each melody was known by a special name and often several different poems were sung to the same air. This air is known as the "Moreen." Another well-known Irish tune is "Londonderry Air."

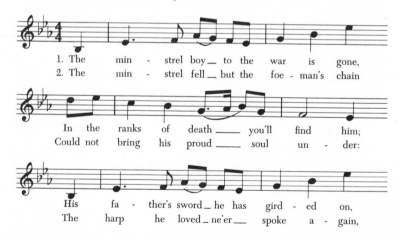

1. The min - strel boy __ to the war is gone,
2. The min - strel fell __ but the foe - man's chain

In the ranks of death _____ you'll find him;
Could not bring his proud _____ soul un - der:

His fa - ther's sword __ he has gird - ed on,
The harp he loved __ ne'er __ spoke a - gain,

Record 2   Side A   Band 4.   VOICES: men's ensemble.
ACCOMPANIMENT: brass ensemble, percussion.
FORM: Introduction, 8 meas.; Vocal, v. 1; Interlude, 8 meas.; Vocal, v. 2; Coda, 8 meas.

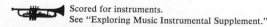

Scored for instruments.
See "Exploring Music Instrumental Supplement."

And his wild harp slung ___ be - hind him.
For he tore its chords ___ a - sun - der. And

"Land of song," said the war - rior bard,
said, "No chains shall ___ sul - ly thee,

"Though all the world be - tray ___ thee,
Thou soul of love and brav - ery

One sword at least ___ thy ___ rights shall guard,
Thy songs were made ___ for the proud and free,

One ___ faith - ful harp ___ shall praise thee."
They shall nev - er sound ___ in slav - ery."

FOLK STYLE: The Irish poet Thomas Moore (1779-1852) was one of the first to recognize the importance of preserving the musical heritage of one's country. During his lifetime many ancient Irish airs were in danger of being forgotten because the words were in Gaelic. Since this language was no longer spoken by the young people, the songs meant little to them. Moore helped to keep these songs alive by writing new words for many of the airs. He turned to Irish history for inspiration in many cases. Thus his poetry not only helped preserve the musical heritage of Ireland, but also provided a living record of their ancient history. The words of many of the Irish songs which are most popular today were written by Moore.

The word "air" means "melody." Folk collectors often use the term to identify melodies, such as this one, which are used with several different texts. Each "air" is given a name so that it can be easily identified. Hymn tunes are also often designated in this manner.

Help children identify the traits which make this a typical Irish song: the text is patriotic, the song is sixteen bars long, and the four phrases are of equal length. It covers a wide range, the rhythms constantly change, and the melody is rhapsodic in nature.

Cockles and Mussels

Key: F Starting Tone: C (5)
Meter: 3/4 (3/♩)
Piano accompaniment on page 232

* **EXPRESSION:** This song probably grew out of a street cry. Help children decide the difference between this type of a "work song" and other work songs they know. In the songs of workers such as sailors or lumbermen, the rhythm of the music is dictated by the rhythm of the work. The purpose of such work songs is to help the work flow more smoothly and easily and to keep the workers in a happy state of mind as they do their work. The street cry, "cockles and mussels," was actually a part of this person's work. Words and music were designed to convey a message to the potential purchaser. As the marketwoman passed through the streets, she drew attention to the things she had for sale by describing them in song.

Ask the children to recall modern applications of these "work songs." Modern advertising jingles serve a similar purpose. So do the bells on ice cream wagons which are to be found in many neighborhoods.

RHYTHM: Learn the rhythm of this song by following the steps outlined on page 9. Discover the repeated rhythm pattern: ♩ | ♩. ♪♪ | ♪♪ ♩ HOW MANY TIMES DOES IT APPEAR? (Six.) Tap the rhythm, making sure that the syncopated pattern is performed correctly.

* **MELODY:** The melody of the opening phrase contains a **sequence.** A sequence occurs when a melodic pattern is repeated at a different pitch. Point out to children that recognition of sequential patterns will help them learn a melody more quickly. WHAT ELSE DO YOU NOTICE ABOUT THE MELODY OF THIS FIRST PHRASE THAT WILL HELP YOU LEARN THIS SONG? Guide children to use their awareness of the sequence as an aid in learning the melody. The melodic pattern in measures one and two makes use of the tones from the I chord (F-A-C). In measures three and four the pattern is repeated a step higher and makes use of the tones from the V7 chord.

Cockles and Mussels

Irish Folk Song

Versions of this melody are found in England as well as in Ireland. The Irish, English, and Scottish have moved from one country to another for centuries; and it is not surprising that the same melodies are often found in all sections of the British Isles.

1. In Dub - lin's fair cit - y, where girls are so pret - ty,
2. She was a fish - mon - ger, but sure 'twas no won - der,
3. She died of a fe - ver and no one could save her,

I first set me eyes on sweet Mol - ly Ma - lone,
For so were her fa - ther and moth - er be - fore;
And that was the end of sweet Mol - ly Ma - lone;

As she wheeled her wheel - bar - row through streets broad and nar - row,
And they wheeled their wheel - bar - row through streets broad and nar - row,
Now her ghost wheels her bar - row through streets broad and nar - row,

Cry - ing, "Cock - les and mus - sels, a - live, a - live oh!"

Refrain
A - live, a - live oh! — A - live, a - live oh! — Cry - ing,
live oh! live oh!

Record 2 Side A Band 5. VOICE: tenor.
ACCOMPANIMENT: alto flute, harp.
FORM: Introduction, 8 meas.; Vocal, v. 1; Interlude, 4 meas.; Vocal, v. 2; Interlude, 4 meas.; Vocal, v. 3; Instrumental (vocal on refrain).

F   F   F C7 F

"Cock-les and mus-sels, a - live, a - live, oh!"

"Cock-les, ___ mus-sels, ___ live, live, oh!"

Irish minstrels accompanied themselves on the harp as they sang. Listen for the harp accompaniment on your recording. You may create a "harp-like" effect on the autoharp by stroking the strings slowly to imitate the rippling sound of the harp.

The alto part may be sung as written, or it may be sung as a descant an octave higher than written. This part may also be plucked on the autoharp. On the recording, it is played on an **alto flute**.

* HARMONY: To create a harp-like effect, strum the strings of the autoharp with the fingertips or with a soft felt pick. Play on the accented beat of each measure, stroking the strings slowly in a rippling sound so that individual pitches can be heard.

Learn the harmonizing part to the refrain. This harmony part may be played on a recorder, bells, or clarinet. (See page viii for discussion of melody instruments.) This part can also be sung with the verse. On the verse the boys could sing the melody, and the girls could sing the harmonizing part an octave higher. On the refrain the girls could sing the melody, and the boys could sing the part as written. Some children might create their own chant or descant for this song.

Discuss the differences and similarities between chants and descants. Both must be based on the same harmonic progressions found in the melody and must use tones from those chords. A chant is made up of a single pattern, usually one or two measures long, which is repeated over and over. It is usually below the melody. (See example, pages 16-17.) A descant is an independent melody which moves in contrast to the main melody; it is usually higher than the main melody. (See example, pages 10-11.)

FOLK STYLE: Review the discussion on page 35 and locate the qualities of this song which make it representative of Irish music.

Turn Ye to Me

Key: E   Starting Tone: B (5)

Meter: $\frac{3}{4}$ ($\frac{3}{\downarrow}$)

Piano accompaniment on page 234

* EXPRESSION: This song is a seaman's prayer as he describes the lonely marsh of the Scottish highlands and calls out for notice and protection of himself. The "sea mew" is the marshy ledge where the water birds nest.

The quiet melody of the opening and closing measures of the song lies in the lower part of the scale and contains tones held for more than one beat. In the middle section, the higher part of the scale and the even rhythm give a different feeling. The repetition of the words "cheerily," "wearily," "drearily," and "merrily" give special charm to the song. Ask the class to read the words aloud, enjoying those sounds as well as the sounds of "Mhairi-du" (mah-ree-doo), "sea mew," and other words. The class should sing pure, bright vowels to make this song sound "Scottish" and to match the mood of the text.

RHYTHM: The main charm of the song is in the expressive melody which is made up of long phrases. The underlying rhythm should therefore be only lightly accented in order to preserve the phrase lines. The rhythm is simple to read and can be studied as a review of basic $\frac{3}{4}$ meter. In the first section, the most important rhythm pattern is uneven ($\downarrow.$ $\downarrow\downarrow$); in the second section, even ($\downarrow$ $\downarrow$ $\downarrow$).

* FORM: The song is in two distinct sections. The first section is composed of an eight-measure melody and its repetition. The second section is composed of four shorter phrases, four measures each. The fourth phrase consists of four measures of the first section repeated as a closing. The shorter phrases and the even rhythm give a feeling of quicker movement which provides contrast.

HARMONY: The first section of the song (the first 16 measures) and the closing phrase are composed almost entirely of the tones of the pentatonic scale E, F♯, G♯, B, C♯. (Although the A is used as a passing tone in some measures, it will not interfere with the pentatonic sound.) Using these tones of the resonator bells or of a low octave on the piano, children can improvise a harmony part that sounds well with the melody they sing. They might find a "rhythm of the sea" for their accompaniment.

Turn Ye to Me

Scottish Folk Song
Words by John Wilson

This song from Scotland is considered to be unusually beautiful. As you listen to the recording, try to discover the expressive musical qualities which give it charm and appeal. In what part of Scotland did this song probably have its origin? In order to answer this question, read the discussion on the next page.

Follow the directions on page 9 for reading the rhythm as you learn this song. Study the form; notice the slight changes in melodic line which add to the interest of the song.

Record 2   Side A   Band 6.   VOICE: tenor.
ACCOMPANIMENT: oboe, harp.
FORM: Introduction, *4 meas.;* Vocal, *v. 1;* Interlude, *4 meas.;* Vocal, *v. 2;* Coda, *4 meas.*

40

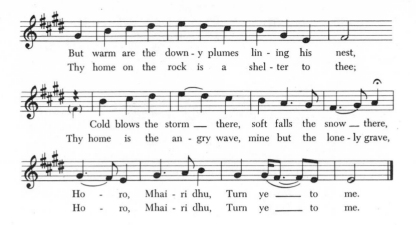

But warm are the down - y plumes lin - ing his nest,
Thy home on the rock is a shel - ter to thee;

Cold blows the storm ___ there, soft falls the snow ___ there,
Thy home is the an - gry wave, mine but the lone - ly grave,

Ho - ro, Mhai - ri dhu, Turn ye ___ to me.
Ho - ro, Mhai - ri dhu, Turn ye ___ to me.

Music of Scotland

The music of Scotland is as varied as the terrain of the country. The songs from the Highlands are often wild and passionate with wandering melodies that may change from major to minor within a single measure. The "Scotch snap," (♪♩) made up of a short-long pattern, comes from the Lowland country. The melodies of the Lowlands may be either slow and tender or sparkling and gay.

The bagpipe gives Scottish music a unique flavor. Its wailing drone on an open fifth is a characteristic sound. The "Scotch turn"—up and down or down and up—helps give the melodies a distinctive sound.

Two unusual happenings helped to preserve the heritage of Scottish folk music. Robert Burns, an important poet, wrote song texts for many old melodies. Several important European composers, including Beethoven, wrote sophisticated accompaniments for the folk songs which the Scottish people had enjoyed for generations. Performers often included these folk songs in concerts. Composers, such as Mendelssohn and Chopin, have echoed the unusual melodies and rhythms of the Scots in their compositions.

Notation for the harmonizing part played by the oboe on the recording is given here so that a clarinet or oboe player may play it.

Music of Scotland

As the class studies "Turn Ye to Me," ask members to read this article, as suggested in their book. They should read it again when they study "Comin' Thro' the Rye." The first song is from the Highlands of Scotland, the second from the Lowlands. The "Scotch turn" (downward) is found on the word "ye" in "Turn Ye to Me" and in "Comin' Thro' the Rye" (upward) on the words "ha'e I."

The five-tone or pentatonic scale is often the basis for Scottish songs. The reason may be that early bagpipes could play only the five tones. The "drone bass" on the open fifth is a characteristic accompaniment in Scottish music. It may be sounded continuously through a song.

Because of the unique sounds of Scottish folk music, it has interested many great composers. Mendelssohn wrote a "Scotch" symphony; Haydn, Beethoven, and Schubert arranged Scottish folk songs. Robert Burns knew and loved his country's folklore. Using folk tunes, he set to music dozens of his own poems depicting the hardships and simple pleasures of his own people.

The similarities of Irish and Scottish music are mentioned on pages 34-35. Listen to the recording of "Turn Ye to Me" and "Cockles and Mussels." In both songs the harp accompaniment is used. This instrument is common to both countries. In the recording of "Turn Ye to Me," the oboe suggests the sound of the bagpipes.

Comin' Thro' the Rye

Key: G♭   Starting Tone: D♭ (5)
Meter: 4/4 (♩)
Piano accompaniment on page 236

* FOLK STYLE: The song is a classic example of Scottish folk music, and it contains many of the typical Scottish musical characteristics.

The "Scotch snap," the syncopated quick rhythm ♫. is repeated many times in the song. The "turn" is found on the words "ha'e I." The song is based on the pentatonic scale: G♭, A♭, B♭, D♭, E♭. The "drone bass" (G♭ and D♭) is often used as an accompaniment to the song. When the children have heard the recording once with books closed and once with books open, help them locate and understand the Scottish characteristics. The song should be sung carefully so that the style derived from these characteristics is observed in performance. Note that this is one of the Robert Burns song texts referred to on page 41. "Comin' Thro' the Rye" is from the Lowlands. The Lowlands refers to the "low road," or the southern section of Scotland; the Highlands refers to the "high road," or the northern part of Scotland.

* HARMONY: Ask class members to play a "drone bass" on the accented beats of the song with tones of the open fifth in a lower octave of the piano or on the bells. Review page viii concerning the use of the piano in the classroom.

* MELODY: So that they gain further experience with the pentatonic scale, ask class members to practice playing the song on the black keys of the piano or on the bells. Begin on D flat. (One tone not in the scale will be needed: B natural [notated C flat in the music] in next to the last measure.)

Comin' Thro' the Rye

Old Scottish Air
Traditional adaptation
of a poem by Robert Burns

Where in this song do you find the "Scotch snap" and the "Scotch turn"? Is this song from the Highlands or the Lowlands?

1. If a bod-y meet a bod-y, Comin' thro' the rye,
2. If a bod-y meet a bod-y, Comin' frae the town,
3. A-mang the train there is a swain I dear-ly love my-sel', But

If a bod-y kiss a bod-y, Need a bod-y cry?
If a bod-y greet a bod-y, Need a bod-y frown?
what's his name or where's his hame, I din-na choose to tell.

Refrain
Ev-ery lass-ie has her lad-die, Nane they say ha'e I;

Yet a' the lads they smile on me, When comin' thro' the rye.

As with the Irish, Scottish history is closely bound to its struggle for freedom from England and dates from 1296 when King Edward I proclaimed himself King of Scotland. The final battles were waged five hundred years later when Bonnie Prince Charlie, the heir to the Scottish throne, and his band of Highlanders were defeated at Culloden Moor.

Many songs tell of the Bonnie Prince, his fight for freedom, his tragic defeat, and his daring escape over the stormy seas to France. One of these songs is "Come O'er the Stream, Charlie," found on the next page. The song is not really an invitation to dine. It is rather the Highlanders' promise of loyalty and devotion to Prince Charles. After his defeat at Culloden Moor, Prince Charles fled to a hiding place in the Highlands where he was protected by Sir John MacLean and his troops.

Record 2   Side A   Band 7.   VOICE: soprano.
ACCOMPANIMENT: recorder, harpsichord.
FORM: Instrumental; Vocal, v. 1; Interlude, 2 meas.; Vocal, v. 2; Interlude, 2 meas.; Vocal, v. 3; Coda, 2 meas.

Come O'er the Stream, Charlie

Scottish Folk Song
Words by James Hogg

Read the lusty words of this song aloud and enjoy the vigorous sound of the Scottish language. Discuss the meaning of the unusual words. Imagine how the song must have sounded as it was sung by a group of men from the Highlands, their voices ringing out in an invitation to the Bonnie Prince.

Refrain

Come o'er the stream, Char-lie, dear Char-lie, brave Char-lie,
And though you be wea-ry, we'll make your heart cheer-y,

Come o'er the stream, Char-lie, and dine with Mac-Lean;
And wel-come our Char-lie and his loy-al train.

Verse

1. We'll bring down the red deer, we'll bring down the black steer,
2. If aught will in-vite you, or more will de-light you,

The lamb from the brack-en and doe from the glen;
'Tis read-y, a troop of our bold High-land men

The salt sea we'll har-ry and bring to our Char-lie
Shall range on the heath-er, with bon-net and feath-er,

The cream from the both-y and curd from the pen.
Strong arms and broad clay-mores, three hun-dred and ten.

Record 2   Side A   Band 8. VOICES: men's ensemble.
ACCOMPANIMENT: woodwind quartet.
FORM: Introduction, *8 meas.;* Vocal, *v. 1;* Interlude, *4 meas.;*
Vocal, *v. 2;* Instrumental fade-out.

Key: D   Starting Tone: A (5)
Meter: 3/4 (3/♩)
Piano accompaniment on page 237

* EXPRESSION: The class should read the words of this song as suggested in their books. For first hearing, read the words aloud or call on a class member whom you have previously coached in reading them expressively:

bothy—small stone hut where milk is kept, pen—small enclosure for farm animals, harry—make a raid on, claymores—swords, bracken—wild growth of flax or hemp, curd—coagulated milk, as in cottage cheese, heather—a tract of wasteland covered with a vegetation of low flowering shrubs, found all through Great Britain, bonnet and feather—refers to the dress of the Highland soldier.

When the children know the meaning of the words of the song and have discussed the circumstances of its being sung (see pupil's page 42), they will enjoy reading the words in choral speech. The song should be sung with style and vital tone quality, as demonstrated on the record. This is a good song for boys to sing alone. Encourage them to sing in full voice and in the style of the Highlanders. The class might review another Prince Charlie song, "Skye Boat Song," in *Exploring Music 5.*

* RHYTHM: After studying the words, learn the rhythm before the record is played or the song is sung. The song is highly rhythmic and the rhythm patterns are simple and familiar. Put the three patterns on the board ( ). Ask class members to clap them, play them on rhythm instruments, or say them with "ta" as you point in any order to these patterns with whatever repetitions you indicate. Then ask them to clap, play, or say the patterns separately, then two patterns together, and finally all three patterns together as they follow the notation of the entire song.

FORM: The song is in two sections (two-part form). The second section gives contrast to the first in two ways. The rhythm is mainly even in contrast to the important uneven rhythm of the dotted quarter and eighth note in the first section. The tones of the melody of the second section are mainly in the high part of the scale in contrast to the lower tones of the first section.

Migildi Magildi

Key: D   Starting Tone: D (1)
Meter: $\frac{4}{4}$ ($\frac{4}{4}$)
Piano accompaniment on page 238

*FOLK STYLE: The Welsh say that when you've found the heart of a good song, you will one day find yourself right in the heart of the place and the people from which the song came. In a visit to Wales, we would surely discover that the spirit of the sturdy Welsh people is reflected in this song.

The Welsh men love to sing. This hearty song, derived from the work rhythm of the blacksmith, should be sung as a man's song in robust style with strong accents and a deliberate tempo. The words of the title have no special meaning and are just rhythmic syllables imitating the sound of the hammer and anvil.

This is a good song for boys to sing alone especially when classes can be combined so that there is a large group of boys. If the boys "will allow" the girls to join in, the girls might sing the upper part, the boys the lower.

*RHYTHM: The class should study the rhythm patterns of the song carefully because they are easily sung incorrectly. The charm of this song depends greatly upon accurate reading of the rhythm. Put the patterns on the board and make a game of playing them on rhythm instruments, clapping them, or speaking them with words from the song. Ask the class to do these things with each pattern separately, repeating it several times, then with two patterns together, and finally with three or all four patterns together. Keep the beats steady. Make sure that the three eighths which make up the triplet are even. See page 12 in the teacher's book for a discussion of triplets.

hi   now   ho   now,

What   a   fine   and   pleas - ant   sight,

Mi - gil - di   ma - gil - di   hi   now   now,

Ho   boys,   to - geth - er   we'll   sing,

Migildi Magildi

Welsh Folk Song
Arranged by Kurt Miller
Words by Jack Dobbs

The Welsh have an interesting musical custom in which a person must improvise a descant "on the spot" for a well-known tune played by a harpist. Harp music has long been a favorite of the Welsh, and many of the Welsh melodies are inherited from the ancient wandering harpists.

Heartily

Ho boys, to-geth-er we'll sing, with a mi-gil-di hi now now.

We'll sing you

1. What a fine and pleas-ant sight,—
2. What a fine and pleas-ant race,—   Mi-gil-di ma-gil-di hi now now,
3. What a fine and pleas-ant sound,—

hi   now   ho   now,   Mi-gil-di ma-gil-di hi now now,

In the smith - y warm and bright;
For the warm -est, bright-est place;   Mi-gil-di ma-gil-di hi now now,
When the songs and tales go round;

Hi   now   ho   now,   Mi-gil-di ma-gil-di hi now now,

Record 2   Side B   Band 1.   VOICES: children's choir.
ACCOMPANIMENT: French horn, harp, percussion.   FORM: Vocal, v. 1 (choir on melody which skips from part to part, instruments on second part); Vocal, v. 2 (choir on lower part, instruments on upper part); Vocal, v. 3 (choir on both parts).

44

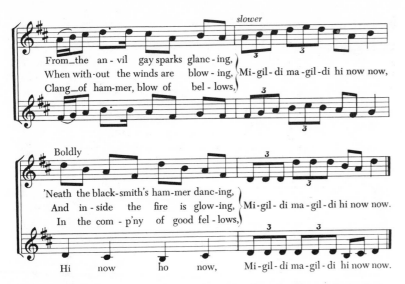

From—the an - vil gay sparks glanc - ing,
When with-out the winds are blow - ing, Mi - gil - di ma - gil - di hi now now,
Clang—of ham - mer, blow of bel - lows,

slower

Boldly

'Neath the black-smith's ham-mer danc-ing,
And in - side the fire is glow-ing, Mi - gil - di ma - gil - di hi now now.
In the com - p'ny of good fel - lows,

Hi now ho now, Mi - gil - di ma - gil - di hi now now.

Although the Welsh have long been famed for their singing, we know few of their songs because translation from the ancient language is difficult. The Welsh folk songs are simple in character and often describe love or the beauties of nature. Some songs grew out of the rhythms of movement of people as they worked. "Migildi Magildi" is an example. The ring of hammer and anvil may be sensed in the words and music of the song.

Someone might imitate the steady rhythm of the anvil on the triangle or cymbals as the class sings the song.

A Survey of the History of Chamber Music

Chamber music, derived from the Italian term, *musica da camera,* originally referred to music performed in the chamber, that is, home, in contrast to *musica da chiesa,* music performed in the church. In its modern meaning, chamber music designates compositions written for a small group of performers each of whom carries an individual part. The individualization of the parts is the essence of chamber music with the resulting subtle exchange of musical ideas. In orchestral music, musical ideas are presented by sections of players—particularly strings—producing a collective or mass-produced statement.

The earliest specimens of chamber music are the seventeenth century trio sonatas. These compositions were usually scored for two soprano instruments with a keyboard and bass instrument accompaniment. The classic era witnessed the birth of the string quartet, which differed from the earlier trio sonata in both texture and form. Instead of the accompanied trio sonata, the quartet strove for the equalization of the four parts. The simple dance forms of the trio sonata were replaced by the complex forms derived from the symphony. Although the string quartet remained the most favored form of chamber music, other instrumental combinations were added to the repertory.

The romantic composers of the nineteenth century were divided in their attitude toward chamber music; some completely neglected this form of expression, while others contributed an occasional piece to its literature. Among the composers who continued the great chamber music tradition, Schubert, Mendelssohn, and Brahms should be mentioned. (See Schubert's, *Piano Quintet in A,* p. 80.)

In the twentieth century the string quartet maintains its eminent position as seen in the output of Bartók, Schoenberg, Hindemith, and others. (See Schoenberg's, *Fourth String Quartet, Opus 37,* p. 160.) In general, modern composers are more favorably inclined toward writing for small groups than for orchestral forces. (See Hindemith's, *Kleine Kammermusik, Opus 24, No. 2,* p. 162.) Many new instrumental combinations have emerged, among which are the combination of the human voice with a small group of instruments and the employment of percussion instruments with conventional strings and winds. (See Milhaud's, *Creation of the World,* p. 177.) Finally, with the advent of electronic music, electronic sounds were brought into combination with the sound of standard instruments.

Greensleeves

Key: E minor   Starting Tone: E (1)
Meter: $\frac{6}{8}$ ($\frac{2}{\text{♩.}}$)
Piano accompaniment on page 240

* **EXPRESSION:** This is one of the best-known and most loved English ballads. The melody has been used as a setting for many different lyrics. Some children may know the Christmas carol version "What Child Is This." The words in the pupil's book are probably the oldest of the many different settings. They help to give a feeling for the life of the fifteenth century. Instruments of the period are heard in the recording of this song and are discussed on page 156.

MELODY: After children have listened to the recording to enjoy the words and the general style of the song, ask them to listen again to hear the **tonality** of the song. They should quickly recognize that it is in a minor key. Review the information regarding minor scales on page 23. This is the **harmonic minor** scale. As children listen and study the notation, help them realize that the first two measures in phrases three and four are major in quality. Sing these two measures, ending on the G of the third measure. Notice that this seems to be the "home tone," giving a sense of rest or completion. As the melody moves on, the use of the D♯ brings us back to E as home tone.

* **FOLK STYLE:** In Elizabethan England, this song was the basis for a stately dance. When the children can sing the song, they may learn the dance. Form a large double circle, facing clockwise, girls on partners right. Partners clasp hands at shoulder height holding a small pine bough in their hands. In the dance two couples work as a group; designate these groups before the dance begins.

Measures 1-4:   All walk forward eight steps; begin on inside foot.

Measures 5-6:   Two couples join hands to form a right-hand star; walk four steps clockwise.

Measures 7-8:   Reverse direction and form a left-hand star; walk four steps counterclockwise.

Measures 9-10:   With all couples again facing clockwise, first couple of each group bends forward and walks backward four steps under the arched arms of the second couple who meanwhile walks forward four steps.

Greensleeves

Old English Folk Song

This song is mentioned in Shakespeare's plays and was a favorite of Queen Elizabeth I. The title refers to the fact that the nobility were known by the color of silk that they wore on their sleeves. Each house or family had a distinctive color.

Notice the change from minor to major in the third phrase. Such changes of mood are typical of music all over the British Isles.

1. A - las! my love, — you do me wrong, — To
2. Ah, Green - sleeves, now — fare - well, a - dieu, — To

cast me off — dis - cour - teous - ly; For I have loved — you,
God I pray — to pros - per thee, For I am still — thy

oh, so long, — De - light - ing in — your com - pa - ny.
sweet - heart true; — Come once — a - gain — to meet — me.

Refrain
Green - sleeves — was all my joy, — And oh, Green - sleeves — was

my de - light, Green - sleeves, — my heart of gold, — And

all — for La - dy Green - sleeves.

Record 2   Side B   Band 2.   VOICE: baritone.
ACCOMPANIMENT: recorder, lute, viola da gamba.
FORM: Instrumental; Vocal, *vv. 1-2.*

46

This song is recorded with the instruments that were popular during the time of Queen Elizabeth I: viola da gamba, recorder, and lute. Pluck this descant on a string instrument to suggest the sound of the lute.

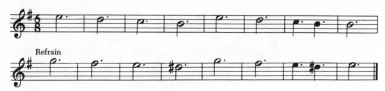

In Elizabethan England "Greensleeves" was the basis for a stately dance. When you can sing the song artistically, learn the dance. Combine the two and, for a few moments, imagine that you are English people of that time.

Tallis' Canon

Music by Thomas Tallis
Words by Thomas Ken

Religious music has always been an important part of English musical life. This lovely **canon** was written by one of the most important composers of sacred music, Thomas Tallis. He has been called the "Father of English Cathedral Music."

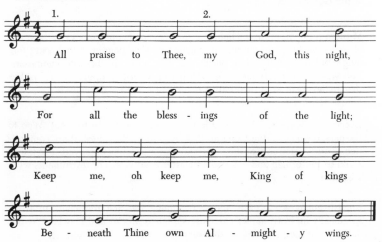

All praise to Thee, my God, this night,

For all the bless - ings of the light;

Keep me, oh keep me, King of kings

Be - neath Thine own Al - might - y wings.

Record 2 Side B Band 3. VOICES: children's choir.
ACCOMPANIMENT: brass quartet.
FORM: Instrumental; Vocal (unison); Vocal (2-part round).

Measures 11-12: Repeat formation for measures 9-10 with the second couple of each group going under the arch of the first couple.

Measures 13-16: Repeat movement for measures 9-12. (This portion of the dance is called "turning the sleeves inside out.")

Key: G   Starting Tone: G (1)

Meter: $\frac{4}{2}$ $\left(\frac{4}{\text{\musical}}\right)$

No piano accompaniment

Tallis' Canon

* COMPOSER'S STYLE: Thomas Tallis (c. 1505-1585) was one of the most famous composers of church music during England's Golden Age. His compositions are especially noteworthy because of their singable melodies. The melodic contour is closely wedded to the natural cadence of the words. Notice how important words are given proper stress.

* MELODY: The melody moves primarily by steps. After children have scanned the notation, challenge them to sing the song with words or on a neutral syllable. Ask them to listen to the recording and check their own performance for accuracy.

* HARMONY: Sing as a round, keeping the rhythm steady with good accents. This canon can be played on trumpets and trombones if there are brass players in class. The trombone part must be written in the bass clef. (See page 113 for names of lines and spaces of bass clef.) The trumpet part must be transposed a step higher to the key of A. (See page x for directions for transposition.)

Music of England

As preparation for studying the music of this section of the book, reread with the class the paragraph on page 33 which deals with England. Then read this page aloud with the class. Encourage class members to describe English life of the sixteenth century in more detail. Possibly they have seen movies, attended plays, or read books in which there were descriptions of the elaborate court dresses and wigs, the social life of nobility, and the very different, simple life of rural people.

Until this time much of the music had been composed for use in the church. The "popular music" referred to in the pupil's book consisted mainly of songs for solo voice, songs for several voices often with parts for recorders or lute, and compositions for keyboard instruments. The virginal, ancestor of the harpsichord and piano, was played especially in the houses of royalty.

While the pupil's page deals only with music of Elizabethan England, the country has always made significant contributions to the world of music. From the time of the bards and minstrels to the present, English songs have been enjoyed in all parts of the world. Keyboard music became important in the time of William Byrd (1543-1623), who was among the first to publish collections of pieces for the virginal and harpsichord. In addition to keyboard compositions, Byrd wrote church music, madrigals, songs, and chamber music. He was considered the most versatile composer of his day.

The seventeenth century produced Henry Purcell who is often regarded as England's most distinguished composer. He was organist at Westminster Abbey and was important in the courts of Charles II, James II, and William and Mary. After Purcell, German-speaking composers dominated the English musical scene for some time: Handel, who lived in England in the eighteenth century; Haydn, who traveled to England to compose and lecture during the late eighteenth century; and Mendelssohn, a composer, conductor, and pianist, who traveled to England several times in the mid-nineteenth century.

From the late nineteenth century to the present time, English composers have influenced their country's music. Included among these composers are Sir Edward Elgar, Ralph Vaughan Williams, Gustav Holst, Sir William Walton, and Benjamin Britten.

Ask the children to study the Time Line on pages 60-61, noticing the contributions of England.

Music of England

By the sixteenth century, England had developed a rich culture which was in sharp contrast to the wild and primitive life in Scotland, Ireland, and Wales. The elegant life of the English nobility, which revolved around the court of Queen Elizabeth I, was unequaled. As English sailors roamed the world, they discovered new lands to add to the wealth of their country. English power was extending around the globe.

The theater flourished, and William Shakespeare's latest "hit plays" were performed everywhere. Music was a regular part of the daily routine in the court of "Good Queen Bess." Musicians were part of her staff of servants. Their job was to play music for the enjoyment of the queen and her friends. It is little wonder that this period in English history is known as the **Golden Age.**

Music was important in the homes of the common people, too. Friends would often gather to spend an evening making music. Sometimes they sang folk songs, but more often they performed new music by favorite composers. This was the period when composers began to write "popular music" rather than to devote most of their efforts to writing music for the church.

Everyone was expected to be able to play at least one instrument. Woe to the person who could not sing his part by reading the notes! Many compositions were written so that the parts could be either sung or played. The music could be performed and enjoyed no matter what voices or instruments were available.

English composers of this age were among the first musicians to write specifically for instruments. Composers, such as Morley and Dowland, wrote dances, fantasies, and airs for different combinations of instruments.

Golden Age of English Music

The Golden Age is a good description of English musical life in the sixteenth century. Probably no other country has produced so many fine composers and so much beautiful music in so short a period of time. The compositions described on this page will help you to become familiar with the sound of this imaginative music. It is as pleasant to perform and hear today as it was four hundred years ago.

Watkin's Ale and Munday's Joy   Anonymous

These dances are performed by a **consort** or ensemble of **recorders**. Notice the ornamented melodies, freely changing rhythms, and distinct phrases which make these dances very typical of the Golden Age.

My Lady Hunsdon's Puffe   by John Dowland

The delicate sound of the many-stringed **lute** made it a favorite instrument. As they sang the latest ballads, young men often accompanied themselves by plucking both melody and accompaniment on the lute. As you listen, notice how the main melody is varied each time it is repeated.

Lure, Falconers, Lure   by John Bennet

Madrigals are probably the best-known music of the Golden Age. Madrigals are **polyphonic** songs, usually about love or nature. In polyphonic music each voice is important with a distinctive and individual melody of its own. Try to hear each individual voice part as you listen to this madrigal about the hunt.

Fantasia in G   by Alfonso Ferrabosco II

This music is performed by an ensemble or **chest of viols**. Viols are string instruments, ancestors of our present-day strings. Their tone quality is more delicate and less resonant. A chest of viols included several viols of different sizes. One of these is the viola da gamba, which you heard on the recording of "Greensleeves." The "Fantasia in G" is in two sections; each develops a different musical idea in a contrasting tempo and meter. The music is polyphonic with each independent melody adding interest to the composition.

Record 8   Side B   Band 1.
1a   Taylor Recorder Consort. **1b**   Desmond Dupre, lutenist.
1c   The Deller Consort. **1d**   Consort of Viols.
August Wenziger, conductor.

Introduce and study separately each of the compositions which are included in this lesson. Give the children an opportunity to listen to each one before reading the discussion in their book. Ask them to identify the instruments and to comment on all that they heard in the music. Refer to page 156 for a detailed discussion of the instruments heard in this recording. Notice the delicate sound of this music. Return to these compositions several times to observe the charm and beauty of the music.

On later hearings, call attention to the characteristics which make these compositions representative of the Golden Age. The music is often made up of contrasting sections, alternating between **polyphony** (two or more independent parts—voices and/or instruments—sounding simultaneously) and **homophony** (lower voices moving with and harmonically supporting the main melody). Imitation is often heard, as in a round. This music contains much rhythmic interest and often freely changing meter.

Watkin's Ale and Munday's Joy

ANONYMOUS

The two dances are characteristic instrumental pieces of the period. After children have enjoyed the lighthearted mood of "Watkin's Ale and Munday's Joy" and discussed the instrumentation, draw attention to the design. The dance is made up of six phrases. Listen for the distinctive contour of the melody of the first phrase and notice how each subsequent phrase grows out of this first melodic idea.

On subsequent repetitions, the main melody is ornamented, the rhythm is altered, and fragments of the melody are treated in various ways.

The step-wise melody of "Munday's Joy" creates a graceful mood which contrasts with the more energetic "Watkin's Ale." The eight phrases are grouped in twos, with each pair seeming to form a "question" and an "answer."

(Continued on page 51.)

Now Is the Month of Maying

Key: G   Starting Tone: G (1)
Meter: $\frac{4}{4}$ ($\frac{4}{\downarrow}$)
Piano accompaniment on page 242

* MUSICAL STYLE: Listen to the recording. Discuss the various musical qualities which give the madrigal its distinctive musical style. This madrigal is an example of a special type developed by English composers. Songs such as these were sometimes called "falas" because of the use of nonsense syllables in the refrain. It is more **homophonic** than **polyphonic.** In homophonic music, the voices move together in harmony with the most important melody in the top voice. This is in contrast to polyphonic music where each voice sings an independent melody. The dance-like character of the English madrigal is due to its rhythmic interest. The form of these madrigals is usually A A B B. The lighthearted spirit of the music reflects the mood of the words which usually deal with nature or love.

COMPOSER'S STYLE: Thomas Morley (1557-1602) was one of the composers who developed the English madrigal style. In addition to many madrigals, Morley also wrote numerous instrumental pieces. Morley tried to reflect in his music the expressive and pictorial descriptions of the words. His melodies follow the natural accents of the words.

RHYTHM: Compare the rhythmic notation of the two parts. Discover measures in which the voices move with the same rhythm and measures in which the voices move in contrasting patterns. Divide the class into two groups; practice tapping the rhythm of the two parts simultaneously; then chant the words. Discuss how the contrast in rhythm adds interest.

* HARMONY: Ask children to follow the notation of their part as they listen to the recording. Then establish tonality and encourage the class to sing as much of the first section as possible, both parts together. When problems arise within a part, practice the pattern separately, then immediately sing the section in harmony. Play the recording again and suggest that children may sing softly as they listen to make sure they have learned their part correctly. Learn the second section in the same way.

This two-part arrangement might be performed by voices and instruments. Choose an instrument of light quality such as a flute to perform one part. Beginning flutists have difficulty in the lower range; they may play the melody one octave higher.

Now Is the Month of Maying

Music by Thomas Morley

Thomas Morley was one of the most famous writers of madrigals during England's Golden Age. Study the Time Line on pages 60-61 and discover what world events were taking place during this period.

Record 2   Side B   Band 4.   VOICES: mixed choir.
ACCOMPANIMENT: 2 recorders, lute, organ, viola da gamba.
FORM: Instrumental; Vocal, v. 1 (5-part madrigal); Vocal, vv. 1-2 (2-parts).

("Golden Age of English Music" continued from page 49.)

(1.) Each with his bon - ny lass, A -
(2.) And to the bag - pipes' sound The

(1.) Each with his bon - ny lass, A -
(2.) And to the bag - pipes' sound The

danc - ing on the grass. } Fa la la la la,
nymphs tread out the ground. }

danc - ing on the grass. } Fa la la la la, Fa la
nymphs tread out the ground. }

Fa la la la la la la la la la la la.

la la la. Fa la la la la la la.

Learn this **madrigal** now and remember to sing it later on **May Day. It** is written here for you to sing in two parts. Listen to the recording. The first time it is sung, voices sing the five parts of the original madrigal. The second time, the voices sing the two parts as they appear in your book, and instruments play the other three parts.

My Lady Hunsdon's Puffe

BY JOHN DOWLAND
BORN 1562   DIED 1626

John Dowland was famed as a lutenist as well as a composer. After children are familiar with the melody of the first phrase, they should be able to hear the ornamentation in the second phrase, the condensed repetition of the opening melody at a lower pitch in phrase three, the contrasting rhythm of the fourth phrase, and the expanded last phrase. Suggest to the children that they tap the beat lightly as they listen for the irregular rhythms which add to the charm of this lute dance.

Lure, Falconers, Lure

BY JOHN BENNET
C. 16TH-17TH CENTURIES

Discuss the title of the madrigal before children listen to the record. A falconer is a person who trains and hunts with hawks or falcons. Falconry was a popular sport during the Golden Age. The nobility hired falconers to breed and train hawks for their amusement. Notice that the lower voices are subordinated to the main melody during the narrative sections (homophony), while each voice has its own melody during the "hey lo!" refrain (polyphony).

Fantasia in G

BY ALFONSO FERRABOSCO II
BORN C. 1575   DIED 1628

The word "fantasia" may be defined as a fantasy. Fantasias are short instrumental compositions which follow no set rules of design; they are freely developed "fancies," almost improvisatory in character. As children listen, draw attention to the imitation between voices in the opening measures. The slower second section contrasts with the more vigorous rhythm of the first part. Compare the tone quality of the viols with their modern counterpart, the violin family. The voice of the viol is softer and more delicate than the more brilliant violin. The sound, however, is well suited to the ornamented melodies of the music of the Golden Age.

Merry Minstrels

Key: C   Starting Tone: C (1)

Meter: $\frac{3}{4}$ ($\frac{3}{\downarrow}$)

No piano accompaniment

DANCE A ROUND: The class will devise original movements if given a chance to experiment. The "style" of the movement is important and should match the style of the song. Lead the class to discuss this aspect of planning the dance.

It may be helpful to see an example of how one class developed the movement. There are three groups, each of which continues the three parts of the dance as it sings the three parts of the round.

Part 1—The group walks forward with four steps (one step to accented beat of each measure), backward with four steps.

On word "enjoy" raise arms and face in gesture of pleasure.

On word "destroy" move fists in gesture of emphasis.

Part 2—The group stays in place, rocking forward and backward with accents of the music, in attitude of carefree life. First four measures, have left foot far forward; then keep right foot in place and move left foot far back for last four measures. Keep body erect; lift each foot completely off the floor in the rocking motion.

Part 3—The group stays in place. On first accent, step to side (away from group two) with weight on one foot. Raise opposite arm in high arc over head in "hailing" gesture. On second accent, return weight to center as arm comes down. Repeat in other direction and do both again, changing weight with each of the four hailing gestures.

When the class has experimented with various steps and gestures and has agreed on those to be used for each part of the song, various positions may be tried for the three groups. The diagrams indicate some possibilities.

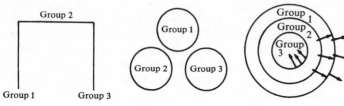

Merry Minstrels

Old English Round

The traveling storytellers and musicians of the Elizabethan age were often actors and dancers as well. They used gestures, pantomime, and dance to help tell their stories and make their songs interesting. When you know this song and can sing it well as a round, make up some steps and gestures that help express the mood of each of the three sections of the music. Performed in this way, the round can be seen in your movements as well as heard in the melodies.

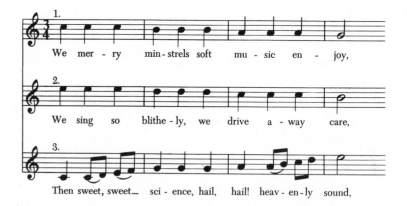

1. We mer-ry min-strels soft mu-sic en-joy,
2. We sing so blithe-ly, we drive a-way care,
3. Then sweet, sweet— sci-ence, hail, hail! heav-en-ly sound,

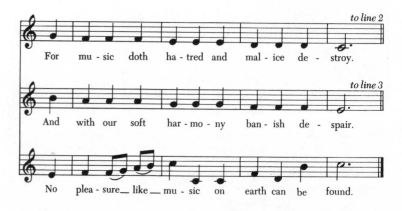

to line 2

For mu-sic doth ha-tred and mal-ice de-stroy.

to line 3

And with our soft har-mo-ny ban-ish de-spair.

No plea-sure— like — mu-sic on earth can be found.

Record 2   Side B   Band 5. VOICES: children's choir.

ACCOMPANIMENT: recorder, organ, viola da gamba.

FORM: Vocal (unison); Vocal (3-part round); Instrumental (3-part round).

Come, Follow Me

Round by
John Hilton

Come, fol-low, fol-low, fol-low, Fol-low, fol-low,

fol-low me! Whith-er shall I fol-low, fol-low, fol-low,

Whith-er shall I fol-low, fol-low thee? To the green-wood,

to the green-wood, To the green-wood, green-wood tree.

Record 2 Side B Band 6. VOICES: children's choir.
ACCOMPANIMENT: recorder, rauschpfeife, viola da gamba.
FORM: Vocal (unison); Vocal (3-part round); Instrumental
(3-part round).

Key: C   Starting Tone: C (1)
Meter: 2/2 (2/♩)
No piano accompaniment

* COMPOSER'S STYLE: John Hilton (1599-1657) was one of the last of the madrigal composers of England's Golden Age. He, like his contemporaries, also wrote rounds. In a round, each section must be of equal length with the melodies designed so that they are interesting when sung alone, yet will create pleasing harmony when combined. The playful spirit, the sprightly rhythm, and the contrasting melodies make this round an excellent example of the music of the Golden Age.

The instruments used in the recording are appropriate to the style of the round. They are instruments which John Hilton might have used.

* HARMONY: As children sing or play this round, draw attention to the contrasting phrases. It is a good example of simple polyphony. Phrase one starts high and moves gradually downward. Phrase two moves in the opposite direction. Phrase three remains higher than the other phrases and is different rhythmically as well as melodically. Each phrase is interesting to hear as a solo melody. When the three phrases are combined, they create pleasing harmony.

* RHYTHM: This is a good song to review the relationship of note values to the meter:

Clap the rhythm of the melody as a rhythmic round. For contrast between the three lines, tap the rhythm of the first phrase on the knees; clap the rhythm of the second phrase lightly; clap the rhythm of the third phrase with cupped hands.

When V and I Together Meet

Key: C minor   Starting Tone: G (5)

Meter: $\frac{3}{4}\left(\frac{3}{\text{d}}\right)$

No piano accompaniment

COMPOSER'S STYLE: Henry Purcell (c. 1659-1695) was one of the outstanding composers who helped England gain its reputation as a leader in music. In addition to an opera and many choral works, Purcell wrote a number of short vocal compositions, including a number of rounds. Purcell's love for song is revealed in this quotation: "Music is the exaltation of poetry. Both of them may excel apart but surely they are most excellent when they are joyn'd. Because nothing is then wanting to either of their proportions; for thus they appear like wit and beauty in the same person."

* **MUSICAL STYLE:** Rounds have been popular ever since the thirteenth century. They are sometimes called "circle canons" because each voice returns from the end of the melody to the beginning, around and around in a circle. (See page 68 for definition of canon.) Composers of this period enjoyed writing "riddle canons." The singers had to study the notation to decide how they were to be sung. Some were written to be sung backward as well as forward. Others could be sung by reading the notation upside down. Sometimes the text was a riddle or a play on words as in this round. Enjoy this song and notice the clever way in which Roman numerals V and I can have several meanings:

1. The Roman V was the symbol for the English letter U. (The children may remember seeing this in ancient documents in museums, places of historical interest, or libraries.)
2. Since the Roman V was pronounced as the English vowel U, the syllables when sung are the personal pronouns "you" and "I."
3. V and I are, of course, mathematical symbols for five and one.

Listen to the recording. Ask the children to speculate on who (or what) is posing the mathematical problems. Is it the Roman numeral I? Also note the instruments used on the recording. They reflect the humorous quality of the song. These are instruments of Purcell's day.

* **HARMONY:** Return to this song frequently over a period of time before attempting to sing it as a round. Experiment with various combinations of instruments or voices and perform the round as it might have been done in Purcell's day.

When V and I Together Meet

Round by Henry Purcell

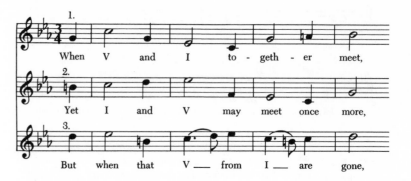

Henry Purcell is one of the most famous English composers. He wrote music for the theatre as well as many madrigals, instrumental compositions, and music for the church.

The text of this amusing round is a play on words. You may have to read it through several times in order to understand how the things described can happen! Listen to the record for a clue to help you.

Record 2   Side B   Band 7. VOICES: children's choir.
ACCOMPANIMENT: recorder, rauschpfeife, harpsichord, regal.
FORM: Vocal (unison); Vocal (3-part round); Instrumental (3-part round).

54

A Great Composer of the Present, Benjamin Britten

The contemporary composer Benjamin Britten is a musician of great invention and charm. He evidently likes to compose for young people; in addition to the *Young Person's Guide to the Orchestra*, he has written an opera for young people which is titled, *Let's Make An Opera*. In another short opera, *Noye's Fludde (Noah's Flood)*, many children sing in the chorus and act the parts of the birds and animals that went into the ark. In the score of this opera, one instrument of the orchestra is called "slung mugs"—a set of coffee mugs with different pitches! This composer thinks of ingenious ways to make new sounds!

As with all great composers, Britten developed his own musical style, yet never ceased to study and appreciate the music of others. He is a great admirer of the music of Henry Purcell who lived three hundred years before him. He has studied and performed the music of Schubert extensively. Of Schubert's music he has said, "The standard of inspiration, of magic, is miraculous and past all explanation." Great composers have much in common as they try to express musical ideas which will have meaning for people of all time.

Old Abram Brown

Music by Benjamin Britten
Words Anonymous

Old A - bram Brown is dead and gone, You'll nev - er see him more.

He used to wear a long brown coat That but-toned down be - fore.

Record 2 Side B Band 8. VOICES: children's choir.
ACCOMPANIMENT: piccolo, oboe, clarinet, bassoon.
FORM: Vocal (unison); Vocal (4-part round); Vocal (choir on augmented version, instruments on part as written in book).

A Great Composer of the Present, Benjamin Britten

Born in 1913, Britten has been referred to by many as "the greatest English composer since Purcell." He has written an impressive number of works. His operas include those referred to in the pupil's book, *A Midsummer Night's Dream* (a setting of the Shakespearean play), *Billy Budd, Peter Grimes,* as well as several others. He has composed many songs and choral works and has arranged numerous English folk songs.

In 1964 Britten received the first Aspen award in the amount of $30,000 presented by the Aspen Institute for Humanistic Studies. This award is given annually to the person who has made the greatest contribution to the understanding of man.

Old Abram Brown

Key: E minor   Starting Tone: E (1)
Meter: $\frac{4}{4}$ $\left(\frac{4}{\quarter}\right)$
No piano accompaniment

* MELODY: To study the minor melody of this song, have children arrange the tones of the song in scale order and play the scales on the bells. Notice that the descending four-note pattern in the second phrase forms a sequence (E D C B, D C B A, C B A G).

* HARMONY: As children sing the round, have them listen to the harmony of the four parts. When all four parts have joined in the round, notice that the low E acts as a pedal point and continues throughout the song. The dissonance of the I$_7$ chord (E-G-B-D) moving through another dissonant chord (F#-A-C-E) is heard on the first beat of each measure. This dissonance resolves to the I chord (E-G-B). It will help to play the entire chord progression (E-G-B-D, F#-A-C-E, E-G-B) in order to hear the unusual harmony in this round.

RHYTHM: This round can also be sung with one part in augmented rhythm and the other part as originally written.

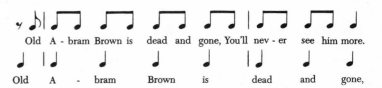

Old A - bram Brown is dead and gone, You'll nev - er see him more.

Old A - bram Brown is dead and gone,

A New Year Carol

Key: Eb   Starting Tone: G (3)
Meter: 3/4 (3/♩)
Piano accompaniment on page 244

* EXPRESSION: Play the recording so that children can discuss the general character of the song and the meaning of the words. Explain that the carol, usually sung later in the school year, is placed here in the book as an example of a song by a contemporary English composer who uses an old theme for a text. The origin of the words Britten used is unknown, but the words are reminiscent of the "waits" of the Middle Ages. The "waits" were musicians who stood at the gate of the royal dwelling ready to play for entering guests. The "seven bright gold wires" might refer to strings of some type of lyre or lute.

Review with the children the meaning of the marks of expression:

mf, cresc., **pp**, dim., rall., molto

Write the complete words for each on the board and see that children know how to say them correctly. (See page 329 of the teacher's book for explanations.) As the class members hear the recording of the song again with books open, suggest that they note the singer's observance of the marks of expression.

* COMPOSER'S STYLE: Discuss with the class the folklike quality of the melody as Britten has written it: the narrow range of scale tones; the repeated patterns of rhythm and melody. Help the class discover what it is that makes Britten's song different from a folk song and what makes it sound "new." (The harmony played in the piano accompaniment is not the traditional harmony for such a song. Although Britten uses the fundamental chords, he consistently adds the dissonance of the seventh tone of the chord and emphasizes the seventh by its placement in the rolled chord.)

A New Year Carol

Music by Benjamin Britten
Words Anonymous

1. Here we bring new wa-ter from the well____ so clear,
2. Sing ____ reign of Fair_ Maid, with _ gold up-on her toe,
3. Sing ____ reign of Fair_ Maid, with _ gold up-on her chin,

For to wor-ship God with this hap-py New Year.
O-pen you the West Door and turn the Old Year go.
O-pen you the East Door and let the New Year in.

Chorus 1., 2.

Sing le-vy dew, sing le-vy dew, the wa-ter and the wine;

The sev-en bright gold wires and the bu-gles that do shine.

Sing le-vy dew, sing le-vy dew, the wa-ter and the

wine; The sev-en bright gold wires and the bu-gles that do shine.

Observe the composer's marks of expression carefully.

Do you remember these musical symbols? **p** **f**

Record 3   Side A   Band 1.   VOICES: children's choir.
ACCOMPANIMENT: piano.
FORM: performed as written by composer (see page 244 for piano accompaniment).

Young Person's Guide to the Orchestra

by Benjamin Britten

First four measures from the full score:

Young Person's Guide to the Orchestra
(Variations and Fugue on a Theme of Purcell)

BY BENJAMIN BRITTEN

BORN 1913

This page shows the first four measures of the full orchestral score of *Young Person's Guide to the Orchestra*. Children will be interested to know that this is the way the conductor's music looks. He must be aware of what each instrument is playing so that he can cue each player's entrance at the proper time, indicate tempo changes, dynamics, phrasing, and so on. After children have studied the lesson on pages 58-59, return to this score page and help children follow the music as they listen to the opening measures. Listen several times and suggest that they try to follow a different line each time—perhaps the violins at first, then the cello or bass, then the percussion, and so on. Discover which instruments are playing the same patterns. Notice that the piccolo, two flutes, first oboe, first clarinet, and first and second violins all have the main melody.

Some children may notice that the clarinets and French horns have a different key signature. That is because these are transposing instruments. The clarinet sounds one step lower than the pitch which appears on the staff, therefore its part must be written one step higher —in the key of G rather than F. French horns sound a fifth lower than written. Therefore, in this composition, their parts must be written in the key of C. Notice the different clef sign for the viola part. This is an **alto clef.** On this clef, middle C is on the third line.

Young Person's Guide to the Orchestra
(Variations and Fugue on a Theme of Purcell)

BY BENJAMIN BRITTEN
BORN 1913

This composition was originally conceived to accompany a documentary film "Instruments of the Orchestra." The composer also prepared a concert version using the spoken commentary from the film. Although it is still often performed in this way, the music speaks so well for itself that the words are not necessary to its enjoyment or understanding. The recording heard in this lesson does not, therefore, have the commentary. As an introduction to the study of the composition, it would be well to play the complete recording before the commentary in the pupil's book is read. With only the title written on the chalkboard as a clue to the musical content and the composer's name, let the class hear the composition. Conduct a discussion about all the details that class members discovered in the first hearing. See pages 62, 104, 118, and 142 for information on the various instruments of the orchestra.

On another day, ask the class to read the analysis of the music from the book. Reread the information about Purcell on page 48. Play the first section of the composition—the statements of the Purcell theme played first by the full orchestra and then by the four main families of the orchestra (the first band). Discuss the melodic characteristics of the theme as analyzed in the pupil's book. Play the beginning of the recording again and ask children to sing the theme by following the notation. Identify the leaps, turn, and sequence by singing the measures indicated. Listen again to the first section of the recording.

The Purcell theme comes from "Rondeau" which was part of an opera entitled *The Moor's Revenge* by Henry Purcell. The complete "Rondeau" may be found in the *Exploring Music 1* record album. Children may enjoy listening to the complete Rondeau after they have studied Britten's adaptation of it.

In the same lesson or at another time, play the first section and the second, or variation, section of the composition (the second band). Ask children to follow the instrumentation listed in their book. Read aloud the description of Britten's use of the three melodic characteristics of Purcell's melody. Play the first four variations again so that children can follow these more closely.

At another time, play the last, or fugue, section of the composition. Have the class follow Britten's theme played by the various instruments, and finally Britten's theme and Purcell's theme played together.

Young Person's Guide to the Orchestra
(Variations and Fugue on a Theme of Purcell)
by Benjamin Britten

As a basis for this composition, Benjamin Britten used a theme by the great English composer Henry Purcell and a theme of his own. Britten developed a series of thirteen variations on Purcell's theme which is stated at the beginning of the composition. From his own theme, stated near the end of the composition, Britten developed a fugue.

Henry Purcell's Theme

Purcell's theme has interesting melodic characteristics: the upward leaps of measure 1, the turn upward and downward as in measure 2, the sequence found in measures 3, 4, 5, and 6.

The Purcell theme is played by: full orchestra (D minor), woodwind section (F major), brass section (E flat major), string section (A major), percussion section (A major), full orchestra (D minor).
◉

Record 9   Side B   Band 1.
Philadelphia Orchestra,
Eugene Ormandy, Conductor.
Symbol (◉) for visible intermediate bands appears on reduced pupil's page.

Then follow Britten's variations on the theme, each featuring a particular instrument: (1) flutes (and piccolo), (2) oboes, (3) clarinets, (4) bassoons, (5) violins, (6) violas, (7) cellos, (8) double basses, (9) harp, (10) French horns, (11) trumpets, (12) trombones (and tuba), (13) percussion.

Notice how Britten makes use of the three melodic characteristics found in Purcell's theme. In the flute variation and in the bassoon variation, he uses the upward melodic leaps. In the oboe variation and in the clarinet variation, he employs the turn upward and downward. In the bassoon variation the sequence is played by the second bassoon.

When the variations are finished, Britten's fugue subject is played, first by the piccolo, and then by the other instruments in the same order as in the variations. Finally, Britten's theme and Purcell's theme are played together.

Britten's Theme (Fugue subject)

Musical quotes copyright 1947 by Hawkes & Son (London) Ltd.
Used by permission.

Play the section again so that the children can listen for the instruments. They might be asked to close books and write the names of the instruments in the order in which they are heard.

At another time review the entire composition. Replay it at various times throughout the year. Emphasize that, although the composition was intended to be a lesson for young people on the sounds and capabilities of orchestral instruments, it is so exciting and colorful that young and old alike find it a rewarding musical experience.

Developing a Theme and Variations

When children have studied Britten's variations they may enjoy developing their own composition based on the variations form. Choose a familiar melody such as "Tallis' Canon," page 47. Discuss different ways that a melody may be varied. Divide the class into groups. Give each group a different instrument for which to plan a variation (or they may improvise vocal variations). Children who play orchestral instruments may bring their instruments to class. They can develop a different variation for each instrument or combine several instruments to make a single variation.

Some possible variations are:

Changing the melodic line through added notes:

Changing the rhythm pattern:

Changing the meter:

Changing from major to minor:

A Time Line for Exploring Music

Three **time lines** have been included in the pupil's book covering the period from 500 A.D. to the present. These time lines have been included to help children develop a sense of historical perspective and to relate the music they study to other historical events with which they may be familiar. Specific dates have not been included. Work for awareness of large historical periods rather than memorization of specific dates.

The knowledge of the music of a time and place adds to our understanding of the people of that time. There is no other form of expression which so clearly reveals the feelings, attitudes, and activities of a people as music does. Help children become sensitive to this as they discuss, listen to, and perform music of different times and places. Ask them to think of times when music has helped express feelings in their own lives or in the lives of the people around them.

Refer to the time lines regularly as new songs are learned. Ask children to study the time line to find out when specific composers lived. When studying the music of a particular country, look for references to that country in the historical section of the time line.

A number of projects related to the time line may become part of the music activities at different times during the year.

1. Make a large time line for the classroom bulletin board. As the children study various countries and periods in music or social studies, they can add new items to their time line.

2. After a new song has been learned, add the name of the song or the composer, if it is not present, to the time line.

3. Encourage children to do independent research into historical periods, lives of composers, or specific countries and to report their findings to the class.

4. Correlate the development of the time line with art activities. Assign various groups to illustrate different historical periods with a bulletin board display.

5. Extend the time line and add current events which may have an effect on present-day music. List important musical events.

6. Some children may wish to look up the specific dates of the events listed in the time line.

A Time Line for Exploring Music

500

Legends of King Arthur and his knights of the Round Table spread throughout Britain.	Monks chant **plainsong** in their worship.
Moors invade Spain.	Two-part singing begins with voices a fifth apart.
Norwegians settle Iceland.	
Vikings sail to the New World.	

1000

Christians set out on Crusades.	The musical **staff** is invented.
Tales of Robin Hood are told in songs and stories.	
Richard the Lion-Hearted is crowned King of England.	Bards, troubadours, and minnesingers roam the country, singing ballads.

1200

St. Francis of Assisi founds an Order of Friars.	Composers write **polyphonic** music.
Marco Polo visits the Orient.	
Edward I is proclaimed King of England and Scotland.	Composers write both sacred and secular music.
William Tell frees the Swiss.	

1400

Joan of Arc leads the French against the English.	Keyboard instruments are in common use.
Gutenberg invents movable type.	Music printing is introduced.
Columbus discovers America.	Hans Sachs, famous Mastersinger, is born in Germany.

1500

Portuguese and Spanish sailors explore South America.	Thomas Tallis, composer of religious music, is born.
Cortez conquers Mexico.	
Martin Luther introduces reforms in church music.	**Chorales** are written to be sung in church services.
Egmont, Dutch patriot, fights the Spanish.	Palestrina composes church music during the **Renaissance**.
Elizabeth I becomes Queen of England.	**Madrigals** are composed by Morley and other English composers.
Shakespeare writes his famous plays.	

1600

Summary

──────────── 500 ────────────

The church was the center of religious life, of all education, and of music. An early leader of the Catholic church, Pope Gregory, helped make music an important part of religious services.

──────────── 1000 ────────────

People were dependent for news on "musical reporters" who wandered from village to village reporting the important events of the day in song. Everyone looked forward to the visit of the roaming minstrel.

──────────── 1200 ────────────

A new music called **polyphony** became more and more popular in Italy. People began to travel more freely. As they visited different countries, they discovered new ideas, new foods, new inventions, and new music. They carried these discoveries back to their homelands.

──────────── 1400 ────────────

With the invention of printing, music could be easily reproduced; and more people could have copies of music. Composers began to write music for the "amateur musician" as well as for church musicians. People would gather to enjoy the latest popular songs.

──────────── 1500 ────────────

The **Golden Age** unfolded in England. Queen Elizabeth encouraged musicians to perform in her court. Everyone learned to play and sing. The other arts—literature, painting, poetry, architecture—also flourished.

Martin Luther made church services more simple and conducted them in the native language of the people rather than in Latin. Easy melodies called **chorales** were used so that all the people could join in the church service.

──────────── 1600 ────────────

Music is not alone in its value as a key to the feelings and attitudes of a people. All art acts in this capacity. Correlate music study with a study of other arts. Find and display pictures, reproductions of architecture, etc. which were created during different periods. Share poetry and prose, written during specific eras, with children in language arts classes. Following are some poems by writers who lived during the period outlined in the first time line.

Instructions of King Cormac

(Irish, ninth century)
An excerpt from the larger work

Be not too wise, nor too foolish,
Be not too conceited, nor too diffident,
Be not too haughty, nor too humble,
Be not too talkative, nor too silent,
Be not too hard, nor too feeble.
If you be too wise, men will expect too much of you;
If you be too foolish, you will be deceived;
If you be too conceited, you will be thought vexatious;
If you be too humble, you will be without honour;
If you be too talkative, you will not be heeded;
If you be too silent, you will not be regarded;
If you be too hard, you will be broken;
If you be too feeble, you will be crushed.

God Be in My Hede

from *The Sarum Primer, 1558*

God be in my hede
And in my understandyng,
God be in myne eyes
And in my lokyng,
God be in my mouth
And in my speakyng,
God be in my harte
And in my thinkyng,
God be at myne end
And in my departyng.

The String Family

The string section is the backbone of the orchestra or, as it is sometimes called, the heart of the orchestra. Without the full-throated strings, the musical sound lacks richness.

When string instruments are played, the sound is created by bowing or plucking a taut string. The player "stops" the string by pressing his finger at a particular point, thus changing the length of the string which is free to vibrate. As the length of the vibrating string is altered, the pitch is changed: the shorter the string, the higher the pitch.

Much of the versatility of the string family arises from the fact that the instruments can be played in a variety of ways. They may be bowed either **legato** (smooth and connected) or **staccato** (short and detached). For special effects they may be played **pizzicato** (plucked). The player may also create a **vibrato** (a slight variance in pitch caused by moving the finger back and forth quickly on the string). A **glissando** can be created by sliding the finger quickly up or down the length of the string. The player may produce a **tremolo** by moving the bow rapidly back and forth across the string. **Double-stopping** refers to playing two strings simultaneously, thus changing a melody instrument to one capable of producing harmony. **Harmonics,** which are flutelike tones in the very high register, are produced by lightly touching the string at certain points instead of pressing it firmly in the usual way. The tone quality of a string instrument may be softened by placing a **mute** on its bridge.

Violin: Often called the soprano of the string family, the violin owes its important position in the orchestra to its remarkably versatile qualities. It can produce expressive sounds ranging from the softest lyricism to the highest dramatic excitement.

This instrument is capable of great agility, and rapid and complex passages can be played with amazing rhythmic precision.

The violin's four strings are tuned in fifths: G D A E. The brilliant or ethereal melodies (depending on the composer's demands), produced on the high E string, are in striking contrast to the warm, full, sonorous tones created on the low G string.

Viola: Known as the alto of the string section, the viola is larger than the violin; and its four strings are tuned in fifths: C G D A. The upper three strings of the viola correspond in pitch to the three lower strings of the violin. The tone quality is the least assertive of the string family. The low register can be somber or mysteriously veiled. The higher register is eloquent and can be romantic but with less brilliance than the violin. The viola is not often used as a solo instrument but usually plays harmony or accompaniment parts in the orchestra.

Violoncello: Popularly known as the cello, this deep-throated string is a favorite of composers. While its vibrant tone quality is darkly resonant in the lower register, it is songful and lyric on its higher strings. The cello often plays intense, soaring melodies; at other times it supplies the harmonic foundation for the string choir. The cello is about double the length of the violin; the player rests it between his knees. The cello's strings are each tuned an octave lower than those of the viola.

Double Bass: The double bass is the largest and deepest-voiced of the string family. The instrument stands over six feet high, and the performer sometimes sits on a high stool while playing. The strings on a double bass are tuned in fourths: E A D G. Rarely, for weird or comic sounds, the double bass is singled out as a solo instrument. However, its function in the orchestra is primarily to provide a harmonic foundation. It is very often played pizzicato to good effect.

Harp: The harp is one of the most ancient of musical instruments. It remained in much the same form from primitive times until the eighteenth century when various improvements were made which allowed the harpist to play all the tones in the chromatic scale. It has over forty strings, each of which can be altered by foot pedals to play three tones: the pitch of the open string, the pitch one-half step higher, and the pitch a whole step higher. The tone of the harp cannot be confused with any other instrument. The lower and middle strings produce a warm, lush tone while the upper strings are more brilliant. The characteristic utterance of the harp is the **arpeggio** (a chord in which the notes are played in rapid succession rather than simultaneously).

Full page painting in pupil's book.
See page 209 for explanation of art.

62

Music of Europe

The countries of Europe are comparatively small and close together. Yet, through the ages, each country has maintained national characteristics which can be observed in its music. American travelers in Europe are always impressed by the rich musical culture of the people there and by the way in which large numbers of people participate in musical activities. Music has been an important part of the lives of European people for centuries. Perhaps this accounts for the great achievements in music which Europe now shares with the entire world.

One can observe that the church has been one of the important roots of music. The visitor goes to an ornately decorated little church in a German village to hear music of Bach's time played on a baroque organ. He visits the great cathedrals of France where, for generations, great organ sounds and great organists have been heard. He walks in the garden of an Italian monastery where, centuries ago, monks engraved by hand on parchment some of the earliest written music.

As the visitor goes from music hall to music hall, he is impressed with the musical specialties of the various countries. He sees ballet on the stages of France where the dance style was developed and where many composers wrote music specifically for the ballet. He hears the great chords of Wagner operas coming from the massive chorus, full orchestra, and dramatic singers in the large open halls of Germany. In rooms elegantly decorated, he will hear small groups perform the chamber music of Mozart or Schubert. In Italy he may visit famous opera houses, such as La Scala, and hear great choirs in the cathedrals of Rome.

The traveler will be entranced by red boots stamping the vigorous dance rhythms of the Czech and Russian countries. He will tap his foot as the gypsy dancer of Spain twirls and claps in a flamenco dance. As he moves from seashore to mountain peak, across warm lands and cold, he will be charmed by the varied customs and the folk songs which reflect the lands, work, and lives of the people.

If any members of the class have visited Europe, ask them to describe their experiences, especially the music they heard. When the class has read the page, conduct a discussion of the ideas and encourage children to relate what they already know of the music of European countries (songs and compositions they can recall) to music of European origin heard in our own country.

Survey with the class the entire section of the book and notice which European countries are represented (Italy, Switzerland, Austria and Germany, France, Czechoslovakia, Hungary). Notice pictures and invite comments. Play a few songs from the recordings as an introduction to the entire section.

On a map of Europe, locate the countries whose music the class is to study. Invite discussion of customs, geographic characteristics, history, and any facts or points of interest children already know.

Encourage children to do individual reading of books, stories, and articles related to the six countries as they study the music of each. Have them report their reading to the class. Children's libraries have many colorful books, written for the reading level of sixth-graders, based on lives of people of various lands.

Refer to this page often as children study the music of this section. After studying the music of each country, the class may wish to plan a culminating activity of some sort. It might be a program of song and dance; an original class drama, story, or essay; an assembly sing; or an oral discussion of all that was learned. Remember that identification of success is the last step in learning. Rather than going on and on, children need to stop for a synthesis of what they know. The culminating activity and the identification of success are a part of the learning process.

Ma bella bimba

Key: B♭   Starting Tone: F (5)
Meter: $\frac{3}{4}$ $\left(\frac{3}{\textbf{J}}\right)$
Piano accompaniment on page 246

* MELODY: Listen to the recording to enjoy this typical Italian melody and to learn the pronunciation of the Italian words. As children learn the melody, help them realize that the A section (which is the refrain) is in **B flat major** while the B section (which is the verse) is in **G minor.** Compare the melodies of the two sections. The A section centers around the B flat chord (B♭-D-F) while the B section centers around the G minor chord (G-B♭-D). The F♯, the seventh step of the G harmonic minor scale, also helps us know that the verse is in minor.

* FOLK STYLE: Read the discussion "Music of Italy" on page 66 and determine the characteristics which are present in this song. It changes to major at the refrain; the form is A B A. The rhythms are made up of dance patterns. The strong upward skip at the beginning of each measure in the refrain gives the melody a distinctive lilt. Listen for the accompaniment on the recording.

Experiment with different patterns and combinations of instruments so that the children can choose those which fit the folk flavor of the song. Accompany the verse with the autoharp; add the following pattern on the tambourine during the refrain.

shake   tap   tap   tap

FORM: Review page 32, "Dance in the Study of Music." This song was probably once a dance. Some children may wish to make up a dance to perform for the rest of the class. Suggest that their dance design should match the design of the music and that the accents of the rhythm should be seen in their dance movements.

Help the group plan movements which are characteristic of Italian dance style. The Italians dance easily, swaying their bodies to the music. Usually the boy holds his arms upward while the girl's hands are on her apron or held akimbo. Occasionally, solo dances interrupt the dancing of the couples with stamping and heel tapping by the boys. The simple dance steps include skipping, waltzing, and step-hops. Italian dances have a simple design usually made up of four or six different patterns. Within the pattern, individual dancers may break away for a solo improvisation.

Ma bella bimba

Italian Folk Song
Arranged by Kurt Miller
Words Adapted

Review the discussion "Reading the Melody" on page 13 as you learn this song. Study the melody of the A and B sections of the song separately. You will discover that some of the steps must be completed differently for the two sections.

Allegro

Ma   co - me bal - li, bel - la   bim - ba, bel - la

Ma   co - me   bel -

bim - ba,   bel - la   bim - ba, Ma   co - me bal - li, bel - la

la   bim - ba, Ma   co -   me

Record 3   Side A   Band 2.   VOICES: soprano, alto.
ACCOMPANIMENT: guitar, mandoline, concertina.
FORM: Introduction, *4 meas.;* Vocal (one voice on melody, mandolin on second part); Interlude, *4 meas.;* Vocal (voices on 2 parts).

bim - ba, bel - la bim - ba, bal - li ben! *Fine*

bel - la ben!

Verse

Bel - la bim - ba, la vil - la - nel - la,
Bel - la bim - ba danc - es so gai - ly,

Guar - da che pas - sa la vil - la - nel - la,
See how the pret - ty girl danc - es so gai - ly,

D. S. al Fine

Bel - la bim - ba sa ben bal - lar! Ma
Bel - la bim - ba whirl - ing a - round!

A - gi - le e snel - la sa ben bal - lar! Ma
Dressed in a pret - ty gown, whirl - ing a - round!

Read the discussion "Music of Italy" on the next page. Which of the characteristics described can you find in this song? Favorite Italian folk instruments are the guitar, mandolin, and concertina. You will hear these instruments on the recording. Plan an accompaniment for this song using the autoharp to suggest the guitar or mandolin.

Permanent Repertoire and Assembly Singing

Incorporated in Book 6 and other books in *Exploring Music* is the plan for building a permanent song repertoire. At each grade level, children will memorize a body of heritage songs which become a part of the lifetime repertoire. Songs will be memorized naturally and with ease by singing them rather than by a separate process of work memorization.

This list selected for sixth grade is also the basic list for assembly singing. Singing together in a group larger than one class has many values as a regularly planned school activity. It provides inspiration and the stimulus to do one's best. It can be a special occasion greatly anticipated by the children. As a point toward which to work, it can have an important effect upon the classroom singing of the school.

A piano accompanist may play for some or all of the songs; autoharps, percussion instruments, and/or resonator bells will sometimes be effective; and some songs may be sung unaccompanied. Songs should be memorized and studied in the classroom before they are sung in assembly. If carefully prepared, the assembly may very well sound like a large choir of selected voices. An attitude of "making beautiful music together" will make the "sing" an inspiring musical experience. A teacher might conduct the singing group, or the classes may sing with accompaniment only. A guest artist as a musical treat can help make the occasion an outstanding educational experience.

The following songs are recommended for these purposes in the sixth grade:

p. 4	Roll On, Columbia	p. 90	The Herdsman
p. 6	Peace of the River	p. 106	In Summer the Sunshine Is Brightest
p. 8	God of Our Fathers		
p. 12	Swinging Along		
p. 15	These Things Shall Be	p. 114	All Hail, Fridolin
p. 30	Let Us Break Bread Together	p. 120	Carmen, Carmela
		p. 121	La Vidalita
p. 40	Turn Ye to Me	p. 124	Río, Río
p. 42	Comin' Thro' the Rye	p. 150	Mystic Lights
p. 46	Greensleeves	p. 155	Arirang
p. 68	Alleluia	p. 164	Beautiful Dreamer
p. 74	Jesu, Joy of Man's Desiring	p. 166	Jacob's Ladder
p. 75	My Heart Ever Faithful	p. 170	Cindy
p. 81	My Homeland	p. 184	Wonderful Copenhagen
p. 86	Evening Prayer		

Buon giorno

Key: F   Starting Tone: C (5)
Meter: $\frac{2}{4}$ ($\frac{2}{\text{♩}}$)
No piano accompaniment

* EXPRESSION: The words of this happy round mean "Good morning, dear little baby. Many kisses to you!" Listen to the recording to learn the pronunciation of the Italian words. As children sing the song, remind them to sing lightly and crisply with light accents and clear enunciation. They will enjoy adding the Italian greeting *buon giorno,* "good day," to their vocabulary of foreign words.

* FORM: As with all rounds, this song is made up of phrases of equal length. Notice that the rhythm is exactly the same for each of the three phrases. Contrast comes in the movement of the melodies. This song might be played by an instrumental ensemble as a round. (See page x.)

Music of Italy

Read the discussion and talk about characteristics of Italian folk music. Emphasize the close relationship between composed music and the musical life of the folk. There is probably no other group of people who supports the musical life of their country as enthusiastically as the Italians. Even the poorest people find time and money to go to the opera. The Italian conductor Arturo Toscanini (1867-1957) is considered one of the most eminent conductors of the twentieth century.

Italians are proud of their many contributions to music throughout the centuries. The fact that Italy has long been the center of the Catholic Church may be a contributing factor. As pointed out in the Time Line on pages 60-61, the church first developed music as an art form. The earliest composers were church musicians; the first notation was developed by monks. Almost every form of music that Italy has produced originated in, or was given impetus by, the church. The first operas were sacred music dramas. The madrigal was influenced by the sacred motets. Composed music and folk music have influenced each other in Italy. Folk music reflects the carefully structured design of composed music. The more complex melodies of some folk songs may have originated in composed music. At the same time, many composers have used Italian folk themes in their orchestral and choral compositions.

Buon giorno
Italian Folk Song

1. Buon gior-no, mi - a ca-ra bam - bi - na, mol-ti ba - ci,

2. Buon gior-no, mi - a ca - ra bam - bi - na, mol-ti ba - ci,

3. Buon gior-no, mi - a ca - ra bam - bi - na, mol-ti ba - ci!

Music of Italy

World travelers often think of Italy as a favorite country because of its bright and varied landscape, a long coast line, and plenty of sunshine. They also remember the musical life of the country because performances of great music are found everywhere. The common people of the country love music and sing or whistle songs from operas as frequently as they sing their folk songs.

Italy is a country of many provinces, each with its own distinctive music. There are the boat songs of Venice, the street songs of Naples, and the colorful melodies of Sicily. Italian folk songs and dances are often lively and bright and reflect a people whose nature is as sunny as their climate. Many of the folk tunes change from minor to major at the refrain. Melodies are romantic and florid and cover a wide range. The rhythms are lightly accented and danceable. A sprightly refrain may follow a more restrained verse.

Italy might be called the birthplace of composed music of the Western World, because many forms of vocal and instrumental music were first created there. Italy was the birthplace of opera, and Italian operas are still the most popular throughout the world. Madrigals, which you studied in the music of the British Isles, were first composed in Italy.

Record 3   Side A   Band 3. VOICES: women's ensemble.
FORM: Vocal (unison); Vocal (3-part round).

Sanctus, Sanctus, Sanctus, Dominus Deus Sabaoth!

With these words, great choirs sang praises hundreds of years ago in Italy. The same words can still be heard in cathedrals and churches all around the world.

Sanctus

from *Pope Marcellus Mass*

by Giovanni Pierluigi da Palestrina

Listen to Palestrina's setting of the *"Sanctus."* To Palestrina, words were of the greatest importance. He believed that music should help people understand the meaning of the text. As you listen, notice how his music supports the idea of praise. Long, ornamented melodic lines give emphasis to important words. Voices weave about, sometimes imitating each other, sometimes introducing new fragments of melody. The tapestry of sound is as colorful as the stained glass windows of the cathedral where this music first was heard.

Palestrina lived in Italy about the time of the Golden Age in England. In Europe, this colorful, exciting period in history is known as the **Renaissance.** This word means "rebirth" and refers to the "rebirth of learning" which spread through Europe from 1450 to 1600.

This was the age of great *a cappella* singing; that is, singing without accompaniment. Instrumental accompaniments were not used because they might interfere with the words. Palestrina once urged his choir to sing "in a suitable manner so that everything can be heard and properly understood." This is still good advice to a singer today!

Record 8   Side A   Band 4.
Pro Musica Choir of Vienna,
Ferdinand Grossman, conductor.

Sanctus

from *Pope Marcellus Mass*

by GIOVANNI PIERLUIGI DA PALESTRINA
Born c. 1525   Died 1594

The **Renaissance** was an age of curiosity and adventure, an age of scholarship and culture. Columbus, Magellan, and others explored new lands. Scientists, including Galileo, made important discoveries about man, nature, and the universe. Leonardo da Vinci, Raphael, and Michelangelo, among others, were the masters of painting, sculpture, and architecture.

The influence of the church extended to all of the fine arts of the Renaissance. Italy has a long religious tradition; and it is not surprising that great composers, such as Palestrina, spent their time writing beautiful religious music.

Encourage children to look for examples of Renaissance painting, sculpture, and architecture. Add names of artists and explorers to the time line.

After children have discussed the information in their book, play the short *"Sanctus"* in its entirety. Give children an opportunity to listen to it quietly. On another day, listen to the composition again and discuss the music.

This composition is written for six voices. There are three main sections in the *"Sanctus."* In the first section, *Sanctus Dominus Deus Sabaoth* (Holy Lord God of Hosts), a soaring melody is stated by the sopranos. Fragments of it are echoed by the other voices. Notice how the phrases overlap with some voices ending a phrase while others begin a new phrase. The second section is more strongly accented. The words are *Pleni sunt coeli et terra gloria tua.* (Heaven and earth are full of Thy glory.) The opening tones of the altos and tenors are imitated by other voices. The final section *Hosanna in excelsis* (Hosanna in the highest) brings the *"Sanctus"* to an exciting close.

The *"Sanctus"* is part of a larger composition called a **mass.** The mass is the most solemn service of the Catholic Church. Music for the mass usually includes the following sections: *Kyrie, Gloria, Credo, Sanctus,* and *Agnus Dei.*

The *"Sanctus"* is taken from the *Mass for Pope Marcellus,* one of the most famous of the many masses written by Palestrina. Palestrina's music is characterized by long phrases, changing rhythms, and melodies which move primarily stepwise or with small skips. His harmony is pure and pleasing with little dissonance. The resulting music is serene and calm, emphasizing the important words.

Alleluia

Key: D   Starting Tone: D (1)

Meter: $\frac{3}{2}$ $\left(\frac{3}{\downarrow}\right)$

No piano accompaniment

* MUSICAL STYLE: "Alleluia" is typical of a type of church hymn that was developed during the sixteenth and seventeenth centuries. Martin Luther introduced many changes into the church service in order to give the people a more active part. The melodies of hymns were often drawn from familiar folk music, and the words were sung in the native language instead of in Latin as had previously been the custom. The hymns were based on religious ideas that the people could easily understand. The words for many hymns were written by Martin Luther himself. Some hymns were adaptations of Bible verses or were taken from the writings of Christian saints such as this one by St. Francis of Assisi.

Ask children to find Martin Luther (c. 1483-1546) and St. Francis of Assisi (c. 1181-1226) on the Time Line on page 60. Discover other events that occurred during these men's lives.

The word "canon" means "law." The musical composition "canon" follows the law, or the rule, that each part must have the same melody but must start at a different time. However, "Alleluia" is not an exact canon. Notice that the second melody is slightly altered in some places in order that the voices may complete each section of the song at the same time.

* HARMONY: Compare the two voices. AT WHAT POINT DOES THE SECOND VOICE FAIL TO IMITATE THE FIRST? (Measure four.) Determine the relationship of the two voices during the "Alleluia" section at the end of the song. (The voices move in unison and then in thirds.)

Learn the imitative sections as you would learn a round; that is, learn the melody in unison, then divide into two parts. Learn the "Alleluia" sections by singing both parts simultaneously; stress the value of listening carefully to the harmony created by the two voices.

Alleluia

German Melody
Translated by William H. Draper
from a poem by St. Francis of Assisi

The influence of the church can be noted in the music of all parts of Europe. The melody of this ancient hymn comes from Germany; the words are attributed to St. Francis of Assisi. Study the Time Line on page 60 to find out when St. Francis lived.

Notice that there are only two patterns of rhythm in this song. This song is similar to a canon; however, the melody of the second voice part is slightly different from the first. Study the differences carefully.

All crea-tures of our God and King, Lift
All crea-tures of our God and

up your voice and with us sing Al - le -
King, Lift up your voice, sing Al - le -

lu - ia! Al-le-lu - ia! Thou burn-ing sun with gold-en
lu - ia! Al-le-lu - ia! Thou

Record 3 Side A Band 4. VOICES: mixed choir.
ACCOMPANIMENT: 2 trumpets, organ.
FORM: Instrumental (unison); Vocal (unison); Instrumental (2 parts); Vocal (2 parts).

Scored for instruments.
See "Exploring Music Instrumental Supplement."

68

RHYTHM: Ask children to recall the steps necessary for reading the rhythm of a new song. Determine that the meter moves in threes with the half note as the beat note. In this song the half note receives one beat; there are two quarter notes to a beat. The beat should move in a moderate walking tempo. Help children realize that, although the beat note is a half note, the tempo does not become slower. Have them write out the first phrase of the song as though the meter were $\frac{3}{4}$, then $\frac{3}{8}$:

WHICH OF THESE PHRASES WOULD WE SING "FASTER"? Help children realize that neither the meter nor the note used as the beat note have anything to do with the tempo that is set. Each of the above patterns would sound exactly the same as long as the tempo of the basic beat remains the same. Clap each of the patterns and discover that each sounds exactly alike because the relationship between note values is the same.

Spinn, spinn, meine liebe Tochter

Key: F   Starting Tone: C (5)
Meter: 3/4 (3/♩)
No piano accompaniment

* FOLK STYLE: When the class has heard the recording of the song and has studied the words, read with the class the article "Music of Austria and Germany" (page 73). Discuss the sentences which apply to this song (the last sentence in paragraph one, all of paragraph three). The words of the song are defined as follows:

> *spinn*—spin; *liebe Tochter*—dear daughter;
> *liebe Mutter*—dear mother; *ja*—yes;
> *ich kauf dir'n paar Schuh*—I'll buy you a pair of shoes;
> *auch Schnallen dazu*—and buckles too;
> *kann ja nicht spinnen*—cannot spin;
> *es schmerzt mich mein Finger und tut mehr so weh*—
>   it hurts my finger and gives me pain;
> *ich kauf dir ein Kleid*—I'll buy you a dress;
> *nicht zu lang, nicht zu weit*—not too long, not too wide;
> *ich kauf dir 'nen Mann*—I'll buy you a man;
> *dann streng ich mich an*—then I shall make an effort;
> *ich kann ja schon spinnen*—I can already spin;
> *es schmerzt mich kein Finger*—
>   none of my fingers is hurting me;
> *und tut nicht mehr weh*—and I have no longer any pain.

* HARMONY: Since this is one of the first three-part songs of the year, it should be taught carefully so that the class will be successful in learning it as quickly as possible and desire to sing other songs in three-part harmony.

The words of the song dramatize a conversation between a mother and her daughter. The mother's voice is always the lowest part. The mother's part has the melody in the first phrase; the daughter's part has the melody in the rest of the song.

Ask the class to listen to the song on the recording. Discuss word meanings and the style of the song. When they have heard the song several times, ask the children to sing the mother's part throughout the song. In the last half of the song, the mother's part is an accompaniment figure repeated several times.

Spinn, spinn, meine liebe Tochter

German Folk Song

Which of the characteristics discussed on page 73 can you observe in this song?

Record 3   Side A   Band 5.   VOICES: women's ensemble.
FORM: Vocal, *vv. 1-3.*

70

O spinn mei-ne lie-be Toch-ter, O spinn, spinn, O spinn.

und tut, und tut, und tut mir so weh!

Toch - ter, und tut nicht mehr weh!

tut, und tut nicht mehr weh!

Choose the most capable singers of the class to sing the middle part. Ask two groups of children to sing the two parts notated on the upper staff. On the first four words *"spinn,"* sing scale numbers 1 and 3, 3 and 5. When they can sing these, ask the third part to sing also *"Spinn, spinn, meine liebe Tochter."* Being able to sing well the first measures in three-part harmony will encourage the children to work further. Complete the learning of the first phrase. Let the group on the second part practice separately, singing numbers and noticing the step-wise pattern on the tones 1-2-3-4-3. The melody of the next phrase is the same as that of the mother's part, but it is an octave higher (the last two notes are different). The second part of this phrase is in thirds with the melody (except the last two notes). Practice the two parts together. Sing the first two phrases completely.

The rest of the song may be learned in the same lesson if the children are used to singing in harmony. Sing the upper and middle parts of the rest of the song with numbers until the parts move easily. Review the mother's part below and sing all three parts with a syllable such as "ta." Then sing the song with words from the beginning. On other days, work on other verses.

Review the song from time to time. When the whole class knows the song, the girls might enjoy keeping it for "their own." There are songs in the book which the boys may claim although the entire class learns them at first. It is good to have some songs which are the specialty of each group, along with many that everybody sings.

Du, du liegst mir im Herzen

Key: E♭   Starting Tone: G (3)
Autoharp Key: F   Starting Tone: A (3)
Meter: 3/4 (1 / ♩.)
Piano accompaniment on page 248

STYLE: The Germans love to sing. They sing at school festivities, at church, when they are hiking, and in restaurants and cafes. This song is representative of the type one might hear sung in cafes or by German students on an outing. Read the discussion "Music of Austria and Germany" on page 73 of the pupil's book and note the characteristics of German music found in this song.

German songs are often accompanied by small orchestras composed of violins, clarinets, zithers, and double bass. When children know the song, they may work out an arrangement similar to that suggested for "The Herdsman."

* RHYTHM: The rhythm of this song is typical of German folk songs with its vigorous patterns and strong accents which group the beats in threes. Each phrase is a single rhythmic idea. Invite children to tap the rhythm of the song while one child maintains a beat. The accent falls on the first beat of each measure. Remind children that this song should be sung with well-marked rhythm, slightly emphasizing each accent, and holding out dotted notes for their full value. Give the song the swing of an old-fashioned *Ländler,* a rather slow waltz danced in a country style.

* HARMONY: Help children answer the question in their book. Discover that the two voices move at an interval of a third most of the time. Play the chords for each measure while the children follow the notation. With the autoharp providing harmonic support, challenge children to sing as much of the song as possible on a neutral syllable. Isolate spots and work on parts individually if necessary. Listen to the recording to learn the pronunciation of the German words. The translation of the words is as follows: "You, you lie in my heart. You, you lie in my mind. You, you cause me much pain. You don't know how much I love you."

Du, du liegst mir im Herzen

German Folk Song
Arranged by Mary Val Marsh

Reread the discussion of intervals on page 5. Study the notation of this song. What intervals do you find between the two voices? Sing as much of the song as possible by reading the notes.

Record 3   Side A   Band 6.   VOICE: baritone.
ACCOMPANIMENT: 2 trumpets, clarinet, trombone, tuba, percussion.
FORM: Instrumental; Vocal.

Scored for instruments.
See "Exploring Music Instrumental Supplement."

Music of Austria and Germany

Songs expressing every activity of daily life were a part of the German culture five hundred years ago. Through these songs, many people of Germany received part of their education. As they listened to folk songs and church hymns, the people learned to love their language and to express themselves in it. Students, farmers, soldiers, and housewives had their own songs which reflected the character and interests of the people.

Many of the German folk songs are solid and vigorous; others are sentimental. Most of the songs are based on the major scale and use intervals taken from the basic chords. Part singing is very common among the German people. They usually harmonize in thirds and sixths. Many German folk songs are strongly accented with dance rhythms. The dances often move in threes. They grew out of the Ländler, the ancestor of the modern waltz.

No part of the world has gained so fine a reputation for music as have the German-speaking countries of Austria and Germany. Since the eighteenth century, music has been one of their greatest exports to the world at large. For centuries before this, music was a deep-rooted part of German life. You will find, as you study this section of your book, that many great composers lived in Germany and Austria. Their compositions have influenced the development of music all over the world. Many of the designs which are considered to be ideal musical forms were developed by these composers.

A Great Composer of the Past, Johann Sebastian Bach

Johann Sebastian Bach lived in Germany during the early part of the eighteenth century, a hundred years after England's Golden Age. He spent his life as a church musician and teacher. It was his responsibility to write and prepare music for the church service. In addition to his church music, Bach wrote music for small instrumental ensembles and for the harpsichord. Some of these compositions were written as study pieces for his own children. Today, boys and girls studying piano often play pieces that Bach wrote for his children. Some of his children became distinguished musicians.

The great number of compositions that Bach wrote and the perfection of their form are an overwhelming accomplishment. The German word "*Bach*" means "brook"; but as a musician the man was not a quiet, flowing brook. He was a great torrent of talent which poured out in hundreds of compositions known and performed throughout the world.

As the children read the discussion in their books, refer to the songs they have learned that are examples of the characteristics described.

Draw attention to the number of compositions included in their book that were written by German and Austrian composers. Represented are Bach, Mozart, Beethoven, Schubert, Wagner, Brahms, Humperdinck, Webern, and Hindemith. Also mentioned in their book is Schoenberg, an Austrian composer who became an American citizen. Long before the time of Bach, great composers, such as Schütz and Buxtehude, were contributing to Germany's musical life. Many outstanding composers including Handel (who lived in England), Haydn, Mendelssohn, Schumann, Wolf, and Richard Strauss were from Germany and Austria. This musical heritage continues to affect the development of music throughout the world.

A Great Composer of the Past, Johann Sebastian Bach

The biographical sketch of Bach has been included because of the historical importance of this man in the development of music through the centuries even to the present time. Although many of the forms and musical organizations that he used had been developed by composers before him, Bach brought them to perfection. Probably no other man of musical genius has influenced composers and the evolution of music to a greater extent than Bach.

Children who study piano may have played some of Bach's music. Invite them to perform for the class. Other children may enjoy finding additional information about Bach's life and his music. Encourage children to present biographies of other composers as well.

Jesu, Joy of Man's Desiring

Key: G   Starting Tone: B (3)

Meter: $\frac{3}{4}$ ($\begin{smallmatrix}3\\ \rule[0.4ex]{0.6em}{0.07ex}\end{smallmatrix}$)

Piano accompaniment on page 250

* MUSICAL STYLE: Discuss the term **chorale** as described in the pupil's book. Chorale tunes arose after Martin Luther initiated his reforms in the Protestant church service. Some of the hymn tunes were adaptations of folk songs; others were taken from the old Catholic service; some were composed by Protestant musicians. Bach and other composers often used chorale melodies as the basis for their religious compositions. They arranged them in parts for choirs to sing and added elaborate organ accompaniments. Sometimes they used the melodies as themes for instrumental compositions.

Listen to the recording. It is sung first as a chorale, then as arranged by Bach. Discuss how Bach has added interest to the simple chorale tune by means of the extended instrumental interludes. The music alternates between polyphonic and homophonic styles. (See pages 50-51.) Be sure to observe the expressiveness of each phrase. Notice how the dynamics rise and fall to a climax within each phrase. The characteristics of Bach's style are listed on page 75. On several different days, have children listen to the song, follow the notation, and then sing it with the recording. The children might recall the recording of "Now Thank We All Our God" in the fifth grade. The arrangement by Bach, used on that recording, is very similar in form and style to his arrangement of "Jesu, Joy of Man's Desiring." If the recording of "Now Thank We All Our God" is available, play it for the class and compare it with "Jesu, Joy of Man's Desiring." Point out the similarities such as the use of instrumental interludes between phrases of the chorale sung by the choir.

* FORM: Study the design of the chorale as notated in the pupil's book. It consists of eight four-measure phrases. Phrases three and four are a repetition of phrases one and two. Review the function of the **repeat sign** (:‖). Notice that phrases five and six are a variation of phrase one. Phrases seven and eight are almost an exact repetition of phrases one and two.

Jesu, Joy of Man's Desiring

Melody by Johann Schop
Arranged by Johann Sebastian Bach

Listen to Bach's arrangement of this **chorale** on the recording. A chorale is a choral hymn intended to be sung in unison by the congregation. In Bach's day organists found that the people often paused at the end of each phrase. This pause allowed time for the organist to improvise a brief interlude on the organ. Gradually, these interludes became more and more important and elaborate. The chorale was sometimes arranged in parts for the choir to sing, and the interludes were given to instruments of the orchestra.

Je - su, joy of man's de - sir - ing,
Drawn by Thee, our souls as - pir - ing,

Ho - ly wis - dom, love _ most _ bright,
Soar to un - cre - a - ted _ light.

Word of God, our flesh that fash - ioned

With the fire of life im - pas - sioned.

Striv - ing still to truth un - known,

Soar - ing, dy - ing round _ Thy _ throne.

Record 3 Side A Band 7A. VOICES: mixed choir.
ACCOMPANIMENT: string quartet, harpsichord.
FORM: as originally written by Bach.

Record 3 Side A Band 7B. VOICES: children's choir.
ACCOMPANIMENT: organ.
FORM: Introduction, *4 meas.;* Vocal.

My Heart Ever Faithful

by Johann Sebastian Bach

Listen to the recording of this **aria**. The composer of an aria is interested in writing a beautiful melody that is expressive of a musical idea. You will hear the aria sung first as Bach originally wrote it and with Bach's original instrumentation. Listen especially for the harpsichord. You will then hear the short version which is printed in your books.

* EXPRESSION: Listen to the recording of this lovely aria. Discuss how the music conveys the joyous, worshipful mood of the words. Sing it expressively with each note in the richly ornamented melody clearly defined.

COMPOSER'S STYLE: As children listen to "My Heart Ever Faithful" and to "Jesu, Joy of Man's Desiring," help them identify some of the characteristics of Bach's music which make it typical of the period during which he lived: melodies are ornamented with turns and embellishments; the tempo rarely varies within a single composition; dynamic interest is attained through contrast of loud and soft phrases instead of making use of gradual crescendos or diminuendos; the phrase structure of this music is easily defined; a moving bass can be heard below the main melody. This period is known in the arts as the **baroque** period.

MELODY: To help children understand what is meant by ornamentation, play the melody, leaving out the sixteenth note "turns." Discuss how the ornamentation adds interest to what is basically a very simple tune.

* FORM: This song is a short version of a long aria from one of Bach's cantatas, "God So Loved the World." A **cantata** is a composition somewhat like an opera in that the words tell a story. Unlike an opera, there is no action in a cantata; the singers "tell a story" but do not dramatize it. Bach's cantatas usually include choruses, recitatives, and arias. A **recitative** is a section in which the narrative of the story is presented; the music is simple and follows the natural rhythm of speech. An **aria** is a solo song used in operas, oratorios, and cantatas. It does not contribute to the unfolding of the story but gives the singers an opportunity to express their feelings about what is happening.

Record 3   Side B   Band 1A.   VOICE: soprano.
ACCOMPANIMENT: oboe, violin, cello, harpsichord.
FORM: as originally written by Bach.

Record 3   Side B   Band 1B.   VOICES: children's choir.
ACCOMPANIMENT: organ.
FORM: Introduction, *4 meas.;* Vocal.

Egmont Overture

BY LUDWIG VAN BEETHOVEN
BORN 1770   DIED 1827

Beethoven wrote the *Egmont Overture* as incidental music for a play by the great German author Goethe. The play is based on the facts of the unjust rule of Spain in the Netherlands and of the courage that resulted in victory over that rule.

In the sixteenth century the famous Spanish Armada sailed the seas, spreading Spanish rule wherever possible. Spain easily conquered the little country of the Netherlands. A wealthy nobleman Count Egmont urged the people to fight back. He was imprisoned and eventually hanged, but his death served to inspire a new spirit which quickly spread and resulted in the victory of the Dutch people.

Read the first two paragraphs of the pupil's page with the children. Ask the class to concentrate on the music with books closed as you play the entire overture. Encourage class members to comment on ways in which the ideas of the first two paragraphs are expressed musically. How does the music express the woe of the people, their confidence, etc.? Discuss each idea separately and play short segments of the record again to help the class recall the music discussed.

Read the rest of the pupil's page with the class and play the coda section. After discussion, play the entire overture once more to close the first lesson on the overture.

On another day, play the overture again and review the first page of the lesson. Then discuss one by one the musical devices listed on the second page of the lesson. Play segments of the music to help the class locate the passages. All children may not hear all the passages discussed in one or two lessons. Play the overture at various times throughout the year and invite further comments from class members as they discover "more and more of the musical details."

Egmont Overture

by Ludwig van Beethoven

Of the many musical messages of freedom, none is more stirring than this overture. It is named for Count Egmont who inspired the Dutch people to rise and fight their Spanish conquerors. Egmont's leadership continued even after he was imprisoned. After his execution a strong spirit of defiance spread through the land. Because of that spirit, the Dutch were eventually victorious.

Listen to Beethoven's overture and enjoy the powerful music for the story it tells and the feelings it inspires. The overture begins with a great chord in which all the instruments of the orchestra unite as did the people of the Netherlands. The music which follows expresses the woe of the people, their restlessness, the confidence they developed, the uprising, and finally, the proclamation of victory.

The proclamation is heard in the coda which is considered to be a masterpiece. Beethoven called it his "Little Symphony of Victory." The coda begins with a restless murmuring of the kettledrums and strings and then the call to arms.

The coda moves on with the theme of battle

and closes with the triumphant theme of victory.

Record 8   Side B   Band 2.
New York Philharmonic,
Bruno Walter, conductor.
Symbol (◉) for visible intermediate bands appears on reduced pupil's page.

This is a composition one can hear many times, each time discovering something new. As you listen to it at various times, try to hear more and more of the musical details. Discuss each of the musical ideas as you identify them.

1. The strong chords of the opening section.
2. The melody pattern played first by the violins and repeated many times in sequence.

3. Theme One, Egmont's theme, a descending melody played first by the cellos which are soon joined by the other strings.
4. Theme Two, the question-answer passage between the strings and the woodwinds.

(strings)

(woodwinds)

5. The scale passages.
6. The repetitions of the two main themes.
7. The question-answer passage between the brass and string sections of the orchestra.
8. The mournful chords.
9. The coda section.

Ludwig van Beethoven is considered by many to be the greatest of all composers. He wrote hundreds of works, including nine symphonies, many chamber works, compositions for violin, piano, voice, and for almost every instrument and combination of instruments known in his time.

Yet there is something more than any of these that seems most important to the many lovers of Beethoven's music. It is the composer's unusual ability to reach the hearts and minds of those who perform his music and those who listen to it. The *Egmont Overture* is a good example of Beethoven's orchestral style. It is also a fine example of the way in which the man and his ideals are expressed in his music.

You might play Theme One (number 3 in pupil's book) on the piano for the class or write it on the board.

When the class has discussed the last two paragraphs of the pupil's page, suggest further study of Beethoven and his music. Some children may have recordings of their favorite compositions by Beethoven at home. Some may play his compositions on instruments. A guest artist of the community might be invited to play a composition for the children. Many children's libraries contain books about the composer. If it is available, show the film *Beethoven and His Music,* a Coronet Color Film, 25 minutes in length.

The Trout

Key: B♭ Starting Tone: F (5)
Meter: $\frac{2}{4}$ (²♩)
Piano accompaniment on page 253

* STYLE: This is one of the best known of Schubert's songs which number over six hundred. Schubert is especially known for composing **lieder.** This German word literally means "songs" but is used to describe songs of a particular type—the **art song** developed in the nineteenth century in which there is a perfect union between the words and the music. The music may be either **through-composed,** or it may be **strophic** (the same melody is used for each verse). The piano accompaniments are works of art in themselves and require great artistic ability on the part of the accompanist. Lieder are notable for their appealing melodies which are appropriate settings for the descriptive and expressive poetry and for the artistic accompaniments which are such an important part of these songs. Other great composers of German lieder are Schumann, Brahms, Wolf, and Richard Strauss.

When the children have heard the recording of the song and have read Benjamin Britten's comment about Schubert (see page 55), conduct a discussion about the source of the song. Invite the children to tell what they know of the composer and his music. The words of this song suggest a typical scene in Germany where fishing streams are plentiful and trout is a favorite food.

Play the recording again and ask the class to notice the leaping figure in the piano accompaniment which suggests the darting fish. The illustration on page 79 also suggests the leaping figure in the accompaniment. This changes in the second section to a darker figure, which helps express the idea of the words.

* EXPRESSION: As an art song, "The Trout" has nuances of expression not found in simpler folk songs and will require careful performance. The song should be sung lightly with crisp sixteenth notes. The words must be clearly enunciated. Expressive dynamics will follow the ideas expressed in the words. Since the accompaniment is very important, the song should be sung with the recording or with the piano accompaniment.

The Trout

Music by Franz Schubert
English Words by Elizabeth Fiske

Listen to Schubert's piano accompaniment on the recording. How does it suggest the scene described in the words? In an art song the piano accompaniment is as important as the vocal melody. It helps to set the mood of the song.

Original Key: D♭

Record 3 Side B Band 2. VOICE: baritone.
ACCOMPANIMENT: piano.
FORM: Introduction, *5 meas.;* Vocal, *vv. 1-3;* Coda, *5 meas.*

The man is set on slaugh - ter; he knows a trick, And fast he churns up mud - dy wa - ter, And makes ___ a luck - y cast. The fish, de - ceived, was tak - en; The an - gler, the an - gler soon went on. I stayed a - lone and shak - en; My hap - py dream was gone. I stayed ___ a - lone and ___ shak - en; My hap - py dream was gone.

* FORM: "The Trout" is a modified version of strophic form. Notice that the first section of the song is one melodic idea. Some phrases are developed out of the preceding one. For example, the last phrase is basically the same as the preceding one but decorative notes are added. The melody of this section is repeated, and the words of the second verse continue the story. The second section of the song is a new melodic idea which follows the mood of the text. Notice that the last two phrases are borrowed from the first section.

Piano Quintet in A ("The Trout")
Fourth Movement

BY FRANZ SCHUBERT
BORN 1797   DIED 1828

When the class has studied Schubert's song "The Trout," introduce the quintet by playing the recording of the fourth movement as children listen without reference to books. Conduct a discussion in which children comment on the fact that the music is based on the song, that it is in the form of theme and variations, that it is played by a few instruments, etc. Some children will probably be able to identify the instruments of the quintet.

On another day, use books in the study of the music. Read the pupil's page with the class to make sure that everyone can read the ideas stated there. Play the recording of the movement as children listen and follow the description of the variations in their books.

Questions asked in the pupil's book may be answered as follows:

. . . In the second variation, the violin plays a decorative counter-melody. The cello often plays in close harmony with the main melody of the viola. The piano plays chords beneath the strings.

. . . In the third variation the cello and double bass play the melody in octaves. The rhythm of the first measure is made even (all eighth notes instead of the dotted eighth and sixteenth). The piano is playing rapid passages of thirty-second notes (four notes to each eighth note of the melody). The accompaniment played by the viola and violin is in syncopated rhythm.

(Continued on page 80.)

("Piano Quintet in A" continued from page 79.)

. . . In the fourth variation the strings and piano play alternately in chords which include only part of the melody notes. Later the piano plays only a bare outline of the melody while the strings play embellishments.

. . . The fifth variation is again in a major key (B flat major). The melody is somewhat changed, for although the rhythm is the same as the original, some of the notes are different.

. . . In variation six, the theme is divided between the violin and cello while the piano plays the darting figure of the original song accompaniment.

Help children notice that although the quintet is in the key of A major, the fourth movement is in D major. The statement of the theme and the first three variations are in D major. The fourth variation has the same tonic note D, but is in minor. In the next variation, Schubert introduces a new key, B flat major. The final variation is once more in D major.

To help children identify key changes in the composition, write signatures for the three keys with tonic chord notes on the board. Ask class members to play the tones on the bells.

D major   D minor

Bb major

This composition is an example of chamber music (music played by a small group of instruments and meant to be played in a small room for a small audience—see page 45).

Some children might do research to learn more about the circumstances of performance in Schubert's time. They might find pictures depicting general life and musical life of that time. Current articles about present-day performances of chamber works might be reported to the class. If it is available, show the film titled *Listening to Good Music* (Encyclopaedia Britannica Film). In this film a string quartet performs music of the style and period of Schubert. If available, show the film titled *The Elements of Music* (National Education Television Film) in which a woodwind quintet demonstrates the elements of musical composition.

Piano Quintet in A   ("The Trout")
Fourth Movement

by Franz Schubert

This **piano quintet** is played by a piano and four string instruments—violin, viola, cello, and double bass. Schubert began the composition of the quintet in the summer of 1819, and it was the first important work written for this combination of instruments. The quintet takes its name from Schubert's song "The Trout," the melody of which is used as the fourth movement theme. The movement is in **theme and variations** form. Review what you know about this form.

As you listen to the statement of the theme by the strings alone, follow the notation of the melody in your book on page 78. Compare the melody of the song with the melody used in the quintet.

◉
In the first variation the piano plays a decorated version of the theme. The violin and cello echo each other as they play triplet figures that remind us of the song accompaniment.

◉
In the second variation the viola plays the theme. What do the other instruments play?

◉
What instruments play the theme in the third variation? How is the rhythm altered in this variation?

◉
How does Schubert change the melody in the fourth variation? Why is it more difficult to hear the melody in this variation?

◉
What key change do you hear in the fifth variation? The theme is played by the cello; the double bass accompanies with pizzicato notes.

◉
In variation six the theme is restated in the original key of D major. What instruments play the theme? Describe the accompaniment.

After you have discussed each variation, listen to the entire movement again. Notice that the theme sounds interesting and fresh in each new version.

Record 9   Side A   Band 1.
Mieczyslaw Horszowski, piano; members of the
Budapest Quartet; Julius Levine, double bass.
Symbol (◉) for visible intermediate bands appears on reduced pupil's page.

As you listen to the recording, notice how Brahm's accompaniment gives support to the melodic line and adds color with its changing harmonies. The broken chords and the strong bass line, which has a melody of its own, add interest to the simple folk song.

My Homeland

German Folk Melody
Arranged by Johannes Brahms
English Words by
Franz Wilhelm

Key: E♭   Starting Tone: E♭ (1)
Meter: $\frac{3}{4}$ $\left(\frac{3}{4}\right)$
Piano accompaniment on page 258

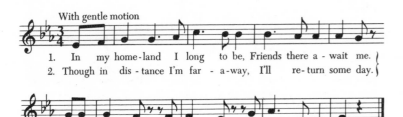

With gentle motion

1. In my home-land I long to be, Friends there a - wait me.
2. Though in dis - tance I'm far - a - way, I'll re - turn some day.

O my home - land, my home - land, My home - land so fair!

COMPOSER'S STYLE: Johannes Brahms (1833-1897) arranged many folk songs; one of his most famous is the beloved "Lullaby." (See *Exploring Music 4*.) Read and discuss information given about Brahms and his love for his homeland. Brahms belongs to a group of composers called **romanticists,** who were interested in the freedom and development of the individual. They aimed for independence from the restraint and control of the musical forms of the classic period. The romanticists expressed their feelings about life and their personal experiences through music composed in an overflowing and unrestrained manner. This romantic nature was also reflected in their interest in the music of the folk.

Dein blaues Auge

by Johannes Brahms

Brahms was a master composer of original art songs as well as an arranger of folk songs. Listen to this art song and notice the beauty of the melody. Like many other art songs, this is a through-composed song; that is, a continuing melody is written for the entire text. Notice the expressive piano accompaniment and its importance to the song. This song is another of the German Lieder. It is a love song and the title means "Your Blue Eyes."

Dein blaues Auge hält so still,
Ich blicke bis zum Grund.
Du fragst mich, was ich sehen will?
Ich sehe mich gesund.

Es brannte mich ein glühend Paar,
Noch schmerzt das Nachgefühl:
Das deine ist wie See so klar,
Und wie ein See so Kühl.

Dein blaues Auge

BY JOHANNES BRAHMS
BORN 1833   DIED 1897

When children have studied the song and the ideas in their book, discuss with them the fact that only the Brahms accompaniment is original in "My Homeland," whereas, "Dein blaues Auge" is Brahms' original composition throughout. The children may remember (and you may wish to borrow the records and review with them) Brahms' music studied in *Exploring Music 4*: "Lullaby," "The Blacksmith," "Liebeslieder Waltzes, Opus 52," and "Trio in A Minor, Opus 114."

Help children identify the characteristics of Brahms' compositional style: flowing melody in simple style with important accompaniment which contributes greatly to the beauty of the song. The climax of the melody occurs in the fifth and sixth lines of the text by use of high tones of the scale, greater dynamic intensity, and more passion in interpretation demanded by the text. The singer is a baritone. The words of the song were written by the poet Groth, and the translation is as follows:

Your blue eyes stay so still,
I turn mine to the ground.
You ask me what I would see
  in them.
I see myself made whole.

A glowing pair has branded me,
The burning lingers still;
Those eyes clear as a lake,
  and as cool.

Record 3   Side B   Band 3.   VOICE: baritone.
ACCOMPANIMENT: piano.
FORM: Vocal, *vv. 1-2.*

Record 7   Side B   Band 1.
Mahon Bishop, baritone
Kelly Hale, pianist.

A Time Line for Exploring Music

Follow the same procedure suggested on pages 60-61 and study this time line. Return to it frequently while studying the music of Europe to help children begin to develop an interest in the historical aspects of the development of music. Continue to stress the fact that the arts, including music, reflect the feelings, attitudes, and activities of the people. Following are some examples of poems from various periods which might be shared with the children.

The following poems come from the Golden Age of English music and the days of Purcell.

The Bell Man

Robert Herrick, English poet, 1591-1674

From noise of scare-fire rest ye free,
From Murders—Benedicite.
From all mischances, that may fright
Your pleasing slumbers in the night:
Mercy secure ye all, and keep
The Goblin from ye, while ye sleep.
Past one o'clock, and almost two,
My Masters all, Good day to you!

As the World Turns

Jonathan Swift, English poet, 1667-1745

I'm up and down and round about,
Yet all the world can't find me out.
Though hundreds have employed their leisure,
They never yet could take my measure.
I'm found in almost every garden,
Nay, in the compass of a farthing:
There's not a chariot, coach, nor mill,
Can move an inch except I will.
(answer to riddle: a circle)

A Time Line for Exploring Music

———— 1600 ————

First colony is founded at Jamestown. | **Homophonic** music is emphasized.

Champlain establishes a settlement at Quebec. | **Opera** becomes an important musical form.

| Composers write instrumental music: **dances, suites,** and **overtures.**

———— 1650 ————

La Salle explores the Mississippi. | Purcell is recognized as the greatest composer in England.

Newton discovers the law of gravity. | Bach and Handel are born in the same year.

———— 1700 ————

Scotland and England form the United Kingdom of Great Britain. | Stradivari makes violins.

China orders all foreigners to leave.
George Washington is born. | Haydn is born.
Bonnie Prince Charlie is defeated at Culloden Moor. | Bach perfects the **fugue,** writes church music.

———— 1750 ————

Wolf captures Quebec. | Mozart is born.

First Industrial Revolution begins.

Robert Burns, Scottish poet, is born. | Beethoven is born.

———— 1775 ————

Declaration of Independence is signed. | The modern **symphony** is developed.
American Revolution brings freedom.
French Revolution ends in liberty. | Mozart writes *Symphony in G Minor.*

| Haydn writes the *"Surprise" Symphony.*

Eli Whitney invents the cotton gin.
Thomas Moore, Irish poet, is born.

———— 1800 ————

Napoleon is crowned Emperor.
Lewis and Clark explore the Northwest.
Abraham Lincoln is born. | *Egmont Overture* is composed by Beethoven.
Bolivar frees northern South America.
Grimm Brothers publish collections of fairy tales. | German composers such as Schubert perfect the solo **art song.**

---1825---

Hans Christian Andersen writes children's stories. Gold is discovered in California.	Rossini writes *William Tell*. Bizet is born. **Symphonic tone poem** is introduced.

---1850---

Summary

---1600---

The exploration of new lands, the development of new inventions, and the exchange of ideas among peoples of different countries were reflected in the life of the people. New scientific ideas were discovered. The works of artists and musicians reflected the excitement of the times.

---1700---

The age from 1600 to 1750 is known as the **baroque** period. Architects built elaborate cathedrals with ornate trim. Artists painted heavenly land- scapes, and their portraits were surrounded by angels and cherubs. Music was also ornate and exuberant.

---1750---

Life in the late 1700's still centered around the royal courts. Each prince had his own group of musicians to perform for his friends. This is known as the **classic** period. It was marked by interest in rules and by restraint. People believed that everything must be done with precision, organization, and clarity, whether it was science, social life, or music.

---1775---

As people came to the New World, they brought their own songs with them. The music was changed to fit the changing life. English and Irish tunes began to tell of events in a new land.

---1800---

With a new century came a new way of life. The revolutions brought free- dom to govern oneself, to have an education, to worship as one wished, and to choose one's own occupation. Musicians wrote music about heroes of freedom. Music was performed in public concerts for everyone to hear.

---1825---

As pioneers moved westward, music went with them. Songs of cowboys, lumberjacks, and riverboatmen echoed across the plains and down the streams. The cotton gin caused plantations to spring up all over the South. With the plantations came Negro spirituals and the songs of Stephen Foster.

---1850---

The rise in interest in Nationalism—period of Beethoven, Mozart, etc.

My Heart's in the Highlands

Robert Burns, Scottish poet, 1759-1796

My heart's in the Highlands, my heart is not here;
My heart's in the Highlands a-chasing the deer;
A-chasing the wild deer, and following the roe,
My heart's in the Highlands wherever I go.

Farewell to the Highlands, farewell to the North,
The birthplace of valor, the country of worth;
Wherever I wander, wherever I rove,
The hills of the Highlands forever I love.

This poem reflects the Romantics—Schubert, Brahms, etc.

My Heart Leaps Up When I Behold

William Wordsworth, English poet, 1770-1850

My heart leaps up when I behold
    A rainbow in the sky:
So was it when my life began;
So is it now I am a man;
So be it when I shall grow old,
    Or let me die!
The Child is father of the Man;
And I could wish my days to be
Bound each to each by natural piety.

Blacksmith's Dance

Die lustigen Hammerschmieds Gesellen (dee loostigen hammer-shmeeds guhzellun, with hard "g" in both words) means "The Happy Blacksmiths' Fellowship," referring to the apprentice organization.

The instruments in this German band are the accordion, clarinet, and guitar. The accordion is the basic instrument and the clarinet plays the countermelody.

As the children listen to the music to discover repetitions and instrumental variations, write the diagram on the board. Use strokes of the chalk to represent measure accents.

Introduction (4 measures)

Melody (8 measures)

/ / / / / / / /	accordion melody
/ / / / / / / /	clarinet descant
/ / / / / / / /	accordion melody
/ / / / / / / /	clarinet descant
/ / / / / / / /	accordion melody
/ / / / / / / /	clarinet melody
/ / / / / / / /	guitar melody
/ / / / / / / /	accordion descant
/ / / / / / / /	guitar melody
/ / / / / / / /	accordion descant
/ / / / / / / /	accordion melody
/ / / / / / / /	clarinet descant
/ / / / / / / /	accordion melody
/ / / / / / / /	clarinet descant

The sequence of patterns to form the complete dance is as follows:

Clap Pattern
Right- and Left-Hand Circles
Clap Pattern
Right- and Left-Hand Stars
Clap Pattern
Do-Si-Do
Fireworks Ending

Blacksmith's Dance

German Folk Dance

A rollicking favorite dance of German men and boys is "Die lustigen Hammerschmieds Gesellen" done in waltz rhythm. The music on your record is typical German dance music used for folk dances of the country.

Listen to the music all the way through. What instruments form this German dance band? Discover how the instruments are used to vary each statement of the melody.

Listen to the opening section again and clap the accents of the waltz rhythm. Count the measures of the introduction. Count the measures of the melody. Make a diagram showing accents and instrumental highlights of the fourteen repetitions of the melody.

Record 8   Side B   Band 3.

The dance is done by a group of four boys in a square. It consists of four patterns and a "fireworks" ending. Each pattern is completed in sixteen measures of the music. In the clap pattern a fascinating rhythm is established when the two sets of partners begin clapping at different times as in a round. A step-hop foot pattern is used for the right- and left-hand circle, the right- and left-hand star, and the do-si-do. The fireworks ending gives a rollicking close to the dance.

Practice each dance pattern without music. Then practice each one with music. Dance the entire dance.

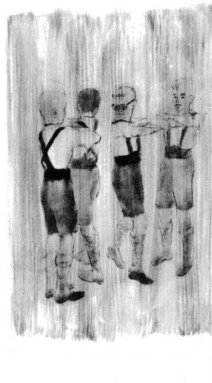

The complete clap pattern is done eight times in the 16 measures by the first pair; but the second pair, beginning on the second measure, finishes one measure early, stopping at the same time as the first pair. In the fireworks ending, the clap pattern is done four times, with the second pair again finishing early.

The Clap Pattern: 16 measures—boys 1 and 3 begin on the first measure, boys 2 and 4 on the second measure.	Clap both hands on thighs. Clap both hands on chest. Clap own hands together. Clap partner's right hand. Clap partner's left hand. Clap partner's both hands.
Right- and Left-Hand Circles: 16 measures—8 measures in each direction.	Group joins right hands and circles left with step-hop. Group circles right in same way.
Right- and Left-Hand Stars: 16 measures—8 measures in each direction.	Group joins right hands in center and circles left with step-hop. Group circles right in same way.
Do-Si-Do: 16 measures—4 measures for each do-si-do.	Boys 1 and 3 fold hands on chest and do-si-do around each other with step-hop. Boys 1 and 4 do likewise. Both pairs repeat pattern.
Fireworks Ending: 16 measures.	Do the clap pattern for 8 measures. Then, everyone stamp floor 3 times. All hit floor with palms 3 times. Slap knees 3 times. Slap thighs 3 times. Stamp right foot, at the same time clapping 3 times. Throw hands over head and shout "Yeow!"

Evening Prayer

Key: C   Starting Tone: C (1)
Meter: $\frac{4}{4}$ ($\frac{4}{4}$)
Piano accompaniment on page 260

* EXPRESSION: Most children will be familiar with the story of *Hansel and Gretel,* and some may have heard the opera. Review the story with the class. The complete story, with recorded excerpts from the opera, may be found in *Exploring Music 3.* This song is sung at the point in the opera when the children, realizing that they are lost, decide to sleep in the forest until morning. They proceed to say their prayers.

Review the suggestions on page iv, "Exploring Music through Singing," and help children sense the importance of expressive performance. Play the recording so that the class can enjoy this beautiful song known by many people throughout the world. Ask the class to discuss all that they observed which contributes to its beauty. Discuss with children the importance of **climax** to musical expressiveness. (See page 30.) Ask them to listen again to the recording and decide where the main climax of this song occurs. (Last phrase.) WHAT THINGS CONTRIBUTE TO THIS CLIMAX? Guide children to discover that both the melodic and rhythmic movement contribute to the climax. The melodic line of the last section rises constantly; each short pattern ends on a higher pitch until the climax is reached in the last measures. Notice that, prior to the last phrase, the rhythmic movement has been in short two-measure patterns. In the last phrase, however, the rhythm moves steadily onward for three measures without a break until the climax is reached on the highest note of the

song and held for two beats (). As children listen to the record-

ing, ask them to note things about the performance which also add to the feeling of climax, such as the gradual crescendo and the slight ritard on the climactic measures.

Observe the notation; notice the dynamic and tempo markings which indicate the manner in which the composer wishes the song to be performed. Review the meaning of these markings. (See glossary, page 329.)

Evening Prayer
by Engelbert Humperdinck

Humperdinck, like Brahms, often turned to folk music for his musical ideas. The prayer is taken from the opera *Hansel and Gretel* which is based on a folk tale and contains many folk melodies.

This song is a good example of two types of harmony. Notice that the parts move together during the first phrase. This type of harmony is called **homophonic. Homo** means "one"; **phonic** means "sound." Therefore, **homophonic** means "tones sounding together as one." In the last part of the composition the voices move independently, each with an important melody of its own. Do you remember the name of this type of music? Refer to page 49 if you cannot recall the name.

Very peacefully

pp

When at night I   go to sleep,   Four-teen an-gels watch do keep,

pp

When at night I   go to sleep,   Four-teen an-gels watch do keep,

Two my head are   guard - ing,   Two my feet are   guid - ing,

Two my head are   guard - ing,   Two my feet are   guid - ing,

Record 3   Side B   Band 4.   VOICES: children's choir.
ACCOMPANIMENT: string quartet, harp.
FORM: Introduction, *2 meas.;* Vocal; Coda, *10 meas.*

* HARMONY: Observe the score carefully before the children begin to sing the song. Listen to the recording. This song uses two kinds of harmony. (See page 50.) In the beginning the two voices move together. Review the name for this kind of harmony. (Homophony.) Beginning with measure nine, the voices move in opposite directions. NOW WE HEAR NOT TWO VOICES MOVING TOGETHER, BUT TWO INDEPENDENT PARTS WITH EACH VOICE SINGING ITS OWN MELODY. DO YOU RECALL THE NAME OF THIS KIND OF MUSIC? (Polyphony.)

Notice that in the last section of the song the second voice often imitates the first voice at a lower pitch. Compare the two parts and discover the melodic and rhythmic differences between them. Notice the use of **sequence** (the same melody repeated at a different pitch) in each voice.

COMPOSER'S STYLE: Humperdinck (1854-1921) was one of the last of the **romantic** composers. He was influenced in much of his writing by Wagner. (See pages 100-103.) From Wagner came many of Humperdinck's ideas for the rich harmonies, colorful orchestrations, and the use of *Leitmotif* (leading motive) to represent people or events within his operas. Although Humperdinck is remembered almost exclusively for the opera *Hansel and Gretel,* he also wrote several other operas and some short orchestral compositions. Much of his music, like *Hansel and Gretel,* reflects the interest of the artists and musicians of the romantic period in the music and life of the folk.

Symphony No. 40 in G Minor
First and Third Movements

BY WOLFGANG AMADEUS MOZART (mo-tsart)
BORN 1756   DIED 1791

Third Movement

To introduce children to this movement, play it at a time when books are not being used. Ask them to discuss what they hear in the music. Encourage them to mention such things as the instruments used, the form, the period in which it might have been written, etc. On another day, read aloud the first two paragraphs in the pupil's book. Refer to the Time Line on page 82 and discuss the period in which Mozart lived. Help children recall the information they know about a symphony. There are usually four movements in a symphony which are in the following order: fast, slow, dance, fast.

Review what children know about **design.** WHAT ARE SOME MUSICAL DESIGNS THAT YOU KNOW? WHAT HELPS TO CREATE DESIGN IN MUSIC? Emphasize that design is dependent on **repetition** and **contrast.** It is the order in which repetition and/or contrast of musical ideas occurs that creates a particular design. **Variety** is also important because it provides interest. Repetition gives a composition **unity.**

Read the questions in the fifth paragraph and play the two themes on the piano. After children have listened to the recording of the minuet and trio, write the design: A B A. Each part also has its own small design made up of short contrasting sections, some of which are repeated.

The $\frac{3}{4}$ meter, the graceful melody, and the balanced phrases characterize minuets of Mozart's day. On subsequent hearings, discuss the instrumentation. The full orchestra plays the Minuet. The Trio is scored for woodwinds and strings, which pass the themes from one to another as in a conversation.

First Movement

After children are well acquainted with the design of the third movement, listen to the first movement of the symphony with books closed. Play the themes on the piano so that children will readily

---

Symphony No. 40 in G Minor
First and Third Movements

by Wolfgang Amadeus Mozart

Mozart was one of the greatest composers of **symphonies**. He lived at a time when the symphony orchestra was first being developed. Mozart and other composers, including Haydn, created a design for the symphony which is still used by many composers today.

What do you know about a symphony? Do you know how many large sections or movements there usually are? How do these movements usually contrast with each other?

Listen to the third movement of Mozart's *Symphony in G Minor* and discover the design.

It is based on a musical form that you already know. It is a minuet, a dance which was popular in the ballrooms of Mozart's day. Composers of this period usually based the third movement of their symphonies on this familiar dance form. Listen for these two themes.

In what ways does the second theme give **variety** to this movement? What gives the movement **unity**? How many different sections did you hear? Write the design of the movement with letters.

After you have discovered the design for the third movement, listen to the first movement of this symphony. As you listen, you will discover that its design is similar to the design of the minuet.

Record 9   Side A   Band 2 and 3.
Cleveland Orchestra,
George Szell, conductor.
Symbol (◉) for visible intermediate bands appears on reduced pupil's page.

There are three large sections.
The last section is a repetition of the first.
There are two main themes.

Theme One

Theme Two

The middle section contrasts with the first and third sections.

Listen to the entire movement. Try to hear the three large sections. You will know when the second section begins because the music comes to a stop at the end of the first section. How will you know when the third section begins? After you have discovered the A B A form of this movement, study each section separately.

A section
The two main themes are stated during the opening section.
The themes are in great contrast to each other.
The two themes are connected by a **bridge**.
The section ends with a short **closing section**.

B section
The music in this section is based on the first theme heard in the A section. The theme is **developed**; that is, the musical material of the theme is used in different ways.

A section
The first theme is heard exactly as it was at the beginning.
The second theme is now heard in minor.
A long **coda** brings the movement to a close.

After you have studied the three sections, listen again to the entire movement. See if you can follow the design as you listen.

This complex A B A design is known as the **sonata allegro** form. Each section also has a specific name. The A section is called the **exposition**, the B section is called the **development**, and the return of A is titled the **recapitulation**. Discuss the meanings of these terms. Why are they good names to describe the sections of sonata allegro form?

recognize them. CAN YOU FIND SIMILARITIES BETWEEN THE DESIGN OF THIS MOVEMENT AND THE DESIGN OF THE MINUET? Invite children to discuss their ideas before reading the discussion in the book.

Help children identify the three large sections. (The recording is banded so that you can easily locate the beginning of each section.) When similarities have been noted, listen again; discover the differences between the two movements. Help children realize that, while this movement also can be considered a "giant" A B A form, the differences are very important. Emphasize that all themes are presented in the A section and that contrast is now derived from the development of the first theme. In the Minuet, however, the B section contains new ideas not heard previously.

Exposition: The first theme is stated by the strings. It is repeated with a slight change at the end and leads directly into a vigorous sounding bridge. The quiet second theme is stated by clarinets and bassoons, answered by strings. Echoes of the opening theme are heard as the first three notes of this theme are played again and again. The coda is announced by full orchestra.

Development: The entire section is based on material from the first theme. The section begins with the theme repeated almost the same as in the beginning of the movement. It is passed from instrument to instrument and played in many different keys. Listen for it in the bass against a high countermelody. A three-note fragment from the theme is the subject of a dialogue between violins and woodwinds. Now it is heard upside down. The flutes and oboes prepare for the return of the theme with soft chords under which can be heard the violins softly answering the opening tones of the first theme.

Recapitulation: The last section is much like the first. The main difference is that the second theme is now in minor. The bridge between the themes is extended, as is the elaborate coda.

Discuss with children the appropriateness of the terms exposition, development, and recapitulation. In the exposition, the composer presents or "exposes" the musical material of the movement. In the development, he manipulates or "develops" his original ideas. In the recapitulation, he restates with some changes the material of the first section.

On another day, draw attention to the characteristics of the music which are representative of Mozart's style. His music is characterized by the lyric quality of the melodies, the imaginative treatment of the themes, careful attention to design, light transparent orchestration, and frequent changes of mood.

The Herdsman

Key: C   Starting Tone: C (1)

Meter: $\frac{3}{4}$ ($\frac{3}{\text{♩}}$)

Piano accompaniment on page 262

* FOLK STYLE: Tiny Switzerland is divided into four language regions: German, French, Italian, and Romanic. This song is from the German section. Wordless yodeling refrains, phrases that end on the third of the scale, and four-measure phrases are typical of music from this section of Switzerland. Let the children enjoy the recording and discuss their own observations. Ask them to listen again to the accompaniment which makes use of **arpeggios** (tones of a chord played in rapid succession rather than simultaneously). Then play the "William Tell Overture" for the class. Focus discussion on the third section of the overture which reflects the music of the Swiss people.

An instrument often associated with the Swiss is the alp-horn, a kind of trumpet which is four to sixteen feet long. The alp-horn has long been used to call the herds in the mountains or to send messages from mountain peak to mountain peak. The alp-horn is restricted to the tones of a major chord in the lower range, although it can move step-wise in the higher range. Yodels often follow this same pattern, and some people believe that yodels developed out of alp-horn calls. Observe that in the yodeling refrain of "The Herdsman," the melody moves by skips and steps, using tones from the I chord or the V7 chord.

In contrast to folk singers of many countries, the Swiss often sing in harmony. This may be because of the long choral tradition in Swiss churches, or it may be due to the influence of the accordion. Its strong chordal accompaniment makes it easy for a singer to hear the harmony and to improvise a second part.

HARMONY: The melody is in the lower part on the verse and in the higher part on the refrain. Learn the melody first, then add harmonizing parts.

Children who are studying instruments which are characteristic of Switzerland may plan their own arrangement of this song. (See page x, "Playing Orchestral Instruments.") Violins and clarinets traditionally play the melody in Swiss dance songs, a double bass usually plays the roots of the chords, and the accordion fills in the harmony.

The Herdsman

German-Swiss Folk Song
Arranged by Kurt Miller

1. Hol - la, Hol - li, sings all day long;—
2. Hol - la, Hol - li, climb moun-tains tall;—

(Melody)

1. The herds-man is mer - ry, he sings all day long,
2. The cows keep Hans bus - y as they climb moun-tains tall,

Hol - la, Hol - li, sings this gay song.
Hol - la, Hol - li, ech - o - ing call.

And while he is tend - ing, he sings this gay song.
And at eve-ning Hans waits for Hei - di's ech - o - ing call.

Refrain
(Melody)

Hol - li - a, Hol - li - a, li - a - lo; Hol -

Hol - li - a, la - lo;

li - a, Hol - li - a, li - a lay.   lay.

Hol - li - a, la - lay.   lay.

Record 3   Side B   Band 5.   VOICES: children's choir.
ACCOMPANIMENT: piano.
FORM: Introduction, *1 meas.*; Vocal, v. 1; Interlude, *1 meas.*; Vocal, v. 2.

Glockenjodler

Austrian Folk Song
Arranged by Egon Kraus

For class experiences the clarinets might play the lower part (transpose to D) while the violin plays the descant. A child who plays cello or bass may play the chord roots indicated in the autoharp markings. Help him write his part in the bass clef. He will use only two tones, C and G. (See page 113 for explanation of the bass clef.) The autoharp may substitute for the accordion and fill in the harmony. The cello or double bass should play on beat one of each measure while the autoharp plays on beats two and three.

Glockenjodler

Key: D   Starting Tone: D (1)
Autoharp Key: C   Starting Tone: C (1)
Meter: ¢ ($\frac{2}{J}$)
No piano accompaniment

* FOLK STYLE: This song is also typical of the German-Austrian-Swiss section of Europe. Children who have visited Europe will be familiar with the fascinating bell sounds heard there and will enjoy this combination of *"Glocken"* (bells) and *"jodler"* (yodeling song). The bell sound of the low parts should remain steady while the upper voices move against it with light tones. Boys may enjoy singing the low parts and girls may sing the upper parts.

Help the class notice that the upper parts move in thirds throughout while the lower parts are in intervals of the fifth or octave. The song uses only two chords. The chords will have slightly different sounds because different tones are doubled—sometimes the root of the chord, sometimes the fifth. With such emphasis, the chord has a somewhat different color.

Record 3   Side B   Band 6.   VOICES: children's choir.
ACCOMPANIMENT: *a cappella.*
FORM: Vocal.

91

Le premier mois d'l'année

Key: C minor (Aeolian Mode)
Starting Tone: G (5)
Meter: $\frac{6}{8}$ $\left(\frac{2}{\unicode{x2669}.}\right)$
Piano accompaniment on page 264

* FOLK STYLE: To answer the question in the pupil's book, help children recall that "Alouette" is a French cumulative song. (See *Exploring Music 3.*)

Read the discussion "Music of France" which follows this song. Observe the characteristics of French folk music which can be found in "Le premier mois d'l'année": it has a narrow range and moves primarily by steps; the melody is modal; the phrases vary in length to suit the text.

The first two verses of the song are written out in the pupil's book. For each succeeding verse, repeat the first two measures of the seventh line on page 92 (within the thin double bars) as many times as needed to list all of the different things one would "give my darling." The French words mean:

1. The first month of the year,
      what would I give my
      darling?
   The first month of the year,
      what would I give my
      darling?
   One partridge flying, a-flee,
      a-flo, a-flying.
   One partridge flying,
      a-flying through the woods.

2. The second month of the
      year, what would I give
      my darling?
   The second month of the
      year, what would I give
      my darling?
   Two turtledoves,
   One partridge flying, a-flee,
      a-flo, a-flying.
   One partridge flying,
      a-flying through the woods.

3. The third month . . .
      Three proud pigeons.
4. The fourth month . . .
      Four ducks all in the air.
5. The fifth month . . .
      Five rabbits running.
6. The sixth month . . .
      Six wolves howling.
7. The seventh month . . .
      Sev'n dogs barking.
8. The eighth month . . .
      Eight white sheep.
9. The ninth month . . .
      Nine cows a-milking.
10. The tenth month . . .
      Ten strong oxen.
11. The 'leventh month . . .
      'Leven boys prancing.
12. The twelfth month . . .
      Twelve girls dancing.

Le premier mois d'l'année

Traditional French Folk Song

The cumulative song is a favorite among the French people. Can you recall another cumulative song you know in French?

Record 3   Side B   Band 7. VOICES: soprano, baritone.
ACCOMPANIMENT: guitar, accordion, double bass.
FORM: Introduction, *4 meas.*; Vocal, *vv. 1-12.*

3. Le troisième mois d'l'année,
   que donn' rai-j' à ma mie?
   Le troisième mois d'l'année,
   que donn' rai-j' à ma mie?
   Trois ramiers au bois,
   Deux tourterelles,
   Une perdriole qui va,
   qui vient, qui vole.
   Une perdriole
   qui vole dans le bois.
4. Le quatrième mois. . .
   . . .Quatr' canards qui vol't en l'air. . .
5. Le cinquième mois. . .
   . . .Cinq lapins grattant la terr'. . .

6. Le sixième mois. . .
   . . .Six lièvr's au champ. . .
7. Le septième mois. . .
   . . .Sept chiens courants. . .
8. Le huitième mois. . .
   . . .Huit moutons blancs. .
9. Le neuvième mois. . .
   . . .Neuf vaches à lait. . .
10. Le dixième mois. . .
    . . .Dix boeufs au pré. . .
11. L'onzième mois. . .
    . . .Onze beaux garçons. . .
12. Le douzième mois. . .
    . . .Douze demoiselles. . .

Music of France

The folk music of France reflects her several distinct provinces. There are songs of the farmers of Normandy and of the Basques who live near the border of Spain, as well as street songs of the city dwellers. Songs of workers form a large part of the folk repertoire. Other songs are religious in nature. Some of the most charming of our Christmas carols come from France. France has had a stirring history, and much of her music was inspired by historical events. As in other countries, the folk music of France has been passed down through generations in various ways. The troubadours, poet-musicians who went about telling stories in song, helped keep French folk music alive.

The most ancient folk melodies were based on the old church **modes**; other melodies seem to be pentatonic. The melodies usually move by scale steps with little ornamentation. The range of the work song is narrow, while more romantic songs move over a wide range. Phrases vary in length to suit the text. The opening musical phrase of a French song is often repeated at the end. The rhythms of many of the songs grow out of dance rhythms. In other songs the rhythm follows the natural word stress, resulting in irregular measures. Many charming dance rhythms are found in French music.

* MELODY: Study the notation; discover that only five tones are used in the melody (C D Eb F G). Play these five tones on the bells and discover the sequence of whole and half steps (whole-half-whole-whole). If the scale were completed with the Ab and Bb indicated in the key signature, it would be the natural minor scale.

Ask the children to sing up and down the five-tone scale on the syllable "loo" to establish a feeling of tonality. Encourage them to sing as much of the first verse as possible with a neutral syllable.

Music of France

As children read and discuss this page, ask them to compare the folk music of France to the folk music of other European countries they have studied. The music of France tends to be more modal than the music of Germany or Italy. The rhythms are freer and follow the natural word stress quite closely, whereas music of other European countries is more likely to move in regular measures.

French folk songs are almost always sung in unison; harmonizing melodies such as those heard in Germany and Switzerland are rarely found in France. Music of France is functional—created for a specific purpose. Many of the folk songs are religious or ceremonial in nature. Work songs make up a large portion of the folk music. Songs purely for entertainment are relatively rare.

Listen again to "Farandole" by Bizet. (See page 26.) Discover the characteristics of French folk music which are apparent in this composed music by a well-known French composer.

Impressionism

Debussy is sometimes called the "Father of Modern Music." He was one of the first to experiment with different harmonies and helped to free music from restrictions of harmony and form that had grown up through the centuries. Debussy attempted to do in his music what the school of painters known as the **impressionists** tried to create in their art. These painters, including the artists Monet, Degas, and Renoir tried to reproduce the play of light and color on a scene as it might look at different times of day: at dawn, in the noontime sun, at evening. They wanted to create visual impressions, not realistic views. Debussy tried to express the same kind of impressions musically. If possible, show children paintings by impressionistic artists.

Plowing Song

Key: F minor (Aeolian Mode)
Starting Tone: C (5)
Meter: $\frac{3}{4}$ ($\frac{3}{4}$)
No piano accompaniment

* FOLK STYLE: Many of the characteristics of French folk songs listed on page 93 can be found in "Plowing Song." It has a narrow range; it moves primarily by steps; the changing meter is a result of the natural stress of the words; it is modal.

Songs of workers, such as this one, make up a large group of French folk songs. The words of the refrain are directions to the oxen pulling the plow. The humorous thoughts expressed in the verse are typical of the gaiety of many French songs.

* RHYTHM: Discuss the fact that changing meters can often be found in folk music. When word accents dictate musical accents, changing meters often result. This same device is often used by contemporary composers. (See "Elements of Music: Rhythm," page 138.)

Practice clapping beats which have been grouped in different meters:

Discuss the fact that the beat remains the same; it moves steadily and evenly although the meter changes often. The only thing that is altered is the position of the accent.

As the children listen to the recording, suggest that they clap the beat softly, accenting the first beat of each measure lightly to help them become accustomed to the changing meters.

MELODY: As children listen to the melody, draw attention to the lack of repetition of phrases. This is also a characteristic of some French songs. Sing the following pattern to establish a sense of tonality; sing the song on a neutral syllable.

HARMONY: Add an accompaniment as suggested in the pupil's book. Clarinets or oboes might also play the open fifth. The drum should be high-pitched and bright in quality. Have children listen to the sound of the bagpipe on the recording. This will help them with ideas in making their own accompaniment.

Plowing Song

French Folk Song
Words Translated

Which characteristics of French folk music do you find in this song? Chant the words lightly until the irregular rhythms move smoothly.

1. "O plow, farm-er, plow! My fence is sure to
2. "O no, farm-er, no! I said that you must

break." "O did you say, my mas-ter, I must not
plow." "O did you say, my mas-ter, I'd bet-ter

work so late?"__ O - lay. O - lay, O-lay, O -
feed the cow?"__ O - lay.

lay, O - lay, ___ O - lay, O-lay, ___ O - lay. ___

A common French folk instrument was the **musette** which was much like the bagpipe. Play an open fifth on the piano at the beginning of each measure to imitate the sound of the musette.

Someone who is studying the flute might play the melody of this song.

Add a small drum and play on the beat.

Record 4   Side A   Band 1. VOICES: men's ensemble.
ACCOMPANIMENT: bagpipe, percussion.
FORM: Instrumental (bagpipe plays the melody twice in B♭ minor); Vocal, *vv. 1-2* (sung in F minor).

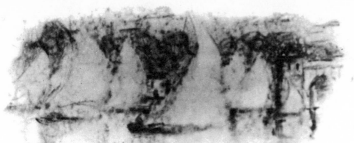

Voiles

by Claude Debussy

Sailboats are anchored in port as the wind gently flutters the sails

The scene described above inspired Debussy to write his composition for piano, "Voiles" (Sails). He has tried to capture in sound the play of light and the shimmering colors of the scene.

In order to create such an atmosphere, Debussy had to search for a new musical style. The scales and forms used by other composers limited him when he attempted to create **impressionistic** music. As you listen to "Voiles," you will hear some of the different kinds of musical organization that Debussy developed.

The melody and harmony are based on a **whole tone scale,** a scale in which the tones are one whole step apart and there is no feeling of **home tone.** For this reason the melody creates a vague impression of the scene.

Here is the opening theme.

Listen for the interesting variety of **tone colors.** By sustaining tones, blurring chords together, and contrasting very high tones with extremely low ones, Debussy creates an illusion of mystery.

The form is also interesting to study. Listen for the repetition of the opening musical idea. Notice how one musical idea grows out of another. Phrase endings are indefinite; one phrase flows into the next like the unwinding of a thread.

Debussy's new style, **impressionism,** helped other composers realize that music did not always have to be based on the same rules. They also began to search for new ways to organize musical sound. Today, composers are still inventing new ways of writing music based on ideas first developed by Debussy.

Record 8   Side B   Band 4.
Robert Casadesus, pianist.

Voiles
from *Piano Preludes, Book I*

BY CLAUDE DEBUSSY (deh-biu-see)
BORN 1862   DIED 1918

Play the recording of "Voiles" (vwahl) before the children have read the discussion in their books. Tell them that the composer is trying to capture an impression of a scene. Ask them to decide the kind of scene they think he may be suggesting.

As the children discuss their impressions, encourage them to verbalize the reasons for their reactions in terms of the melodies, rhythms, tone colors, and harmonies.

After the class members have had ample opportunity to discuss what they have heard, read the discussion in the pupil's book. Discover the notes that make up the whole tone scale by studying the notation of the opening theme. Write the whole tone scale on the chalkboard as children name the notes; then play and sing the scale.

Listen again to the composition and discuss the ideas stated in the book. How does the use of the whole tone scale, the variation of tone color, and the free design contribute to the impression the composer had in mind?

Listen for the form. The opening musical idea is heard four times. Each repetition is slightly altered and different harmonies support it. The third statement leads into a middle section which is based on this pattern:

A series of rippling scale passages brings us to a final statement of the opening theme, again with different harmonies sounded beneath it. Some children might paint their impressions of the scene Debussy is suggesting. Others might write a poem about the scene. (For a discussion of Debussy and impressionism, see page 93.)

Czech Riding Song

Key: D   Starting Tone: F# (3)
Autoharp Key: C   Starting Tone: E (3)
Meter: $\frac{3}{4}$ ($\frac{3}{\downarrow}$)
Piano accompaniment on page 266

* FOLK STYLE: The bright melodies and rhythms of songs like "Czech Riding Song" help us understand why the music almost demands to be sung! As children hear the recording, ask them to listen for the different characteristics listed in their book.

The song was probably a dance at one time. The regular rhythm and the use of the exclamation between verse and refrain are typical characteristics of Czech music. The refrain should be sung at a quicker tempo than the verse, another characteristic of Czechoslovakian dance songs.

* RHYTHM: As children learn the rhythm by following the steps on page 9, review the relationship of dotted eighth notes to sixteenth notes. (See page 31.) Note the rhythms which move in some variation of a short-short-long pattern (♩. ♬ ♩) or short-long pattern (♩ ♩). This is a common characteristic of Czechoslovakian songs.

The *"Hey!"* at the end of the verse should be done in a half-singing, half-shouting manner. Be sure that the rhythm is not interrupted by the shout. The refrain must start promptly on the very next beat.

Hungarian Round

Key: D minor   Starting Tone: D (1)
Meter: $\frac{4}{4}$ ($\frac{4}{\downarrow}$) No piano accompaniment

* MELODY: The melody of this song may be considered to be in D minor. Because there is no B flat in the melody, it has a pentatonic quality, characteristic of Hungarian music. Practice singing the melody with numbers or neutral syllables. Remind children that the C in measure five is a whole step lower than D, rather than a half step, as usually occurs between steps seven and eight.

RHYTHM: Notice the change in rhythm between the first and last phrases and the middle section. Lightly accent each of the quarter notes to emphasize the contrast between the eighth note patterns of the first and last phrases and the slower moving quarter notes of the middle section.

* HARMONY: This can be sung as a two- or four-part round. Voices enter two beats apart rather than at the end of the phrase as in most rounds.

Czech Riding Song

Czechoslovakian Folk Song
Words by Martha C. Ramsey

This spirited, rhythmic melody is typical of the music of Czechoslovakia. The triple meter, the long tone at the end of the phrase, the stepwise melody, and the insertion of the exclamation between the verse and refrain are characteristic of Czech music.

With spirit

1. Came a-rid-ing on a day,
2. Oft he asked in man-ner bold,   } Zum-ta-dy-ja-dy-ja;
3. Now my heart I'd give to you,

A suit-or jaun-ty, bold and gay,
ᵧ How could I my heart with-hold? } Zum-ta-dy-ja-dy-ja, *Hey!*
Could I be sure your own were true,

Refrain

Zum-ta-dy-ja-dy-ja,   zum-ta-dy-ja-da,

La   la la   la   la la la la

Used by permission of the Cooperative Recreation Service, Inc., Delaware, Ohio.

Record 4   Side A   Band 2. VOICES: baritone, children's choir.
ACCOMPANIMENT: clarinet, accordion, guitar, double bass.
FORM: Introduction, *2 meas.;* Vocal, *vv. 1-3.*

Review the discussion on page 63 as you learn these songs from Czechoslovakia and Hungary.

Hungarian Round

Hungarian Folk Song
English Words by
Betty Askwith

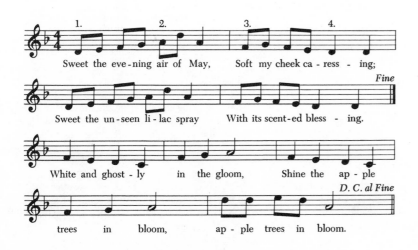

Record 4 Side A Band 3. VOICES: children's choir.
ACCOMPANIMENT: flute, alto flute, clarinet, cello.
FORM: Vocal (unison); Vocal (4-part round); Instrumental (4-part round).

("The Moldau" continued from page 98.)

Analysis:

1. The Source of the Moldau—The composition begins with a rippling figure played by the flute to suggest a small stream. The clarinet soon joins with a similar melody, and as the two instruments begin to play in thirds, we envision the joining of two small streams. Pizzicato strings and harp accompaniment add further suggestion. Additional instruments (the bassoon and then the strings) play the rippling figure as the broad, lyric river theme emerges. The theme is played first in minor key by violins, oboes, and bassoons. It is repeated in minor key and then is beautifully transformed to major by raising the G to G sharp.

2. The Forest Hunt—A hunting call, at first remote, is sounded by the horns. The call is built from a single chord, growing spirited in a steady crescendo of oboes, horns, and bassoons. It dies away and closes with a long note played by the horn.

3. Peasant Wedding—All instruments of the orchestra except the French horns join in the rustic polka, a dance which originated in Bohemia. The dance is part of the wedding festivities on the river bank. The polka swells to a fortissimo and then fades.

4. Moonlight and Dance of the Nymphs—The high strings suggest moonlight, while flutes, piccolos, and clarinets play figures that suggest frolic. Horns, trombones, and tuba intone stately chords in the rhythm of a march as from afar, perhaps suggesting the "past glory of chivalry and martial fame."

5. St. John's Rapids—The string section plays upward swirling figures to describe the surge of the rapids. The river theme appears again and the sound becomes violent as different rhythmic patterns are played. A huge climax is built up and then sinks into quietness just as do the waters after the rapids are passed.

6. The Moldau in Its Wide River Bed—The river theme returns triumphantly in major key as it is played by a swelling chorus of woodwinds, accompanied by the full sound of the other instruments.

7. Vysehrad (vi-sheh-rahd)—A chant which might have come from the cathedral of the ancient castle Vysehrad is played in fortissimo chords. The river theme finally soars from the string section, giving unity to the colorful composition. The chant dies away as the Moldau "disappears in the distance from the composer's vision."

The Moldau

BY BEDŘICH SMETANA (smeh'-tah-nah)
BORN 1824   DIED 1884

Read this page in the pupil's book with the class and conduct a discussion as suggested. The subject of this composition is the Vltava River, on which Prague is situated. The Vltava is also called the Moldau. Play the recording of the first section of the composition and complete the discussion. Ask the class to concentrate on the music with books closed as you play the entire composition to finish the first lesson.

In subsequent lessons, the details of the seven sections can be discussed as segments of the record are played. Play the composition for review and enjoyment throughout the year.

A **symphonic poem,** or **tone poem** as it is also called, is a comparatively recent form in the literature of music. It first appeared in the nineteenth century. Such works are large designs in which the composer expresses a definite "program" or poetic thought. The program may be a story or a description. The composer usually gives a descriptive title to the work to help convey his ideas to the listener.

Nationalism in music refers to the composer's expression of love of his country. During the nineteenth century when a wave of national feeling swept Europe and Scandinavia, such composers as Grieg in Norway, Smetana in Czechoslovakia, and Rimsky-Korsakov in Russia made nationalism in music an important idiom. Bartok was a later composer with great interest in national expression. It is not as evident in the music of countries that already had a strong musical tradition of their own, such as France, Italy, and Germany. Many elements can be a part of nationalistic expression in music, but it often depends upon national stories and/or characteristic folk rhythms and melodies. The composer may intend to express patriotic feelings, or he may intend to keep alive tales and pictures identified with his country. Often common patterns of rhythm and melody are developed into compositions which promote understanding of the country and its unique qualities.

The seven sections of "the Moldau" as designated by Smetana are outlined in detail on page 97.

The Moldau

by Bedrich Smetana

Smetana's love for his country is expressed in practically all of his music. In 1874 he undertook the great task of writing six symphonic poems under the title *My Fatherland*. The pieces are all dedicated to the city of Prague. "The Moldau" is one of these. It is a picture in sound of the chief river of Czechoslovakia and of the scenes and activities along the river bank.

When Smetana had finished writing the score, he wrote this preface to the work:

> Two springs start their courses in a shady Bohemian forest: one is warm and sparkling, the other cool and tranquil. Their clear waters that run so gayly over stone and pebble unite and sparkle in the morning sun. The rapid forest brook, rushing on, becomes the River Moldau. As it takes its course through the fields and valleys of Bohemia, it grows into a mighty river. The river flows through dense forests from where the joyous clanging sound of the hunter's horn seems to approach the listener.
>
> It makes its way through meadows and farms. A rustic wedding is being joyfully celebrated with music and song and dance. The water nymphs are seen by moonlight in the river's glittering waters. Reflected towers and castles are reminders of the past glory of chivalry and martial fame. At St. John's Rapids the stream winds its way through the foamy rapids of the cataract and through the deep and narrow rocky cleft into the broad river bed. It rolls majestically on to Prague, welcomed on its way by the old castle Vysehrad, and disappears in the distance from the composer's vision.

Discuss the first paragraph of Smetana's preface and describe the music that you would expect to hear. Then listen to the first section of Smetana's composition to discover how the ideas of the paragraph are expressed in the music.

Although "The Moldau" is one continuous composition, it has seven sections designated by the composer. When you have studied the entire composition, use it as an example and try to define **symphonic poem**. Use this composition as an example and try to define **nationalism** in music.

Record 10   Side B   Band 1.
Cleveland Orchestra,
George Szell, conductor.
Symbol (◉) for visible intermediate bands appears in the teaching suggestions.

Farewell, Beloved Homeland

Music by Bela Bartok
Words Adapted

Key: C minor   Starting Tone: C (1)
Meter: $\frac{3}{4}$ $\left(\frac{3}{\downarrow}\right)$
No piano accompaniment

Farewell, Beloved
Homeland

Bartok is a modern Hungarian composer. He became interested in Hungarian folk music early in the twentieth century and collected and arranged many long-forgotten songs. Music composed by Bartok also shows his interest in the music of his homeland. The dissonant harmonies, exotic scales, unusual intervals, and changing rhythms of the folk song can be heard in many of his compositions.

O fare-well, be-lov-ed home-land.   Sad   I   leave my Mag-yar

home-land.   Oft in my dreams,__   I   see your hills,__

Mem-'ries of their beau-ty   haunt me.   Oft in my dreams,__

I see your hills,__   Mem-'ries of their beau-ty   haunt me.

"Elindultan Szep Hazambul" by Bela Bartok, copyright by Zenemukiado Vallalat.
Reprinted by permission of Boosey and Hawkes, Inc., sole Agents for Kultura.

Record 4   Side A   Band 4.   VOICE: baritone.
ACCOMPANIMENT: piano.
FORM: Instrumental; Vocal.

* COMPOSER'S STYLE: The interest in music of the folk which began with the rise of nationalism in the late 1800's has continued into this century. Many composers have collected and studied the scales, harmonies, rhythms, and designs used in the folk music of their homelands. Much of Bartok's music was influenced by his study of Hungarian folk music. He arranged many Hungarian folk tunes for piano, including "Farewell, Beloved Homeland."

Bartok's accompaniment may be heard on the recording. As children listen, ask them to notice how his accompaniment supports the mood of sadness conveyed by the folk melody. Its simplicity is folklike and adds to the beauty of the melody line.

* RHYTHM: Note the short-long rhythm patterns (♩ ♩ and ♫ ♪) which give a feeling of syncopation to the melody. This pattern, common in Hungarian folk music, results from the natural stress of the original Hungarian words. Tap the rhythm lightly to make sure that these patterns are performed correctly in relation to the beat.

The Mastersingers of Nuremberg

BY RICHARD WAGNER (vahg-ner)
BORN 1813   DIED 1883

In the first lesson, discuss opera as a musical form. Encourage children who have seen an opera to share their experience. Make sure the class knows the components of an opera: the individual singers who take the parts of characters in the story, the chorus which assists in dramatizing and singing the story, the orchestra that plays the accompaniment, the stage settings. Sometimes composers will use ballet as part of the opera. Identify the opera by its title, to make sure that children can pronounce it. Mention Richard Wagner as an important German composer known especially for his operas. The style of his operas is described briefly in the third paragraph on page 63 in the pupil's book.

To motivate interest in the opera, ask children to tell what they think the subject and setting of the opera may be. To answer the question, the class may read the four paragraphs of description. Conduct class discussion of the ideas found there.

Help the children understand the function of the Mastersingers Guild. The members of this guild were not professional composers or singers; they worked at many different trades and occupations in order to earn a living. The guild provided a cultural and recreational diversion from daily work.

Remind the class that the overture is the orchestral introduction to the opera. Play the overture of the opera. Ask the children to close their books and listen for the general atmosphere of grandeur which the overture portrays.

In the same lesson or in a later one, read with the class "Festival Scene" in the pupil's book and play the rest of the music on the recording. The children will enjoy hearing the contrast between the songs sung by Beckmesser and Walter, and the final triumphant chorus. Having had an overall view of the opera, they are ready to study, in subsequent lessons, the overture and Festival Scene in detail.

The Mastersingers of Nuremberg

by Richard Wagner

The walled city of Nuremberg in Germany is well known to people everywhere. Visitors in Nuremberg today marvel at the sturdy walls built in medieval times to protect the city from attack. In the cathedrals, visitors view with wonder some of the world's most beautiful wood carvings. They watch the mechanical figures of the tower clock in the old city square. They visit the magnificent museums in which are seen the first watches and clocks, the oldest musical instruments, and many of the world's oldest and most important scientific and technical objects.

Today's Nuremberg, bustling with traffic, still has many reminders of the time four hundred years ago when the Mastersingers was an important guild. Even then, the city was a busy one, dependent on commerce and the work of people of many occupations. Each occupation had its own guild or union. Membership in the Mastersingers Guild was the greatest honor of all. Most of the people hoped to compose a song so fine that it would be known as a "mastersong." By singing it, they might gain membership in the guild.

Bakers, grocers, tailors, and many others were represented in the musician's guild. They developed strict requirements which one had to meet in order to be a member of the guild. Each mastersong had to have three stanzas; and each stanza, three sections. There were thirty-four rules covering everything from breathing to leaving the stage gracefully. Any singer who broke more than seven rules could not be called a Mastersinger.

Wagner's opera gives us a perfect picture of the life and customs of medieval Nuremberg. Some of the characters are patterned after real people. The most famous of the Mastersingers, Hans Sachs, a cobbler, died in 1576. He was said to be the author of six thousand poems. In the opera he is head of the guild. Beckmesser is another character of the opera patterned after a real person. He was the town clerk and chief "marker" for the guild.

The Story of the Opera

The opera is concerned with a midsummer festival in which the Master-singers are to award a prize to the one who sings the best song. The hand of Eva has been offered to the one who receives the prize. Walter is in love with Eva. Wishing to marry her, he decides that he must be admitted to the guild and somehow win the prize. His rival for Eva's hand is Beckmesser who uses his position as marker, and every other means, to keep Walter from entering the guild.

Walter is at first rejected from the guild for not knowing the rules. Later, he sings a song of such beauty that the guild members are overcome with pleasure. The charm of the song and of Walter's singing lay in the fact that they were free from the very rules which were thought important. Hans Sachs at once recognizes that this freedom can lead the Mastersingers to new and loftier ideals of performance. Walter is awarded the festival prize and wins Eva for his bride.

The Overture

The overture to *The Mastersingers of Nuremberg* is considered to be one of the greatest of all overtures. Called the *Vorspiel* (Prelude), it presents most of the main themes of the opera and summarizes the action. It fulfills Wagner's purpose of showing that art which is free and inspired by human feeling is greater than that which is bound by very strict rules.

Record 10   Side A   Band 1.
Columbia Symphony Orchestra,
Bruno Walter, conductor.
Symbol (◉) for visible intermediate bands appears in the teaching suggestions.

Help the children understand that the opera is concerned with an important part of the life of the period and requires a great stage setting depicting an outdoor festival and a large chorus of men to represent the Mastersingers.

The Story of the Opera

Read the story of the opera with the class. Identify the three main characters mentioned (Eva, Walter, Beckmesser). Remind children that Hans Sachs, who is the head of the guild in the opera, actually lived in sixteenth century Nuremberg. The "marker" is the one who judges the singing of the candidates for the guild, "marking" all the mistakes on his slate as he listens.

The Overture

Three lessons will be required in the study of the overture. Read with the class and discuss the information concerning the overture in their book. Review the names of the four *Leitmotif* (light moteef) themes. Play the first section of the music (to the first small band). This section includes the Mastersinger Theme, the Love Theme, a cadenza for the violins which is used as a bridge to the new mood, and the Banner Theme. The opening measures of the Mastersinger Theme are heard twice. The opening measures of the Love Theme are heard four times, played by flute, oboe, flute, and clarinet respectively. Strings and woodwinds complete the theme. The violin cadenza follows, and the brasses at once introduce the Banner Theme with the harp joining in playing the chords. The opening pattern of the Banner Theme is heard six times.

When the children have discussed all that they heard in the first section of the overture, study the first three themes in their books. The class might sing the Mastersinger Theme, being careful that the rhythm is accurate. You might play the Love Theme on the piano, a flute player might play it for the class, or the class might tap the rhythm or sing the melody in the lower octave. The class can sing and tap the Banner Theme or the rhythm might be played on class-room percussion instruments. Play the section again as children follow the notation of the themes in their books.

After a stirring passage by the full orchestra, the woodwinds begin a section based on the Mastersinger Theme in a faster tempo and a lighter mood. This charming portion of the music is a development of a brief pattern by woodwinds. It is played first by the clarinet, then tossed about, with flutes and bassoons taking their turns. The strings echo parts of other melodies or chatter along with the woodwinds. The strings and woodwinds, with French horns below, then develop a great crescendo. Discuss this portion of the overture, and give children a chance to hear it as many times as they need to discover the musical content.

In another lesson, play the first two sections of the overture as a review and then go on to the end of the composition. The great crescendo (just before the second band) leads into the magnificent last section in which three of the themes are heard at once. The violins and cellos play a version of the Prize Song Theme, the double basses, tuba, and bassoons are playing the Mastersinger Theme, and the middle-range woodwinds are playing the Banner Theme. Along the way, the trumpets sound out the opening pattern of the Banner Theme. Finally, the Banner Theme is played twice by the whole orchestra in grand manner, with violins playing decorative figures against it. The Mastersinger Theme returns to close the overture.

Play the new section of the music several times for the class. Discuss the use of the three themes in a passage showing remarkable skill in **counterpoint.** (In early times the word "point" was used to mean "note"; thus the term means literally "note against note.") The combination of melodies of "voices" in instrumental music is a great art. This work of Wagner is considered an excellent example of counterpoint since each melody keeps its own distinguishable characteristics, yet the blend of all three develops a new sound.

Return to the overture many times during the year for restudy or for listening without discussion.

Wagner was skilled in the technique of establishing a theme called a *Leitmotif* (leading motive) to represent a character or situation. Whenever one hears the motive, he immediately associates it with the character or part of the story represented. There are four such themes in the overture. Each is an important theme of the opera.

The Mastersinger's Guild Theme
This theme reminds us of the very respectable members of the group, of their dignity, and of their conservative rules.

The Love Theme
Contrast is immediately provided in the overture by the theme which represents the love of Eva and Walter.

The Banner Theme
This theme is heard many times in the opera, most notably when the Mastersingers march in for the great festival. Each guild carries a banner, and the long procession is very colorful. In the overture the composer uses this important theme in several ways.

The Prize Song Theme
Portions of the melody from Walter's prizewinning song are heard throughout the opera. It becomes the climax of the opera when Walter sings it at the festival. It has an important position in the overture, too, and is surely one of the best known of all operatic melodies.

Listen for the skillful way in which the composer has combined three of the themes in counterpoint near the end of the overture. Listen for the repetition of the Banner Theme and the Mastersinger's Theme with which the overture closes. The overture is in itself a great composition and is often performed by symphony orchestras apart from the opera.

Act Three: Festival Scene

Although Walter had been refused membership in the Mastersinger's Guild because he did not know the rules, Hans Sachs thought Walter had a good voice and encouraged him. Walter's love for Eva compelled him to keep on trying. One day he told Sachs of a song that had come to him in a dream. As Walter sang parts of it, Sachs wrote down the words and promised to help him perfect his song and to perform it well. Beckmesser secretly found the notes Sachs had made. Thinking that Sachs had written the poem, he decided to sing the song at the Festival. Any song by the head of the Mastersingers should surely win the prize!

Your record begins at this point in the story. You will be able to follow the humor of the scene as Beckmesser sings, the excitement which follows Walter's beautiful singing of the aria, and the glorious chorus with which the opera closes.

Although Beckmesser carefully follows the rules, his song is a farce. The words as Sachs had written them are not complete, and those Beckmesser fills in are anything but poetic. His ornamental phrases are only funny as he becomes confused and forgets the words. As the Mastersingers express unbelief at the performance, and as the people watching the Festival ridicule and laugh at him, Beckmesser becomes more and more confused. He finally leaves the stage in disgrace.

Walter's performance of the song is as beautiful as Beckmesser's was disgraceful. Soon the people and the Mastersingers are murmuring with surprise and then demanding that Walter be given the award. Eva places a wreath on his head while the chorus sings an ode to the German masters and to their sacred art. The crowd cries out in homage to Hans Sachs.

Record 10   Side A   Band 2.
Soloist; Saxon State Orchestra;
Dresden State Opera Chorus.
Symbol (◉) for visible intermediate bands appears in the teaching suggestions.

Act Three: Festival Scene

In studying the Festival Scene of the opera, ask the class to reread the description of the scene. Play the recording of Beckmesser's song. Lead the children in a discussion of the tones of the lute, the elaboration of melody which makes humor of Beckmesser's bad musical taste, and of the choral and orchestral interjections. Beckmesser's bass voice is a strong contrast to the tenor voice for which the song was intended and adds to the humor.

◉
Play the tenor aria "The Prize Song" sung by Walter. Review the notation of the opening measures of the melody on page 102. Discuss the elements that make the song a great aria: the dramatic rise and fall of the melody, the climactic tones, the rhythmic movement in the accompaniment. Discuss the dramatic tenor voice which is a high and powerful man's voice, often singing the most important and dramatic male roles in opera and oratorio.

Walter's Prize Song

Dort unter einem Wunderbaum,	There, under a wondrous tree
von Früchten reich behangen,	richly hung with fruit
zu schau'n im sel'gen Liebestraum,	I could see in my blissful love dream
was höchstem Lustverlangen	with greatest longing and desire
Erfüllung kühn verhiess—	fulfillment boldly promised—
das schönste Weib,	the most beautiful maiden
Eva im Paradies.	Eva—in Paradise.
Morgenlich leuchtend in rosigem Schein,	The morning was gleaming with rosy light,
von Blüth' und Duft	The air was filled
geschwellt die Luft,	with the scent of flowers
voll aller Wonnen	and all delights
nie ersonnen,	exposed by the sunlight—
ein Garten lud mich ein,—	a garden lured me in.

◉
The great chorus of Mastersingers and village people on stage sings the ode to the art of music in words that mean, "Hail, German Masters, Hail our sacred German Art!" The chorus begins with a dramatic exclamation under which the orchestra plays the strains of the Banner Theme, and all join in the Mastersingers' song for the triumphant closing.

Play Beckmesser's humorous song, Walter's Prize Song, and the entire Festival Scene many times throughout the year.

103

The Woodwind Family

Members of the woodwind family include instruments whose tone is produced by blowing into a tube or pipe. They are, or were originally, made of wood. There are four main members of the woodwind family: **flute, oboe, clarinet,** and **bassoon.** To each of these, another instrument is closely related: the **piccolo** is related to the flute; the **English horn,** to the oboe; the **bass clarinet,** to the clarinet; and the **contrabassoon,** to the bassoon. As the children listen to woodwind instruments on various occasions, help them to develop their own vocabulary of descriptive words by which they can identify the characteristics of each instrument.

Flute: The flute is held horizontally and the player blows across a hole near the upper end. In the high register the flute is brilliant and penetrating, while the low register is soft and velvety. The middle register is smooth and clear. The flute is used for important melodic passages in the middle and upper registers and brilliant decorative figures.

Piccolo: The piccolo is a small flute, played in the same manner, but pitched an octave higher. Its tone is piercing and easily heard in the upper register, but it is rarely used in its lowest octave. The piccolo's gay, sparkling quality adds color to orchestral climaxes.

Oboe: The oboe is a double-reed instrument. It is almost as agile as the flute. Its intense tone and versatility of expression make it one of the important members of the orchestra. In the upper range the tone is bright and reedy; the low tones are round and haunting. The oboe gives the A to which the whole orchestra tunes.

English Horn: The English horn is actually an alto oboe. Its pear-shaped bell accounts for the unusual timbre. The dark, nasal quality is somewhat melancholy and meditative in character with a plaintive quality which is peculiarly its own. It is a most effective solo instrument if not required to play too loud.

Clarinet: The clarinet is a single-reed instrument. Its sound is caused by vibrations of the reed against the mouthpiece. It creates a tone which is fuller than that of the double-reed instruments and yet markedly different in different ranges. In the low range the clarinet is dark, and its sonorous tone is sad and haunting. The bright quality of the clarinet in the middle or "clarion" register is polished and capable of singing pure, clear melodies. The high register is brilliant and penetrating.

In the orchestra the clarinet adds a variety of tonal colors that no other woodwind can contribute. It is also noted for its agility. The clarinet holds the place of importance in the modern band that the violin holds in the orchestra.

Bass Clarinet: As its name implies, this clarinet adds to the bass of the woodwind choir. Its tone is more powerful, rounder, and less reedy than its higher-pitched brother. The low tones, used most often, are remarkably rich and resonant.

Saxophone: The saxophone has only comparatively recently become a part-time member of the symphony orchestra. Today it is a regular member of popular or jazz bands. The saxophone, a single-reed instrument, is built in different sizes, including soprano, alto, tenor, baritone, and bass.

Bassoon: A double-reed instrument, the bassoon is a long wooden pipe doubled back on itself. It is often called the clown of the orchestra, yet it is also capable of many other moods. It provides the bass for the woodwind choir but is also assigned melodic parts. Its tone color varies considerably in different registers.

Contrabassoon: This instrument has a tube over sixteen feet long, doubled back on itself four times. It has a dark, growling quality peculiar to itself. It can play lower notes than any other orchestral instrument.

Full page painting in pupil's book.
See page 209 for explanation of art.

Music of Scandinavia

The glorious countries of the northland are sometimes referred to as "Norway, the land of the midnight sun," "Denmark, a storybook land," "Sweden, the land of the Goths," and "Finland, the land of a thousand lakes." They are rich in scenic beauty and tales of adventure which are expressed in their songs. These watery lands, with their long, dark winters and vividly bright summers, are countries of great contrast. There is also great contrast in the songs—vigorous songs of the sea, poetic songs about spectacular beauty, and melancholy songs that depict loneliness.

The people of Norway have a strong national feeling. We find here some of the oldest folk songs on earth. Norwegian dances are merry ones and are often accompanied by a fiddle. Norway's greatest composer Edvard Grieg succeeded in capturing in his compositions the Norwegians' love of nature, their stories, and the strong rhythms of their gay dances.

Denmark and Sweden are countries of fertile lands and beautiful gardens. Because of their nearness to the countries of Europe, their songs often resemble those of other countries, especially France and Germany. Danish songs are chiefly composed, but they are known and sung by the Danes in the same way that people of other countries sing folk songs. Denmark and Sweden are especially rich in folk dance music. Their dances are charming to watch and to dance.

Loneliness and sorrow are common topics in the songs of Finland. Finland is a land of dense forests and cold, bleak winters. Its people have struggled for generations to maintain liberty. Although the country had six centuries of Danish rule and a century of Russian domination, Finland has persistently preserved her language, legends, and songs. Her great composer Jean Sibelius has written into his compositions the rugged strength of the people and of the land.

Read the prose page with the class and encourage discussion of ideas. Review what the children know of the Scandinavian countries. Allow the class to leaf through this section of the book to notice pictures, titles, and musical ideas. Play the recording of one or more songs from this section as motivation and basis for discussion of the ideas stated on the prose page.

Return to this page as children study the section and learn examples of music from each country.

Edvard Grieg (1843-1907), the best-known Norwegian composer, was steeped in Norwegian folk music throughout his life. He absorbed it so thoroughly that its idioms are very much at home in his compositions. In Grieg's works, Norway has its finest expression of nationalism. He wrote neither symphony nor opera but is remembered for countless songs and short works, many for piano. His "Piano Concerto in A Minor" is one of the most regularly performed compositions of its kind. The incidental music which he wrote for the play "Peer Gynt" has become popular in the form of two orchestral suites.

The Finnish composer Jean (pronounced yahn) Sibelius (1865-1957) found the inspiration for practically all of his music in the strong feeling he had for his nation. His interest in the natural beauty of the country and its legends is evident in his music. His works include seven symphonies, eight tone poems, and many songs and short compositions.

In Summer the Sunshine Is Brightest

Key: B♭ Starting Tone: F (5)
Autoharp Key: C Starting Tone: G (5)
Meter: 4/4 (♩)
Piano accompaniment on page 268

* FOLK STYLE: Listen to the recording and discuss the musical characteristics described in the pupil's book. Read again the discussion on page 105. IN WHAT WAYS DOES THIS SONG RESEMBLE THE MUSIC OF EUROPEAN COUNTRIES WHICH YOU HAVE STUDIED? The major tonality, the melody which uses tones from the common chords, and the reference to nature are also characteristics of German folk songs.

FORM: Ask children to listen to the recording with books closed to determine the form. It is in two parts. Ask them to listen carefully to the two sections. WHAT IS SIMILAR ABOUT THE TWO PARTS? WHAT IS DIFFERENT? Help children realize that the basic melody is the same for the verse and the refrain; the rhythm is different, and some passing tones are added in the refrain.

Analyze the structure. Each part of the song is made up of four two-measure phrases. Write the design of each part in letter names: A A' (repeated one step lower) B C.

* MELODY: Follow the steps on page 13 to learn the melody. Draw attention to the patterns which use tones from the I, IV, and V7 chords. (Measure one outlines the I chord; E flat and A flat are **passing tones.** Measure two uses tones from the IV chord. Measure three is based on tones from the V7 chord.)

Sing the melody of the verse with numbers, then with a neutral syllable, and finally with words.

* HARMONY: Since the melody of the refrain is the same as the verse, children should be able to learn this section quickly. Notice that the voices move at an interval of a **third** apart during the first two phrases. Establish tonality; sing the two parts simultaneously. Remind children to listen to each other to be sure that the parts are "in tune."

Assign some children to learn to harmonize this song at the piano. Encourage those children who have studied piano to improvise an interesting accompaniment. See page viii.

In Summer the Sunshine Is Brightest

Swedish Folk Song
Words Adapted

Discuss how musical characteristics contribute to the mood and purpose of the song: the major tonality, the dotted rhythm, and the harmony in thirds.

1. In summer the sunshine is bright-est;
2. In winter when cold winds are blow-ing,

The time when our hearts are the light-est.
We'll sit by the fire when it's snow-ing,

We walk through the wood and the mead-ow,
And dream of the bright sum-mer days When

And sing a joy-ful song, Hal-la, Hal-la!
we sang a joy-ful song, Hal-la, Hal-la!

Refrain
O come a-long and join our song;

The day is bright, our hearts are light.

When win-ter's done and fun's be-gun,

Record 4 Side A Band 5. VOICES: soprano, baritone.
ACCOMPANIMENT: accordion, guitar, clarinet, double bass, snare drums.
FORM: Introduction, *4 meas.;* Vocal, *v. 1;* Instrumental; Vocal, *v. 2.*

Key: D minor   Starting Tone: D (1)
Meter: $\frac{2}{4}$ $\left(\frac{2}{\downarrow}\right)$
No piano accompaniment

Summer Magic

Swedish Folk Song
Arranged by Kurt Miller

Li - mu, li - me, li - mu, Let the sun be - gin to shine.

Li - mu, li - me, li - mu, Let the sun be - gin to

Melt the moun - tains of snow, set the for - est lakes a -

shine.   Melt the moun - tains of snow, set the for - est

glow;   Warm the earth, light the skies; Bright sun, a - rise!

lakes a - glow; Warm the earth, light the skies; Sun, a - rise!

* **MELODY:** Ask children to study the notation of this song and recall the steps which will help them learn the melody. Discover that it is in **minor.** The melody moves around the tones of the D minor chord. The seventh step of the D harmonic minor scale, C sharp, appears in two places.

Notice the repetition of melodic patterns within the first voice (measures five through eleven). Draw attention to the fact that the melody of the first voice has a range of six tones (C♯ to A). The second voice also uses this range except at the end of the song.

HARMONY: Learn each voice part separately. When children are secure with the melody of each part, sing as a two-part song. Notice how the second voice imitates the first voice in measures five through eleven. BE SURE TO STAY ON YOUR OWN PART! Be sure children singing the first voice part sing the E securely in the second measure. Because they are only one step above the second voice at this point, they may tend to sing D.

FOLK STYLE: The narrow range of this melody and the use of the word "Limu" (lee-moo) indicate that this song is probably ancient. The word "Limu" is no longer in the Swedish language. It may refer to an ancient deity.

Record 4 Side A Band 6. VOICES: children's choir.
ACCOMPANIMENT: 2 French horns. FORM: Introduction, *4 meas.;*
Vocal (choir on melody, 1 French horn on lower line); Vocal (1 French horn on melody, choir on lower line); Vocal (choir on 2 parts).

Icelandic Prayer

Tonality: Modal
Starting Tone: F
Meter: $\frac{4}{2}$ $\left(\frac{4}{\textstyle{}}\right)$
No piano accompaniment

FOLK STYLE: Discuss the information in the pupil's book. On the Time Line (pages 60-61), locate the date of the Norwegian immigration to Iceland. Discuss the musical events of that historical period.

Several characteristics of this song are typical of the church music of the medieval period. The melody is modal; it moves by steps or very small skips; the rhythm matches the rhythm and accent of the words. The two voices remain an interval of a fifth apart throughout the song. This type of harmony, known as **parallel organum,** was common during the ninth and tenth centuries. Organum may come from the word *organare* meaning "to organize." The two voices are strictly organized; that is, they remain exactly the same distance apart throughout the entire composition.

HARMONY: Compare the two voices. They always remain exactly the same distance apart (except for the two unison notes at the beginning). Analyze the interval between the two voices and discover that it is made up of seven half steps. This is called a **perfect fifth.** The D flats are added in the lower part in order to keep the voices at the same interval. If D natural were sung against A flat, the interval would include only six half steps.

To help the children get a feeling for the harmony in this song, practice singing a pattern made up of perfect fifths. Start the two groups on F and C; move up and down by half steps.

Encourage children to sing both parts of the song simultaneously. Sing first on a neutral syllable, then with words.

EXPRESSION: Listen to the recording. Members of the brass family are among the oldest known instruments. At the beginning of the recording a French horn plays the melody; the ancestors of this instrument were the primitive hunting horns. (See page 118 for a detailed description of all instruments in the brass family.)

Men's voices in unison singing the first verse capture the vigorous spirit of this ancient music. On the second verse women's voices sing in parts at the notated pitch in order for the pupils to hear clearly the parallel fifths.

Icelandic Prayer

Icelandic Folk Song

The Norwegian Vikings settled Iceland in the ninth century. The ancient language and music which they brought with them have survived since that time. The music is much like the church music of the ninth century, particularly the use of the interval of the fifth between the voice parts. Singing in parallel fifths was the earliest kind of harmony.

1. O great God of the earth,
2. O great mak - er of life,

Hear now my prayer ris - ing up - ward,
Give now my spir - it Thy beau - ty,

(Melody in lower part)

Wak - en my soul to Thy good!
Fill all my days with Thy work!

Wak - en my soul to Thy good!
Fill all my days with Thy work!

Record 4   Side A   Band 7.   VOICES: mixed choir.
ACCOMPANIMENT: 2 trumpets, 2 trombones, French horn.
FORM: Instrumental (melody only); Vocal, *v. 1* (male voices, melody only); Instrumental (2 parts); Vocal, *v. 2* (women's voices, 2 parts).

I Came Home Late One Evening

Norwegian Folk Melody
Words Adapted

1. I came home late one eve - ning con - tent - ed and at rest,
2. I went _ to the sta - ble and bri - dled my grey steed;
3. I rode _ through the dark - ness and trav - eled five long miles.

But soon at my door came a knock - ing. _____
I knew he could run fast as light - ning. _____
The town was at rest sleep - ing sweet - ly. _____

A mes - sen - ger stood, and he said, "Go to your love,
The sad - dle was sil - ver, the reins were made of gold,
And when I ar - rived at the house _ of my love,

Ride quick - ly now to her dwell - ing."
And in the pale moon they shone bright - ly. _____
Her broth - er was wait - ing to meet me. _____

O my love, my on - ly love, my dear one. _____

4. We quickly went inside and I asked about my love.
   He burst out in sorrow a-crying.
   So sad were his words, that I thought my heart would break
   To hear that my loved one was dying.
   O my love, my only love, my dear one.

5. I walked for a while through the meadows and the hills,
   And nearby the church bells were tolling.
   My heart was so sad, that I could not bear to stay;
   I knew far away I'd be going.
   O my love, my only love, my dear one.

Record 4 Side A Band 8. VOICE: tenor.
ACCOMPANIMENT: guitar. FORM: Introduction, *4 meas.;* Vocal, *v. 1;*
Interlude, *4 meas.;* Vocal, *v. 2;* Interlude, *4 meas.;* Vocal, *v. 3;*
Interlude, *4 meas.;* Vocal, *v. 4;* Interlude, *4 meas.;* Vocal, *v. 5.*

Key: A minor Starting Tone: D♯ (4♯)
Meter: $\frac{2}{4}$ ($\frac{2}{\text{♩}}$)
Piano accompaniment on page 270

I Came Home Late
One Evening

* FOLK STYLE: This song in minor key expresses the melancholy text well. Such a text is found in the folk songs of many countries. Observe the wailing sound in the last phrase of this song.

* MELODY: When the children know the song, lead them to discover the intervals from which it derives its strong minor sound and much of its appeal. They should play the pattern E G♯ A to hear the strong pull of the seventh step of the minor scale to the resolution. They should notice that in the first and third phrase of the song the D is sharped, while in each answering phrase the D is natural. The sharped fourth step of the scale (D♯ in this song) is very common in Norwegian music.

* RHYTHM: The even rhythm of quarter and eighth notes throughout the song is relieved in the last phrase by the uneven dotted rhythm. Classes that have not mastered these patterns will benefit from tapping and clapping them before chanting the words in correct rhythm.

The tied note over the bar should be noticed and sung correctly.

Solveig's Song
from *Peer Gynt*

BY EDVARD GRIEG
BORN 1843   DIED 1907

Read the pupil's page with the class. Play the recording of the song. Assist the children in following the instructions in their books to compare the song of Grieg with the folk song "I Came Home Late One Evening," page 109.

The measures specified in the pupil's book contain the same descending melody patterns but begin on different pitches. In the ballad, the pattern begins on C and then outlines the tones of an E minor chord. In the Grieg song, the pattern begins on F and then outlines the tones of an A minor chord. Both patterns move in eighth and quarter notes. The rhythm and melodic contour of the songs is similar throughout.

Remind children to listen for dynamic expression in the performance of the singer. The singer observes the crescendo and decrescendo markings of the first line and similar markings throughout the song. As the melody rises to the climax, the level grows louder; and as it falls, the level becomes gradually softer. The building and receding of each phrase of the melody is one of the charms of the song.

Children may have music from *Peer Gynt* at home or may have heard parts of it at concerts. "In the Hall of the Mountain King," "Morning" and "The Death of Ase" are well known. The Ibsen play "Peer Gynt" is a popular one on the stages of Scandinavia and Europe, and the incidental music of Grieg contributes to the moods of the story and action.

See page 105 for information concerning Grieg.

Solveig's Song

from *Peer Gynt*
by Edvard Grieg

"Solveig's Song" comes from the music Grieg composed for *Peer Gynt*, a play written by another great Norwegian, Henrik Ibsen. Grieg wrote songs for the drama and some **incidental music** for the orchestra to play between scenes. The play is named for the main character Peer Gynt, a selfish young man who, unmindful of others, spent his life searching for adventure. Solveig is the girl who loved him and waited for him.

The verse of her song begins with this line:

and ends with this line.

This music is an excellent example of the influence of Norwegian folk music on Grieg's compositions. Because his music contains many melodies and rhythms from the folk music of Norway, it is often referred to as **nationalistic music**.

In fact, part of Grieg's melody in this song is exactly like that of the folk ballad "I Came Home Late One Evening." Compare the melody of measures three and four in the ballad with measure two in "Solveig's Song." Notice also the minor tonality of each and the general similarity in mood.

Record 7   Side B   Band 2.
Mary Sue Berry, soprano
Charles Burkhart, pianist.

Peasant Dance for Norwegian Fiddle

Transcribed by Johan Halvorsen

Listen to the fiddle tune and enjoy the typical Norwegian folk melody. The tune is used as accompaniment for the halling, a folk dance from the Hallingdal district of Norway. Try to imagine the dance as you listen to the fiddle tune. The dance is a vigorous reel popular also in Scotland and other northern countries. The dancers do a great deal of high kicking, and some good dancers turn somersaults to the steady pulse of the music.

As you listen again, discover how many sections the folk melody contains. Write the design, using letters to name the sections. Count accents and discover whether all phrases are the same length.

Halling, Opus 72, No. 4

by Edvard Grieg

This piano composition by Grieg is named for, and based on, the folk tune. It is a fine example of Grieg's interest in transcribing folk melodies and, as Grieg himself said, "raising them to an artistic plane."

What is the design of Grieg's composition? Which section is developed into music sounding like Grieg's own? What musical devices did Grieg use in this development? How did Grieg preserve the harmony of fifths heard in the fiddle tune?

Grieg's development from the fiddle tune.

Record 10 Side B Band 2.
2a Felix Galimir, violinist.
2b Fritz Jahoda, pianist.
Symbol (◉) for visible intermediate bands appears in the teaching suggestions.

Peasant Dance for Norwegian Fiddle

TRANSCRIBED BY JOHAN HALVORSEN

Halling, Opus 72, No. 4

BY EDVARD GRIEG

These two pieces are included for further study of nationalism in music, specifically Grieg's use of the dance tune as a basis for a piano composition. Call attention to the Latin word *"opus,"* meaning "work," and suggest to children that they will often see this designation or numbering of a composer's works or compositions.

Read the first paragraph with the class and play the recording of the fiddle tune. After discussion, read the second paragraph and play the tune again. The fiddle tune is made up of three different melodies heard in a three-section structure:

> A—8 measures (first melody)
> B—9 measures (second melody)
> —6 measures (third melody)
> B—Repeated

Read the first paragraph regarding the Grieg composition and play it for the class. After hearing the children's observations, read the rest of the page and play the piano composition again. It is in A B A design, since Grieg developed a new section out of the first melody of the fiddle tune. The A section of Grieg's composition includes all three melodies from the fiddle tune. Except for the addition of a short introduction, the piano composition is like the fiddle tune in both the first and last sections. In the first section of the piano composition, Grieg preserved the harmony of the open fifth by using the chord in the left-hand part.

In the middle section, Grieg reduced the rhythm of the first melody to less than half speed. He changed it to a minor key and harmonized it in his own way as seen in the notation in the pupil's book.

Structure of Grieg's composition:
> A—Fiddle tune A B B
> ◉ B—Grieg's development
> A—Repeated
Coda—8 measures

My Little Bird, Where Do You Fly?

Key: C minor   Starting Tone: E♭ (3)

Meter: $\frac{6}{8}$ ($\frac{2}{\text{♩.}}$)

No piano accompaniment

* STYLE: Carl Nielsen (1865-1931) has written a great deal of music for voices and various instruments. In the United States he is primarily known for his symphonies which have been performed by major orchestras. Most of his songs are folklike. When the children know this song, ask them to identify ways in which it is like a folk song. (The text is simple and concerns a subject understood by everyone. All three stanzas are sung to the same melody.) The song requires a choral tone and should not be sung too fast. The children should hear and enjoy the harmony as they sing.

* HARMONY: The lowest part might be sung better by the boys with some girls' voices added, if needed. In learning the parts, it may be better for some classes first to practice the upper and lower parts together, and then the middle and lower parts, in order to hear the relationship of two parts. Some classes will be able to sing all three parts very early in the teaching process. The song is in the key of C minor and the lowered sixth step of the scale (A flat) and the raised seventh step (B natural) should be sung carefully. In this song the C minor scale uses the same key signature as its relative major, E flat.

MELODY: Ask the class to observe an interesting sequence in the two phrases "Ah, do you not remember me" and "My heart is aching just for you." The second part of the sequence begins a half step lower than the first.

Bass Staff: Play the scale tones on the piano so that children can hear the pitches usually sung by men. Point out the difference in staff names between the bass and treble staves and help them discover that the same sequence of note names (A to G) is used for the lower staff but that the lowest line is G. Play the alto part of the song in octaves (the tone as written and the one an octave lower) as the boys sing so that they can hear that the lower note of the octave is the range in which they will sing when their voices change.

My Little Bird, Where Do You Fly?

Music by Carl Nielsen
Arranged by William Reynolds
Words Translated by William Reynolds

Carl Nielsen is as well known to the Danish as Grieg is to the Norwegians. Both composers had the ability to write folklike music which has strong appeal. The words Nielsen used for this song were written by the well-known Danish storyteller Hans Christian Andersen, in whom the Danes take great pride.

1. My little bird, where do you fly
2. You said that you would come to me,
3. My little bird, you do not come

A - mid the for - est branch - es?
Yes, just like all the oth - ers.
Out from the for - est branch - es;

Ah, do you not re - mem - ber me?
If you could real - ly un - der - stand,
So I must go my si - lent way.

Record 4   Side B   Band 1.   VOICES: children's choir.
ACCOMPANIMENT: flute, 2 alto flutes.   FORM: Introduction. *2 meas.;*
Vocal, *v. 1* (choir on 2 parts, flute on lower part); Vocal, *v. 2*
(choir on 2 parts, flute on middle part); Vocal, *v. 3* (choir on 3 parts).

My   heart   is   ach - ing   just   for   you;
Your   song   would bring   my   soul   new   joy,
Ah,   no   one   ev - er   cared   as   much;

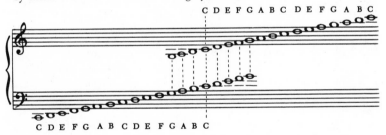

A - las, — I am — so   lone - ly.
And   I — would not — be   lone - ly.
A - las, — I am — so   lone - ly.

The **grand staff** with the **bass clef** below the treble **clef** shows notes sung by men's voices as well as those sung by women.

C D E F G A B C D E F G A B C

C D E F G A B C D E F G A B C

When the boys' voices have changed, the notes they sing may be written on the **bass staff.**

Men's voices usually sing in this range.

Women's voices usually sing in this range.

Some boys might make an individual project of rewriting the alto part on the bass staff, or this might be done by the class as you put notes on the board. It would be good to use the treble staff above so that the children can see the same notes on both staves. They should notice that middle C belongs to both staves.

Middle C

All Hail, Fridolin

Key: F   Starting Tone: A (3)

Meter: $\frac{6}{4}$ $\left(\frac{6}{\flat}\right)$

No piano accompaniment

* COMPOSER'S STYLE: See page 105 for information about Sibelius. Sibelius wrote many choral compositions. This one was originally for male voices. It should be sung in **legato** style with unbroken phrases. As the children listen to the recording for the first time, have them follow the suggestions in their books. Play the recording again and ask them to listen especially for the phrasing and style of singing. This haunting melody contains the unusual beauty for which the songs of Sibelius are noted.

RHYTHM: This song is another example of the art song. The cadence at the end of the fourth phrase leads directly into the next phrase, and care should be taken to sing the rhythm accurately. The $\frac{6}{4}$ meter allows the rhythm to flow with two accents to the measure.

* Bass Staff: When the children know the song, follow the suggestion in the pupil's book and assist the boys (girls, too, if they wish) in singing the lower part from the bass staff notes. They might sing with a neutral syllable first, concentrating on note position. A challenge then would be to sing with note names, since these are different from the treble names to which the children are accustomed. Review the bass staff on page 113 as a preparation.

The Child's Voice

Children at the age level of a sixth grade class should maintain a flexible voice with considerable range. The range usually increases in the pre-adolescent years if all available tones continue to be used. The child's attitude toward singing and toward his singing voice is a most important factor. Girls often develop the idea that they can only "sing high" and wish always to sing soprano. Boys, in the desire to take on masculine traits, sometimes refuse to sing high even when their voices show no sign of changing. Sometimes, because a child has gained skill in singing harmony parts, he will declare himself an "alto" and not wish to sing a melody which requires full range.

Although some children, especially boys, develop voice qualities at this age which give the voice a new color and limited or extended ranges of tones, the great majority will have a good range of tones (usually two octaves from G to G and often A to A). Children should be helped to realize that they can sing both high and low;

All Hail, Fridolin

Music by Jean Sibelius
Arranged by William Reynolds
Words Adapted

Fridolin is the name of an old man who still enjoys life. Can you picture Fridolin in his fine clothes, setting out to enjoy life as in former times?

1. The salm-on scarce-ly be-gin to jump, The win-ter scarce-ly is o'er, Be-fore you rise up as of old With eag-er glance once more. In spite of dis-ap-point-ments past, Of

2. Your cloth-ing is of the fin-est cut, With silk-en tie in a bow; You walk as grace-ful-ly as of yore With tall silk hat you go. Ah, I shall watch you swing-ing by, Your

Record 4   Side B   Band 2. VOICES: children's choir.
ACCOMPANIMENT: 3 clarinets.
FORM: Introduction, 8 meas.; Vocal, v. 1 (choir on 2 parts, clarinet on lower part); Vocal, v. 2 (choir on 3 parts).

114

man - y bro - ken dreams, — Your soul still finds _ its
cane hangs light on your arm, — Your step re - veals _ your

joy in life, So all hail, Fri - do - lin. —
joy in life, So all hail, Fri - do - lin. —

If the alto part of this song were written on the bass staff, it would sound the same as when it appears on the treble staff; but it would not look the same. Boys, try singing the part as you read from the bass staff.

The salm - on scarce-ly be - gin to jump, The win - ter scarce-ly is
o'er, _ Be - fore you rise up as of old With
eag - er glance once more. _ In _ spite of dis - ap -
point - ments past, Of man - y bro - ken dreams, _ Your
soul still finds its joy in life, So all hail, Fri - do - lin. _

and by doing so, the voice will develop more range and strength. Singing alto at this age depends upon the ability to sing independently and to hear and read harmony parts rather than a contralto voice quality. Harmony and melody parts should be assigned to the children alternately so that they do not feel themselves permanently assigned to one voice range. Almost all children of this age have stronger voices with more color and beauty than they had in previous years. They should be encouraged to develop good singing habits (see page iv, "Exploring Music through Singing") and to adopt an attitude of pleasure in using the singing voice in its full tonal range and dynamic possibilities.

Toward the end of the year, there may be several boys in the class with indications of the changing voice; some voices may be completely changed. Again, the boy's attitude toward his voice and acceptance by the teacher and class are most important. His voice should not be treated as some undesirable sound in the class singing; the new tones should be enjoyed as a good addition to singing in harmony. The boy can often develop new high tones at the same time the low ones become available, but this is sometimes neglected because of the boy's attitude. If possible, the class should hear a boys' choir or recordings of such a choir in order to realize the range and color possibilities. (In the recordings that supplement this book, a boys' choir sings "Jacob's Ladder," "Music in the Air," and "The Swan.") If the boy can develop an unusual range, he should be encouraged to take pride in it. If his range becomes narrow, he can often sing the lower harmony part; or he can sing chord roots as harmony. Boys should become aware of the new sounds and different notation they will sing when their voices change. Such preparation will help them adjust to the new vocal conditions and maintain an interest in singing.

Occasionally, boys who cannot "sing a tune" or match pitch as an elementary student will be able to do so in at least a limited way when their voices change. If there are boys or girls in your class who do not sing on pitch, give them special help in singing and playing chord roots and encourage them to believe they will be able to sing. Often it is a habit of inattention which underlies the inability to sing on pitch.

The attitude toward the singing voice and its range is largely due to the experiences of the child in singing and hearing others sing. This book and the records give special attention to the several kinds of voices and to choral singing. The teacher's own singing range need not limit the children if he uses all resources as models and if he emphasizes expressive use of the child's voice as one of the objectives of classroom music.

Totur

Totur (toh-toor) depends upon the two-step as explained in the pupil's book. In the first lesson, play the music so that children can enjoy the folk melody and become acquainted with the dance rhythm. Help them analyze the folk melody so that they hear the introduction and the two parts.

In another lesson, allow children to practice the two-step individually, then in couples. When they are at ease with the step, play the part of the music which follows the introduction so that they can practice the step with music. Ask children to practice moving in the several directions they will need to move when doing the folk dance: toward the center, away from the center, around the circle, turning as they go.

Good style will develop as children learn to turn their bodies slightly to the side in the direction they move, raising and lowering arms with the turns. They should "feel light" with the music, letting the accents carry them along. These concepts of style are best demonstrated by children who seem to practice them naturally. Watch for good examples and point them out to the rest of the class. Accomplished folk dancers of the community are often willing to demonstrate for classes.

The circle "walk" can become a step-together-step of the two-step when children know the dance well. When the grand right and left pattern is finished, if some girl is left without a partner, she should step to the center of the circle (called the "lost-and-found department" by some folk dancers) where the lost boy will find his partner.

Totur

Danish Folk Dance

"Totur" means "two around," and the dance of this name is a couple dance done in a circle. It is a "mixer" and is a popular dance in the United States as well as in Denmark. The dance is based on the "two-step," which is done in the pattern, step-together-step.

With partners in ballroom position, practice the two-step in preparation for learning "Totur." Listen to the record to get acquainted with the rhythm; then practice the two-step with the music.

The dance is composed of an introduction and two parts. During the introduction, partners walk in the circle 16 steps to the left, 16 steps to the right.

In part one of the dance, partners move to the center of the circle in the pattern: step-together-step, walk, walk. Return to your place with the same steps. Then do four two-steps, turning as you move around the ring.

Repeat all of part one and finish facing your partner.

In part two of the dance, do a grand right and left for 16 measures.

Take a new partner.

Repeat part one of the dance.

Record 9   Side B   Band 2.

116

Far in the Mountains

Finnish Folk Song
Words Adapted

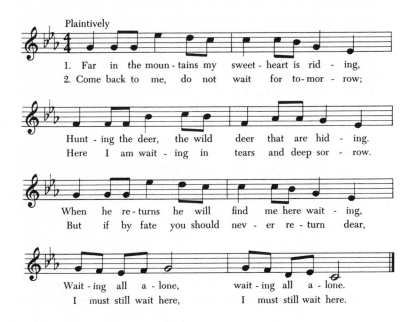

1. Far in the moun-tains my sweet-heart is rid - ing,
2. Come back to me, do not wait for to-mor - row;

Hunt - ing the deer, the wild deer that are hid - ing.
Here I am wait - ing in tears and deep sor - row.

When he re-turns he will find me here wait - ing,
But if by fate you should nev - er re-turn dear,

Wait - ing all a - lone, wait - ing all a - lone.
I must still wait here, I must still wait here.

* EXPRESSION: Listen to this beautiful melody; ask the children to discuss its expressive qualities. WHAT IN THE MUSIC ADDS TO THE MOOD OF LONELINESS AND MELANCHOLY EXPRESSED IN THE WORDS? Children may comment on the minor tonality, the tempo, and the dynamics. Draw attention, also, to the melodic contour. The large skip upward at the beginning of a phrase followed by a descending line seems almost like a "wail." The low range of the last phrase contrasts with the higher tones of the first three phrases and reinforces the sense of desolation. Work for an expressive performance of this lovely melody. Refer to page iv for suggestions on "Expressive Singing."

* FOLK STYLE: Loneliness and sorrow are common topics for songs of this remote land. This song may have come from the Eastern section of Finland which is adjacent to Russia. The minor tonality, descending melodic line, and repetitive long-short-short rhythm patterns are typical of Russian songs.

The **kantele,** a favorite Finnish instrument, is similar to a psaltery. On the recording, the harp suggests the sound of the kantele.

Play the following descant on an appropriate instrument such as the flute, oboe, or violin. On the recording the descant is played by the French horn an octave lower than written here. Listen for the distinctive sound of this instrument accompanied by the harp.

Record 4   Side B   Band 3. VOICE: soprano.
ACCOMPANIMENT: French horn, harp.
FORM: Instrumental; Vocal, vv. 1-2.

The Brass Family

Members of the brass family include those instruments whose tones are produced by blowing through cup-shaped mouthpieces into long metal tubes which are coiled in one of several different shapes. The player can, by pressing the valves in various combinations, change the length of the air column and thus alter the pitch.

Brass instruments existed in ancient cultures but were not useful as musical instruments because of their limited range. Because they lacked valves, the primitive instruments could play only a few tones, mostly those making up the tonic chord (1-3-5-8). For this reason, most military and hunting calls are made up of just these four tones. The modern valved instruments were developed during the nineteenth century, making it possible to sound all of the pitches within the range of the instrument.

Ancient instruments were used primarily for signals during military maneuvers, in religious ceremonies, and during the hunt. The Jewish shofar is described in the Old Testament. Its terrifying sound was commanding and hoarse in great contrast to the tones of modern-day instruments. The earliest horns were made from animal horns.

The brass choir adds color, accent, richness, and body to the orchestral texture. A cone-shaped **mute** inserted into the bell makes the sound of a brass instrument become more nasal or more subdued, depending on how loud it is played.

Trumpet: The trumpet is the soprano of the brass choir. Its tubing is four and one-half feet long, coiled into a narrow rectangle, with three valves. Its tone can be noble, defiant, sharp, and heroic.

The **cornet** is very much like the trumpet with shorter, thicker tubing. Its tone is less brilliant but it is more agile and easier to blow. It is found more often in bands than in orchestras.

French Horn: Often described as the most beautiful of all the brass instruments, the French horn is also the most difficult to play. Its seventeen feet of tubing are wound into a circle, and it may have three or four valves. The French horn is a descendant of the ancient hunting horn; and its tone still suggests the out-of-doors, the remote, the romantic. Its mellow, full tone can be exceedingly powerful and majestic; it can also be dreamy and mysterious. The tone of the French horn blends equally with either woodwind or brass, and it is often used as if it were a member of the woodwind family.

Trombone: The trombone is unique among the brass instruments in that the player changes pitch by moving a slide, thus lengthening or shortening the air column. The trombone can be pompous and heavy or majestic and noble. Its tone is very powerful and most effective when played in groups. The bass trombone contributes strength to the lower register of the brass choir.

Tuba: This "brass bass" is the largest and lowest member of the brass family. It can add robust power and weight to the entire orchestra. When played softly, it adds a plush smoothness to the bass line.

Full page painting in pupil's book.
See page 209 for explanation of art.

118

Music of Latin America and Spain

The arts of a people usually reflect the land. This is especially true of Latin America and Spain where the click of castanets and the strumming of guitars seem to go with the brilliant colors of the flowers and birds.

The folk music of Latin America is a blend of three influences—Indian, African, and Spanish. The Indians of such countries as Ecuador and Peru contributed plaintive, slow-moving melodies, often based on the ancient pentatonic scale. In Haiti and Cuba we find rhythms which were brought to the New World by the African Negro. From Spain came sentimental love songs and intricate dance rhythms.

Many Latin-American customs and musical traditions are well known by North Americans. The fiestas and the Posadas of Latin-American countries are often celebrated in communities of the southwestern United States. The love songs of Mexico are often heard in restaurants and places of entertainment in the United States. The songs are appealing because of the pleasing harmony, the long phrases, and the simple texts.

Many popular dance rhythms have been imported to the United States from the South American countries. The **tango** had its origin in Buenos Aires. Brazil gave us the **samba**, which was originally a rural dance of the Indian natives and later was taken up by the people of the cities. The guitar, the accordion, and various percussion instruments are favorite instruments in all the countries of Latin America.

As children read the description of musical life in Latin America and Spain, help them relate their knowledge about the history of these countries to the development of music in Latin America. Discuss the effect that colonization has on a people. Many things are altered when one country rules another; in this case, even the music was drastically affected. The music we hear today in Latin America is much closer in sound to the music of Spain than it is to the music of the South American native Indian. Compare this development with the development of folk music in our own country. Our music reflects the characteristics of the people who conquered this country, while the music of the American Indian is rarely heard.

The sound of Latin-American music may be more familiar to children than the music of the other countries which they have studied. Some children may have visited Mexico and brought back maracas, castanets, etc. which they can show the class. Some may have seen a fiesta which they can describe to the other students.

When discussing various kinds of Latin-American dances, identify the characteristic rhythm of each.

The tango is:

The basic samba rhythm is:

Another famous Latin dance which was introduced from Cuba is the habanera:

The bolero is Spanish in origin:

Carmen, Carmela

Key: F   Starting Tone: C (5)
Meter: 2/4 (2♩)
Piano accompaniment on page 272

FOLK STYLE: This Mexican folk song is similar to the music of Latin America. The melody, based on the major scale, moves in either scale- or chord-line patterns. The A B form, the repetition of melodic and rhythmic patterns, and the harmonization in thirds and sixths are all traits found in Mexican music. The rhythm pattern which alternates between groupings of three and groupings of two

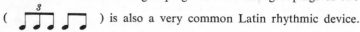

) is also a very common Latin rhythmic device.

As children listen to the recording, ask them to notice each characteristic. Listen also for the typical accompaniment: violin, guitar, double bass, marimba, castanets.

* **HARMONY:** Study the notation of the two voice parts. Discover that the two voices usually move at an interval of a **sixth** apart. Find the patterns in the refrain where voices move at an interval of a **third.** Play the autoharp chords softly and ask children to sing their part lightly on a neutral syllable.

Experiment with different kinds of rhythm patterns on the autoharp. Any of the following might be suitable:

* **RHYTHM:** Refer to page 9 to learn the rhythm of this song. To help children feel the rhythm of the alternating groupings of twos and threes, suggest that they chant and clap this pattern over and over:

Car-men Car-me - la   Car-men Car-me - la

Add an accompaniment using representative percussion instruments. (See page x i.) On the recording, the following two-measure pattern is played during the refrain by the castanets.

Castanets
[musical notation]

Carmen, Carmela

Mexican Folk Tune
Words Adapted

The marimba and two violins that you hear on the recording suggest the kind of accompaniment you might hear in Mexico.

Not too fast

1. When day is done and the sun-set glows in the dis-tance,
2. And when the shad-ows are fall-ing, night birds are call-ing

light-ing a dusk-y sky, I wan-der back to the val-ley
as they de-scend in flight. The stars are glim-mer-ing bright-ly,

where my Car-me-la waits for my joy-ful cry.
clouds drift-ing light-ly, soft-ly we say "good night."

Car-men, Car-me-la, my gold-en sun-beam,

You ban-ish sor-row with one sweet smile.

May all good for-tune a-wait your plea-sure,

My gold-en trea-sure, Car-me-la, mine.

The constant shifting from three to a beat ([♪♪♪]) to two to a beat ([♪♪]) is a very typical Latin-American rhythmic device. What other characteristics mentioned on page 119 can you find in this song?

Record 4   Side B   Band 4.   VOICES: tenor, baritone.
ACCOMPANIMENT: 2 violins, guitar, marimba, double bass, castanets.
FORM: Introduction, *4 meas.;* Vocal, *v. 1;* Interlude, *4 meas.;* Vocal, *v. 2.*

Gaucho tunes can be heard on the pampas and ranges of Uruguay and Argentina. *Vidalitas* are simple, plaintive melodies that are favorites of the gaucho as he sings and accompanies himself on the guitar.

La Vidalita

South American Cowboy Song
Arranged by Kurt Miller
Words Adapted by Kurt Miller

1. Ev - ery day I ride, cross - ing prai - ries wide,
2. Night with star - ry light, at the camp - fire bright,

Ah, _____ La, La Vi - da - li - ta.
(Melody)

La Vi - da - li - ta, sí!

(Melody)

(1.) Cat - tle mill - ing 'round, dust clouds hide the ground,
(2.) Noth - ing stirs the air, peace is ev - ery - where,

Ah, _____ La, La Vi - da - li - ta. La Vi - da - li - ta.
(Melody)

La Vi - da - li - ta, sí! sí!

Record 4 Side B Band 5. VOICES: tenor, baritone.
ACCOMPANIMENT: 2 guitars, double bass.
FORM: Instrumental (one guitar on melody); Vocal, *v. 1;* Instrumental (one guitar plays the harmony part); Vocal, *v. 2.*

Key: D minor   Starting Tone: E (2)   La Vidalita
Meter: $\frac{3}{4}$ $\left(\frac{3}{\downarrow}\right)$
Piano accompaniment on page 274

* EXPRESSION: Read aloud the explanation of *vidalitas* in the pupil's book. "*Gaucho*" means "cowboy." Listen to the song. Compare its mood with that of familiar American cowboy songs such as "Home on the Range." Although the melodies and rhythms are not typical of American cowboy music, the acceptance of the lonely life on the broad prairies or pampas is revealed in the songs of both groups. The guitar is a favorite instrument of cowboys on both sides of the border, because it is easy to play and easy to carry.

FOLK STYLE: Many of the gauchos are descendants of the South American Indians; the music of the *vidalitas* incorporates some characteristics of Indian music. This may account for the lack of strong key feeling, the relatively narrow range, and the repetitive character of this song. Compare "La Vidalita" to "Carmen, Carmela." Many characteristics are common to both songs: the two-part form, the repetition of melodies and rhythms, and the harmonization in thirds. The $\frac{3}{4}$ meter and dotted rhythms are also typical of Latin-American music.

MELODY: Ask the children to listen to the recording. IS "LA VIDA-LITA" MAJOR OR MINOR? CAN YOU HEAR A HOME TONE? After children have listened to the recording and discussed their views, have them look at the notation. Discuss the fact that, although the key signature indicates D minor, the many accidentals and the phrases starting on the second step of the scale and ending on the third step make it difficult to identify any single tone as a strong home tone.

* HARMONY: Suggest that the boys sing the melody and the girls sing the descant. As the girls learn their harmonizing part, allow them to practice the descant for measures three and four of the first section on a neutral syllable before adding it to the melody sung by the boys. This descant is repeated in measures three and four of the second section using the first ending. Have the class notice that, in the first two measures of the second section, the part lies a **third** above the melody.

Add an autoharp accompaniment. The following pattern would be appropriate:

Me gustan todas

Key: E♭   Starting Tone: B♭ (5)
Autoharp Key: F   Starting Tone: C (5)
Meter: 2/4 (2/♩)
Piano accompaniment on page 276

* FOLK STYLE: Following is a translation of the Spanish words: "I like them all, in general I like them all. But that blonde, I like the best. We walk always, and in the sunlight, her eyes then shine, her smile is gold."

After children have listened to the recording to learn the Spanish words, ask them to list all of the characteristics they heard which are representative of Latin-American music. This lighthearted song contains many of the characteristics previously discussed: the romantic words, the syncopated rhythm, the alternating patterns of three and two, the melody which moves by scale- and chord-line patterns, and the harmonization in thirds.

* RHYTHM: Review pages 9 and 13 to learn the rhythm and melody of this song. Clap the beat and chant the words; remind children to watch carefully for the frequent changes in pattern. Develop a percussion accompaniment. Choose rhythm patterns from the song for each instrument to play. Some of the following might be suitable:

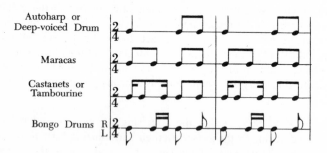

Autoharp or Deep-voiced Drum
Maracas
Castanets or Tambourine
Bongo Drums R L

* HARMONY: When children have heard the recording and have studied the notation of both the melody and the descant on page 123, they should learn the two voice parts simultaneously. Notice that on the recording the A section is in unison; the B section moves in thirds. The return of A is harmonized with the descant played by a trumpet. The children themselves may play this descant on a trumpet, clarinet, or flute; or it may be sung by voices on the syllable "la."

Me gustan todas

Spanish-South American Folk Song
Words Adapted

Refrain

Me gus-tan to-das, me gus-tan to-das, me gus-tan to-das en ge-ne-ral. Pero e-sa ru-bia, pero e-sa ru-bia, pero e-sa ru-bia me gus-ta más. *Fine*

Verse

No-so-tros an-da-mos siem-pre, y den-tro la luz del sol, sus o-jos en-ton-ces bri-llan; su son-ri-sa de o-ro es. *D.C. al Fine*

Record 4   Side B   Band 6.   VOICE: tenor.
ACCOMPANIMENT: trumpet, guitar, marimba, double bass.
FORM: Instrumental; Vocal.

122

The trumpet is a favorite instrument in Spain and some Latin-American countries. Listen for this brass instrument on the recording. It plays the following descant with the refrain of the song. You can play this descant or sing it on "la."

Music of Mexico and South America

The musical traditions of Mexico are old and varied. Centuries before the Spanish arrived, music was a part of the life of the Aztecs. With the arrival of Cortez and the rule of the Spanish, the music of these ancient Aztecs was almost forgotten. The Spanish priests taught the Indians the music of the church. Spanish nobles sang their songs and danced the latest European dances. The Mexicans listened and absorbed the music from Spain until it became their own.

The music of South American countries also shows the imprint of Portuguese and Spanish colonization. As the huge coffee plantations were developed, Negroes were brought from Africa and their music was blended into the new music of the people. Thus, the folk music of South America is a blend of many cultures. Little trace is left of the music of the Indians except in Peru. There, one may still find remnants of the ancient Inca pentatonic melodies played on the primitive flutes used by their ancestors.

Melodies of Mexican and South American songs are almost always major. They are in simple patterns and are repetitive. The rhythm often changes from a feeling of two to a feeling of three. Harmony is almost always based on the I and V chords. Harmony which sounds in thirds or sixths with the melody is characteristic of this music.

Some children may be able to form a *marachi* band to perform this composition. Trumpets or clarinets may play the melody. (Transpose to the key of F. See page x for directions.) The violin may play the descant. Fill in the harmonies with the autoharp. A cello or double bass player may pluck the roots of the chords at the beginning of each measure. Add the percussion accompaniment which the children have previously developed.

Music of Mexico and South America

Refer to this discussion as the children learn songs from various Central and South American countries. Encourage the class to speculate as to the origin of different songs and the effect of European, African, and Indian music on each.

Summarize the musical characteristics of Latin-American music which have been discussed as the children studied various songs. Locate these traits in other songs.

Rhythms: Meter often moves in threes; rhythm patterns may alternate between groupings of two and three; syncopated patterns are common.

Melodies: Melodies are usually major; they move in scale- or chord-line patterns. They are often repetitive and make use of sequences. Those of Spanish influence have wide ranges and are "romantic" in nature. The Indian influence is revealed in some pentatonic songs with narrow ranges and lack of strong key feeling.

Harmony: Melodies are generally accompanied with the I and V7 chords. Many songs can be harmonized vocally by adding a second part a third or a sixth above or below the main melody.

Instrumentation: The guitar, castanets, and tambourine come from Spain and Portugal. Drums and various kinds of rattles are inherited from the Indians. The *marachi* band is a familiar sound in Mexican cafes. It generally consists of a guitar, a violin, and a trumpet or clarinet.

Encourage children to do additional research into Latin-American music: its history, musical characteristics, and major composers including Chávez, Villa-Lobos, and Ginastera.

Río, Río

Key: F   Starting Tone: C (5)

Meter: $\frac{6}{8}$ $\left(\frac{2}{\text{♩.}}\right)$

Piano accompaniment on page 278

* EXPRESSION: The sentimental words and the romantic melody of this song are characteristic of folk music found in the cities of South America. Many of the popular ballads descended from the Spanish and Portuguese serenades. They are usually accompanied by guitar or ukulele. Sing the song slowly and smoothly to emphasize its romantic nature.

MELODY: Follow the steps on page 13 to learn the melody. Notice that it moves primarily by steps. Skips are within the I or V7 chord patterns. Draw attention to the **sequence** in measures eight through twelve. The same four-note pattern is repeated four times, each time beginning one step higher. The melody in measures twelve through sixteen is also of a sequential character, although the repetition is not exact.

* RHYTHM: Ask children to locate interesting rhythm patterns in the notation. Practice clapping the syncopated patterns as one member of the class plays the accented beats on a drum. Study the relationship of pattern to beat:

Pattern:

Accented Beat:

HARMONY: The refrain of the song is harmonized in two parts. When the children are familiar with the complete song, encourage them to improvise their own harmonization for the verse. Remind them that Latin-American songs are usually harmonized in thirds and sixths. The first two measures of the verse can be harmonized a sixth below the melody, while measures three and four will sound well harmonized in thirds. The sequential pattern in measures eight through twelve can also be harmonized in thirds.

Río, Río

Chilean Folk Song
Words Adapted

Watch carefully for the changing rhythm patterns as you sing this song. Its romantic melody is typical of the music of the nineteenth century in South America.

O fast flow-ing rí - o, rí - o, _____ Swirl-ing on to the
O fast flow-ing rí - o, rí - o, _____ Swirl-ing on to the

sea; _____ O fast flow-ing rí - o, rí - o, _____
sea; _____ O fast flow-ing rí - o, rí - o, _____

Swirl-ing on to the sea; _____ In the black-ness _____ of your
Swirl-ing on to the sea; _____ Tears of sor-row _____ in your

chan-nel, _____ In the white-ness _____ of your foam, _____
wa-ters, _____ Joy-ous whis-pers _____ deep be-low, _____

O what se-crets, what ad-ven-tures,. If your sto-ry _____ we could know.

Refrain

Rí - o, rí - o, _____ rí - o, rí - o, _____ with your

Record 4   Side B   Band 7.   VOICES: tenor, baritone.
ACCOMPANIMENT: 2 violins, trumpet, guitar, marimba, double bass.
FORM: Instrumental; Vocal, v. 1; Interlude, 2 meas.; Vocal, v. 2.

124

tales you — o - ver - flow. — O what se - crets, — what ad -

ven - tures, — If your sto - ry — we could know. —

Dansa
from *Bachianas Brasileiras No. 4*
by Heitor Villa-Lobos

Villa-Lobos may be described as a **nationalistic** composer. His music is as colorful and full of striking contrasts as the Brazilian land. There is the Brazil of the jungles, with exotic foliage and birds of flashing plumage, where people still live as they did thousands of years ago. There is also the Brazil of the cities like Rio de Janeiro, which is modern and up to date, a melting pot of many cultures.

This fiery composition seems to tumble breathlessly from beginning to end. The effect is exciting and may call many colorful images to mind. As you listen again and again, you will discover that it is a very carefully planned composition with a design which you can follow.

The opening section is based on the following theme played in the middle range of the piano. It is surrounded by a rapidly moving rhythmic pattern in the high range and strong, repeated fifths in the bass. Listen for a repetition of this theme, slightly changed, in the upper range. An arpeggio cascading down the keyboard brings us to the quiet opening of the middle section. This section develops some of the material already heard in the first section. Then listen for the repetition of the musical ideas you heard at the beginning of the composition.

As a young man, Villa-Lobos collected thousands of Brazilian folk songs. When he began to compose music of his own, the rhythms, melodies, harmonies, and tone color of these folk songs became a part of his compositions.

Record 7   Side B   Band 3.
Fritz Jahoda, pianist.

Dansa
from *Bachianas Brasileiras No. 4*

BY HEITOR VILLA-LOBOS
BORN 1887   DIED 1959

Read the first two paragraphs in the pupil's book. Discuss the meaning of the term "nationalistic composer." Such a composer draws on the folk melodies and dance rhythms of his country for musical ideas. He often chooses historic national themes as subjects for his compositions. Ask children to think of other composers who might be considered nationalistic (Smetana, Grieg).

Listen to the composition. Although this composition does not use specific folk themes, the complex rhythms and percussive sounds have their roots in Brazilian dances.

Read the remainder of the discussion. Listen again to the composition and follow the design as explained in the pupil's book.

The middle section opens with this theme:

The repetition of the opening section is easily identified because there is a slight pause just before the restatement of the opening melodic idea.

Draw attention to the interesting tone colors which Villa-Lobos has created. Listen for the sustained tones in the low register sounded against the sparkling arpeggios in the upper voices. Listen for the marked melody surrounded by rapid rhythmic figures.

"Dansa" is the last movement of *Bachianas Brasileiras No. 4*. Villa-Lobos wrote nine such compositions. The title indicates the composer's intention: to combine elements of Bach's polyphonic style (see page 50 for explanation of polyphony) with elements of Brazilian folk music.

In Bahía

Key: F   Starting Tone: A (3)
Meter: $\frac{2}{4}$ $\left(\begin{array}{c}2\\\text{♩}\end{array}\right)$
No piano accompaniment

FOLK STYLE: Discuss the characteristics described in the pupil's book. Listen to the recording and locate other characteristics of South American music.

The samba has become a popular dance in the United States. The basic samba rhythm can be found in the first measure of this song. This dance rhythm, like the rumba and calypso, reflects the influence of the African slaves who were imported into Brazil to work on the huge plantations.

Some children might enjoy writing new verses. Suggest that they do research to discover what products are native to Brazil. They might describe these in their added verses.

* RHYTHM: Chant the words in rhythm until the syncopated patterns move smoothly. Compare the syncopation of the refrain with the more straightforward rhythm of the verse. Divide the class into two groups; ask one group to clap the refrain while the other claps the verse. When the song is familiar, add the percussion accompaniment suggested in the pupil's book. Add one pattern at a time until children can maintain each rhythm independently. When the basic rhythm patterns are learned, encourage children to improvise variations as they play.

HARMONY: The verse of this song is in three voice parts. Study the parts and name the different chords in each measure:

I | I | V7 I | V | IV V7 IV | I | I V7 | I ||

Ask children to listen to the chord sequence on the autoharp and then sing their parts lightly, listening carefully to each other. If children find it difficult to sing all three voice parts together, have them sing the two upper parts. Later in the year when they are more accustomed to singing in three parts, they can return to this song and sing all parts.

In Bahía

Brazilian Folk Song
Words Adapted

Bahía is a state in eastern Brazil. The music in this section of Brazil is noted for its complex rhythm and the use of syncopation. A choral refrain often answers a solo stanza. This song probably had its origin in a street call. It is based on the samba rhythm.

Record 4   Side B   Band 8.   VOICES: children's choir.
ACCOMPANIMENT: percussion.
FORM: Vocal, vv. 1-2.

Add the following accompaniment.

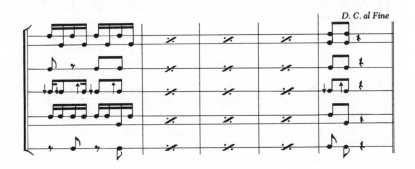

As you observe the growing musical awareness, musical independence, and musical skill of your class members, you will take great pride in the contribution of classroom music to the life of each human being. In some children you may note more confident and secure personalities because of musical success and recognition of musical accomplishments. You may note more responsiveness to beauty of all kinds. You may notice a new and deep interest in music that will last a lifetime. As you work with your class through the year, you may wish to evaluate quite often the effectiveness of their experiences in music. The following questions may be of help in noting evidences of growth.

Performance Skills—Are children performing music by singing, playing instruments, and dancing? Are they working individually, in small groups, and in the class group? Are their performances becoming more expressive, more musical, and more independent?

Listening and Analysis Skills—Are class members listening to music and discussing music with enjoyment and enthusiasm? Are they acquiring listening habits and analysis skills that contribute to intelligent listening to music? Are they hearing in greater detail the elements of music, musical design, and composer's style? Are they developing broader interest in more types of music? Do they often listen to music outside the classroom and discuss it in class?

Discussion Skills—Is vital experience with music resulting in the desire of class members to express opinions and feelings concerning music? Are children growing in ability to speak intelligently and expressively on musical topics? Is classroom discussion a planned part of the music class?

Creative Skills—Are children developing musical imagination and interest in experimentation? Are dancing, playing instruments, vocal improvisation, and other activities which require originality practiced by individuals and small groups? Do children share their original work with the class?

Reading Skills—Are your class members observing the music page with an understanding of what they see? Are they relating sound patterns of rhythm, melody, and harmony to notation patterns? Are they becoming more aware of good phrasing and other aspects of performance through study of the music page? Are they gaining confidence in their ability with these skills so that they feel they can read music? Are their reading skills practiced in both playing and singing?

Music of the West Indies

Discuss the explanation of calypso music given in the pupil's book. Although calypso originated in Trinidad, it is heard in varied forms all over the islands. The influence of its rhythms can be found in music of other Latin-American countries.

Discuss the history of the West Indies and its effect on calypso music. The islands were owned in turn by the Spanish, the French, and the English, each of whom imported Negro slaves from Africa to work on the sugar plantations. The language of the Negro gradually became a mixture of Spanish, French, and English; their music and songs reflect the same influences.

The slaves were not allowed to talk as they worked; consequently, they sang the news of the day, plots to escape, and funny insults about their masters. A "chantwelle" was the leader. To keep the workers interested, he would make up new verses about different topics. Modern calypso songs also comment on topics of current interest. The best calypso singers improvise words as they sing.

Other songs and dances, in addition to the calypso, have come from the West Indies. The rumba, a popular dance, originated in Cuba as did the habanera. Calypso has become very popular in the United States, and children may have recordings of calypso songs that they can share with the class.

Water Come A Me Eye

Key: E♭   Starting Tone: B♭ (5)
Autoharp Key: F   Starting Tone: C (5)
Meter: ¢ (²⁄₂)
Piano accompaniment on page 280

EXPRESSION: Although many of the characteristics of calypso music described in "Music of the West Indies" are apparent in this song, its plaintive quality sets it apart from the lighthearted mood commonly associated with calypso music. This song should be sung smoothly at a moderate tempo with rhythms still clearly defined.

* RHYTHM: Clap the rhythm of measures three and four while some children play a steady beat. Discuss the relationship of pattern to

Music of the West Indies

Calypso, the music most often associated with the West Indies, actually came from only one island, Trinidad. Calypso music has distinctive musical characteristics. Calypso singers have always improvised their songs "on the spot" to fit a particular situation. As they add new verses, they shift the word accents to accommodate the existing rhythm of the melody rather than alter the rhythm to fit the words. The melodies are simple and usually move in chordal patterns which outline the I and V7 chords in a major key. A variety of Latin instruments may be used for accompaniment in a modern calypso band: conga and bongo drums, claves, maracas, cowbells, guiro. The guitar plays the harmony. Listen for these instruments on the recordings of the calypso songs in your book. How many of them can you identify?

Water Come A Me Eye

Jamaican Folk Song
Words Adapted

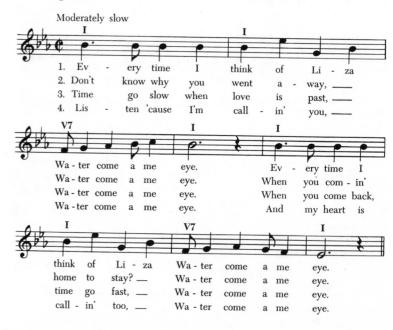

Moderately slow

1. Ev - ery time I think of Li - za
2. Don't know why you went a - way, ___
3. Time go slow when love is past, ___
4. Lis - ten 'cause I'm call - in' you, ___

Wa - ter come a me eye.

Ev - ery time I
When you com - in'
When you come back,
And my heart is

think of Li - za Wa - ter come a me eye.
home to stay? ___ Wa - ter come a me eye.
time go fast, ___ Wa - ter come a me eye.
call - in' too, ___ Wa - ter come a me eye.

Record 5   Side A   Band 1.   VOICES: baritone, children's choir.
ACCOMPANIMENT: cowbells, guitar, conga drums, maracas.
FORM: Introduction, *4 meas.;* Vocal, *vv. 1-4.*

Refrain

I   I   V7   I

Come back, Li-za, come back, girl, Wa-ter come a me   eye.

I   I   V7   I

Come back, Li-za, come back, girl,   Wa-ter come a me   eye.

Improvise Your Own Calypso

The use of colorful word phrases to describe a feeling, an idea, or an event is typical of **calypso** music.

You can improvise your own song by imitating the distinctive patterns of calypso music.

First, make up a four-line verse about a current event or a famous person. Establish a steady beat and chant your verse. Do not worry if you have to shift the accent on some words; this helps to give your song a typical calypso rhythm. You may want to mispronounce a word deliberately in order to get the desired syncopated effect. Choose a home tone and establish tonality by playing the I and V7 chords on the autoharp.

Sing a melody for the first phrase or play it on the bells. Remember that calypso melodies are usually made of tones from the I and V7 chords.

You may repeat the same melody for more than one phrase; sometimes you will need to change the ending of the phrase.

After you have worked out a melody, add a calypso accompaniment as suggested on page 132.

beat. Be sure that the second, third, and fourth notes in the pattern are clapped on the offbeat.

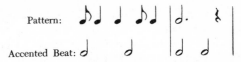

Pattern:

Accented Beat:

Experiment with various combinations of instruments until children are satisfied that the accompaniment is appropriate to the mood of the song. Use only a few instruments. An autoharp might play the accented beats while a light drum repeats the pattern (♩. ♪♪ ♩).

Play the pattern found in measures three and four on the claves or maracas.

FORM: Analyze the structure. It is an A B form with each section made up of two four-measure phrases. Notice that the same rhythm is repeated each time the words "Water come a me eye" are sung. Sing the song as a question and answer with one child singing the narrative sections while the class joins in on the repeated phrase "Water come a me eye."

* MELODY: The melody of this song is very simple; it moves in scale- or chord-line patterns. Establish tonality and challenge the children to sing as much of the song as possible at sight. Review the steps for reading a new song outlined on page 13. Listen to the recording to correct errors they may make in the melody and rhythm.

Improvise Your Own Calypso

This project might be carried on by the entire class but will be more effective if children work in small groups or as individuals. After the children have developed their songs, have them share the songs with the class. Choose those which seem to be most typical of calypso music and perform them for other classes in the school or for parents.

Children who do not wish to make up their own melody may write new words to the melody of "Hosanna," "Water Come A Me Eye," or some other calypso song. The custom of setting new words to familiar melodies is common.

Hosanna

Key: E♭   Starting Tone: B♭ (5)
Autoharp Key: F   Starting Tone: C (5)
Meter: ₵ ($\frac{2}{J}$)
Piano accompaniment on page 282

FOLK STYLE: Discuss the characteristics which make this song representative of calypso music: the syncopated rhythm patterns cause changes in word accent; the melody moves by chord-line patterns alternating between the I, IV, and V7 chords. The subject of this song is also typical. Calypso songs often comment on events of the community life; many times a moral of some sort is drawn from the observations.

* **MELODY:** Study the notation and analyze the chordal structure of the melody line. Ask one child to play the autoharp accompaniment as the class sings the melody with words or a neutral syllable. Practice difficult intervals with numbers.

* **RHYTHM:** Chant the words while someone plays the accented beats on a drum or claves. To emphasize the interesting character of calypso rhythms, chant the words without the syncopation.

Ho - san - na, me build a   house, oh, Ho - san - na

Add an accompaniment as suggested on page 132.

HARMONY: Some children may learn to play this song on the piano. Encourage them to learn the melody first, then to add a harmonizing accompaniment. Children who are studying the piano may be encouraged to develop an accompaniment in an appropriate rhythmic pattern.

Hosanna

Jamaican Folk Song

The building of a house is an important occasion in the West Indies as it is in many parts of the world. The words come from the Biblical parable about the wise man who built his house on rock and the foolish man who built his house on sand.

Record 5   Side A   Band 2.   VOICES: baritone, children's choir.
ACCOMPANIMENT: cowbells, guitar, conga drums, maracas, claves, guiro.
FORM: Introduction, *4 meas.;* Vocal, *v. 1;* Interlude, *4 meas.;* Vocal, *v.2.*

An important objective of classroom music is musical independence of the individual class members. Independent activities and individual and small group practice are essential in this development. Also essential is willingness of the teacher to provide leadership in initial study of a song or other compositions and, thereafter, to exert less and less leadership. Conducting, although it is occasionally useful, should not be a regular part of the teacher's role in the elementary classroom. It may lead to mechanical singing and too much dependence upon the teacher.

The following questions may be of help as you plan and observe the development of musical independence in your class.

Can class members take responsibility for preparatory steps as well as for performance of a song: can they set the tempo, play an introduction, find the starting pitch? Can they sing songs they know with good intonation, interpretation, diction, and appropriate style without undue reminding? Can they play accompaniments and various kinds of instrumental embellishments?

Do class members know and enjoy songs well enough to sing them outside the classroom? Can they explain to parents with some degree of accuracy and detail what they have learned about the instrumentation and form of an orchestral composition?

Do children who play orchestral instruments sometimes take responsibility for working out a harmony part to play with class singing? Do they sometimes learn to play themes of orchestral compositions for the class?

Are class members developing the freedom and poise necessary to compose an original dance as a part of the music class or apart from it? Can they dance folk dances they have learned, making their own preparation, and with a minimum of organization by the teacher?

Do class members show ability to use the elements of music and various musical devices as they improvise or as they experiment with original musical ideas?

Do children assist in keeping instruments and musical materials in good condition and in a convenient place? Can they prepare the setting for the class music period, making sure that necessary equipment is ready?

Compose Your Own Percussion Accompaniment

Follow the suggestions in the pupil's book for adding calypso accompaniments. The children will enjoy playing these patterns as a rhythmic exercise as well as for an accompaniment. Encourage them to improvise additional patterns as they become more skilled.

A Calypso Game

After children have learned the calypso songs on pages 128-131, they may enjoy playing this game which was created by a group of children. The words and rhythm pattern might be written on a large chart, or the children may learn the chant by listening to the teacher.

Establish a steady beat; then chant the words in rhythm.

Choose one person to be the leader. He chants the first phrase, naming anyone he wishes. The person named must be ready to tell where he is "hiding" during measures five and six. He can be hiding any place he wishes as long as he says it in rhythm. The game is then repeated with "William" becoming the leader. Anyone who does not say his part in rhythm must drop out of the game. Continue to play until everyone is eliminated.

Compose Your Own Percussion Accompaniment

The interesting cross rhythms created by the percussion patterns are one of the unique features of calypso. Rhythms to accompany a calypso song or dance are built upward like layers of a cake. You can build your own accompaniments by using this plan.

Begin with a solid foundation:

Deep-sounding drum

Next add the shakers or maracas:

Maracas

Then add a counter rhythm:

High-sounding drum

Now a more difficult rhythm is joined to the others. In this case, we can use the rhythmic pattern from the first measure of "Hosanna":

Claves or something metal

Practice these patterns separately. Then combine them until you can play them easily and can hear the intertwined rhythms.

Key: G minor   Starting Tone: D (5)

Meter: $\frac{2}{4}$ $\left(\frac{2}{\downarrow}\right)$

No piano accompaniment

La Tarara
Spanish Folk Song

The Spanish often use hand-clapping alone as an accompaniment. Clap your hands or snap your fingers in a rhythmic accompaniment as you sing this song. Improvise different patterns as you sing. Add a sharp *"¡Olé!"* at the end of the refrain.

Refrain

La Ta - ra - ra, sí, la Ta - ra - ra, no,

Fine

la Ta - ra - ra, ni - ña, que la he vis - to yo.

Verse

1. Lle - va mi Ta - ra - ra un ves - ti - do ver - de,
2. Lu - ce mi Ta - ra - ra sus co - las de se - da

D.C. al Fine

lle - no de vo - lan - tes y de cas - ca - be - les.
en - tre las re - ta - mas y la hier - ba - bue - na.

Record 5   Side A   Band 3.   VOICE: tenor.
ACCOMPANIMENT: trumpet, tambourine, wood blocks, castanets, tom-tom.
FORM: Introduction, *4 meas.;* Vocal, *v. 1;* Instrumental; Vocal, *v. 2;*
Coda, *4 meas.*

* FOLK STYLE: Listen to the recording. Ask the children to read the description of Spanish music on page 135 in the pupil's book. IN WHICH OF THE SPANISH PROVINCES DID THIS SONG PROBABLY ORIGINATE? (Andalusia.) The interesting minor melody with its dotted rhythms reminds us of the gypsy music from this province. The tambourine and castanets' accompaniment heard on the recording is also typical of Andalusian gypsy music.

As children listen to the accompaniment, notice the following patterns which they may use in their own accompaniment:

* FORM: The design of this dance song is A B A. People in Spain often improvise rondos as they sit about in the sunny plazas. Everyone joins in on the A section. One person improvises new verses and melodies for the B section. Then the A section is repeated between each verse. It can go on and on as long as someone is ready with a new melody (A B A C A D and so on). "La Tarara" might be used as the basis of an improvised rondo. Suggest that everyone join in on the refrain each time. Encourage individuals to improvise new melodies (or new words for the original melody) for the middle section. The new melody must be the same length as the A section.

Listen to the recording to learn the Spanish words. The translation is: "Tarara, yes, Tarara, no, my friend, I have seen Tarara. My Tarara wears a green dress, covered with ruffles and little bells. My Tarara displays her silken trains among the flowering plants and the peppermint."

Los gallos cantan

Key: E♭   Starting Tone: B♭ (5)
Autoharp Key: F   Starting Tone: C (5)
Meter: $\frac{6}{8}$ $\left(\frac{2}{\text{♩.}}\right)$
Piano accompaniment on page 284

* FOLK STYLE: Listen to the recording to learn the Spanish pronunciation. Read the discussion on page 135 and discuss the characteristics which are present in this song. It is from the province of Castile. This morning serenade may have been sung by a Spanish suitor under the window of his sweetheart.

When the song is familiar, children may wish to add an accompaniment as described on page 132. Improvise a pattern on a small, high-pitched drum. Encourage children who have studied the flute to make up a descant.

DESIGN: Determine the form of the song; write it in letter names (A B C B). Review the function of the repeat sign 𝄆 and first and second endings.

* HARMONY: The voices move in thirds throughout the entire song. Help children to learn both parts simultaneously. Sing on a neutral syllable until notes are learned; then sing with the Spanish words.

Los gallos cantan

Castilian Popular Song
Words Adapted

Record 5   Side A   Band 4. VOICES: tenor, baritone.
ACCOMPANIMENT: 2 violins, guitar, double bass, percussion.
FORM: Introduction, *4 meas.;* Vocal (Spanish); Instrumental; Vocal (English).

134

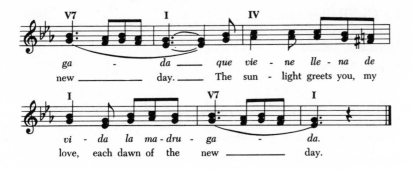

ga - da ___ que vie - ne lle - na de

new ___ day. ___ The sun - light greets you, my

vi - da la ma - dru - ga - da.

love, each dawn of the new ___ day.

Music of Spain

The whir of a tambourine, bright skirts swirling, heels tapping as guitars play intricate rhythms—this is the picture many people have of Spanish music. Yet these gay sights and sounds are only one part of the colorful folk music of Spain.

Music in Spain has as many contrasts as its land which reaches from the rugged northern mountains to the sunny southern slopes along the Mediterranean. In the northern Basque country we can hear haunting modal melodies moving in irregular rhythms. The lively **jota** is danced in the Basque country.

The distinctive rhythm of the **bolero** had its origin in Castile. The custom of serenading also comes from this province. The young men often sang their serenades unaccompanied. Other songs were accompanied on a small flute or a little drum. From Catalonia come beautiful carols of Christmas and the New Year.

The music that we most often associate with the Spanish comes from Andalusia in the south. Many of the musical customs, such as the **flamenco** songs and dances, were introduced by the African Moors who invaded Spain in the eighth century. The exotic melodies with unusual intervals and exciting rhythms were adopted by the wandering gypsies.

If you visit Spain today, you may still see the Andalusian gypsies gather in a circle to play their guitars, clap an intricate accompaniment, and shout "¡Olé!" as one of their group stamps his heels and snaps his fingers in a breathtaking flamenco dance.

As children read this description of music in Spain and learn the Spanish songs in their book, ask them to locate characteristics which they have also noted in Latin-American music. The distinctive rhythms, the romantic ballads, the harmonization in thirds, and the use of the guitar came originally from Spain.

No other country has such a variety of folk dances as Spain. The **jota** is a dance in rapid triple time, performed by couples, and accompanied by castanets. The distinctive rhythm of the **bolero** was made famous by the French composer Ravel in an orchestral composition which bears the name of the dance. The **flamenco** dance is marked by its frequently changing rhythms and by the character of the performance which is typified by the rapid stamping of heels and toes and clapping of hands.

Spanish-composed music has a history as long and rich as that of its folk music. Spanish composers were writing beautiful music for the Catholic Church and composing instrumental music for recorders and viols at the same time the English composers of the Golden Age were adding to the rich musical heritage of Europe.

The creative rhythms, colorful melodies, and harmonies of Spanish folk music have captured the imagination of many composers from other countries as well as from Spain. De Falla, Albéniz, and Granados are three of the best-known Spanish composers who used folk themes in their music. Ravel, Liszt, Debussy, Rimsky-Korsakov, Bizet, and Chabrier are only a few of the European composers who have been inspired by Spanish folk themes.

Le Cid Ballet Suite
Castillane, Andalouse, Aragonaise, Aubade

BY JULES MASSENET
BORN 1842   DIED 1912

The national hero of Spain is El Cid (el theed in Spanish), but Massenet, being French, used the French name Le Cid (le seed) for the opera and French names for the dances from the opera.

Castillane (cah-sti-lahn). After playing the composition once and discussing it, play the music again and write the design on the chalk board as children call out the letters indicating the order of the melodies. They will first establish the fact that the music begins with a brief rhythmic introduction followed by the main, or A, melody played on the flutes. When they are familiar with the A Theme, they will be able to hear the complete design: Introduction A B A C A D A B C A Coda (based on A). Class members may be asked to discover changes in the playing of the A Theme, such as the addition of a scale-wise pattern and to discover the short bridge passages between the themes.

One class member might play the castanets with the A Theme each time it is heard. Another might play the tambourine with the B Theme, striking it with the palm on the accents, shaking it on other beats. The accents of the C and D Themes can be effectively played on claves. The class, divided into three groups, might also become part of "the orchestra" by clapping the rhythms of the themes as they listen. (Although there are three main tunes, all of which are repeated, the brief fourth tune is heard once and the accents may be played on a different instrument and dramatized in a different dance pattern.)

One class worked out the dance in this way. Formation: A line of boys facing a line of girls, the lines about ten feet apart, space of two-arms length between children of each line. Each boy has hands clasped behind him at waist height, elbows out in usual Spanish dance style throughout the dance. Boys alternate feet in light stamping steps accenting the stamp with the music. They step in place during the introduction and bridge passages of the music. With the A Theme, using the same step, they move across to partners and back to place

Le Cid Ballet Suite
Castillane, Andalouse, Aragonaise, Aubade

by Jules Massenet

The dances of this suite are examples of Spanish influence in music. Massenet and many other French composers were fascinated by the music they heard and the folk dances they saw when they visited Spain.

Originally prepared as ballet music for a festival scene in the opera *Le Cid*, the dances are most often performed in the United States as concert pieces for orchestra. The rhythms and melodies are typically Spanish; and it is easy for us to imagine the original street dances, songs, and instruments which inspired Massenet to write the music for orchestra.

"Castillane," an animated dance in $\frac{6}{8}$ rhythm, takes its name from the Spanish province of Castile. It is a rondo—the rhythm and melody of the first theme returns many times and alternates with less important themes.

A special feature is the rhythm

which is heard through most of the composition. Listen to the dance and enjoy the Spanish characteristics. Discuss all that you hear. Listen again and write the design; use letter names for the melodies. Choose an appropriate instrument for each of the four tunes. A class member might play each instrument as you listen to the composition a third time and follow the design.

Later, compose your own Spanish dance. Use Spanish dance ideas you have seen and experiment until you find an appropriate foot pattern and dance movement for each melody. Decide on a formation, combine your dance ideas, and dance the entire "Castillane" as you listen to the record.

Let four class members accompany your dance with instruments.

Record 11   Side B   Band 1a-1d.
Israel Philharmonic,
Jean Martinon, conductor.

"Andalouse" takes its name from the southern province of Andalusia and shows the Moorish influence in Spanish music. The melodies are typical of this region. They move slowly over the habanera rhythm:

$$\frac{2}{4} \quad \text{♩. ♫ ♩ | ♩. ♫ ♩ |}$$

Both themes are in the key of A minor and the design is one with which you are familiar. Listen for the three elements of music and discuss the charm of each as heard in the brief composition. Discover the design.

"Aragonaise" is based on sounds heard in the province of Aragon. Listen to the record and discuss ways in which the composer gave the music a Spanish sound. Why is the music exciting even though it includes only one important melody? Compose a dance for the Aragonaise. Let the boys dance the rhythmic figure heard throughout the music while the girls develop whirling patterns with the melody.

"Aubade" means "morning serenade." What sounds of the orchestra give the music its charm? The girls will enjoy dancing the Aubade. Using only a small circle of space, each girl might experiment with foot patterns until she finds one that fits the mood and rhythm of the music. Find an appropriate point in the music for dancing away from your place. Try soft hand-clapping with some accents of the music.

in parallel line, stamping forward, then backward (8 accents in each direction).

With the B Theme, the girls twirl toward partners with two wide swirls and stamps, then smaller turns. They return to place with the same pattern, but turning in the opposite direction. With the C and D Themes, the boys move in a line, turning in brisk half-turns on the accents, facing one direction and then the other. The line moves to the left with seven steps and back to place with the same twisting movement, as boys spin on first one foot, then the other.

Andalouse (an-duh-looź) The rhythm pattern played on the cello at the beginning of the composition is repeated throughout. The cello and woodwinds play a kind of duet in the opening and closing sections, with the other strings being prominent in the middle section. The harmony is interesting in the change to major at the end of the B section. The design is A B A, the middle section being brief.

Aragonaise (aŕ-a-gon-aźe) The composer used a typical Spanish rhythm, swirling melody, and changes of tempo and dynamics to remind us of music of the province of Aragon.

In composing the dance, the boys might stamp the basic rhythm throughout the music, changing their formation for some of the repetitions. One girl, a few girls, or all girls as a class might follow the melody with turning, swirling dance patterns. Sudden endings are typical of Spanish dances, and each dancer should plan a statue-like pose that can be executed gracefully.

Aubade (oh-bańd) "Morning serenade" melodies, called "Alborado" in Spanish, have been heard in Spanish folk music since the time when troubadours serenaded their ladies. The class might conjecture that such a serenade as this was originally played on a lute or guitar. Plucked strings and woodwind instruments give a special sound to the delicate orchestral music.

Each girl might dance an original foot pattern, and when the patterns are established in small spaces, the girls might "dance away," continuing to use the same foot movement. They might dance back to place and close the dance with a hop or bow.

Elements of Music: Rhythm

The study on pages 138-41 should be used as an opportunity for children to review and synthesize their knowledge about the elements of music. It should also help them begin to develop an understanding of the historical development of music. Begin the discussion with the historical approach. Ask the children to tell how they think music might have begun. Lead them to discover the different kinds of music (folk songs and composed music—all styles and from all periods of history). Summarize the children's ideas on the chalkboard.

Continue with a discussion of rhythm. Encourage children to develop their own definition. Suggest that they refer to various sources, such as the encyclopedia, the dictionary, or other books in this series.

Read each paragraph aloud and discuss each idea presented in the pupil's book. Emphasize the fact that all music has rhythm of some kind, made up of sounds and silences of varying duration. Although people of different times and places have organized rhythms in various ways, there is always some kind of organization. In most of the music we know, the rhythm is organized around the meter grouping. Beats are divided by accents into groups of twos or threes (or some combination of these). Patterns made up of tones of varying length are woven around this grouping of beats. These tones are organized in relationships to each other (and to the beat). Some of these relationships are:

Contemporary composers still use these same basic rules of organization. However, they combine them in new ways. Ask children to look for examples in their music books (or in music they are studying in private lessons) of the different kinds of rhythmic groupings described in the last paragraph of the pupil's page.

As the information on the pupil's page is discussed, play the recordings at appropriate times. Examples on the recording include: African drumming, Viennese waltz, military march, Spanish bolero, Scottish snap, calypso rhythms (examples appear in this order on the recording).

Elements of Music: Rhythm

Rhythm has been called the heartbeat of music. It is the element which gives music life. Rhythm was probably the element that man first discovered in his search for ways to express his feelings musically.

A steady pulse or beat is the basis of rhythm.

/ / / / / / / / / /

Some beats are accented. This results in an organization of the beats into groups.

/ / / / / / / / / / /

Intricate rhythm patterns, made up of sounds of different lengths, may be woven around the steady pulse.

— — — — — — — — — — — —

Rhythm is present in various styles and forms. On your recording there are several examples of rhythm. Listen carefully and identify as many different examples of rhythm as you can.

Modern composers are especially interested in finding new ways to use rhythm in their music.

They organize music in unusual meters.

Sometimes they change meters within a single composition.

Two meters may be sounded at once.

Their music may include unusual rhythm patterns.

Record 11   Side A   Band 1.

Elements of Music: Melody

From the time when man first created a crude melody, he has searched for ways to expand his melodies by using a wider and wider range of tones. The earliest songs or **chants** probably included only two or three tones a second or third apart.

Oh,   Rain God,   Bring   us rain.

Many of the primitive songs which have been collected are based on a **pentatonic scale** of five tones.

whole   whole   step and   whole
step   step   a half   step

As the years passed, more tones were added to melodies. Many of the early Christian **plainsongs** were based on **modes** made up of eight tones. There are six different modes, each of which has a different arrangement of whole and half steps. For example, the **Dorian mode** begins on D and the whole and half steps are arranged in this sequence.

whole   half   whole   whole   whole   half   whole
step   step   step   step   step   step   step

Much of the music we know today is based on the familiar **major** or **minor** scales. In the late nineteenth century and early twentieth century, composers grew curious about the possibilities of other kinds of melodic organization. Some composers used the **whole tone** scale.

whole   whole   whole   whole   whole
step   step   step   step   step

Other composers used all the tones of the **chromatic scale** as the basis of their composition.

No longer do musicians base their music on major or minor scales alone. In writing music the composer may use any of the twelve tones he wishes and may create his own principles of organization for each new composition. There is often no "home tone" as found in music based on traditional scales.

Elements of Music: Melody

Begin the class by asking the children to define "melody." After they have made various suggestions, read the explanation in their books.

As children read and listen to the examples of melody, stress the fact that the history of melody has been one of constant expansion. From the earliest chants of primitive man to music of today, man has explored the limits of the melodic range. Ask children to think of ways in which melody might continue to expand. Some may suggest that we could add more than twelve tones to the chromatic scale. This is possible, of course, and has been done. Our present tonal system is based on twelve half steps to the octave. Some tonal systems in the Orient are based on quarter steps. Contemporary Western composers have also used this means of expanding their melodic range. Another way to expand melodies is to increase the range from high to low. This is possible with electronically controlled instruments. (See page 187.)

A second important concept is that all melody is based on some kind of **tonal organization.** The different tones which make up a melody are always selected because they belong to some kind of a group. No composer selects the tones of his melody by accident. The choice determines the specific tones that will be used in that melody.

The sound of the church modes can be easily illustrated at the piano. Start on each of the six white keys C, D, E, F, G, A in turn and play up eight tones, always playing on the white keys. Notice that the mode which starts on C is the same as the major scale and the mode which starts on A is the same as the natural minor scale. The Dorian mode which starts on D is often heard in folk music as well as in ancient religious chant. Modal songs are found on pages 94, 108, and 193.

In reference to the whole tone scale, review the composition by Debussy on page 95.

Additional discussion of contemporary tonal organizations is included in "Music of the Twentieth Century," pages 160-162.

Elements of Music: Harmony

As children read the opening paragraph, ask them to think of music they have heard which contains no harmony. "La Tarara" (page 133) and "O Come, O Come, Emmanuel" (page 193) are two examples of songs in their books which are single-line melodies.

To help children grasp the concept of **consonance** and **dissonance,** play the chord pattern illustrated in their book. Pause after each chord and ask children to describe their reaction. DOES THE CHORD LEAVE YOU WITH A FEELING OF REST (CONSONANCE) OR DO YOU WANT TO MOVE ON TO ANOTHER CHORD (DISSONANCE)? **Dissonance** is a sound which creates tension and demands to move on. Whether or not a chord is dissonant depends upon its placement in a chord sequence, as well as the sound of the chord itself.

Like melody, the history of harmony has been one of expansion through a variety of ways. Some of these are described in the pupil's book: adding more thirds to chords; building chords with seconds, fourths, and fifths.

Review the construction of chords given on pages 16-17. Encourage children to experiment with the construction of different kinds of chords as described in their book. Listen to recordings of various songs and study the harmonic progressions. Notice how the harmony adds interest and helps to build to a climax.

The last phrase of "Evening Prayer," (page 87,) is a good example of how constantly changing harmonies can help to build a musical climax. Compare this song with the mood of "He's Got the Whole World in His Hands" in which the chords are sustained for two measures.

Elements of Music: Harmony

Harmony is the most recent of the elements of music. Primitive man played or sang only one melody at a time. If more than one pitch occurred at once, it was probably an accident!

Harmony is created by combining tones so that they sound together. The combined sounds create feelings of **consonance,** or rest, and **dissonance,** or unrest.

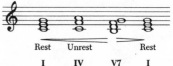

The harmony we are most accustomed to hearing was developed during the sixteenth and seventeenth centuries. This kind of harmony is usually created by combining three tones to form a chord in which the tones are a third apart. The chords used most frequently are those based on steps 1, 4, and 5. However, composers use chords built on every step of the scale.

Modern composers have used new harmonies just as they have used new rhythms and melodies.

They have added more thirds to chords.

They have sounded chords from two different keys at the same time.

They have built chords of tones a fourth apart, a fifth apart, or a second apart.

Unity and variety are important in our lives. We enjoy doing one thing and then doing something else. We like doing things in new ways.

Our minds function in a similar way when we listen to music. We enjoy the challenge of hearing something new and the satisfaction of hearing something already experienced.

In planning music which has unity and variety, composers have developed various designs. It is important that the listener understand design in music so that he can notice the details which give beauty to the composition. In discovering the design in music, listen for introductions, bridge passages, and special endings which signal changes and help outline the structure. Listen for different sections or divisions in the music. In a song the sections are short. In a longer composition the sections may be long.

Listen for changes in harmony. A common way of giving variety to music is to go into a new key. In two-part form, for example, the composer often uses one home tone in the first section and another home tone in the second section. One section of a composition may be in a major key, and another section may be in a minor key.

Listen for changes in melody which help the composer build the design:

decoration of the melody,
imitation of the melody in different choral or instrumental voices,
extension of the melody,
changes in the rhythmic movement of the melody,
introduction of a new melody.

Find examples of these common musical forms in songs you know and instrumental compositions you have heard:

two-part form, referred to as A B
three-part form, referred to as A B A
rondo form, referred to as A B A C A
theme and variations
fugue
sonata allegro form, with sections referred to as exposition, development, and recapitulation.

The first paragraph may be the basis for discussion of the principle of unity and variety. Encourage thoughtful observation of the principle as related to daily life and to design in nature, architecture, painting, and even in clothing. Children may recall the example of the tree with a main trunk and many branches which are similar, yet different.

From the second paragraph, encourage discussion of design in music. Relate design to basic structure. The basic structure depends upon what it is the composer wishes to express. After years of experimentation with the various ways of expressing musical ideas, some basic forms have been established.

From these examples children may deduce that a long process of development took place as composers tried to express musical ideas with various combinations of instruments and voices. A number of basic forms resulted from this development. Experimentation and growth are still in process. Contemporary composers sometimes use basic designs already outlined in older compositions, or they sometimes deviate greatly from the basic designs as they seek expression of their own musical ideas. Nevertheless, the principle of unity and variety is basic to all design.

In other lessons, as a special project, have the class recall and locate specific examples of each form or element of form referred to on the pupil's page. Use recordings to review the examples. Below are examples pertaining to the different musical forms.

Introductions	
short introduction	the beginning of the folk dance melody "Totur," page 116.
long introduction	an overture to an opera, page 101.
Bridge passages	"Farandole," page 26.
Sections	the "Kalvelis" folk dance melody, page 24.
	the "William Tell Overture," page 7.
	the song "The Trout," pages 78-79.
Movements	the one movement of the "Piano Quintet in A," page 80.
	the two movements of the "Symphony No. 40 in G Minor," pages 88-89.

(Continued on page 151.)

The Percussion Family

The most ancient of all instruments are the percussion family (whose sounds are made by striking or shaking). The earliest percussive sound-makers were our hands and feet. There is evidence that primitive man made much use of these in his first experiments with rhythmic sound. Next came sound-making instruments of wood, gourds, skin, clay, and metal, depending on which materials were easily available.

Percussion instruments in the modern orchestra are of two types: those of definite (tuned) pitch and those of indefinite (non-tuned) pitch.

Instruments of Definite Pitch

Timpani: The timpani, the only drums of definite pitch, are some of the most important percussion instruments in the orchestra. They are like huge copper kettles with skins stretched over the tops; hence, they are also called "kettledrums." Screws placed around the top change the tension of the skin head and alter the pitch. Foot pedals are also used to alter the pitch and may be employed for rapid pitch change.

A minimum of two timpani are found in the orchestra. They are used to build up the orchestral volume of sound, to create dramatic suspense, and to add to thunderous climaxes. Mallets of different types—made of sponge, felt, rubber, or wood—are used to produce special effects.

Glockenspiel (Orchestra Bells): Horizontal steel bars are arranged ladder-like in two parallel rows and are struck with various kinds of mallets. Orchestra bells have a bright, crystalline quality. The penetrating tone color is used sparingly for special effects.

Xylophone: The xylophone consists of a series of tuned wooden bars struck with wooden mallets. Its dry, hollow sound is somewhat grotesque and wooden in quality. The **marimba,** a type of xylophone, has a softer tone quality.

Chimes: Metal tubes are suspended from a metal frame and struck with a hammer. They produce a solemn sound reminiscent of church bells.

Celesta: The celesta looks like a miniature upright piano. Its sound is created by striking a series of steel plates with tiny hammers which are controlled by a keyboard. Its silvery, liquid tone is delicate and is especially suitable for light, ethereal effects. One of its first appearances was in the "Dance of the Sugar Plum Fairy" from *The Nutcracker Suite* by Tchaikovsky.

Instruments of Indefinite Pitch

Snare or **Side Drum:** The snare drum is a shallow cylinder closed at both ends by skin. Gut or wire snares are stretched across one head of the drum. They vibrate against the skin when the other head is struck. The crisp, rattling tone of the snare drum is often used for martial effects. It accentuates the rhythm and can also create suspense.

Bass Drum: The bass drum is essentially a huge snare drum without snares. The pitch is very low and, because of the great body of vibrating air enclosed, the sound is exceedingly resonant and powerful.

Cymbals: Cymbals have come to us virtually unchanged in form since Biblical times. The two large, slightly cupped discs of brass add to the brilliance of an orchestral climax when struck together.

Triangle: The triangle is a rod of steel bent into a triangular-shaped form and open at one of the corners. It is struck with a thin steel bar, producing a light, tinkling sound which can cut through the sound of the full orchestra.

Gong: This large disc of hammered metal is of Chinese origin and is struck with a soft mallet. Its sound can be ominous and solemn or soft and mysterious.

Tambourine: This instrument is actually a miniature drum with a single parchment (skin) head. Small metal discs are inserted into the wooden hoop, creating a metallic jangling sound when shaken or struck.

Other percussion instruments are discussed on pages xi, xii and xiii.

Full page painting in pupil's book.
See page 209 for explanation of art.

142

Music of Asia and the Orient

Music in the Far East today is a strange mixture of the very old and the very new. The old music is composed of tones from scales unlike Western scales and rhythms unlike Western rhythms. It is often sung in a nasal voice and played on instruments of ancient origin. The people still enjoy music composed many centuries ago and played on the instruments used by their forefathers. In the cities one can also hear music played on Western orchestral instruments and songs that sound like American popular songs. We can see children learning to play the violin, and we can hear symphony orchestras. Operas, symphonies, and other Western classics are heard on the radio and in concert halls.

The Chinese regard music as an image of the universe. They believe music expresses the accord of heaven and earth. The importance of music was taught by Confucius, the Chinese philosopher who lived in 550 B.C. He taught that music should represent great virtues in man's life including humanity, justice, charity, wisdom, and honesty.

The old music of India, China, and Japan is based on ancient modes of five, seven, or sometimes six tones. Decoration is a feature of the melodies. Long notes are adorned with ornamental shorter notes. Improvisation is an important part of Oriental music. Musicians improvise as they perform by developing original musical material or by adding melodic and rhythmic embellishments. Music for the theater developed very early in the Orient, and there is a great deal of theatrical music still performed in the style of ancient court music. Percussion instruments of many kinds often accompany the dances from this part of the world.

Although the Japanese have carefully preserved the great tradition of their own music, Western music has been included in their musical studies since the late nineteenth century. As a result, Japan has the most widespread tradition in Western music among all Asian countries. Western folk songs have been enjoyed in Japan for more than half a century. Today the young Japanese of the big cities also delight in our popular music.

Read the pupil's page with the class. Encourage comments concerning Eastern people, customs, and geography. Discuss especially the "old" and "new" aspects of the life—the remote villages with primitive tools and housing and the big cities that are modern and efficient. Help the class analyze the reasons why old and new music would also be heard.

The Chinese beliefs regarding music can be seen in various ways. For example, their instruments are divided symbolically into eight classes according to their materials. Instruments made of metal represent dampness; those made of stone represent heaven; those of clay, earth; of skin, water; of silk, fire; of wood, wind; of gourd, thunder; of bamboo, mountain.

In discussing the modes which form the basis of Oriental music, children may be interested to know that Chinese music is usually based on either seven-tone (heptatonic) or five-tone (pentatonic) modes. Most of the Chinese compositions we hear in the West usually sound pentatonic. In a Chinese pentatonic scale, no half steps are used. In some of the Japanese pentatonic modes, half steps are used. The well-known Japanese song "Cherry Bloom," which appears in *Exploring Music 3,* is based on such a scale.

Engage the children in a discussion of the meaning of terms used in their book: decoration, improvisation, embellishments. As an introduction to this section of the book, play the recording of the Chinese song "Purple Bamboo," the Japanese folk dance tune "Tanko Bushi," and the "Ancient Classical Chinese Music." With these sounds as a basis, discuss the characteristics of Asian and Oriental music stated in the third paragraph of the pupil's page.

Encourage children to think of world changes brought about by air transportation, television, and radio. Discuss with them the fact that customs of living are becoming similar around the world. Help them to name unique contributions of various peoples and to think of ways of preserving them.

The Purple Bamboo

Tonality: Pentatonic (D E F♯ A B)
Starting Tone: A
Meter: 2/4 (2/♩)
Piano accompaniment on page 285

FOLK STYLE: Read the discussion "Music of China," page 146, and ask children to identify musical characteristics in this song as they listen to the recording. It is based on the pentatonic scale and the rhythm matches the accents of the words. Phrases are irregular and alternate between four, three, and two measures in length.

* **MELODY:** Follow the suggestion in the pupil's book and locate the tones which make up the pentatonic scale (D E F♯ A B). Review the structure of steps in this scale: whole-whole-whole and a half-whole. Practice singing up and down the pentatonic scale on the syllable "loo" until children feel at home in this tonality. Sing the melody on a neutral syllable.

Assign some children to learn this melody on recorder, bells, or flute. See page viii, "Exploring Music through Melody and Harmony Instruments."

Discuss reasons why Chinese songs sometimes seem monotonous to our ears. One reason may be due to the limited number of scale tones. This does not allow for as much melodic variation as we are accustomed to hearing in our melodies which are based on eight-tone scales. Actually, Oriental music is very interesting when we learn to listen for constantly changing tone color and the variations in rhythm.

HARMONY: Encourage children to improvise a countermelody using the steps of the pentatonic scale. They can play the melody on the bells as the class sings the song.

Discuss ways to make their countermelody interesting. The melodic line should have a contour that is different from that of the main melody. It should also contrast rhythmically.

RHYTHM: Add the percussion accompaniment given in the pupil's book. Encourage children to improvise variations after they are familiar with these patterns.

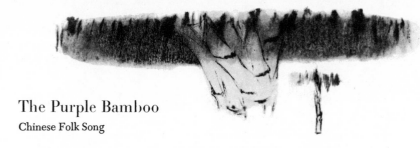

The Purple Bamboo

Chinese Folk Song

Find the tones which make up the pentatonic scale on which this melody is based. Improvise an accompaniment using these same tones.

Play it on a flute or recorder.

1. See I bring to you pur-ple bam-boo shoot,
2. You must try and grow like the bam-boo tall,

Now 'twill make a love-ly flute;
Then those part-ing lips so small

But those lips so small Can-not play at all
Soon will play the flute Made from bam-boo shoot;

On a love-ly gold-en __ flute.
Sil-v'ry tunes will gent-ly __ fall.

Refrain

Ee-tee-tee, Soon will come the hap-py

1. day.
2. day. My son the flute will play.

Record 5 Side A Band 5. VOICE: soprano.
ACCOMPANIMENT: ch'in, recorder, percussion.
FORM: Introduction, 4 meas.; Vocal, v. 1; Interlude, 4 meas.; Vocal, v. 2 (percussion instruments play parts in Pupil's Book); Coda, 4 meas.

144

Add this percussion accompaniment to give an oriental flavor to the song.

Haiku Poetry

All of the arts are important to the Oriental people. At one time it was considered important for an educated young man or woman to be able to write poetry, arrange flowers, and paint, as well as perform on some musical instrument.

One well-known kind of Japanese poetry is known as "haiku." These poems are usually three lines long; the first line must contain five syllables, the second line seven syllables, and the third line five syllables. In translation to English, the number of syllables does not always remain the same. These little poems are impressions characterized by their imaginative use of colorful words.

Some children may wish to choose one of the poems to set to music. Suggest that they should keep the music in character with the origin of the poem. Make use of pentatonic scales. Encourage children to follow the inflection of the words in their rhythmic organization and avoid forcing the patterns into the same meter throughout as they might do with a poem of the Western world. Suggest that they add a percussion accompaniment using bells, gongs, cymbals, etc.

Little Gray Cuckoo

Sing and sing; and fly and fly
Oh, so much to do!

by Basho

Skylark

Singing clear and loud.
A skylark makes the silver
Ripples on the cloud.

by Seien

Waterfowl

The waterfowl
Lays its beak in its breast
And sleeps as it floats.

by Ginko

Snow

I could eat it!
This snow that falls
so softly, so softly.

by Issa

Music of China
Ancient Chinese Music

Read and discuss the first paragraph in the pupil's book. Help children develop an appreciation for the complexity of Oriental culture and the influence it has had on Western culture. Stress the antiquity of Chinese culture represented in the complexity and sophistication of ancient classical composition. Suggest that children research to discover other examples of the antiquity of Chinese civilization. For example, one reason the Chinese could have such elaborate instruments over three thousand years ago was because by that time they had discovered how to combine tin and copper to make bronze. This is a necessary process before bells, cymbals, and gongs can be developed. The Chinese had discovered the process for making fine porcelain and paper, developed a postal system, and invented printing by the time Jesus was born. None of these evidences of civilization was apparent in the West until much later.

To the Chinese, music is an image of the universe and it plays an important part in Chinese philosophy and in all of their rituals. The Chinese concern for tone color arises from the fact that each class of instruments has a symbolic purpose. (See the discussion of Chinese music on page 143.)

As children listen to this example of temple music, draw attention to various characteristics of ancient classical music. The contrasts in tone color, the single-line melody which is made up of phrases of different lengths, and the complexity of the rhythms are all typical of Chinese music. Note the absence of harmony as we think of it. Unlike Western music, Chinese music is conceived linearly rather than vertically.

And the Fallen Petals

BY CHOU WEN-CHUNG
BORN 1923

Discuss reasons for the influence of the West on the East in the last one hundred years. Ask children to study the time line to determine when Western influence first began to make itself felt in China and Japan. Discuss how modern communication and transportation have speeded the interchange of ideas between the West and the East.

As children listen to "And the Fallen Petals," discuss the traits found in the music which are representative of the two cultures. Note the

Music of China

Ancient Chinese Music

The Chinese musical culture is ancient and has its origin in traditions which began centuries before the time of Christ. From the seventh to the tenth centuries, huge orchestras with as many as a thousand musicians performed at ceremonies of state. In the temples, music by a few performers formed an important part of the religious ritual.

Listen to the example of ancient Chinese music on your record. It is performed in the style of temple music. Notice the changing instrumental tone colors, an important element in Chinese musical composition. In this performance you will hear a number of percussion instruments: high-pitched metal bells, cymbals, and drums of different sizes. A flute, *hsaio*, plays the high melody. A different tone color is added by the *seh*, a kind of harp.

And the Fallen Petals

by Chou Wen-chung

Chou Wen-chung was born in China and now lives in the United States. His compositions blend qualities of both Eastern and Western cultures.

The title of this composition is taken from a poem by a Chinese poet of the eighth century:

> All through the night
> Such noise of wind and rain
> And the fallen petals
> Who knows how many!

The composer describes the section of the composition on your record in this way, "A storm breaks and the furious wind drives the dazed petals far and wide."

As you listen, notice how the composer contrasts and combines the tone colors and ranges of his orchestral instruments. Listen for the wide leaps of the melody and the sharp contrasts in instrumental color.

Record 11   Side A   Band 2.
2a (Buddhist Chanting).
2b Louisville Symphony Orchestra,
Robert Whitney, conductor.

146

This song is a ballad of Tsugaru, and its delicate beauty is typical of songs of northern Japan. The Honsu port of Tosagata was called Tosa long ago. Here, ships carrying rice and lumber to other parts of the world were a common sight. The song is a nostalgic one describing the feelings of the singer as he remembers the view of the city which includes the sandy hill or dune.

Dune of Tosa

Japanese Folk Song

To - sa no —— Su - na - ya - ma ——

na - a - a ya - e

Ko - me na - ra —— yo - ka - ro na ——

Ni - shi - i - i no

Be - en - za - i - shu - u - u ny - a - e

Ta - a - da - tsu - u ma - sho

Ta - da tsu - ma - sho ——

Record 5 Side A Band 6. VOICE: soprano.
ACCOMPANIMENT: koto, recorder, percussion.
FORM: Introduction, *4 meas.;* Vocal.

existence of the same traits discussed under "Ancient Chinese Music." The contrasts in tone color, irregular phrases, complex rhythms, and absence of harmony are all apparent in "And the Fallen Petals." In this music one finds no melody in the conventional sense but a succession of intervals which is passed from one instrument to another. Although it is not apparent in the example on our recording, this characteristic is also typical of ancient Chinese music. The difference between the music of the two cultures lies, of course, in the use of traditional Western instruments which makes possible ranges and tone colors not found in the traditional Chinese instruments.

Many of the characteristics found in Chou Wen-chung's composition, while reminiscent of the classical music of China, can also be found in contemporary music of the Western world. Compare the sound of this composition with that of Webern, page 161. In both compositions the concern with tone color and the use of interval patterns rather than an extended melody are the basis for the composition.

Dune of Tosa

Tonality: Pentatonic (D E F A B♭)
Starting Tone: F
Meter: 2/4 (²♩)
Piano accompaniment on page 286

* FOLK STYLE: This song from Japan reveals some of the same musical characteristics observed in Chinese folk songs. There is little melodic or rhythmic repetition; the phrases are irregular in length; the rhythm matches the accents of the words. The melodic turns are typical of Japanese music. The topic of longing for home is a common one.

* MELODY: Ask children to study the notation and discover that the melody uses only five tones (D E F A B♭): whole-half-two wholes-half. This Japanese pentatonic scale makes use of a half step between tones (in contrast to the Chinese pentatonic modes in which no half steps are used).

Some classes may prefer to only listen to this song while other classes may wish to study the melody and learn to sing it. Listen to the recording several times before singing it on the syllable "la." The Japanese words are written phonetically. Use the following chart as a guide to the pronunciation.

a.........ah, e.........ay, i.........ee,
o.........oh, u.........oo.

Si Pilemon

Key: G   Starting Tone: D (5)
Meter: $\frac{4}{4}$ ($\frac{4}{}$)
Piano accompaniment on page 288

* FOLK STYLE: This amusing song tells of an activity which is very important in all island countries. Discuss the relationship of a country's geographical location to its major occupation and thus the effect on its music. People in island countries sing of sailing and fishing; people on the plains of South America and the United States sing of herding cattle.

RHYTHM: Learn the rhythm by following the steps on page 9. Practice clapping the dotted rhythms. Chant the words lightly.

MELODY: Learn the melody as the class reviews the steps on page 13. Notice the sequential nature of the melody. Phrases one and two make up a sequence; another can be found in the last five measures of the song.

* HARMONY: Some children may sing the descant after the main melody has been learned. Compare the melodic contour of the two melodies. Notice that the descant is usually a third above the main melody. Divide the class into two groups or assign the descant to the girls. Notice that the voices are in unison on the first note; the lower part then skips up a fourth while the higher part skips up a sixth. Practice this skip until the children are sure of the interval. Then encourage the descant singers to sing the descant at sight while the rest of the class sings the melody.

Si Pilemon

Philippine Folk Song
Words Adapted

One would expect this land of islands to have many fishing songs. The words of this song reflect not only the importance of fishing, but also a carefree, playful mood.

Study the changing rhythm patterns carefully. You may wish to review the instructions for reading rhythm on page 9 as you study the song.

Record 5   Side A   Band 7.   VOICES: children's choir.
ACCOMPANIMENT: woodwind quintet.
FORM: Introduction, *3 meas.;* Vocal; Instrumental (vocal beginning on measure 12); Instrumental fade-out.

148

What they gave him was a pen - ny,

What they gave him was a pen - ny; That day he had not

noth - ing ___ at all. ___

an - y good things to eat at all. ___

Music of the Balinese Orchestra

On the tiny islands of Java and Bali one may hear music which is as elaborate and carefully organized as any found in the Western World. The Balinese **gamelan** rivals the European orchestra in the variety of instruments and complexity of its music.

Although most of the instruments in a gamelan are percussion, the many tone colors create a musical sound which is never monotonous. There are various kinds of **metallophones**, pitched percussion instruments made of metal. Gongs of all sizes and pitches form an important section. Some orchestras include a **rebab**, a two-stringed fiddle. There are also various types of drums, small cymbals, bells, and xylophones.

Gambangan

Listen to "Gambangan" and study its design. Each group of instruments has its special role. After a short introduction, the large metallophones play the basic melody at the same time as the small metallophones are playing ornamentations and variations of the same melody. Two small, two-headed drums set the tempo. Changing patterns are played on pitched bamboo rattles. The end of each melodic phrase is marked by the deep-voiced gong.

As you listen, enjoy the strange expressive music which is as colorful and exotic as the beautiful islands from which it comes.

Record 11 Side A Band 3.

Music of the Balinese Orchestra

Play the recording before children read the discussion in their book. Discuss the children's reactions. WHAT COUNTRY DO YOU THINK THIS MUSIC COMES FROM? WHAT DIFFERENT KINDS OF INSTRUMENTS DO YOU HEAR? When children have made various suggestions, read the first two paragraphs in the book. Locate Bali and Java on a map of the world. Stress the important fact that these islands, which in so many ways seem primitive to us, have music which is complex and sophisticated.

Gambangan

Listen again to the recording and notice the things listed in the text. Children's fascination with this music will grow after repeated hearings. Return to the composition on several different occasions. Suggest that children try to identify and tap some of the rhythms that they hear. Notice the design of the composition. It is very similar to music which a Western orchestra might play. The composition is divided into three sections with an introduction and a coda. The middle section contrasts with the opening section. The last section is similar to the first.

Guide children to listen for the sustained melody played on the larger metallophones. The sound of these instruments is mellow and darker in quality than their higher-voiced counterparts. It is difficult to hear, unless pointed out, because the rapidly moving countermelody played on the smaller metallophones is more brilliant. Since this countermelody is higher than the main melody, it is more easily heard.

Suggest that children look for information about the life and history of the people of these islands.

Mystic Lights

Key: C   Starting Tone: G (5)
Meter: $\frac{3}{4}$ ($\frac{3}{}$)
Piano accompaniment on page 290

FOLK STYLE: This song is typical of the romantic songs of Spanish flavor popular in the Philippine Islands. It should be sung in moderate tempo with a tone that is natural and unforced. It is ideal for informal singing by individuals and small groups as well as for class singing. The autoharp, imitating the sound of the guitar, would provide a good accompaniment for this song.

* **MELODY:** Play the recording and lead a discussion of the commentary in the pupil's book concerning the text and Spanish characteristics of this song. Study the words in order to understand the imagery. Play the recording again and ask the class to follow the notation and study the melody. WHICH PHRASE IS THE CLIMACTIC PHRASE OF THE SONG? (The last phrase containing the highest tone and the most important descriptive words.) IN WHAT KEY IS THE SONG? (In the key of C with no signature and ending on C.) LOOK FOR A SEQUENCE. (Second phrase is exactly like the first except that it is one tone lower.) HOW IS THE SIXTH PHRASE "BEAUTY AND FRIENDS WHO DWELL HERE WITH ME REFLECTING" DIFFERENT FROM THE SECOND PHRASE? (The rhythm is different; melody tones are the same.) WHAT EFFECT DO THE SHARPS HAVE IN THIS SONG? (The raised tones add to the romantic and sentimental style of the song.)

* **HARMONY:** When the children know the song, help them add an alto part. The first and second phrases sound well with thirds below the melody notes. The third phrase might be harmonized with the lower voice on E on the word "lights" and remaining at the interval of a sixth throughout the phrase. The entire song can be harmonized similarly.

On another day, have the children play the descant written in their book on page 151. The descant can be played on the bells (as on the recording), piano, flute, clarinet, or violin.

Mystic Lights

Philippine Folk Song
Words by Beth Landis

The Philippine Islands were ruled by Spain for many years, and this song from the Ilocano region of the islands is one of many Philippine songs which have a Spanish sound. Yet, the mystic and philosophic text is more like oriental songs and reminds us that the Philippines are really a part of Asia. Refer to page 135 and find the lines that describe the Spanish characteristics of this song. When you know the song, make up an alto part in thirds and sixths below the melody.

Here be-neath the sky I stand en-chant-ed; ____

Gar-den high a-bove with stars im-plant-ed, ____

Mys-tic lights, how fair you are! ____

Splen-dor shin-ing from a-far, ____

Mir-ror in the sky, the earth pro-tect-ing, ____

Beau-ty and friends who dwell here with me re-flect-ing, ____

Record 5   Side A   Band 8. VOICE: tenor.
ACCOMPANIMENT: 2 violins, guitar, bells, double bass.
FORM: Instrumental; Vocal; Instrumental.

Ra - diant jew - els in the heav'n a - bove,

You are the eyes of life and love! ____

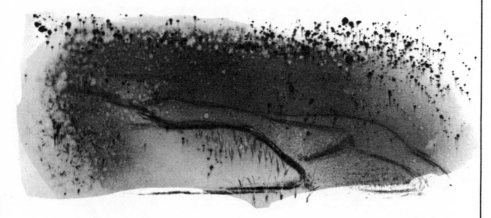

To harmonize "Mystic Lights" in another way, play this descant on any suitable melodic instrument. The bells play it on the recording.

Here be-neath the sky I stand en-chant-ed

("Elements of Music: Design" continued from page 141.)

Harmony changes	the four playings of Purcell's theme in the "Young Person's Guide to the Orchestra," pages 58-59. "The Moldau," page 98. the "Piano Quintet in A," page 80. the song "Greensleeves," page 46.
Decoration of melody	the song "My Heart Ever Faithful," page 75. the "Piano Quintet in A," page 80.
Imitation of melody	the "Fantasia in G" (imitation in voices), page 49. the song "Play on Notes" (inversion and retrograde), pages 188-189.
Extension of melody	the song "Ghost of Tom" (augmentation), page 28. the song "Cindy," pages 170-171.
Change in rhythmic movement of the melody	"Peasant Dance for Norwegian Fiddle," page 111.
Introduction of a new melody	the "Young Person's Guide to the Orchestra," pages 58-59. the "Farandole," page 26. "The Moldau," page 98.
Two-part form	the song "Shule Aroon," page 34. the song "Turn Ye to Me," page 40.
Three-part form	the song "Beautiful Dreamer," page 164. "Symphony No. 40 in G Minor," page 88.
Rondo form	the "Castillane" from "Le Cid Ballet Suite," page 136.
Theme with variations	the "Young Person's Guide to the Orchestra," pages 58-59. the "Piano Quintet in A," page 80.
Fugue	the "Young Person's Guide to the Orchestra," pages 58-59.
Sonata allegro form	"Symphony No. 40 in G Minor," page 88.

151

Tanko Bushi

Play the recording and discuss the Oriental characteristics: the nasal tone quality in the singing, the sound of the unusual instruments, the phrases of unequal length.

Ask the children to listen again and hear the four phrases. It is important that they hear the beginnings of the four phrases of the song, since the movement is designed with the phrases rather than by counting beats or accents.

   The first phrase ends with the "yoi-yoi" of the song (7 accents). The second phrase begins immediately after the "yoi-yoi" (6 accents). The third phrase begins with the highest pitches of the song (6 accents). The fourth phrase begins with the word "sa-go-ya" (8 accents).

The foot movements consist of two forward steps, two backward steps, two forward steps.

The authentic style comes in the manner of stepping. As you prepare to step on the right foot, bring it back behind the left knee, then touch right toe forward on the first accent. Bring the right foot back behind the left knee again, then step forward putting weight on the right foot on the second accent. The preliminary movement is accomplished with a slight bounce of the body as the knees bend and the foot goes behind the knee. Touching the toe and stepping on the foot are on the accents. The complete step is used in the first and fourth phrases. In the second and third phrases, touching the toe is omitted and the foot goes down with the first accent.

There is an instrumental introduction to the dance (8 accents). The dance begins each time with the singer. Do this clap pattern with each instrumental interlude: clap-wait-clap, clap, clap.

This dance is more subtle than other folk dances and demands more stylized movement. If all members of the class do not learn it easily, it is effectively done by a smaller group. Girls especially may enjoy the more delicate movements and the Oriental style of stepping.

Tanko Bushi
Japanese Coal Miner's Dance

Listen to your recording of the music for this folk dance. It is sung and played by Japanese musicians. The instruments are those used in Japan as accompaniment for the dance. Discuss the characteristics of the Japanese music which you hear. Can you hear the four phrases of the song? Do the phrases contain the same number of accents? Hear the song several times until you can raise your hands when you hear each phrase begin.

Record 10   Side B   Band 3.

152

This dance is a favorite of Japanese people. It is made up of the work rhythms of coal miners: digging, shoveling, looking ahead, pushing the cart. One person leads the dance and the others follow, single file, around the circle. The song is sung four times, and the dancers do the same patterns of movement each time. The dancers clap a pattern of rhythm during the instrumental interludes.

Practice the four movements of the dance. When you know the movements and can do them in the rhythm of the music, dance the entire dance. You might enjoy singing the words "yoi-yoi" which come at the end of the first and fourth phrases of the song.

If there is a folk dance group in your community, invite a member to demonstrate the dance for your class.

Practice the entire foot pattern:

> Lift, toe, lift, step (right)
> Lift, toe, lift, step (left)
> Lift, step (right)
> Lift, step (left)
> Lift, step (backward right)
> Lift, step (backward left)
> Lift, toe, lift, step (right)
> Lift, toe, lift, step (left)

The hand movements can then be added.

With the first phrase of the music, dig to the right with the accents when you touch right toe and when you step on right foot (two digs). Dig to the left in the same way.

With the second phrase of the music, throw coal over the right shoulder (once) when you step on right foot. Throw coal over the left shoulder (once) when you step on the left foot.

With the third phrase of the music, shade your eyes with your left hand as you step backward on right foot. Shade your eyes with your right hand as you step backward on left foot. (Each time, let the other arm be straight, pointing behind you, palm up.)

With the fourth phrase of the music, push with both hands with the accents when you touch right toe and when you step on right foot (two pushes). Push with both hands with left step in the same way.

Keeping the same foot position, let arms drop to sides, then raise hands to chest height in a horizontal line as the song ends.

Suliram

Key: E♭ Starting Tone: E♭ (1)
Autoharp Key: F Starting Tone: F (1)
Meter: ₵ (2/♩)
Piano accompaniment on page 292

FOLK STYLE: Compare this Indonesian song with other Oriental folk songs and with the music of Europe. WHAT CHARACTERISTICS MAY HAVE RESULTED FROM THE INFLUENCE OF THE EUROPEANS? (The major tonality, the use of repetition, etc.) WHAT IS TYPICAL OF ORIENTAL MUSIC? (The rhythm which changes to match the rhythm of the words and the irregular phrase lengths.)

After children have listened to the Balinese orchestra, they may add a "gamelan" accompaniment to this song even though it is a Westernized melody. Use a light-sounding drum to establish the tempo. Someone may learn to play the melody on the xylophone or bells. Play the finger cymbals to mark the end of each phrase and softly strike a deep-pitched gong at the end of each larger section. Pluck the root notes of the autoharp chords on a string instrument to suggest the sound of the *rebab*.

* **EXPRESSION:** This song is a lullaby. Discuss the fact that music is used by people everywhere in the same way to express similar feelings. Ask children to recall lullabies they know from other countries. Discuss the similarities and differences between the music of the lullabies they name.

Discuss other kinds of music found in different countries. For example, work songs, songs of nature, and songs of home and worship are found throughout the world. Songs which express feelings of love, loneliness, sorrow, or patriotism are a part of all countries' music. Suggest that children study their books and make lists of the songs of different countries that express the same feelings. Such a list could form the basis of a bulletin board display. A program to be shared with another class or with parents might also be planned around this theme.

MELODY: After the children have studied the notation and have listened to the recording, ask them to sing the melody on a neutral syllable or with numbers. Learn to pronounce the Indonesian words by listening to the recording. The Indonesian words are written phonetically.

Suliram

Indonesian Folk Song

The melody of this Indonesian lullaby is more European than Asian. It shows the influence of the Portuguese sailors who first visited the Indonesian coast and the Dutch who later settled there. The words say: "Suliram, the sweet Suliram, hush my baby; look there, my sweet baby. Now the sun rises very high. I see a water buffalo slain. For a long time I have looked for you. And now I have found you."

Sing this song unaccompanied or with a soft autoharp accompaniment.

Record 5 Side B Band 1. VOICE: soprano.
ACCOMPANIMENT: recorder, percussion, koto.
FORM: Introduction, *1 meas.*; Vocal.

154

Su - dah - lah la - ma sai - ya___ men - cha - ri. ___

D.S. al Fine

Ba - ru se ka - rang sai - ya___ men - da - pat. La su - li -

Arirang

Korean Folk Song
Words Adapted

The pentatonic quality of this song reveals the Chinese influence on Korean music. "Arirang" is one of the most popular songs of Korea. Many Americans who have lived in Korea know the song. It grew out of a legend about Arirang Pass near the city of Seoul.

1. A - ri - rang,___ A - ri - rang,___ A - ri - rang,___ A - ri - rang,___
2. A - ri - rang,___ A - ri - rang,___ A - ri - rang,___ A - ri - rang,___

A - ri - rang,___ A - ri - rang,___ A - ri - rang fair.
A - ri - rang,___ A - ri - rang,___ A - ri - rang fair.

Through the pass___ I watch you___ go___ there. ___
Here I wait for you, wait, wait___ and___ stare. ___

A - ri - rang,___ A - ri - rang,___ A - ri - rang fair.
A - ri - rang,___ A - ri - rang,___ A - ri - rang fair.

Record 5   Side B   Band 2.   VOICE: soprano.
ACCOMPANIMENT: kum, recorder, percussion.
FORM: Introduction, *4 meas.;* Vocal, *v. 1;* Interlude, *4 meas.*
Vocal, *v. 2;* Instrumental fade-out.

* FOLK STYLE: Reread the description of "Music of China" found on page 146. Ask children to listen to the recording and identify qualities in this Korean folk song that are also typical of Chinese music. The pentatonic melody, the uneven phrases, the turns in the melodic line, and the rhythms which flow with the accent of the words are all characteristic of Korean music as well as music of China.

* EXPRESSION: This lovely ballad is a favorite among the Korean people. It is also a favorite of the many Americans who have visited Korea. The words describe the feelings of someone who has been left behind and who must wait for the return of his loved one. Ask the children to recall other songs which deal with this same feeling. ("Johnny Has Gone for a Soldier" and "Shule Aroon.")

* MELODY: Determine the pentatonic scale upon which this song is based (G A B D E). Sing the melody on a neutral syllable, then with words.

Suggest that some children improvise a descant using the tones of the pentatonic scale while the others sing the melody.

FORM: Determine the phrase structure. The first phrase is three measures long; the second phrase is five measures; each of the last two phrases is four measures long. Mark the end of each phrase with a stroke of the finger cymbals.

Ancient Musical Instruments

From earliest times, man has used musical instruments. Primitive man had drums, panpipes, and even rudimentary harps. The Bible mentions such instruments as the psaltery, timbrel, harp, and cymbals to be used in praise of God. It is known that the Greeks used the lyre, harp, a reed pipe called the *aulos,* as well as brass and percussion instruments. These were intended to provide music for both religious and recreational activities.

In the Middle Ages, composers were chiefly concerned with writing church music. Most of the musical literature that has come to us from this period is vocal rather than instrumental. However, instruments were often combined with voices or sometimes substituted for them.

By the sixteenth century, the **organ** had undergone great development from a crude instrument, often lacking a keyboard, to one of considerable complexity. The organs in Germany were the most advanced, possessing a pedalboard and, at times, two keyboards. The organs in Italy, France, and England developed more slowly and were deficient in many respects, especially in not having pedalboards.

Another keyboard instrument, the **harpsichord,** flourished in the Renaissance and baroque era. The characteristic metallic tone was produced by plucking the strings with a quill attached to a jack, which in turn was activated by a key. Members of the harpsichord family had different sizes and shapes and, based on these differences, were called virginals, spinets, and harpsichords. While the harpsichord possessed a large enough tone to be used in concerts, the **clavichord,** due to its small volume, was used primarily in the home. The method of tone production of this instrument was markedly different from that of the harpsichord. The strings were struck or pressed by a metal tangent attached directly to the end of a key. The clavichord and harpsichord were the forerunners of the modern piano. This new instrument, whose strings were struck by hammers, was invented about 1710. However, all three existed side by side until the late eighteenth century. In our own times, the harpsichord has again emerged, both in popular and in serious music. (Listen to "My Heart Ever Faithful" on the song recording.)

The **lute,** an ancient instrument similar to the modern guitar, was originally brought from Persia. Interest in the instrument gradually spread over the entire continent. Schools of lute performers and composers flourished in Spain and Italy, and later in France and England. One of the most renowned of English lute composers was John Dowland, the author of "My Lady Hunsdon's Puffe."

The body of the lute is shaped like a pear cut in half, the stem of the pear representing the fingerboard. Unlike the violin, the lute has no bridge, and the fingerboard has frets; that is, raised strips of wood which facilitate finding the finger positions for the notes. The strings were plucked by the fingers, producing a gentle, subdued tone. Members of the lute family varied in size from very large to quite small.

Another string instrument was the **viol,** a descendant of the medieval vielle, or fiedel. The two main types of viols were the **viola da gamba,** or "leg viol," and its smaller counterpart, the **viola da braccia,** or "arm viol." The latter was similar to the violin but was held upright on the knee, not under the chin. The viola da gamba, or bass viol, was larger and, therefore, was held between the knees like a cello. These ancestors of the violin family differed from them in that they had flat backs, fretted fingerboards, and six strings instead of four. The bows curved outward from the hair, unlike modern violin bows. The viol possessed a tone that was more sombre and less brilliant than that produced by the modern violin. A set of viols of various sizes was called a **chest of viols,** after the method of storing them as a set in a chest or cabinet. (Listen to the recording of Ferrabosco's "Fantasia in G" on the appreciation records.)

The **recorder** family, too, included instruments of various sizes and ranges. A **consort of recorders** might contain from four to eight different recorders. A precursor of the modern transverse flute, the wooden recorder was end-blown like a whistle. Although used as a concert instrument in the baroque period, the soft-voiced recorder was later superseded by the brighter and more resonant flute. Today, many amateur players find pleasure in performing recorder music with their friends, just as might have been done in the sixteenth and seventeenth centuries.

Other wind instruments prominent in the baroque period were the **shawm, pommer,** and **bombarde,** roughly equivalent to the modern-day oboe, bassoon, and contrabassoon. All members of this family were played with a double reed. The sound quality was rather coarse and raucous in contrast to the more refined sound we now expect from the woodwind family.

Brass instruments intended primarily for use in church or out-of-doors were the **sackbut,** an ancient trombone, and the **cornett,** a wooden trumpet sometimes covered with leather. Percussion instruments, such as the snare drum, were usually reserved only for military music.

Full page painting in pupil's book.
See page 209 for explanation of art.

More Music to Explore

As you have studied music of different parts of the world, you have discovered that each country has distinct musical characteristics. Climate, geography, and national history have an effect upon the mood, style, rhythm, and melody of a nation's songs and dances. Much composed music also reflects national individuality.

Much of the music of our country has its roots in Europe. The music of the English countryside can be heard in the ballads of the Appalachian mountaineers. The sound of Spanish rhythms is common in Texas and New Mexico, and in Minnesota the music shows a Scandinavian influence. Some American composers have written music based on traditional European styles.

Music in the United States also has its own special qualities. The songs of the cowboy, the spirituals of the Southern Negro, and the work songs of the riverboatman are examples of America's unique folk music. Jazz is also unique American music. It is a blend of the dances brought by the Frenchmen, the hymn tunes of the English settlers, and the rhythms of the African Negro.

In the twentieth century, composers all over the world have sought to develop new musical styles. They have organized music in different ways, using new kinds of melodies, rhythms, and harmonies. Some composers have created music with sounds made possible by electronically controlled machines. The possibility of music composition by computers has also been explored.

As you continue to study the many different kinds of music, you will realize that there are always new and exciting musical paths to follow. There is always "more music to explore"!

Much of the music included in this section of the book is from the United States. As children read this page, help them to realize the unique qualities of American music and the contribution that Americans have made to music.

Read the pupil's page aloud with the class. Reread each paragraph in order to discuss each idea separately. Ask the class to name any examples of both folk songs and composed music which express national individuality. Have the children look through their book to familiarize them with the countries and regions of the world which are represented. Encourage the children to comment about their personal preferences and interests and to give reasons for their choices.

Discuss the fact that our folk music embodies qualities found in folk music of every section of the world. Ask children to think of specific examples of American folk music which reflect musical characteristics of other countries. Help the class to have some idea of the extent to which our country is populated by people who are, at most, a few generations from their national origin.

American composed music has its roots in Europe as American folk music does. Many American composers have studied in Europe and the sharing of ideas continues. Although the electronic music which is discussed on pages 186-187 was composed in this country, the first electronic musical experiments were made in Europe.

As we have become a more sophisticated country with our own musical contributions in jazz (page 173) and musical comedy (page 180), we have influenced the compositions of musicians in Europe and the Orient (Milhaud, page 177; Bulent Arel, page 187). Gradually the musical differences between countries are disappearing. It is often difficult today to identify the national origin of the composer by listening to his music.

The last paragraph in the pupil's book sums up the attitude which we hope the children will develop: that music is always exciting; that there is always another musical path to follow. Take this opportunity to discuss with the children their specific musical interests and ambitions. They will soon be going into junior high school. Discuss the possibilities of musical participation in their new school. Discuss ways that they can continue to explore music as individuals. Suggest that they make a bulletin board to show different ways one can explore music within his own community.

The Night Piece

Key: G minor   Starting Tone: G (1)
Meter: ¢ (4/4)
No piano accompaniment

* MUSICAL STYLE: Read the discussion in the pupil's book and comment on the fact that, although the words are very old, the music is very new. Listen to the recording. HOW WOULD YOU KNOW, BY LISTENING, THAT THIS MUSIC WAS NOT WRITTEN DURING ENGLAND'S GOLDEN AGE? DOES IT SOUND DIFFERENT FROM THE SONGS YOU LEARNED WHEN STUDYING THE MUSIC OF THAT PERIOD? Some children may realize that this song has only one main melody with a sustained vocal accompaniment. Much of the music they studied from England's Golden Age was polyphonic (two or more independent melodies sounded simultaneously). (See page 50.)

* HARMONY: The harmonic sequence of this song is not typical of old music. (See "Elements of Music: Harmony," page 140.) We are accustomed to hearing chords move I, IV, V7, I, etc. The harmony of this song is primarily made up of a sequence of chords moving up or down by steps. The notes of the melody which do not belong to these chords are **passing tones.** They add color to the chordal sequence and create an interesting melodic line. Here is the basic harmonic sequence for the first phrase:

I   VII   VI   V
G minor F major Eb major D minor

Play the sequence on bells or piano. Divide the class into three groups and sing the chords. Listen to each chord and decide if it is major or minor in quality.

After the children have practiced singing the sustained chords, have them learn the complete song and sing all parts together.

MELODY: Notice that phrases one and two form a sequence. Determine that the song is in G minor; it uses the natural minor scale.

The Night Piece

Music by Arthur Frackenpohl
Words by Robert Herrick

The poet who wrote the lyrics for this song lived in England during the Golden Age. Centuries later, Arthur Frackenpohl, a contemporary American composer, set the words to this music.

Quietly
Let not the dark thee — cum - ber; What
Loo   loo   loo   loo   loo

though the moon does — slum - ber? The stars of the night Will
loo   loo   loo   loo loo   loo   loo

lend — thee their light, Like ta - pers clear with-out num - ber.
loo   loo   loo   loo   loo loo   loo loo loo.

Record 5   Side B   Band 3.   VOICES: children's choir.
ACCOMPANIMENT: 2 flutes, oboe.
FORM: Instrumental; Vocal.

Listen to the recording. During each verse, a different voice part is sung while the remaining parts hum. Listen carefully for your part when it is sung. Listen to the combined harmonies as all voices sing the first verse again.

Lullaby of the Sea

Music by
Arthur Frackenpohl
Words Anonymous

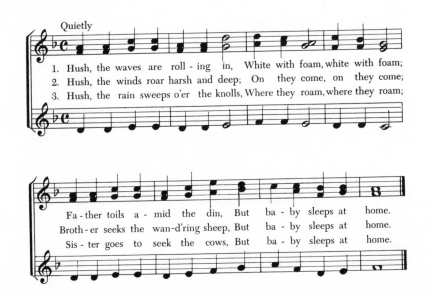

Quietly

1. Hush, the waves are roll-ing in, White with foam, white with foam;
2. Hush, the winds roar harsh and deep; On they come, on they come;
3. Hush, the rain sweeps o'er the knolls, Where they roam, where they roam;

Fa-ther toils a-mid the din, But ba-by sleeps at home.
Broth-er seeks the wan-d'ring sheep, But ba-by sleeps at home.
Sis-ter goes to seek the cows, But ba-by sleeps at home.

Record 5 Side B Band 4. VOICES: children's choir.
ACCOMPANIMENT: *a cappella.*
FORM: *Vocal, vv. 1-3; Vocal, v. 1.*

Starting Tone: A
Meter: **C** ($\frac{4}{\downarrow}$)
No piano accompaniment

Lullaby of the Sea

* HARMONY: This three-part lullaby is to be sung **a cappella** (without accompaniment). Stress the importance of listening to all parts when singing a cappella.

Learn all three voice parts simultaneously. Study the notation of each phrase. Notice the chord structure and the relationships between parts. For example, all three voice parts move in **parallel motion** during the first two measures. The song begins on a D minor chord. The music moves back and forth between minor and major. Draw attention to the dissonant chord at the end of the second measure. Study the remainder of the song in the same fashion. Isolate individual chords, such as the one at the end of the second measure, and practice them, listening carefully to the quality of the chord. Then practice each phrase until children are familiar with the chord sequence. Listen to the recording to make sure the chords are being sung in tune. The song is recorded in such a way that not only the chords (all three parts together) may be heard, but also each of the three parts can be heard clearly at specific times: on the first verse, the soprano is prominent; on the second, the second soprano; on the third, the alto.

For variety, one verse might be sung with a soloist (or a small group) singing the soprano line while the other voices hum their part as an accompaniment.

* EXPRESSION: Ask children to discuss the expressive qualities in the music. Read the words aloud. WHAT KIND OF MUSIC WILL SUPPORT THE MOOD OF THE POEM? WHAT HAS THE COMPOSER DONE IN THIS SONG TO CREATE AN APPROPRIATE MUSICAL SETTING? The melodic contour, the narrow range, and the even rhythm are appropriate to the mood of the song. The recurrent minor chords and the fact that no phrase comes to rest until the end of the song help to create a lullaby feeling. The song should be sung softly and smoothly with a light, delicate tone quality. The musical line should continue without a break from the beginning to the end of each verse.

159

Music of the Twentieth Century

To begin this study of twentieth century music, discuss the opening paragraph in the pupil's book. Review the discussions on pages 138-141 about differences in musical organization. Much of the music we hear today is still based on principles developed before 1900; major and minor scales are the basis for the tonal (harmonic and melodic) organization of much of the music we hear. Rhythms are based on meters that move consistently in groups of twos or threes.

Many twentieth century composers search for different kinds of organization. During the first lesson, listen to each composition and compare the four different kinds of organization. Later, study each composition in greater detail.

Fourth String Quartet, Opus 37
Third Movement

BY ARNOLD SCHOENBERG
BORN 1874   DIED 1951

After children have listened to this excerpt from Schoenberg's quartet, write the melody in the pupil's book on the chalkboard.

Discover that each tone of the chromatic scale is present. Emphasize that the melody is derived from the **row,** or **set.** The composer creates his complete composition by manipulating this row in various ways. In the quartet the row is first played as a melody in unison by all four instruments. It is then played backward and upside down **(retrograde inversion).** Children should be able to hear the interval of a fifth (the interval that ends the first statement of the row) now played by the cello alone. The next three tones are played by the viola and second violin. The first violin plays the remaining seven tones.

Remind children that even the notes of the harmony are taken from the row. For example, a little later in the composition, this pattern may be heard.

The cello, viola, and second violin play the first six tones of the retrograde inversion of the row (transposed) as a chord, while the first violin plays the remaining tones as a melody.

Music of the Twentieth Century

Until the twentieth century, traditional composers used the same musical language as the basis of their compositions. Countless numbers of compositions were written in many different styles and designs, yet they all had certain things in common. All were based on similar kinds of tonal, harmonic, and rhythmic organization. One could quickly understand and enjoy a new composition because it was written in a familiar language.

In the twentieth century, composers have begun to explore different ways to organize the musical elements. Some of their music sounds as if it were written in a new language. This new musical language may seem strange to our ears until we become accustomed to the sounds and begin to understand it.

Fourth String Quartet, Opus 37

Third Movement

by Arnold Schoenberg

Traditional composers had used major and minor scales as the basis of their tonal organization. Schoenberg created a new kind of organization by ordering all twelve tones of the familiar chromatic scale into a **twelve-tone set,** sometimes called a **row** or a **series.** When writing a new composition based on a twelve-tone set, the composer places the tones in any order he wishes.

Listen to the opening section of the third movement of Schoenberg's *Quartet No. 4.* In this movement the quartet plays the twelve-tone set in unison at the beginning. The remainder of the piece grows out of the musical ideas found within the series.

Record 11   Side A   Band 4.
4a   Julliard String Quartet.

160

Six Pieces for Orchestra, Opus 6
First Piece

by Anton Webern

Other composers introduced a short pattern using just a few pitches as the basic musical idea of their composition. Instead of using a scale or row as a basis, the composers build their compositions around the repetition of the intervals and pitches which make up their introductory pattern. This pattern may consist of only two or three pitches, each of which is presented by a different instrumental color. This music is sometimes described as **tone color music** because the choice of instruments is so important. In fact, it is so important that, if the same pitches were played by another group of instruments, the musical structure of the composition would be fundamentally altered. Tone color music is also called **atonal music** when the tones are not related to a home tone.

As you hear this brief composition by Webern, listen for the repetition of the intervals of a third and the succession of tone colors.

Scaramouche Suite
First Movement

by Darius Milhaud

While some composers wrote music which was **atonal** (music which has no home tone or tonal center), other composers were writing music which was **polytonal.** As the name suggests, polytonal music may have several home tones sounding at once. This composition by Milhaud uses two different keys simultaneously. As you listen, notice that the first time the main theme is played, you hear only one key, C major.

When the theme is repeated, still in C major, it is accompanied by chords from other keys. The following combinations of chords result.

Record 11   Side A   Band 4.
4b Columbia Symphony Orchestra,
Robert Craft, conductor.
4c Pierre Luboshutz and Genia Nemenoff, pianists.

Six Pieces for Orchestra, Opus 6
First Piece

BY ANTON WEBERN
BORN 1883
DIED 1945

After children have read the paragraph describing this composition, play a succession of thirds up and down the bells. Listen to the composition and try to hear the repetition of this interval used both melodically and harmonically.

Compare Webern's choice of musical organization with Schoenberg's. While Schoenberg built his composition by repeating the same sequence of tones, Webern achieved unity by repeating the same interval.

Compare the way Webern uses instruments with the way they are used in traditional music. We are accustomed to hearing many instruments playing at once, each with its own musical line. In Webern's music the instruments take turns. We hear only one (or a very few) at a time. Help children identify the different instruments. Phrase one is played by flute, trumpet, and celesta, in that order. The next phrase is introduced by the flute and completed by the French horn and strings. Draw attention to the climax near the middle of the composition. Near the end, the mood created by the descending trumpet melody recalls the rising melodic pattern played by the flute at the beginning.

Scaramouche Suite
First Movement

BY DARIUS MILHAUD (mee-yoh)
BORN 1892

Discuss the meaning of the words **tonal, atonal,** and **polytonal.** The prefix "a" means "non"; "poly" means "many." Therefore, we have tonal music with one home tone, atonal music with no home tone, and polytonal music with several home tones.

As children hear this composition for two pianos, point out that Milhaud alternates between tonal and polytonal music. He first states the theme in the key of C. It is immediately restated in two different tonalities (keys) at the same time. Discuss the fact that each part played separately would sound like traditional music. To illustrate, play the passage in the pupil's book (drawn from the first theme). First play each part separately, then both together.

The polytonality in the middle section is also readily apparent. Suggest to the children that they try to concentrate on one part at a time, listening for its home tone. Compare this composition with the one by Milhaud discussed on page 177.

Kleine Kammermusik, Opus 24, No. 2

Fifth Movement

BY PAUL HINDEMITH
BORN 1895   DIED 1963

The first three compositions discussed on these pages use methods of organization developed during the twentieth century; this composition was deliberately included to show that some composers have continued to use old principles to create new music. This composition has a tonal center. It begins and ends in E.

In response to the suggestion in their books, help children realize that the design of the composition, with its clearly defined phrases and the repetition of the opening section at the end, is similar to the form of many traditional compositions.

The harmony has a contemporary sound because many of the chords are built on the interval of a fourth instead of the traditional third. (See page 140.) Help children hear that Hindemith also uses a twentieth century rhythmic technique. He constantly alternates the meter between measures of two and three. To help children hear this changing meter, suggest that they clap the beat lightly as they listen to the opening section.

At the end of the opening section the clarinet plays a pattern which uses another twentieth century technique. Hindemith has written a five-note melody and placed it in a rhythmic pattern of six notes so that the natural accent of the measure falls on a different note each time:

melodic pattern

rhythmic pattern

New Music of Your Own

The four exercises in the pupil's book may be done on four different days as a class activity with some children experimenting and the rest of the class observing. Or, they might be assigned to certain

Kleine Kammermusik, Opus 24, No. 2

Fifth Movement
by Paul Hindemith

While some composers were exploring new musical principles, such as atonality and polytonality, other composers were writing new music based on traditional principles. This kind of music is called **neoclassic**, meaning "new classic." It is based on principles of design developed nearly two hundred years ago by the **classic** composers, such as Mozart. In many ways, the music of the neoclassic composers does not sound the same as the music of earlier composers. The harmonies, melodies, and rhythms are twentieth century in sound. As you listen to Hindemith's quintet, try to decide what makes it sound "classic" and what makes it sound modern.

New Music of Your Own

Creative people are curious and often have a good sense of humor. They enjoy doing things in new ways. They like to try new schemes and structures that result in new ideas.

In the spirit of exploration, try several ways of making your own original music.

1. Using resonator bells, make up your own scale. Instead of putting the whole and half steps in the usual order of the major scale, put them in a different order. Play your scale until you remember it. Play "Three Blind Mice" and "Twinkle, Twinkle, Little Star" in your new scale.

2. Review page 132 where you learned to build rhythms. Begin with a slow, steady beat as the lesson suggests. Now, instead of the patterns suggested, add original patterns of your own. Keep working until each

Record 11   Side A   Band 4d.
Philadelphia Woodwind Quintet.

player can remember his idea. Repeat your patterns many times. Later, make a more complex percussion composition by starting with two tones to the beat in an uneven pattern.

3. Experiment with polytonality. Choose a familiar melody that you can play by ear, such as "Hot Cross Buns." While one person plays it in the key of C, another person may play it in the key of G. Play it as a round in the two keys. Now try the same experiment in the keys of C and E.

4. Harmonize a familiar song in a new way. Choose a melody that uses only two or three chords. Using the roots of these chords, build a new chord with tones an interval of a fourth apart. Review the discussion on page 140 regarding new harmonies. Play your new chords on the resonator bells or on the piano while the class sings the song.

children or groups of children to be worked out apart from the class and shared with the class when perfected.

1. Children can follow the instructions with very little assistance. Asking them a few questions may help them think through the process. HOW MANY TONES WILL YOU HAVE IN YOUR SCALE? WHERE HAVE YOU DECIDED TO PLACE THE HALF AND WHOLE TONES? (The scale should stay within an octave but might have as many half tones as the child wishes to use from those available. For example, the scale might be made up of seven tones in a sequence of steps such as: whole-half-whole-half-whole-half-whole.) ON WHAT TONE OF THE SCALE DOES "THREE BLIND MICE" BEGIN? (It should begin on the third.) ON WHAT TONE OF THE SCALE DOES "TWINKLE, TWINKLE LITTLE STAR" BEGIN? (It should begin on the first step of the scale.)

2. A small group of three or four children can work together in this exercise after the class reviews page 132. Drums can be used for all the rhythms, or another percussion instrument such as sticks, or a combination of instruments. One group might be assigned to try each plan.

When the children in a group have worked out an interesting percussion composition and have practiced until they can remember it, they should share it with the class. The same children in the same groups may later try the more complex plan of starting with two tones to the beat.

3. Ask the class to review the meaning of polytonality. The first experiment will result in the harmony of parallel fifths. The second will be more interesting in sound. Review with the player the E scale which includes four sharps. Two sets of resonator bells will be required for these experiments. Each player should practice until he can play the melody accurately in the one key or tonality before he joins another player in polytonality.

4. When the class has reviewed harmony as an element of music and has reviewed the traditional way of building chords (in thirds), members can try playing the new chords (in fifths) on the piano or resonator bells. The harmonizing chords might be built on C and G (in the key of C) with tones C-G-D and G-D-A; the children might then sing a song such as "Skip to My Lou," beginning on E. Other simple songs children know can be treated similarly.

Beautiful Dreamer

Key: D   Starting Tone: D (1)
Meter: $\frac{9}{8}$ $\left(\frac{3}{}\right)$
Piano accompaniment on page 295

* COMPOSER'S STYLE: Stephen Foster (1826-1864) composed 189 songs. For most of these he also wrote the words. Ask children to recall some of the Stephen Foster songs they know such as "Old Folks at Home," "Some Folks Do," "Oh! Susanna," and "Jeanie with the Light Brown Hair." Foster was largely a self-taught musician. He learned much of what he knew by studying the music of Mozart, Weber, and Beethoven. He was the first outstanding American song composer. More than any other single composer of the period, Foster caught the spirit of his time and, in so doing, made his music a part of the American tradition.

* EXPRESSION: Listen to the recording. Discuss the importance of singing the long phrases on a single breath. Long tones at the end of the phrases must be sustained for their full value so that the beauty of the long melodic line is maintained. Notice how the melodic contour dictates the changes in **dynamics.** The song should be sung at a moderate **tempo.** Review page iv, "Exploring Music through Singing."

FORM: Analyze the design of the song. There are nine two-measure phrases. Each group of two phrases forms a **period.** The first phrase in each period acts as a question (the musical idea is not complete—it demands to move on). The second phrase is the answer and completes the musical idea. The ninth two-measure phrase is the **coda.**

The design of the song is A (first period) A B A coda. Notice how the last phrase (the coda) adds interest and strength to the song ending. Foster introduces a new musical idea to emphasize the importance of the repeated words.

RHYTHM: Draw attention to the meter signature. It indicates nine beats to a measure with the eighth note as the beat note. Ask children to listen to the recording and tap the beat. Notice that the song seems to move in groups of three rather than in nine. The dotted quarter note serves as the beat note. The meter signature might look like this: $\frac{3}{}$

Beautiful Dreamer

Words and Music by
Stephen Foster

This beautiful melody was written by Stephen Foster, one of our best-known American song composers. Study the Time Line on pages 82-83 to discover when he lived. What events may have affected the music he wrote?

1. Beau-ti-ful dream - er,   wake un-to me,
2. Beau-ti-ful dream - er,   out on the sea

Star-light and dew-drops are wait-ing for   thee; _____
Mer-maids are chant-ing the wild lo-re - lei; _____

Sounds of the rude   world   heard in the day,
O-ver the stream - let   va-pors are borne,

Lulled by the moon-light have all passed a - way. _____
Wait-ing to fade at the bright com-ing   morn. _____

Record 5   Side B   Band 5.   VOICE: tenor.
ACCOMPANIMENT: harp, cello.
FORM: Introduction, *4 meas.;* Instrumental; Interlude, *4 meas.;* Vocal, *v. 1;* Interlude, *4 meas.;* Vocal, *v. 2;* Coda, *4 meas.*

Beau - ti - ful dream - er, queen of my song,
Beau - ti - ful dream - er, beam on my heart,

List while I woo thee with soft mel - o - dy;
E'en as the morn on the stream-let and sea;

Gone are the cares of life's bus - y throng,
Then will all clouds of sor - row de - part,

Beau - ti - ful dream - er, a - wake un - to me!

Beau - ti - ful dream - er, a - wake un - to me!

Stephen Foster's melodies often show the influence of Irish music. "Beautiful Dreamer" has been recorded with a harp accompaniment, which reminds us of the Irish harp.

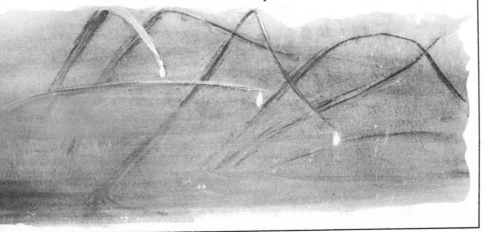

Stephen Foster is sometimes described as "America's Minstrel." It is an apt name because he was the first important American songwriter. Two traditions found in Stephen Foster's music are the European popular ballad and the music of the American Negro. It is this amalgamation of two traditions which gives Stephen Foster's music its unique position in American music.

Foster grew up in a comfortable home in Pennsylvania. He was surrounded by music as a child. He heard ballads sung by his older sisters, work songs by the Negro workers on the riverboats, and spirituals when the maid took him to Sunday evening services at her church.

Foster never had any formal instruction in music because it was not considered a proper occupation for a man at that time. He showed musical aptitude at an early age and had written his first composition, a waltz for piano, when he was fourteen years old.

Foster's songs can be divided into two categories: the comic nonsense song and the sentimental plantation song. The comic songs were written for minstrels, a type of musical show popular during the mid-1800's. "Oh! Susanna" is typical of this type of song. "Old Folks at Home" and "Jeanie with the Light Brown Hair" are examples of the sentimental ballad.

Foster's music is characterized by singable melodies, simple harmonies, and rhythms which often make use of syncopation. His songs are characterized by their repetition with contrast achieved through slight variation.

Foster visited the South only once, yet his best songs deal with the South and plantation life. His songs have a special nostalgic meaning for many Americans.

Foster died in 1864, lonely, ill, and poverty-stricken. He was thirty-seven years old.

Jacob's Ladder

Key: C   Starting Tone: E (3)
Meter: $\frac{2}{2}$ $\left(\frac{2}{2}\right)$
No piano accompaniment

* **EXPRESSION:** This lovely song is one of the most popular spirituals sung today. Many children may be familiar with the melody. Discuss how the words and the melodic line of this song help determine the phrasing and dynamics of the musical performance. Each phrase should "climb" until the climax is reached in the third phrase. See page 172 for information on spirituals.

RHYTHM: Note the meter signature. This song moves in twos with the half note as the beat note. Notice the syncopated effect of the repeated short-long pattern.

* **HARMONY:** Study the notation of the three voice parts. Compare the chord structure of the voice parts with the chords indicated for the autoharp. Place these chords on the chalkboard:

ARE THERE SOME TONES IN THE VOICE PARTS THAT DO NOT BELONG TO THESE CHORDS? (Measures 2, 3, 6, 8, 12, 13, 14.) These "extra" tones are called **passing tones.** Listen to the recording by the boys' choir. Notice how these passing tones add interest to the harmony.

This song has been arranged so that the lower part can be sung by the boys whose voices are beginning to change. If children cannot sing it in this range, **transpose** the song to the key of E flat. (The first chord will include E flat and G.)

The arrangement should be sung a cappella. When sung in unison or in two parts (the top two), the autoharp accompaniment will sound appropriate.

Jacob's Ladder

Spiritual

1. We are climb - ing Ja - cob's lad - der,
2. Ev - ery round goes high - er, high - er,

We are climb - ing Ja - cob's lad - der,
Ev - ery round goes high - er, high - er,

We are climb - ing Ja - cob's lad - der,
Ev - ery round goes high - er, high - er,

Sol - diers of the Cross. _____

Record 5   Side B   Band 6.   VOICES: boy choir.
ACCOMPANIMENT: *a cappella.*
FORM: Introduction, *4 meas.;* Vocal, *vv. 1-2.*

Scored for instruments.
See "Exploring Music Instrumental Supplement."

166

Shalom Alëḥem

The words of this Hebrew song mean "Peace be with you."

Shalom Alëḥem
Jewish Folk Song

Hë - vë - nu   sha - lom   a - lë - ḥem,

Hë - vë - nu   sha - lom   a - lë - ḥem,

Hë - vë - nu   sha - lom   a - lë - ḥem,

Hë - vë - nu   sha - lom,   sha - lom,   sha - lom a - lë - ḥem.

* **EXPRESSION:** Listen to the recording to learn the Hebrew words. The dot under the "h" in the word "alëḥem" indicates that it is to be pronounced similarly to the German "ch."

Discuss how singing style can enhance musical expressiveness. Notice how the melodic contour of phrases one and two suggests a rise and fall in dynamics. The contrasting melody in phrase four suggests that this phrase should be sung in a **marcato** style (slightly accented or marked), while the other phrases should be sung in a **legato** style (smoothly sustained).

* **MELODY:** Review the structure of the natural minor scale. (See page 23.) Sing up and down the scale to establish tonality; ask children to sing the song on a neutral syllable. Notice the similarity in melodic contour between phrases one and two.

Record 5   Side B   Band 7.   VOICES: soprano, baritone.
ACCOMPANIMENT: clarinet, accordion, guitar, double bass, percussion.
FORM: Instrumental; Vocal; Instrumental; Vocal.

Ev'ry Night When the Sun Goes In

Key: C   Starting Tone: C (1)
Meter: $\frac{2}{2}$ $\left(\frac{2}{\downarrow}\right)$
Piano accompaniment on page 299

* EXPRESSION: Children will enjoy learning to sing this "blues" song. Listen to the recording. Notice how the style of performance adds to the expressiveness of this folk melody: tempo, dynamics, slurring of tones, etc.

FOLK STYLE: As children hear the recording, ask them to listen for musical qualities which are typical of the blues. Draw attention to the B flats which do not belong to the key of the song. These are "written out" blues tones. The traditional blues singer flatted these tones unconsciously as a part of his singing style; they were not a part of the original melody line. Listen for chord patterns which use the flatted tones. The repetition of words emphasized by changing the melody for each restatement is also a common "blues" technique.

MELODY: Learn the melody of the song in unison. Observe the notation. Notice that the melody changes for each phrase, yet the character of the contour remains consistent. Each musical idea seems to grow out of the preceding one.

* HARMONY: Choose a small group to learn the harmonizing part. Study its tones in relation to the main melody. Discover the interval between voices at the beginning of each harmonizing pattern. Notice the overall contour of each pattern. Then, while the class sings the melody softly, encourage the children assigned to the harmony part to sing as much as possible at sight.

On another day, suggest to the children that they improvise their own harmonization. This is in character with blues singing because improvisation has always been an important part of this music. Blues singing was one of the sources of jazz.

Ev'ry Night When the Sun Goes In

Southern Folk Song
Arranged by
William S. Haynie

This song is an example of a type of folk music from the southern United States known as the **blues**. This music gets its name from the custom of singing some tones slightly flat. These tones were known as "blue" notes. Find the "blue" notes in this song.

Record 5   Side B   Band 8.   VOICES: children's choir.
ACCOMPANIMENT: piano.
FORM: Introduction, *2 meas.*; Vocal, *vv. 1-2.*

Scored for instruments.
See "Exploring Music Instrumental Supplement."

168

Much of the folk music of the United States has its roots in the countries of Europe. As the people migrated to this country, they brought their music with them. Through the years this music has remained fairly stable. Melodies and texts can still be traced back to the country of their origin. The backgrounds of some of these songs, such as "Johnny Has Gone for a Soldier" and "Green Grow the Laurels," have been discussed in the pupil's book. The fifth grade book in this series emphasizes the study of American music. Ask children to recall songs that they studied in the fifth grade which may have originated in the countries they have studied this year. Sing these songs again; compare them with songs in the sixth grade book from the same country. Some possibilities from the fifth grade book might include "Morning Comes Early" from Czechoslovakia, "The Praties They Grow Small" from Ireland, "Oleana" from Norway." "The Coasts of High Barbary," "Farewell, My Own True Love," and "Springfield Mountain" are all similar to the music of England.

In contrast to the music of the Europeans, which has retained the European characteristics, the music of the Negro has evolved into a distinctly American form. Its musical characteristics have become a part of the American folk and popular tradition. The minstrel songs of the nineties (such as "Cindy"), the "rags" of the early 1900's, the "rock and roll" of the sixties have all been influenced by the music of the Negro. Additional information about Negro music may be found on pages 171-172.

Cindy

Keys: C & F   Starting Tone: G (5)
Meters: $\frac{4}{4}\left(\frac{4}{\downarrow}\right)$ $\frac{2}{4}\left(\frac{2}{\downarrow}\right)$
Piano accompaniment on page 301

* HARMONY: Many children will know the melody of this popular American folk song. Listen to the recording. Ask children to follow the notation and decide which voices are singing the melody. In the first verse the boys sing the melody; the girls sing the melody during the refrain. In verse two the parts are reversed; the girls sing the melody for the verse while the boys sing the melody during the refrain.

Study the notation and discuss the relationship between the two voice parts. Notice that the two voices move in thirds during the introduction. (Measures one through four.) Study the coda and notice several different intervals. (Last six measures of the song.) Practice these two sections separately.

After children have reviewed the melody of the song, add the harmonizing parts. Those singing the main melody might hum their part softly while the others practice the harmonizing part.

* RHYTHM: Draw attention to the changing meter signatures. WHAT WILL BE DIFFERENT BETWEEN THE RHYTHM OF VERSE ONE ("I WISH I HAD A NICKEL") AND VERSE TWO ("I WISH I HAD A NEEDLE")? Help children realize that, although the overall pattern is the same, the total rhythmic movement is "stretched out" during the second verse. In both cases the quarter note is the beat note. Remind children of the term for this kind of rhythmic alteration, **augmentation.** (See "Ghost of Tom," page 28.)

Practice reading the words in rhythm. Make sure that the second verse is sung with one word to a beat while the first verse moves with two words to a beat.

Draw attention to the contrasting rhythmic movement between the two voices. The melody moves in eighth notes and makes use of dotted patterns and syncopation. The harmonizing part usually moves with longer tones, quarter or half notes, in an even rhythm.

Cindy

Southern Banjo Tune
Arranged by Kurt Miller
Traditional Words

Here is a well-known folk melody that comes from the southeastern United States. It is a lively square dance and banjo tune that was popular in the minstrel shows of the late nineteenth century.

Girls
I went to see my, went to see my pret - ty Cin-dy gal,   I

Boys
I went to see my, went to see my pret - ty Cin-dy gal, oh, yes, I

have   no   nick - el;   have   no   dime;   I

wish I had a   nick- el,   I   wish I had a   dime,   I

Verse 1.

Record 6   Side A   Band 1.   VOICES: children's choir.
ACCOMPANIMENT: banjo, fiddle, double bass.
FORM: Vocal.

MUSICAL STYLE: Draw attention to the different musical devices used in this arrangement and often heard in arrangements of popular songs: the use of "flatted tones," the quality of chords (such as the **diminished** chord: last beat, measure 28), the movement of the melody up or down by half steps (as in the introduction), and the syncopated rhythms.

Music of the American Negro: The "Blues"

The blues came out of the fields and levees of the Southland. As the Negro worked, he sang because he found it easier to work in rhythm. Gradually, the field "hollers" and work songs of the slaves mingled with the folk ballads of the white people; and the style known as the "blues" arose. Its style and musical structure has remained almost the same since the blues began.

The three-phrase pattern of the blues grows out of its poetry which always consists of a question, which is repeated, and followed by a contrasting answer.

Blues, Blues, Blues, why did you bring trouble to me?
Yes, Blues, Blues, Blues, why did you bring trouble to me?
O Death, please sting me and take me out of my misery.

Blues melodies are distinctive and easily identified. The melody line usually moves downward and is characterized by the recurrence of the flatted tones, known as "blue notes." These flatted notes help to give blues its plaintive air.

The three phrases of the blues song are always harmonized in the same progression: the first is harmonized by the I chord, the second by the IV and I chord, the last by the V7 and I chord. The harmonies may be expanded with added notes, but the basic progression remains the same.

Usually the blues singer's melody only fills the first three bars of each phrase; the last measure is filled with an instrumental improvisation on the vocal melody. These brief improvisations may well have been the germ from which the whole art of jazz improvisation grew.

Music of the American Negro: Spirituals and Work Songs

In contrast to these two groups which are usually in a quick tempo and excited mood, the quieter "settin'" spirituals are characterized by a long, sustained melody line, as in "Were You There" and "Let Us Break Bread Together."

The work songs of the Negroes were sometimes sung to coordinate the efforts of the group; at other times they sang simply to relieve the monotony. In the latter case the men often sang spirituals. For work such as "hammerin'" or "drillin'," the leader sang while the other men worked. The leader was carefully chosen because of his ability to select the right song and sing it in the proper rhythm.

Examples of both spirituals and work songs of the Negro may be found in *Exploring Music 5*. Suggest to the children that they review examples of each type.

Although the Negro spirituals and work songs are uniquely American, their ties with the African homeland can be seen in many characteristics of the American Negro's music.

The "call-response" form of many of the spirituals and the vitality of their rhythms may be traced directly to the singing style of the Negro in western Africa. The pentatonic quality of many African melodies may be sensed in the melodies of the earliest American Negro songs. Although many of the spirituals and work songs are based on an eight-tone scale, rather than a pentatonic scale, there is a tendency in these songs to avoid the fourth and seventh steps of the scale. The Negroes were unfamiliar with the eight-tone scales on which the gospel hymns were based. When they tried to sing them, they unconsciously erred in repeating certain intervals. The habit of "flatting" the third and seventh steps of the scale may also be traced to the pentatonic tradition.

Many spirituals, such as "Go Down, Moses" and "Swing Low, Sweet Chariot," are based on the call-response form. The repeated part may be very brief or may consist of a complete refrain. The leader always sings the verses while the congregation joins in on the response.

Another large group of spirituals is characterized by short, segmented melodies. These are usually based on a repeated rhythmic pattern,

American Jazz

Jazz has developed in the United States as a new musical form. Although a blending of musical ideas from Africa and Europe was a part of the development, the form is an American product. Many different types of jazz have emerged since it began in New Orleans in the early 1900's including Dixieland (New Orleans and Chicago styles), swing, bop, cool, and progressive. Such piano styles as ragtime and boogie-woogie are also part of the evolution of jazz.

Jazz is not the art of the composer but that of the performer. Although members of the jazz combo may decide on a general arrangement with some sections memorized or read from notes, it is the originality of the performer that makes jazz unique. The performer is free to improvise on a melody or to add a new one. A good jazz musician knows a large number of standard "pop" tunes on which he improvises. He may create a new solo improvisation on the basic tune each time he plays it. He also knows various ways of harmonizing the tune so that he can either take a harmony part or lead out with the melody.

Rhythm is one of the most important elements of jazz. Syncopated rhythms have special importance in jazz music. Jazz musicians build their music from the rhythm section (drums, string bass, guitar, piano). These instruments furnish the driving pulse or beat which holds the music together and gives it vitality. The special tone qualities of the saxophone section, the high trumpets, and the wail of the "blues" singer are characteristic of jazz performance. "Blues" harmonies are often used. They are created by flatting certain tones in the chord or by adding the sixth of the chord as an extra note.

Jazz has an enthusiastic following of people around the world. American jazz combos on tour through Asia, Africa, and the Middle East bring back reports of "standing room only" at their concerts. Jazz has influenced many composers of the twentieth century. Composers of other nations, as well as those of the United States, have adapted jazz styles for use in their compositions. The influence of jazz can also be seen in the art of ballet and other kinds of dance. The continuing development of jazz as an independent musical form makes it a subject of special interest to lovers of music.

generally syncopated. Examples of this type of spiritual are "Little David" and "Soon Ah Will Be Done." These spirituals are marked by a strong rhythmic swing and usually are accompanied by bodily movement: clapping, stamping, etc.

American Jazz

Begin the study of the jazz unit by studying and discussing the material provided on page 173 of the pupil's book. This unit will be of special interest to the children and they will enjoy sharing their listening experiences with jazz with the class.

Below is a listing (and approximate dates) of the eras of jazz.

New Orleans Blues (1895-1917): Created in the South by Negro musicians, blues is a form of jazz that is still popular today. It is a twelve-bar theme, usually played slowly.

Ragtime (1898-1917): A notated form of jazz, primarily for the piano, utilizing exaggerated syncopations.

Boogie Woogie (1912-1942): Primarily a piano style, with fast moving left hand, based on twelve-bar blues.

New Orleans Dixieland (1917-1926): Lighter sound than New Orleans blues, with emphasis on beats two and four. Strong melody, with counterpoint over a harmonic framework.

Chicago Jazz (1925-1935): Tenor saxophone added, rhythm section increased, and ensemble blend became more precise and polished. Solos became more intricate. Jazz interpretations of popular songs were styled by Bix Beiderbecke and Eddie Condon.

Kansas City Style (1927-1934): Bands increased in size. Call and response techniques between the soloist and the band became popular. (Cab Calloway and Duke Ellington)

Swing (1935-1945): Bands increased in size, often including four saxophones and four or five brass instruments. Arrangements were scored for these bands. The jitterbug craze hit the country and the Big Band Era was born. (Woody Herman, Tommy Dorsey, Benny Goodman, Glenn Miller)

Bop (1945-1955): Small combos, clipped phrases, abrupt melodic skips, altered chords, complicated syncopations. (Charlie Parker, Thelonius Monk, Dizzie Gillespie)

Progressive Jazz (1945-1952): The big band sound of screaming brass and hard-driving tempos, characterized by Stan Kenton.

Cool Jazz (1949-1960): Small combos, soft ensemble passages, subtle rhythms. Miles Davis paved the way, followed by musicians such as Stan Getz and Dave Brubeck.

Modern Jazz (1960-present): A mixture of many styles and textures —classical, modal, and modern harmonies, and complex rhythms. (Charlie Mingus, Jerry Mulligan, Lenny Tristano)

Dixieland combos had their origin in the street bands of New Orleans. These bands often played at funerals, and the old gospel song "When the Saints Go Marching In" was an appropriate tune to play on such occasions. Since the bands marched in the funeral processions, the instruments had to be portable. For instance banjo and tuba, rather than piano and double bass, were used.

Study the description of the Dixieland combo in the pupil's book. Play the recording of "the Saints" and have the children follow the illustrations in their books. On the recording each illustration is separated by three beats of rest. A three-second band separates the illustrations and the complete arrangement. The complete arrangement follows the traditional form: introduction and full ensemble; solos in which each instrument has a chance to show-off (clarinet, trumpet, trombone, and rhythm section); a return to the full ensemble, followed by a tag. Have the children indentify the instruments playing the solos.

On the next page, the opening measures of the complete arrangement are reproduced to illustrate the relationship of all the parts when combined.

"Take the 'A' Train" illustrates a later style of jazz that is still somewhat close to Dixieland. In one sense, "Take the 'A' Train" is a "modern spiritual" or "train song." The 'A' Train is a subway line in New York City. The tune was written by Billy Strayhorn, arranger for Duke Ellington's band (see Kansas City Style on page 173).

On your recording there is a demonstration of a jazz **combo** playing in the early Dixieland style of New Orleans. Listen carefully and follow the examples given below.

A favorite tune in this style was "When the Saints Go Marching In."

An early Dixieland combo usually consisted of trumpet, clarinet, trombone, drums, banjo, and tuba.

The **rhythm section** — drums, banjo, and tuba — played an accompaniment such as this:

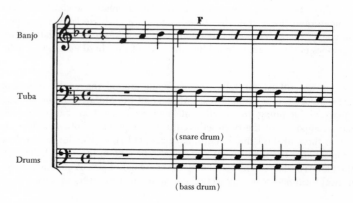

Record 11   Side B   Band 2.
The Burly Five Plus One.

174

The melody was taken by the trumpet. The trumpet player would "decorate" the original melody in a variety of ways:

In a range below the melody the trombone played the most important note of each chord.

The clarinet played a busy part, filled with many notes, in harmony above the melody.

Now hear a complete jazz arrangement of "When the Saints Go Marching In."

Also on your recording is an arrangement of "Take the 'A' Train," a more recent tune that is a favorite of jazz performers today. It is played by a "big band" consisting of five trumpets, four trombones, five saxophones, piano, double bass, and drums. As you listen, try to notice some of the similarities and differences between this style and the early Dixieland style.

Compared to Dixieland, the band heard on the recording of "Take the 'A' Train" is considerably larger, and written music is used. However, the feeling is still four-to-a-bar and there are full ensembles and solos (in this style the solos are often accompanied by the saxophone section, as in this recording when the muted trumpet improvises against the saxophone background).

Green Grow the Laurels

Key: F Starting Tone: C (5)
Meter: $\frac{3}{4}$ $\left(\begin{smallmatrix}3\\ \end{smallmatrix}\right)$
Piano accompaniment on page 305

FOLK STYLE: Read and discuss the explanation of words given in the pupil's book regarding the origins of the song. The laurel has always been the official emblem of authority dating from the time of the Greeks. The significance of the last line "We'll change the green laurel to the bonnet so blue" in the original Scottish song probably refers to the desire to keep Scotland free of British imperialism. The British have used the laurel wreath as part of their official document stamp since the thirteenth century.

WHY IS THE LAST LINE OF THE SONG IN YOUR BOOKS APPROPRIATE FOR THE PEOPLE OF THE UNITED STATES TO SING? Help children recall that we also fought against British imperialism. For the song to fit our situation, the Scottish blue bonnet was changed to the red, white, and blue of the American flag.

* MELODY: Study the melody. Notice repetition of the first phrase. Work on the difficult intervals in the last phrase. Notice that the first measure in this phrase outlines the V chord. However, the first note in the second measure is a D instead of the expected C. The next interval from C to E is a skip of a sixth.

* HARMONY: Study the autoharp chord markings to see what chords are used in the accompaniment. Determine the notes which make up each chord and write them on the chalkboard. Listen to the chords on the autoharp and determine whether they are major or minor.

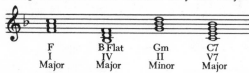

F	B Flat	Gm	C7
I	IV	II	V7
Major	Major	Minor	Major

Encourage children who play piano to improvise an accompaniment. See page viii concerning melody and harmony instruments.
Study the descant. Notice that it uses tones from these same chords. Determine the interval relationships between the two parts. The voices move primarily in thirds and sixths.

Green Grow the Laurels

American Folk Song

Extremely popular at the time of the Mexican War, this song is supposed to be the reason why the Mexicans call Americans "gringos." The song was so widely sung by the American soldiers that the Mexicans identified them by the first two words of the title.

The song dates back to the days of Bonnie Prince Charlie, whose loyal Scotsmen sang, "We'll change the green laurel to the bonnet so blue." Study the Time Line to discover when these various events occurred.

Listen to the recording of this song. The English horn plays the descant. This woodwind instrument is similar in sound to the oboe but has a lower range. Notice that it plays the descant an octave lower than it is written in your book.

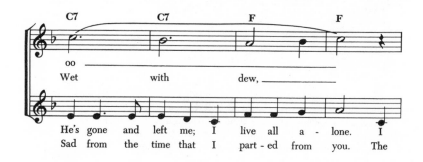

Record 6 Side A Band 2. VOICE: soprano.
ACCOMPANIMENT: English horn, guitar, double bass.
FORM: Instrumental; Vocal, v. 1; Interlude, 4 meas.; Vocal, v. 2.

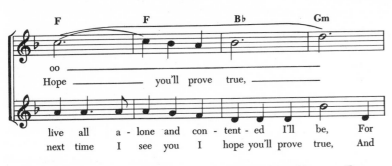

Hope _____ you'll prove true, _____

live all a - lone and con - tent - ed I'll be, For
next time I see you I hope you'll prove true, And

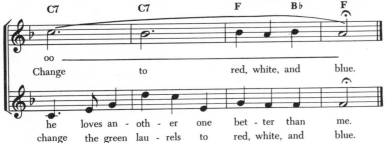

Change to red, white, and blue.

he loves an - oth - er one bet - ter than me.
change the green lau - rels to red, white, and blue.

Creation of the World

by Darius Milhaud

Milhaud is truly a man of the twentieth century. He has experimented with many kinds of new music. He has traveled all over the world and has absorbed the spirit of the life around him. The sounds of the music he has heard have been woven into his own music. When he visited America in 1922, the sounds of American jazz fascinated him.

Shortly after his visit, Milhaud began to work on a new ballet *The Creation of the World*. The music he wrote for the ballet contains many of the jazz elements he had admired in American music.

Review what you have learned about the elements of jazz on page 173. As you listen to the closing portion of Milhaud's ballet, decide which of these elements are present in his music. Listen for characteristic instrumentation, distinctive tone qualities, typical rhythm patterns, and jazz harmonies.

Do you hear anything in the music that is not typical of jazz?

Record 11   Side A   Band 5.
Columbia Symphony Orchestra,
Leonard Bernstein, conductor.

Creation of the World

BY DARIUS MILHAUD
BORN 1892

Play the composition for the children without comment. Ask them if they can decide what kind of music it is and from what country the composer might have come. Children may suggest that it is jazz composed by an American.

Open the book and read the discussion. Emphasize the fact that jazz is an American musical form, which in this case is borrowed by a European composer. Milhaud is an eminent French composer who has spent a major part of his life in the United States. American composers have long borrowed musical ideas from the Europeans; the process has been reversed in this composition.

Listen again and discuss the items listed at the bottom of the pupil's page. Characteristic instrumentation includes trumpets, saxophones, and various percussion instruments. The fact that it is a small ensemble is also typical of jazz instrumentation. Distinctive tone qualities can be heard in the "blue" notes of the trumpet and clarinet, the slurring of tones, and the deliberate distortion of tone quality. Jazz performers often play tones in the extreme high and low ranges of their instruments, such as those heard on the clarinet in this composition. Syncopated complex rhythms over a strongly accented beat are also a typical jazz sound. The chords which use flatted tones or add extra tones are representative of jazz harmonies.

The violin and flute heard in this music are seldom used in standard jazz combinations. The abrupt changes in tempo and mood which occur in the middle of this excerpt are not usually found in a jazz performance. Stress also that the musicians are playing from a printed score. All the notes have been designated by the composer; there is no improvisation.

The music on your recording is an excerpt consisting of the last few minutes of the complete ballet. There are numerous recordings of the complete composition available, and children will enjoy hearing all of it. The theme of the ballet is the creation of the world as it might be described in African folk tales.

A Time Line for Exploring Music

Continue the activities previously begun in connection with the Time Lines on pages 60-61 and 82-83. Encourage children to add to their time line and bring it up to date with current events.

Following are examples of poetry from the period covered by this Time Line.

I Hear America Singing

Walt Whitman, 1819-1892

I hear America singing, the varied carols I hear,
Those of mechanics, each one singing his as it should be blithe and
    strong,
The carpenter singing his as he measures his plank or beam,
The mason singing his as he makes ready for work, or leaves off
    work,
The boatman singing what belongs to him in his boat, the deck-hand
    singing on the steamboat deck,
The shoemaker singing as he sits on his bench, the hatter singing as
    he stands,
The wood-cutter's song, the ploughboy's on his way in the morning,
    or at noon intermission or at sundown,
The delicious singing of the mother, or of the young wife at work,
    or of the girl sewing or washing.
Each singing what belongs to him or her and to none else,
The day that belongs to the day—at night the party of young fellows,
    robust, friendly,
Singing with open mouths their strong melodious songs.

A Time Line for Exploring Music

──────── 1850 ────────

Commodore Perry enters Japan.	Two Scandinavian composers, Sibelius and Nielsen, are born in the same year.
Civil War is waged between the states.	
Juarez helps to free Mexico.	Wagner's *The Mastersingers of Nuremberg* is written.
Italy and Germany become nations.	Grieg writes *Peer Gynt*.
	Brahms composes songs, symphonies.

──────── 1875 ────────

Bell invents the telephone.	Smetana completes "The Moldau."
Edison harnesses electricity.	Massenet writes *Le Cid*.
The western frontier disappears.	Debussy writes **impressionistic** music.
Gold is found in Alaska.	Humperdinck composes the folk opera *Hansel and Gretel*.

──────── 1900 ────────

Wright brothers complete the first air flight.	Stravinsky begins his long career.
	Bartok collects Hungarian folk music.
Panama Canal is completed.	Debussy completes a series of **piano preludes**.
World War I ends in victory for the Allies.	Jazz becomes an important American musical form.
New nations are formed in Eastern Europe.	Composers explore new kinds of musical organization.
Japan rises as a world power.	Milhaud writes *Creation of the World*.

──────── 1925 ────────

First sound movies are made.	Schoenberg composes **twelve-tone** music.
Lindbergh makes the first transatlantic flight.	Webern composes **tone- color** music.
Spanish fight Civil War.	Composers begin to create electronically produced music.
Atomic power is developed.	Hindemith writes "Kleine Kammer-musik."
Allied nations win World War II.	**Musical comedy** becomes an important American musical form.
First United Nations Assembly meets.	
Television becomes popular.	Britten is commissioned to write *Young Person's Guide to the Orchestra*.
Irish gain freedom from English.	

----- 1950 -----

Korean War begins.
First space flight is accomplished.
Alaska and Hawaii attain statehood.

Babbitt completes the first music composed on the **RCA Electronic Sound Synthesizer.**

Summary

----- 1850 -----

The nineteenth century is sometimes called the **romantic** period. People became interested in things faraway and long ago. They dreamed of living like the ancient Greeks. People felt that it was important to express one's emotions freely. Music reflected this in long, flowing melodies, rich and colorful instrumentation, and musical designs which were less rigid than those of the classic composers.

----- 1875 -----

New nations were being formed all over the world. The emphasis on **nationalism** was shown in many ways. People became fiercely loyal to their own country. Writers, artists, and musicians were inspired by the culture and history of their countries. They used these topics as themes for their stories, paintings, and musical compositions.

----- 1900 -----

The twentieth century is an age of invention and discovery in science, technology, government, and art. Men have invented machines to accomplish all kinds of tasks. New sources of power have helped man travel vast distances more and more quickly. He has learned ways to communicate with people in remote corners of the world.

----- 1925 -----

Men have invented new ways of living together. Different kinds of governments were organized, and world organizations have emerged. Musicians also have become inventors. They have invented new kinds of musical organizations and have taken advantage of technological advances to develop new ways to produce musical sounds.

----- 1950 -----

The history of man has been the history of exploration: a search for new frontiers on land, on sea, and in space. Musicians keep on searching, too, for new melodies, new rhythms, and new sounds that will help them to express the feelings, ideas, and activities of twentieth century man.

Requiem

Robert Louis Stevenson, 1850-1894

Under the wide and starry sky,
Dig the grave and let me lie;
Glad did I live and gladly die,
And I laid me down with a will.

This be the verse you grave for me:
Here he lies where he longed to be;
Home is the sailor, home from the sea,
And the hunter home from the hill.

Dust of Snow

Robert Frost, 1874-1963

The way a crow
Shook down on me
The dust of snow
From a hemlock tree

Has given my heart
A change of mood
And saved some part
Of a day I had rued.

Thumbelina

Key: G   Starting Tone: G (1)
Meter: $\frac{2}{4}$ ($\frac{2}{\quad}$)
Piano accompaniment on page 306

* MELODY: Many children may be familiar with the songs from *Hans Christian Andersen* and should be able to sing the melodies with little practice. After scanning the notation of "Thumbelina," challenge the children to sing the melody of the verse at sight. Isolate any problem spots and sing them with numbers. Then immediately sing the complete verse with words.

RHYTHM: Ask one child to establish the beat and chant the words in rhythm. Remind children that they must hold the tied tones for their full value. Review the relationship of the dotted eighth note to the sixteenth note. Suggest that, if children think of the sixteenth note as belonging to the note that follows it, they will be more likely to perform this pattern correctly.

* HARMONY: Study the harmonizing part of the verse. Have sopranos hum the melody lightly while the altos practice their part.

Discover the sections of the refrain which are in unison and those where the voices sing in harmony. Phrases one and three are in unison except for the last tone. Determine these intervals (fourth, sixth). Practice moving from the unison tone to these two intervals. Notice the sequence in the second phrase. The sopranos sing the first two measures of the sequence, and the altos answer with the same melody starting one half step lower. Practice the fourth phrase. Notice that the last four measures are in three parts. Assign a few strong singers to the middle part.

Musical Comedy

The three songs "The Inch Worm," "Thumbelina," and "Wonderful Copenhagen" are from the movie *Hans Christian Andersen*. This movie is similar in form to **musical comedy.**

Musical comedy is often cited as the one purely American form of theatre music. It combines features of the comic opera and the revue (or variety show). The plot of a musical comedy is often realistic and contemporary in contrast to the plots of many nineteenth century operas which deal with the mystic and the fantastic. Interspersed throughout the story are songs and dances which add to the mood, help to communicate the personality of the players, comment on the situation, and often further the plot of the story.

Thumbelina

Words and Music by
Frank Loesser
Arranged by William Stickles

This song and the two on the following pages are from the movie *Hans Christian Andersen*. Plays and movies of this type are often known as **musical comedies.** The composer writes songs, choruses, and dances which help set the mood of a scene or tell the story of the play.

This type of musical play has been developed in America. The American musical is a very popular form of entertainment. Can you name other popular musical comedies?

1. Though you're no big-ger than my thumb, _____
   you're no big-ger than my toe, _____
   than my thumb, _____ than my thumb, _____
   than my toe, _____ than my toe, _____
   Sweet Thum-be-li-na, don't be glum.
   Sweet Thum-be-li-na, keep that glow, _____
   Now, now, now! Ah, ah, ah! Come, come, come!
   And you'll grow, and you'll grow, and you'll grow!

Record 6   Side A   Band 3.   VOICES: children's choir.
ACCOMPANIMENT: piano.
FORM: Introduction, *5 meas.;* Vocal, *vv. 1-2.*

Refrain

Thum - be - li - na, Thum - be - li - na, ti - ny lit - tle thing,

Thum - be - li - na, dance! Thum - be - li - na, sing!

Oh, Thum - be - li - na, what's the dif - f'rence if you're ver - y small?

1. tall. When your heart is full of love, you're nine feet tall, you're nine feet

2. tall. tall. 2. Though nine feet tall, you're nine feet tall.

Composers have borrowed from popular musical forms for many of their musical ideas and have made use of jazz rhythms and harmonies, blues melodies, etc. The orchestra is usually a combination of strings, brass, woodwinds, and a large percussion section—similar to the large dance bands of the thirties.

Dance has become an important part of the musical comedy in recent years. Classical ballet as well as the popular dance styles have influenced dance in the musical comedy.

One of the early composers of musical comedy was George M. Cohan. "You're a Grand Old Flag," pages 10-11, is from an early musical comedy *George Washington, Jr.* Jerome Kern, Cole Porter, Irving Berlin, Richard Rodgers, Meredith Willson, Alan Jay Lerner, and Frank Loesser are all well-known musical comedy writers. Leonard Bernstein, the well-known composer and conductor, has written several excellent musical comedies.

Some children may have seen musical comedies on the stage or watched movie versions of them. Give children an opportunity to tell of their experiences to the class.

Frank Loesser, the composer of the musical score for *Hans Christian Andersen*, was born in New York in 1910. He taught himself to play the piano when he was a teen-ager. For a long time he wrote lyrics for musical comedies while others wrote the music. The first song for which he wrote both words and music was "Praise the Lord and Pass the Ammunition," a popular song during World War II. Some of his most famous musical comedies are "Where's Charley?" "Guys and Dolls," "Most Happy Fella," and "How to Succeed in Business Without Really Trying."

The movie *Hans Christian Andersen* is based on the life of the famous Danish storyteller. He was born in Denmark in 1805. Andersen wrote more than 150 fairy tales as well as other longer stories and poetry. His fairy tales have been translated into forty different languages and are known and loved all over the world. In the movie, Andersen is shown telling his stories to groups of children as he wanders through the streets of Copenhagen. As in many musical comedies, the main function of the plot is to provide a vehicle for the songs and dances. The song "Thumbelina" is sung as Andersen tells the fairy tale by the same name. "The Inch Worm" is not drawn from a specific fairy tale, although the use of insects and flowers to illustrate a moral lesson was a common Andersen device. "Wonderful Copenhagen" is sung as Andersen and the children dance through the streets of the city.

The Inch Worm

Keys: D minor & F   Starting Tone: D (1)
Meter: $\frac{3}{4}$ $\left(\frac{3}{\text{♩}}\right)$
Piano accompaniment on page 309

* RHYTHM: With books closed, write the words of the first two phrases on the chalkboard and ask children to chant them aloud. Clap the beat and decide whether the meter seems to move in twos or in threes. Children will probably read them aloud as though they move in twos:

Two and two are four
1   2   1   2
Four and four are eight
1   2   1   2

With books still closed, listen to the record. HOW DOES THIS SONG MOVE? Help children realize that $\frac{3}{4}$ meter adds interest to the song because of the way accents occur in unexpected places.

MELODY: Study the melodies of the verse and refrain separately. Notice how the opening section has a feeling of moving back and forth between D minor and F major. Call attention to the pattern used for the words "two and two are four." This same contour is used throughout the song, although slight changes in intervals may occur.

Study the melody for the "Inch worm" section which begins at the refrain. Notice the reiteration of the two intervals C to A and B♭ to G. Draw attention to the fact that these intervals are repeated throughout the refrain except for six measures. CAN YOU FIND THESE MEASURES? (6, 7, 8, 14, 15, 16.)

Review the function of the accidentals found in the upper voice during the refrain. Notice that this melody often moves by half steps.

* HARMONY: Play the recording; ask children to pay particular attention to the harmony of the accompaniment. Notice how interest is added by introducing **dissonant** chords in important places. Remember that dissonance does not necessarily mean displeasing but refers, in this case, to chords that demand to move on rather than come to rest. (Note measures two and four of refrain.)

After children learn each melody, combine the parts. Discuss the importance of balance between voices. Decide which part should be stressed.

The Inch Worm

Words and Music by
Frank Loesser

Slowly

Two and two are four, four and four are eight;

That's all you have on your busi-ness-like mind.

Two and two are four, four and four are eight;

How can you be so blind?

Refrain

Two and two are four. Four and four are eight,

Inch worm, inch worm, mea-sur-ing the mar-i-golds,

Record 6   Side A   Band 4. VOICES: children's choir.
ACCOMPANIMENT: piano.
FORM: Introduction, *5 meas.*; Vocal.

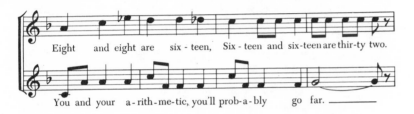

Eight and eight are six-teen, Six-teen and six-teen are thir-ty two.

You and your a-rith-me-tic, you'll prob-a-bly go far.

Two and two are four, Four and four are eight,

Inch worm, inch worm, mea-sur-ing the mar-i-golds,

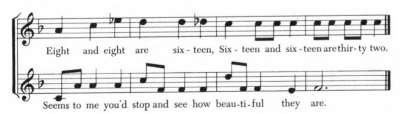

Eight and eight are six-teen, Six-teen and six-teen are thir-ty two.

Seems to me you'd stop and see how beau-ti-ful they are.

The Symphony Orchestra

There are many exciting things one can hear in music played by a symphony orchestra. One can listen for the melody, the rhythm, and the harmony. One can hear melodies being repeated, new melodies being introduced, and contrasting musical ideas. One can also listen for interesting **tone colors** of instrumental combinations or the **timbre** of a single instrument. Every instrument in the orchestra has its own distinctive timbre or tone quality. In the same way one can recognize good friends by the sounds of their voices, so one can learn to identify the instruments of the orchestra when they speak. Becoming acquainted with the individual personalities of the orchestral instruments makes listening to music more enjoyable. Just as it adds to one's pleasure to meet good friends in a strange place, so it is pleasant to recognize familiar instruments as one listens to new and different music.

The orchestra is divided into four families or choirs. Each of these families has some characteristics in common. Yet, just like human families, each member also has a distinctive personality that is a little different from that of any other member. The instruments that belong to a particular family are usually made from similar kinds of materials, and the sound is produced in a similar fashion on each instrument. In the string family the sound is created by bowing or plucking a string. Most of the woodwinds have reeds that vibrate, creating a slightly nasal quality. The brasses all have a cup-shaped mouthpiece which helps to create the full-throated sound which is their trademark. In the percussion family, sound is created by striking the instrument in some fashion.

Within each family, voices range from high to low, just as they do in a choir of human voices. There are sopranos, such as the flute and violin; altos, such as the English horn and the viola; tenors, such as the trombone or cello; basses, such as the tuba and the double bass.

Orchestras, as we think of them today, were first heard nearly two hundred years ago, about the time that George Washington lived. These orchestras had only about twenty or thirty members. All the members of the string family were present but in much smaller numbers than are used today. The woodwinds and brasses were

(Continued on page 185.)

Wonderful Copenhagen

Key: D   Starting Tone: A (5)
Meter: 3/4 (3/♩)
Piano accompaniment on page 312

FORM: Listen to the recording and determine the design of the song. It is A B A B′ coda. Notice how the repetition of B′ extends into the coda to create the climax of the song.

MELODY: Scan the score and discover the differences in the melodic movement of the two sections. The A section moves primarily by whole and half steps. Review the function of **accidentals.** (See page 8.) Notice that the melody during the B section moves by chord-line skips.

Draw attention to the sequential nature of the melody. A sequence may be found in phrase one (measures one through four and five through seven) and in phrase two (measures eight through nine and ten through eleven).

* HARMONY: Scan the score and discover the relationships between the two voice parts. The A section moves in thirds. At the end of the song, the voices move in thirds and sixths. Practice first the sections that are written in two parts. Establish tonality and sing the first phrase with both parts. Remind children to listen carefully to each other to be sure the thirds are "in tune." If problems occur within one voice, isolate the problem area and practice the parts separately. Immediately sing again in harmony. Follow the same process to learn the end of the song; then learn the unison sections.

* EXPRESSION: Discuss how the swing of the melody line and the waltz rhythm help to make this a wonderful song to sing. It should be sung in a moderately fast tempo with a feeling of one beat to a measure. Notice how the melody helps one to know the correct dynamics of each phrase.

Wonderful Copenhagen

Words and Music by
Frank Loesser
Arranged by William Stickles

Record 6   Side A   Band 5.   VOICES: children's choir.
ACCOMPANIMENT: piano.
FORM: Introduction, *8 meas.;* Vocal; Vocal.

won - der-ful, won - der-ful Co - pen - ha - gen,

won - der-ful, won - der-ful Co - pen - ha - gen,

salt - y old queen of the sea, _____

salt - y old queen of the sea, _____ Once I

Sing - ing

sailed a-way, but I'm home to-day, Sing - ing

Co - pen - ha - gen, won - der - ful, won - der - ful

Co - pen - ha - gen, won - der - ful, won - der - ful

Co - pen - ha - gen for me. _____

Co - pen - ha - gen for me. _____

("The Symphony Orchestra" continued from page 183.)

also represented in smaller numbers than are used today. Tubas were never found in these early orchestras. The variety of percussion instruments was not great; the timpani was the most frequently used. How different from the orchestra of today with as many as a hundred players and a wide variety of instruments!

Following is the instrumental makeup of a typical modern orchestra.

Strings	16 first violins
	16 second violins
	12 violas
	10 cellos
	8 double basses
	harp
Woodwinds	3 flutes, 1 piccolo
	3 oboes, 1 English horn
	3 clarinets, 1 bass clarinet
	3 bassoons, 1 contrabassoon
Brass	4 French horns
	3 trumpets
	3 trombones
	1 tuba
Percussion	Timpani, snare, tenor, and bass drums, glockenspiel, celesta, piano, xylophone, triangle, wood blocks, and tambourine.

All of these instruments are not necessarily heard in every composition. Their use depends on the specific needs of the piece. The percussion section may be expanded by a variety of special kinds of instruments. For special compositions a larger brass section is needed. Sometimes saxophones are added for special effects.

A composer has an amazing variety of timbre from which to choose, and he may combine them in many fascinating ways. The same music will sound very different when played on different instruments. A composer may choose combinations of instruments whose tones blend together into a single, rich, vibrant color. He can choose other instruments whose tones are sharply contrasting and create a pattern as vividly variegated as an artist's palette with its many colors. Listening to the music of the orchestra can be a never-ending source of interest and delight.

Compose Your Own Electronic Music

Introduce this project by playing a brief excerpt from one of the electronic compositions described on the next page. With books closed, play the music without comment. Ask children to decide what kind of music they think it might be. At a later time, return to these compositions and analyze them in more detail.

After children have listened to the composition and discussed their reactions, read aloud with the class the directions in the pupil's book. Discuss each idea carefully. Emphasize the fact that the composer of electronic music is searching for ways to expand his musical resources. Compare his efforts to those of other composers to expand musical expression throughout history.

To carry out the experiment you will need at least two tape recorders. These should be the type which can record at two or three different speeds. You will also need blank tape for each machine and a tape splicer.

Before beginning to work on the actual composition, experiment with different sound sources: the human voice, a musical instrument, various natural sounds. Ask children to bring items from home which make interesting sounds.

When children have experimented with a variety of sounds, you may wish to put the most interesting ones on **tape loops.** To make a tape loop, cut a segment of the recorded tape large enough to fit around the two spindles on the recorder. Splice this segment together to make a loop. Thread the tape loop through the tape recorder as you would a regular reel of tape. By using the loop, the same sound can be repeated over and over without having to rewind the tape each time.

Electronic experimentation will be most successful if done as an individual or small group activity. Introduce the techniques involved to the entire class: how to run the tape recorders, how to change speeds to create transformations, how to make tape loops, and so on. Then give those individuals who are interested the time and opportunity to develop their own compositions or encourage them to do so at home.

Specific suggestions for creating transformations may be found on page 190 of the teacher's book.

Compose Your Own Electronic Music

When you listen to a recording of a traditional musical composition, three steps have taken place. The composer has written the music; the music has been performed on a musical instrument; the sound of the instrument has been recorded electronically. When you listen to a record, you are actually hearing electronic music. Everything that you hear is being communicated by the vibrations of the cone of the speaker in your phonograph. If you could control these vibrations, you could control the sound, and thus produce any kind of music you wish.

This is what the composer of electronic music does. He bypasses the second of the three steps which takes place when traditional music is recorded and communicates his decisions immediately to the electronic medium. By directly controlling the sound the speaker produces, the composer is able to create a new kind of music. He is able to use combinations and qualities of sounds, patterns of rhythm, and variations of pitch and dynamics in his music which were impossible when he depended on traditional musical instruments to perform his composition.

On your record, Milton Babbitt, the composer, explains some of the ways that sounds can be transformed through the use of the tape recorder.

Experimenting with a tape recorder will help you understand the basic process involved in composing electronic music. To develop your own electronic composition, follow these steps:

Decide on the sounds which you wish to use as the basis for your experimentation. The source may be your voice, a musical instrument, or some natural sound.

Experiment to discover ways to transform your original sound. Record it on a tape recorder; then replay the tape at different speeds or play it backward.

Record these transformed sounds on a second tape recorder; then replay this tape at different speeds.

Play the original sound on two tape recorders at the same time at different speeds and record this combination of sounds on a third tape recorder.

After you have taped a number of different transformations, splice them in an interesting sequence to make your completed composition.

Record 7   Side B   Band 4.
Milton Babbitt, demonstrator.

Listen to Electronic Music

Contemporary composers who have explored the possibilities of electronic composition have used several different methods to produce their music. The three compositions discussed on this page have each used a different sound source and different kinds of electronic equipment. All three compositions have one thing in common, however. Each composer has communicated everything he wishes to emerge from the speaker directly to the electronic instrument.

Leilya and the Poet   by Halim El-Dabh

Three different sources of sound were used in this electronic composition for tape recorder. Sounds made by the human voice, by instruments, and by electronic means have been manipulated and combined in various ways. The composer changed the speed, altered the character of the sound, played the sound against itself, and spliced the tape in order to eliminate sections or to rearrange the sequence. Finally, he ordered these sound patterns into a sequence to create his musical composition.

Stereo Electronic Music No. 1   by Bulent Arel

Bulent Arel has used the resources of the tape medium in his composition in somewhat the same way as Halim El-Dabh explored them. However, the sound sources for this composition are entirely electronic. Arel began with sounds produced on oscillators and noise generators instead of with natural sounds. To create the completed composition, these sounds were filtered, combined, mixed, and finally organized into a musical design.

Composition for Synthesizer   by Milton Babbitt

Milton Babbitt created his composition on a machine called the **RCA Electronic Sound Synthesizer,** the only one of its kind in the world. In this composition the original sound and all its transformations are created directly on the synthesizer. The tape recorder is used only in recording the completed composition. Babbitt punched his choices on paper tape in order to provide the information needed for the synthesizer to produce the sounds. On this tape he indicated the frequency of each sound, its tone color, duration, and the envelope. (The envelope is the way the sound is to be attacked and allowed to die away.) He also had to indicate how each sound should progress to the next.

Record 11   Side B   Band 4a-4c.
(electronic)
RCA Electronic Sound Synthesizer.

Listen to Electronic Music

As children listen to the compositions discussed on this page, emphasize the idea that the composer of electronic music has the same purpose as the composer of traditional music: to communicate a musical idea to his audience. All three composers named in the lesson have written music for traditional musical instruments as well as for the electronic medium. They have turned to electronic music in order to explore additional possibilities of new musical sounds and structures, just as composers all through history have experimented with new musical ideas.

Introduce each of the compositions on a different day. Return to them at various times; ask children to comment on their reactions and to share their observations of the interesting patterns, sounds, and tone qualities. Electronic music is a very new medium and one that many of us may find confusing because we are not accustomed to hearing this kind of sound or musical organization. The children will need to become accustomed to the sound before they can examine the composition in greater detail. Remind them that they have all heard electronic music; the musical scores for television cartoons and space movies often use the electronic medium to create an atmosphere appropriate to the mood of such stories.

The three pieces included in this lesson are all excerpts from larger compositions. They were selected to represent three different kinds of electronic music.

Leilya and the Poet

BY HALIM EL-DABH
BORN 1921

When children have heard this composition, discuss the various sounds that they heard. Discuss how the composer has added to the expressive excitement of the composition through his transformation and manipulation of the original sounds. He has created variations in tone color, pitch, and dynamics which would have been impossible without the electronic medium. The resulting composition conveys an intense and expressive mood.

("Listen to Electronic Music" continued on page 190.)

Play on Notes

Based on a twelve-tone set
Starting Tone: C
Meter: ¢ (²∕𝅗𝅥)
No piano accompaniment

Begin the study of "Play on Notes" by reading the discussion in the pupil's book and listening to the recording. The commentary in the pupil's book refers mainly to Part I of the song since phrases 6 and 8 of Part II are transposed versions of the prime set.

Ask the class to name the notes found in the first two measures of the voice and bell parts. Place them on a staff.

Play this pattern on the bells and discover that all twelve tones of the chromatic scale are present. The notes of the two parts of the song (bells and voice) combine to make the **twelve-tone** set. Compare this with the Schoenberg composition (see page 160) where the opening melody containing all twelve tones is played in unison by the four string instruments. Discuss the fact that, when a composer has created his twelve-tone set he has, in effect, created his own "scale" or organization which will be the basis for his complete composition, just as the major and minor scales are the basis for the organization of the melody and harmony in traditional music.

Study the score and discover how Babbitt used his set to create the composition. Each two measures of the song is a rearrangement of the set. Help children discover the principle which underlies each rearrangement. Because music based on a twelve-tone set is primarily concerned with the intervals between the different pitches, first help children analyze the intervals which make up the original statement. Compare each subsequent phrase with this statement.

Analyze the voice part first. Give one bell to each of six children (C E F D G A). As each phrase is analyzed, ask children to rearrange themselves in the proper sequence so that the class can visualize the rearrangements as they hear the patterns and observe the notation.

Phrase 1: **Prime;** original statement.

C-E	E-F	F-D	D-G	G-A
major third	second	minor third	fourth	second
up	up	down	up	up

Play on Notes

Words and Music by
Milton Babbitt

"Play on Notes" is based on a twelve-tone set. It was written for you by Milton Babbitt, who also wrote "Composition for Synthesizer," which is discussed on page 187.

In Part I, notice that the entire melody for the voice is made up of only six tones. The bell part uses the other six tones from the twelve-tone set. Review what you learned about twelve-tone music on page 160.

If you study the words carefully, you will discover that this song is also a "play on words." Each word remains with its own tone throughout Part I.

Record 6 Side A Band 6. VOICES: children's choir.
ACCOMPANIMENT: bells.
FORM: Vocal.

Part II

sound the note, and play here.

Hear, play, and note the sound;

sound and play the note here.

Here note the play and sound;

sound the note, and play here.

Phrase 2: **Inversion;** each interval is turned upside down. The phrase begins with the last pitch of the first phrase.

A-F	F-E	E-G	G-D	D-C
major third	second	minor third	fourth	second
down	down	up	down	down

Phrase 3: **Retrograde Inversion;** beginning with the last interval of the set, each interval in turn is inverted.

C-D	D-G	G-E	E-F	F-A
second	fourth	minor third	second	major third
up	up	down	up	up

Phrase 4: Retrograde; the six pitches of the prime set are played backwards.

Phrase 5: Prime

Phrase 6: Inversion, Transposition. This is the same as phrase 2, except that each tone sounds a tritone (six half steps) higher or lower.

Phrase 7: Retrograde Inversion. This is the same as phrase 3.

Phrase 8: Retrograde, Transposition. This is the same as phrase 2, transposed a tritone.

When first learning the song, it may be helpful for children to play both parts on the bells so that they can hear the song as an entity. The harmonic relationship between the two parts consists of thirds and sixths (major and minor) except for the last tone in each section where the two voices are a tritone apart.

When children are comfortable with the sound and familiar with the rhythm, learn to sing the voice part. When this has been learned and children can sing it easily, assign the bell part to one child.

Enjoy the fact that this delightful song is not only a "play on notes" but also a "play on words." The composer has written the text so that the same word (or word sound) stays with the same pitch throughout Part I and phrases 5 and 7 of Part II, thus giving the children one more way of understanding the rearrangement of the twelve-tone set. The song may be sung in its entirety, or either part may be performed separately.

("Compose Your Own Electronic Music" continued from page 186.)

To begin the experiment, choose a single sound pattern and treat it with as many transformations as possible. Do not hesitate to put each sound through a series of transformations because the most interesting effects often occur after the original sound has been transformed several times.

To transform a sound by raising the pitch, follow these steps:

1. Tape the sound pattern at **slow** speed on tape recorder A.
2. Replay the pattern at **fast** speed on recorder A while recording it on tape recorder B running at **slow** speed.
3. Play the sound on recorder B at **fast** speed; record it on tape recorder A at **slow** speed.
4. Continue this process as long as desired. Each sound should be put through several transformations. Remember that the two tape recorders must always be set at different speeds.

To transform a sound by lowering the pitch, reverse the process.

1. Tape the original sound at **fast** speed on tape recorder A.
2. Replay it at **slow** speed on recorder A; record it on tape recorder B at **fast** speed. Continue the process as described above.

Experiment with combinations of sounds. Choose two transformed patterns of contrasting pitch, tone quality, and rhythm. Play one on tape recorder A, the other on tape recorder B. Record the two patterns simultaneously on a third tape recorder.

When children are ready to develop their composition, discuss the qualities which need to be present. A musical composition must have shape and coherence. Discuss ways of attaining these qualities through the repetition and contrast of tone colors, pitch levels, etc. Plan the sequence before beginning to tape. Help children realize that their completed composition must be very short because this process is quite time-consuming. Replay the Webern composition (page 161) to remind children that a composition can be very short and still complete.

The final composition may be put on tape by one of two processes. The selected sound segments may be taped in the chosen sequence onto a third tape recorder, one at a time. Another process is to cut the tapes apart, select the preferred segments, and splice them in the appropriate sequence.

Full page painting in pupil's book.
See page 209 for explanation of art.

("Listen to Electronic Music" continued from page 187.)

Stereo Electronic Music No. 1

BY BULENT AREL
BORN 1918

All the sounds in this composition are derived from an electronic origin; that is, the sounds originated as electrical impulses rather than as the vibrations of some substance such as a violin string or a drum head. The composition is planned around two "sound groups." The first serves as background. Its continuous texture contrasts with the second group which is made up of clearly defined patterns which stand out against the background. The first group remains constant while the second group is developed and expanded. The composer has likened this expansion to the growth of the branches on a tree.

Composition for Synthesizer

BY MILTON BABBITT
BORN 1916

The elaborate instrument, on which Babbitt composed this music, theoretically can produce an infinite number of different pitches, tone qualities, and sound patterns. His compositional technique was different from the other composers in that he dictated his decisions about each sound directly to the synthesizer, which automatically created the desired sound. He did not manipulate preexisting sounds on the tape as did the other composers when they created their compositions. Because of the vast capabilities of the RCA Electronic Sound Synthesizer, the composer is faced with a new problem: it is possible for him to produce a composition made up of pitches we could not distinguish and rhythm patterns moving too rapidly for us to comprehend. As Babbitt created his composition, he had to constantly keep in mind the hearing limitations of his audience.

As children listen to the composition, remind them that Babbitt had to make at least five different decisions for every single note that they hear. Every tone and every variation of sound have been specifically chosen by the composer in contrast to traditional music in which the performer interprets the composer's musical ideas. Draw attention to the wide variety in pitches, tone colors, rhythms, etc. which the composer used in this brief excerpt.

Key: C   Starting Tone: G (5)
Meter: $\frac{3}{4}$ ($\frac{3}{}$)
Piano accompaniment on page 315

Thanksgiving Hymn

Music for Special Times

Thanksgiving Hymn

Netherlands Folk Song
Arranged by Edward Kremser
Words Translated by Theodore Baker

1. We gath-er to-geth-er to ask the Lord's bless-ing,
2. Be-side us to guide us, our God with us join-ing,
3. We all do ex-tol thee, thou lead-er tri-um-phant,

He chas-tens and has-tens his will to make known;
Or-dain-ing, main-tain-ing his king-dom di-vine,
And pray that thou still our de-fend-er will be.

The wick-ed op-press-ing, now cease___ from dis-tress-ing.
So from the be-gin-ning the fight___ we were win-ning;
Let thy con-gre-ga-tion es-cape___ trib-u-la-tion.

Sing prais-es to his name;___ he for-gets not his own.
Thou, Lord, wast at our side, ___ all ___ glo-ry be thine.
Thy name be ev-er praised!___ O ___ Lord, make us free!

Record 6   Side A   Band 7. VOICES: children's choir.
ACCOMPANIMENT: organ.
FORM: Instrumental; Vocal, *vv. 1-3*.

* EXPRESSION: Many children will be familiar with this Dutch hymn. It is sometimes known as the "Netherlands Hymn." A Thanksgiving Day is also traditionally observed in the Netherlands although it is very different in expression from ours. In the Netherlands it is not a national holiday. In our country, it is observed with special services in the different churches. It is not a day of feasting in the Netherlands but a day for solemnity and fasting. The food is very simple.

Read aloud together the words of the hymn; make sure that children understand the meaning of such words as "chasten," "ordaining," "extol," etc. Discuss the importance of singing with careful enunciation. Complete each phrase as one thought so that the meaning of the text is clear.

* MELODY: Establish tonality and ask children to sing the first verse. Listen to the recording and compare performances. Isolate any problem intervals or phrases.

RHYTHM: The song should be sung in a majestic style. In order to maintain the flow of the melody, the $\frac{3}{4}$ meter and dotted patterns must be sung accurately in a sustained manner without strong accents.

191

Scored for instruments.
See "Exploring Music Instrumental Supplement."

Dona nobis pacem

Key: G   Starting Tone: G (1)
Meter: $\frac{3}{4}$ $\left(\frac{3}{\downarrow}\right)$
No piano accompaniment

* EXPRESSION: This beautiful round is a prayer. Discuss the ways that tempo, dynamics, and tone quality can help convey the mood of the words.

Study the melodic line and decide where the **climax** should occur in each of the three phrases. Locate the climax of the complete song. (Middle of second phrase.)

* HARMONY: This ancient round is an excellent example of polyphonic music. It should be learned thoroughly and enjoyed often as a unison song before children attempt to sing it as a three-part round.

It is effective to perform the round by singing each voice part once, then by humming the repetition. Continue humming until the third group reaches the end of the song. Group one will thus close with the second phrase; group two will close with the first phrase.

Dona nobis pacem

Traditional Round

The words of this song mean "Grant us peace." Sing the song in such a way that the meaning is expressed by the sound of your voices. Pay special attention to singing with pure vowel sounds.

This round can be especially effective when you sing it once through with words; then repeat it and hum the melody softly until everyone has sung the complete melody twice.

Record 6   Side B   Band 1.   VOICES: boy choir.
FORM: Vocal (unison); Vocal (3-part round).

O Come, O Come, Emmanuel

Music adapted from Plainsong
Words Translated by John M. Neale

This melody, based on a **plainsong**, is similar to the chants sung by the monks during the early days of Christianity. On the record this song is sung by a **male choir.** Their voices suggest the way plainsong might have sounded. Plainsongs are single-line melodies based on a **mode,** an ancient scale used in the earliest Christian music. Review the explanation of modes found on page 139. Plainsongs are never divided into regular rhythmic groupings or measures. The rhythm grows out of the rhythm of the words.

O come, O come, Em-man - u - el,
Ve - ni, Ve - ni, Em-man - u - el,

And ran - som cap - tive Is - ra - el,
Cap - ti - vum sol - ve Is - ra - el,

That mourns in lone - ly ex - ile here
Qui ge - mit in ex - i - li - o,

Un - til the Son of God ___ ap - pear.
Pri - va - tus De - i Fi - li - o.

Re - joice! Re - joice! Em-man - u - el
Gau - de! Gau - de! Em-man - u - el

Shall come to thee, O Is - ra - el.
Nas - ce - tur pro te, Is - ra - el.

Record 6   Side B   Band 2.   VOICES: men's ensemble.
FORM: Vocal (English); Vocal (Latin).

* MUSICAL STYLE: Ask children to examine the notation of the song. DO YOU NOTICE ANYTHING THAT MAKES THIS SONG APPEAR DIFFERENT FROM OTHER SONGS? Some children may notice the absence of measure bars and meter signature. Others may mention the use of several tones to one syllable.

Listen to the recording. DOES THE SONG SOUND DIFFERENT FROM OTHER SONGS YOU HAVE SUNG? Children may suggest that it seems unfinished and "wanders about."

Discuss the fact that this song is in the style of an ancient **plainsong,** the music that was sung in the earliest Christian churches. Locate this term on the Time Line on page 60. This song is not an original plainsong but is believed to have been composed in the nineteenth century. However, it exhibits characteristics of the ancient chants.

Help children summarize some of the musical characteristics of plainsong: there is no harmony; the rhythm is determined by the rhythm of the words; there are no regularly recurring accents to divide the melody into metric groupings. The melody is based on a mode and moves primarily by steps or small skips. There is no accompaniment. The text is always religious. The important words are stressed by singing several tones on the same syllable, thus giving an ornamental effect to that segment of the melodic line.

MELODY: Examine the melody of this song and discover the tones that are used: D E F G A Bb C D. Determine the scale structure: whole-half-whole-whole-half-whole-whole. This song is in the **Aeolian** mode. It is the same as our natural minor scale.

EXPRESSION: The song should be sung with a pure, clear tone quality in a steady tempo. The dynamics should be consistent throughout. Phrasing is determined by word meaning; each phrase should be sung as one thought.

Traditionally, plainsongs were sung by monks in the churches and cathedrals. The boys may choose to sing this song as their own while the girls listen.

I Wonder as I Wander

Tonality: Modal
Starting Tone: E
Meter: $\frac{6}{8}$ $\left(\frac{6}{♩}\right)$
Piano accompaniment on page 316

* EXPRESSION: Read the words aloud. Discuss how the use of folk expressions, such as "on'ry people," adds to the mood of the song. Listen to the recording. Draw attention to aspects of the performance which support the meditative mood of the song: the moderate tempo, the quiet tone, lack of strong rhythmic accent, simple accompaniment, and rhapsodic nature of the melody which, in this case, seems to "wander."

* HARMONY: Listen to the accompaniment. The simple chordal accompaniment reinforces the mood of the song because it also seems to "wander." The use of a dissonant chord (a chord that wants to move on) at the end of the song adds to this mood.

MELODY: This song seems to be written in A minor, although it ends on D. It is actually modal. (See page 139 for discussion of modes.) Many primitive folk songs are modal, probably influenced by the ancient church music. Compare this song with the hymn "O Come, O Come, Emmanuel." Both have the same plaintive, mystic quality supported by the freely flowing melody and rhythm.

FOLK STYLE: John Jacob Niles has spent his life collecting the folk songs of the American people. He has given lectures and recitals all over the country and was one of the first to bring folk music to the attention of the public. Niles has also written many songs. Like other folk composers, such as Woody Guthrie and Stephen Foster, his music is in the style of the folk song with texts which speak of feelings common to many people, rhythms which are wedded to the rhythm of the words, and simple melodies.

I Wonder as I Wander

Words and Music by
John Jacob Niles

John Jacob Niles is a collector of American folk songs as well as a famous composer. There are two performances of this composed carol on your record. The first one is sung by Mr. Niles. He shows the freedom a folk singer takes with a song as he sings in a high key and accompanies himself on the dulcimer, an old folk instrument. The second recording follows the rhythm and melody that appear in your book.

1. I wonder as I wander out under the sky
2. When Mary birthed Jesus 'twas in a cow's stall,
3. If Jesus had wanted for any wee thing,
4. I wonder as I wander out under the sky

How Jesus our Savior did come for to die
With wise men and farmers and shepherds and all,
A star in the sky or a bird on the wing,
How Jesus our Savior did come for to die

For poor on'ry people like you and like I.
But high from God's heaven a star's light did fall,
Or all of God's angels in heaven to sing,
For poor on'ry people like you and like I.

I wonder as I wander out under the sky.
And the promise of ages it then did recall.
He surely could have it, 'cause He was the King.
I wonder as I wander out under the sky.

Record 6 Side B Band 3A. VOICE: John Jacob Niles.
ACCOMPANIMENT: dulcimer.
FORM: Introduction, *1 meas.*; Vocal, *vv. 1-4.*

Record 6 Side B Band 3B. VOICE: soprano.
ACCOMPANIMENT: piano.
FORM: Intoduction, *2 meas.*; Vocal, *vv. 1-4.*

This expressive melody adds to the beauty of the words. Notice how the rising melodic contour, made up of a melodic sequence, dictates the phrasing and changes in dynamics.

Infant Jesus, King of Glory

Polish Carol
Words Adapted

Gently

1. In - fant Je - sus, King of glo - ry, Sleep - ing
2. In - fant Je - sus, King of glo - ry, We pro -

in a cat - tle stall. Moth - er Mar - y there be -
claim thy ho - ly birth. We have come to tell the

side thee, Watch - ing o'er the king. of all.
sto - ry Of glad tid - ings, peace on earth.

Shep - herds heard the an - gels sing - ing, Sing - ing
Come and join in hap - py sing - ing, Has - ten

car - ols bright and gay; — } Christ the Lord is born to -
now with - out de - lay; — }

softer

day, Christ the Lord is born to - day.

Key: G   Starting Tone: D (5)
Meter: $\frac{3}{4}$ $\left(\frac{3}{2}\right)$
Piano accompaniment on page 317

Infant Jesus, King of Glory

* EXPRESSION: Discuss the ways in which the melodic contour and word meaning dictate the dynamics and phrasing. As each melodic sequence rises, the voice naturally grows louder. WHERE DOES THE CLIMAX OF THIS SONG OCCUR? (At the end with the first statement "Christ the Lord is born today.") Discuss how a song usually has one major climax. Each phrase may also have a climactic point. One must sing each phrase emphasizing its climax, yet also continue to move toward the main climax of the complete song. The dynamics of this carol might be charted as follows:

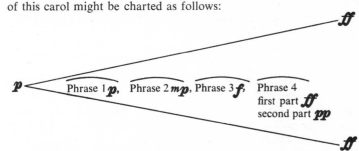

p Phrase 1 p,   Phrase 2 mp,   Phrase 3 f,   Phrase 4 first part ff second part pp ff ff

Remind children that each phrase must be sung as a single thought even though the melody is made up of several motives.

This:
Not this:

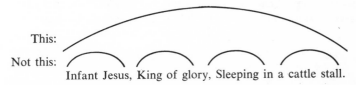

Infant Jesus, King of glory, Sleeping in a cattle stall.

MELODY: Listen to the recording and comment on the discussion in the pupil's book. Note the sequence in the first three measures. A second sequence can be found starting with measures eight through twelve. Note that the melody which is repeated at the end of the song is the same as the melody for measures two through four.

HARMONY: Study the relationships between the two voice parts. Notice that the first two phrases start in unison, then move in contrary motion. Discover the intervals between the two voices. The song moves primarily in thirds and sixths. Draw attention to the dissonant intervals created when the voices are only a half step apart (measure eleven) or a whole step apart (beginning of song, measures four, nine, ten).

The First Noel

Key: D   Starting Tone: F♯ (3)
Meter: ¾ (♩)
Piano accompaniment on page 319

* FORM: Study the form of the song. There is a verse and a refrain. The verse is made up of four phrases (two **periods,** see page 164). The second period is a repetition of the first. The design of the complete song is A A B.

Discuss the importance of singing phrases so that the word meaning is clear. For example, in phrase one a slight break in the middle of the phrase is appropriate because of the comma after "Noel." The same melody reappears in phrase three; but because of the word meaning, the complete phrase must now be sung without a break.

* RHYTHM: Read aloud the words of the poem in rhythm. Remind children to watch carefully for slurs, dotted patterns, etc. Listen to the recording. Note the difference in the slurring of words between verses. Discuss the importance of repeating the vowel of a word that is slurred in order to produce a beautiful sound: "No-o-el."

HARMONY: Assign a few children with high voices to sing the descant on the refrain. This might also be played on the bells.

The First Noel

Sing the descant to the refrain or play it on bells or other melody instruments.

Traditional English Carol

Record 6   Side B   Band 5.   VOICES: children's choir.
ACCOMPANIMENT: organ.
FORM: Introduction, 8 meas.; Vocal, vv. 1-2.

Scored for instruments.
See "Exploring Music Instrumental Supplement."

Christmas Is Coming
Traditional English Round

1. C — F — G7 — C
Christ - mas is com - ing, the goose is get - ting fat!

2. C — F — G7 — C
Please to put a pen - ny in an old man's hat.

C — F — G7 — C
If you have - n't got a pen - ny, a ha' - pen - ny will do,

C — F — G7 — C
If you have - n't got a ha - pen - ny, God bless you.

Record 6 Side B Band 6. VOICES: children's choir.
ACCOMPANIMENT: piccolo, bassoon.
FORM: Vocal (unison); Vocal (2-part round); Instrumental (2-part round).

Key: C   Starting Tone: C (1)

Meter: $\frac{4}{4}$ $\left(\frac{4}{\text{♩}}\right)$

No piano accompaniment

Christmas Is Coming

FOLK STYLE: The words of this charming old English round summarize many of the English Christmas customs. The goose was the traditional food on the English Christmas feast day. The poor would beg in the streets at Christmastide for a treat and pay for it with a song.

This song probably comes from the fifteenth century when rounds were popular in England. Compare the music of this song with other early English songs (pages 46-54).

* MELODY: Study the notation carefully. Sing with numbers until the melody is familiar. Note that the melody of phrases one and three are the same, although the rhythm is slightly altered. This is also true of phrases two and four.

* HARMONY: Sing as a two-part round. Follow the custom of fifteenth century England and assign one or two parts of the round to instruments. Flutes (or recorders) and violins would be suitable for the quickly moving melody.

Go Tell It on the Mountain

Key: A♭ Starting Tone: C (3)
Meter: $\frac{4}{4}$ ($\frac{4}{\quad}$)
No piano accompaniment

*FOLK STYLE: The United States has contributed many beautiful Christmas songs to the folk carol heritage. Spirituals are considered by many people to be the most beautiful songs among that group. This triumphant statement of the Christmas story is an excellent example. Note characteristics of spirituals found in this song: the religious text, the repeated refrain followed by a verse which narrates the story, syncopated rhythms.

RHYTHM: Study the notation. Compare the rhythms of the three voices. Note phrases where all voices move in the same rhythm and where they move in contrasting rhythm.

Have each group chant the rhythm of the words of its own part. Practice the syncopated patterns in measures three, four, and ten.

*HARMONY: Ask children to follow the notation of their part as they listen to the recording. Examine each part. Notice its movement in relation to the other voices and discuss the melodic contour of each voice. Work on the parts phrase by phrase; sing as much as possible of each phrase in harmony. Isolate problem areas in individual parts if needed. Immediately sing the phrase again in harmony.

If children are unable to sing the song in three parts, it may be learned in unison. In this song, the melody is always in the top voice. Some children may learn the refrain in unison and add the harmony for the easier verse section.

Go Tell It on the Mountain

Spiritual
Arranged by
Buryl A. Red

Record 7   Side A   Band 1.   VOICES: children's choir.
FORM: Vocal, *vv. 1-3.*

198

While Shepherds Kept Their Watching

1. While shep-herds kept their watch-ing O'er si-lent flocks by night, Be-hold through-out the heav-ens There shone a ho-ly light.
   Shep - herds watched o'er flocks by night, ———— Through - out heav - ens shone a ———— light. ————

2. The shep-herds feared and trem-bled When lo! a-bove the earth, Rang out the an-gel cho-rus That hailed our Sav-ior's birth.
   Shep - herds feared, a - bove the earth ———— Cho - rus hailed the Sav - ior's ———— birth. ————

3. Down in a low-ly man-ger Our hum-ble Christ was born, And God sent us sal-va-tion That bless-ed Christ-mas morn.
   Low - ly man - ger Christ was born, ———— God sent us that Christ - mas ———— morn. ————

Words for four carols learned in earlier grades are included here because they are especially useful at the Christmas season.

O Come, All Ye Faithful (Key: A)

1. O come, all ye faithful, joyful and triumphant,
   O come ye, O come ye to Bethlehem;
   Come and behold him, born the King of angels;
   Refrain
   O come, let us adore him, O come, let us adore him,
   O come, let us adore him, Christ, the Lord!

2. Sing, choirs of angels, sing in exultation,
   Sing, all ye citizens of heaven above!
   Glory to God, all glory in the highest;
   Refrain
   Adeste fideles,
   Laeti triumphantes,
   Venite, venite in Bethlehem:
   Natum videte
   Regem angelorum:

   Refrain
   Venite, adoremus, venite, adoremus,
   Venite, adoremus Dominum.

Joy to the World! (Key: D)

1. Joy to the World! the Lord is come:
   Let earth receive her King;
   Let every heart prepare him room,
   And heaven and nature sing, And heaven and nature sing,
   And heaven, and heaven and nature sing.

2. Joy to the earth! the Savior reigns:
   Let men their songs employ;
   While fields and floods, rocks, hills, and plains
   Repeat the sounding joy, Repeat the sounding joy,
   Repeat, repeat the sounding joy.

3. He rules the world with truth and grace,
   And makes the nations prove
   The glories of his righteousness,
   And wonders of his love, And wonders of his love,
   And wonders, wonders of his love.

Here We Come A-Wassailing (Key: Eb)

1. Here we come a-wassailing Among the leaves so green;
   Here we come a-wand'ring, So fair to be seen.
   Refrain
   Love and joy come to you, And to you your wassail too;
   And God bless you and send you a Happy New Year,
   And God send you a Happy New Year.

2. We are not daily beggars That beg from door to door;
   But we are neighbors' children, Whom you have seen before.
   Refrain

3. God bless the master of this house, Likewise the mistress too;
   And all the little children, That round the table go.
   Refrain

Deck the Halls (Key: Eb)

1. Deck the halls with boughs of holly, Fa la la la la la la la la.
   'Tis the season to be jolly, Fa la la . . . .
   Don we now our gay apparel, Fa la la . . . .
   Troll the ancient Yuletide carol, Fa la la . . . .

2. See the blazing Yule before us, Fa la la la la la la la la.
   Strike the harp and join the chorus, Fa la la . . . .
   Follow me in merry measure, Fa la la . . . .
   While I tell of Yuletide treasure, Fa la la . . . .

3. Fast away the old year passes, Fa la la la la la la la la.
   Hail the new, ye lads and lasses, Fa la la . . . .
   Sing we joyous all together, Fa la la . . . .
   Heedless of the wind and weather, Fa la la . . . .

Il est né

French Carol

The woodwind quintet accompanies this song on the recording. The bassoon and oboe in open fifths suggest the sound of musettes. The oboe plays the melody during the instrumental section. Can you describe its distinctive tone quality?

Record 7 Side A Band 2. VOICE: soprano.
ACCOMPANIMENT: flute, oboe, bassoon, French horn.
FORM: Introduction, *4 meas.*; Vocal; Instrumental.

Key: F   Starting Tone: C (5)   **Il est né**
Meter: $\frac{2}{2}$ $\left(\frac{2}{\downarrow}\right)$
Piano accompaniment on page 321

Jou - ez, haut - bois, ré - son - nez, mu - set - tes!

Il est né, le di - vin en - fant!

Fine

Chan - tons tous son a - vè - ne - ment!

De - puis plus de qua - tre mille ans,

Nous le pro - met - taient les pro - phè - tes,

De - puis plus de qua - tre mille ans,

D. C. al Fine

Nous at - ten - dions cet heu - reux temps.

The words of this lovely carol mean: "He is born, the divine Infant! Play, oboes; ring out, musettes! Let us all sing of his advent! For more than four thousand years, the prophets promised him to us. For more than four thousand years, we awaited this happy time."

* EXPRESSION: Many of our loveliest carols come from France; this one is an excellent example. Notice the characteristics of French folk music which are apparent in this song: it has a narrow range and moves primarily by steps; the rhythms are dance-like; the opening musical ideas are repeated at the end of the song (A B A).

To add to the folk quality of the song, one child might play an open fifth on the piano to suggest the sound of the bagpipes. At times, this will create a dissonant sound against the melody. This sounds typical of the wailing quality of a bagpipe accompaniment.

If there is a child in the class who plays the oboe, he might play the melody while the class sings.

* FORM: Study the design. It is A B A with each section made up of four two-measure phrases.

MELODY: Scan the melody; discover repeated patterns. Notice that the B section moves primarily by scale steps while the A section moves more often by skips, using tones of the I or V7 chords.

Establish tonality and challenge children to sing the complete song with numbers, then on a neutral syllable. Listen to the recording to learn the pronunciation of the French words.

Pat-A-Pan

Key: G minor   Starting Tone: G (1)
Meter: 2/2 (2/♩)
Piano accompaniment on page 322

* FOLK STYLE: Notice the characteristics of French folk music apparent in this song: the melody based on the minor scale, the dance-like rhythms, the repetition of the opening melodic idea.

While one child plays the percussion pattern on a drum, another might play the melody on the flute. The flute is a common folk instrument in France.

RHYTHM: Using the two rhythm patterns of the song as the basis for movement, some members of the class might dramatize the carol in dance. The march rhythm (two beats to the measure) can be taken for a light, high-stepping march by the drummer and fife player. They can march throughout the song and pretend to play instruments. The rhythm of "Pat-a-pat-a-pan" or "Tu-re-lu-re-ley" might be danced by a few children in four quick steps and a hop throughout. A third group or two or three children might dance when the tambourine plays, stepping with the rhythm pattern in a step-run-run-step movement, hop-run-run-hop, or whatever they choose as a light, quick dance step. When the three groups can dance the rhythm patterns, they might move in three circles: the drummer and fife player in the inner circle, the next circle moving in the opposite direction, and the outer circle in the same direction as the inner circle.

HARMONY: Examine the notation and discover where the voices move together in thirds and where they move in contrary motion (as on the words "on this joyous holiday").

EXPRESSION: This appealing carol should be sung in a steady tempo with crisp enunciation of the words. Suggest to the children that the sound of their voices should imitate the crispness of the drum. In the coda, the percussion should get gradually softer and softer (decrescendo) as though the procession were moving into the distance. Children may enjoy extending the coda by repeating these last four measures.

Pat-A-Pan

French Carol
Arranged by Kurt Miller
Words Adapted by Kurt Miller

In ancient France, carols were both sung and danced to celebrate Christmas. Review the discussion of French music on page 93.

(Tambourine or Drum)

Pat - a - pat - a - pan, _____

Tu - re - lu - re - ley, _____   Fife and

drum to - geth - er play on this joy - ous hol - i - day.

1. Bil - lie,   bring your new red   drum, Rob - bie, get your
2. There is   mu - sic   in the   air,   you can hear it

1. Bil - lie
2. Mu - sic

Record 7   Side A   Band 3.   VOICES: children's choir.
ACCOMPANIMENT: 2 piccolos, percussion.
FORM: Vocal, vv. 1-2.

202

fife and come.
ev - ery - where. } Fife and drum to-geth-er

bring your drum.
ev - ery - where. } Rob -

play, Pat - a - pat - a - pan, Tu - re - lu - re - ley; Fife and

bie, your fife play; Fife and

drum to - geth - er play on this joy - ous hol - i - day.

Pat - a - pat - a - pan.

Some class members may wish to plan a dance for this carol while others play the percussion accompaniment.

Enjoy the following poetry in your class. Some children may wish to develop their own carol melody for one of the poems.

Christmas Carol

Author Unknown

God bless the master of this house,
    And its good mistress, too,
And all the little children
    That round the table go;
And all your kin and kinsmen,
    That dwell both far and near;
We wish you a Merry Christmas
    And a Happy New Year.

Carol, Brothers, Carol

by William Muhlenberg

Carol, brothers, carol,
    Carol joyfully,
Carol the glad tidings,
    Carol merrily!
And pray a gladsome Christmas
    For all good Christian men,
Carol, brothers, carol,
    Christmas comes again.

Haleluyoh

Key: G minor   Starting Tone: D (5)
Meter: $\frac{6}{8}$ ($\frac{2}{\text{♩.}}$)
Piano accompaniment on page 325

* EXPRESSION: Discuss the history of the Passover festival with the children. It is the Jewish festival of freedom and celebrates the Jews' exodus from Egypt. The story of the Passover can be found in Exodus 12:3-40. A destroying angel killed the firstborn child in every Egyptian home but "passed over" the homes of the Israelites. The word "passover" also refers to the passing of the Israelites out of Egypt into a free land. The Hebrew name for Passover is *Pesach*. It is sometimes called the "Feast of Unleavened Bread" because the Israelites baked unleavened bread, or *matzah,* to take with them on their flight from Egypt.

Jewish families celebrate Passover at home with a feast called the *Seder*. The head of the family reads the story of the Passover out of the *Haggadah*.

FOLK STYLE: Compare the music of this song with other Jewish songs from Eastern Europe such as "Tum Balalyka" and "Shalom Alëhem." Certain common characteristics can be observed in all: the minor tonality, the repetitious rhythm patterns, the strong accents.

* MELODY: Study the notation and learn the melody by following the steps on page 13. Discover that the song is in minor. The added F♯ suggests the use of the harmonic minor. See page 23 and review the differences between the natural and harmonic minor scales.

Notice the interval from F♯ to E♭ (one and one half steps, or a minor third). The use of this augmented interval between the sixth and seventh steps of a scale is often found in music of Eastern Europe. Sing up and down the scale to help children feel the tonality.

Have children sing the melody on a neutral syllable. Listen to the recording to learn the Hebrew words which mean:

> Hallelujah, Hallelujah,
> Praise God forever more.
> A rock and refuge is he to us
> Now as in days of yore.
> Hallelujah.

Haleluyoh

Jewish Folk Song

Ha - le - lu - yoh, ha - le - lu - yoh, Ha - le - lu av - dey A - do - noi, Ha - le - lu - yoh, ha - le - lu - yoh, Ha - le - lu es shem A - do - noi. Ha - le - lu - yoh, ha - le - lu - yoh, Ha - le - lu - yoh, ha - le - lu - yoh, Ha - le - lu - yoh, ha - le - lu - yoh, Ha - le - lu - yoh, ha - le - lu - yoh.

Record 7   Side A   Band 4. VOICES: soprano, baritone.
ACCOMPANIMENT: clarinet, accordion, guitar, double bass, percussion.
FORM: Instrumental; Vocal; Instrumental (Vocal on last 8 meas.).

204

Key: G   Starting Tone: D (5)
Meter: $\frac{2}{4}$ $\left(\frac{2}{}\right)$
No piano accompaniment

Lieb Nachtigall
German Folk Song

In Germany this is one of the most popular Christmas songs. The German words are translated as follows:

Lieb Nachtigall—dear nightingale
wach auf—wake up
du schönes Vögelein auf jenem grünen Zweigelein—thou lovely little bird on yonder green branch
wach hurtig ohn' Verschnauf—watch attentively without ever resting
Dem Kindelein auserkoren—to the chosen child
heut geboren—born today
halb erfroren—half frozen to death
sing—sing
dem zarten Kindelein—to the tender child

* HARMONY: When the children have heard the recording and have studied the pronunciation and meaning of the words, they should notice the notation. In the first section of the song, words and notes are identical for the two voices. In the second section of the song, the voices move in harmony, most of which is in contrary motion.

RHYTHM: The meter seems to fit the text of the song. The even rhythm and the $\frac{2}{4}$ meter is right for the words of the first section and for the melodic imitation. The accented $\frac{3}{4}$ measure on the word "sing" reflects an urgency expressed in the words "ohn' Verschnauf." The $\frac{4}{4}$ meter closes the song with steady duple accent.

Record 7   Side A   Band 5.   VOICES: 2 sopranos.
ACCOMPANIMENT: 2 flutes.
FORM: Vocal (soprano on upper part, flute on lower part); Vocal (flute on upper part, soprano on lower part); Vocal (sopranos and flutes on both parts).

Ríu, Ríu, Chíu

Tonality: Modal
Starting Tone: B
No piano accompaniment

* RHYTHM: Read the discussion in the pupil's book regarding the rhythm. This type of rhythm, which makes use of freely changing metric groupings based on the natural word stress, was typical of the music of the early centuries. Bar lines given in the pupil's book are simply for our convenience, because we are accustomed to seeing rhythm patterns grouped by measures. These measure groups are usually of equal length in music of later periods. Examine the notation. Consider the quarter note as the beat note and determine the number of beats in each rhythmic group.

* MUSICAL STYLE: This Spanish carol comes from the sixteenth century. A rich musical life flourished in Spain during this period. Composers wrote music for the church, music for small instrumental ensembles, and secular songs. Review the discussion of Spanish music on page 135. The modal quality of the melody, its narrow range and stepwise contour, the free rhythm, and the lack of harmony are typical of the music of this period.

Create a percussion accompaniment. A tambourine or hand-clapping accompaniment would be appropriate for this Spanish carol from the sixteenth century. One accompaniment pattern might be to play on the first beat of every measure.

Improvise another accompaniment pattern by tapping every fourth beat beginning with the first beat of the song.

This song is recorded in two ways. Voices, accompanied by tambourine, sing the melody only as written in the pupil's book. The second part of the recording presents the song in its original four-part setting for mixed voices (only the first verse is sung).

Ríu, Ríu, Chíu

Spanish Christmas Carol
Words Adapted

This carol is sung in free meter. As in all early music, this song originally had no bar lines. The bar lines added here indicate rhythmic groupings. There is no meter signature because not all measures contain the same number of beats.

Record 7   Side A   Band 6.   VOICES: mixed choir.
ACCOMPANIMENT: percussion.
FORM: Vocal, *v. 1* (choir as originally written); Vocal,
v. 2 (as written in the book).

The rich sounds of a string quartet accompany this song on the record. The words of the song suggest another instrument. Name this instrument and listen for it on the recording.

Music in the Air

Words and Music by
George Root

Key: G   Starting Tone: D (5)
Meter: $\frac{4}{4}$ $\left(\frac{4}{\downarrow}\right)$
Piano accompaniment on page 326

Music in the Air

There's mu-sic in the air, ___ When the in-fant morn is nigh.

There's mu-sic in the air, ___ When the in-fant morn is nigh.

And faint its blush is seen ___ On the bright and laugh-ing sky.

And faint its blush is seen ___ On the bright and laugh-ing sky.

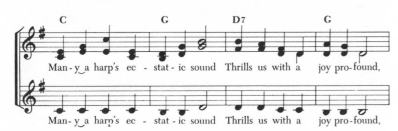

Man-y a harp's ec-stat-ic sound Thrills us with a joy pro-found,

Man-y a harp's ec-stat-ic sound Thrills us with a joy pro-found,

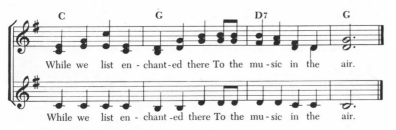

While we list en-chant-ed there To the mu-sic in the air.

While we list en-chant-ed there To the mu-sic in the air.

Record 7   Side A   Band 7. VOICES: children's choir.
ACCOMPANIMENT: string quartet, harp.
FORM: Instrumental; Vocal.

207

FORM: Observe the notation and listen to the recording; conclude that the song is in two sections made up of two phrases each: A A B B′. Remind children that awareness of form will help them learn the music more quickly. As soon as phrases one and three are learned, the entire song has been studied!

* HARMONY: Determine the tonality of the song and write the I, IV, and V7 chords on the chalkboard.

I   IV   V7

Review the terms "homophonic" and "polyphonic." (See page 50.) WHICH KIND OF HARMONY IS FOUND IN THIS SONG? (Homophonic; there is a main melody, and the lower voices simply support this melodic line.)

Analyze the chord structure of the song to discover what chords are being used. The entire song is based on the I, IV, and V7 chords. (The B in measures three and eleven and the A in measure twelve are passing tones.)

Play the chord sequence on the autoharp while children listen to the chord progressions and watch the notation of their own parts. Notice that the lower part often moves a sixth below the melody; the middle voice often moves in thirds with the melody.

Play the autoharp accompaniment as children sing at sight the three parts simultaneously with a neutral syllable. Remind them to "think" the chord progressions as they sing.

* EXPRESSION: Notice the expressive contour of each phrase. There is a high point near the middle of each phrase.

Discuss the contributions that suitable tempo, appropriate changes in dynamics, and correct phrasing make to the expressiveness of the song. In each phrase, the children should make a slight crescendo to the high point, followed by a decrescendo. Avoid breaking the phrase with a breath.

Scored for instruments.
See "Exploring Music Instrumental Supplement."

The American Hymn

Key: E♭ Starting Tone: B♭ (5)
Meter: 4/4 (♩)
Piano accompaniment on page 327

* EXPRESSION: Read the information about the author given in the pupil's book. Discuss the meaning of the word "immigrant" and the fact that all of our ancestors were "immigrants" at one time.

Read aloud the words of the song and discuss the meaning of such phrases as "girdle with virtue."

* FORM: Review the function of the symbol *D. S. al Fine* (return to the sign 𝄋 and sing to *Fine,* the "end").

* RHYTHM: Review the steps for learning the rhythm of a song. Scan the notation; discover that the rhythm pattern ♩ ♩ ♩ is often repeated. Note the dotted patterns in phrases four and five. Remind children to sustain the whole notes at the end of each phrase for the full four beats.

* MELODY: Ask children to recall the steps for learning a melody. Draw attention to the fact that there is no melodic repetition in the song (except for the D. S.). Review the function of the accidental (♮) in phrase two. Notice the sequential pattern in phrase three.

The American Hymn

**Words and Music by
Matthias Keller**

Keller was an immigrant from Germany to the United States during the early 1800's. He wrote many patriotic songs for his adopted country, including "The American Hymn." It was chosen to be sung at a special ceremony celebrating the end of the war between the states.

A brass quartet plays this song on the recording. Why do you think this is appropriate to accompany a patriotic song?

Record 7   Side A   Band 8.   VOICES: mixed choir.
ACCOMPANIMENT: brass quartet.
FORM: Introduction, *4 meas.;* Vocal, *vv. 1-2.*

 Scored for instruments.
See "Exploring Music Instrumental Supplement."

NOTES ABOUT THE ARTIST'S PAINTINGS

In the paintings for the unit opening pages, the artist combined color and form in free flowing designs. As works of art, they point up the relationship between painting and music.

The primary purpose of the paintings, however, is to reflect the musical content of the book. They introduce particular regions of the world, suggest the geography, mood, and music of those regions, and hint at the universal characteristics of music. The dominant color in each unit opener is picked up in the rest of the art work for the unit.

Let's Explore Music   (Page iv)

We see a massive ball and as we look closer, we see that it is almost a globe, with the Americas, Europe, and Africa faintly discernible. Like the rhythmic beat of music, a pulsating line, gradually getting lighter and sharper, climbs upward and across. It is the path of music we are about to explore. Long thin rest symbols and squared notes are used as accents.

Music of the British Isles   (Page 32)

The general shapes of the British Isles are colors: purple for England, deep gray for Wales, rust for Scotland, and green-yellow for Ireland. In them are musical touches: singers harmonizing in Wales, a harp in Ireland, and a hint of a bagpipe in Scotland. The color accents are musical symbols in varying levels of clarity—notes, sharps, and rests. The rests also act as waves traveling back and forth between Britain and the continent, much as the music of those regions interacts. The blue around the outside reminds us that these countries are islands.

Music of Europe   (Page 62)

As before, a map emerges from the shapes and colors. And, as before, musical characteristics are an essential part of the design. Italy is yellow. Antique notes and Roman arches lead up to the pipe organs of France, a blue cathedral. Germany is green. There the yellow breaks into a rococo swirl, contrasting in color, shape, and rhythm to the static beat of boots from Czechoslovakia. Separated from the main design is a flamboyant coral swirl, the flare of Spain and Spanish music. Sound waves of the background color lead to the text opposite.

Music of Scandinavia   (Page 104)

Cold, bleak blues and blue-blacks of the lonely Arctic and dense northern forests press downward and gradually break into the bright colors of Norway, Sweden, Finland, and Denmark. Accents here are tiny splashes of color, suggesting people and the heavily populated part of Scandinavia.

Music of Latin America and Spain   (Page 118)

The flamboyant coral swirl of Spain is here accented by music stops and by castanets. From Spain colors stream across the Atlantic and circle Latin America. Drum beats from Africa pulsate east to west, too, particularly toward the Caribbean area and Brazil. The heart shape of Mexico suggests the sentimental Mexican songs. The vertical lines in the shape that is South America remind us of Indian string instruments and of sound waves.

Music of Asia and the Orient   (Page 142)

The dominant yellow mass is China—and a Chinese lute. To the southwest brilliant colors of Indian silks and a horn form India. Stretching southeastward in a disorganized array, splashes of brown are peppered with darker specks. These are the heavily-populated islands of Southeast Asia. To the north, in contrast, is the neat shape of a musical rest—Japan. The red circle nearby suggests the Japanese flag.

More Music to Explore   (Page 156)

Here we find elements of our American musical background and of contemporary music. Easily recognizable are a piano keyboard along the Gulf Coast (jazz), singers in the deep South (Negro spirituals), other singers in the Appalachians, Texas, and Oregon (folk music). The coral Spanish color shows up in the Southwest, and the blue, green, and blond colors move across from Europe to the Northeast. The irregular sound waves from a guitar pass through an oscilloscope and become mechanical, electronic music. Sharp off beat notes here and there and accents fading out point up the complexities of modern music.

Music for Special Times   (Page 190)

Purple tones and the vague shape of a church suggest the religious origin of many holidays. Bits of bright blue confetti lighten the painting and tell us that holidays are gay, too. Rhythmic lines play against each other: soft, sweeping traditional curves and sharp-edged modern ones. The dominant purples of this painting make us think again of the similar colors in the first painting.

2. The Home Road

Words and Music by
John Alden Carpenter

1. Sing a hymn of free - dom, Fling the ban - ner high!
2. In the qui - et hours _____ Of the star - ry night,

Sing the songs of Lib - er - ty, Songs that shall not die,
Dream the dreams of far a - way, Home fires burn - ing bright,

Refrain
For the long, long road to Tip - pe - ra - ry Is the road that leads me home, O'er

hills and plains, By lakes and lanes, My wood - lands! My corn - fields! My coun - try! My home!

3. Johnny Has Gone for a Soldier

American Folk Song

1. There I sat on But-ter-milk Hill. Who could blame me cry my fill? And
2. Me oh my, I loved him so; Broke my heart to see him go, And

ev - ery tear would turn a mill;
on - ly time will heal my woe; } John-ny has gone for a sol - dier.

4. Roll On, Columbia

Words and Music by
Woodie Guthrie

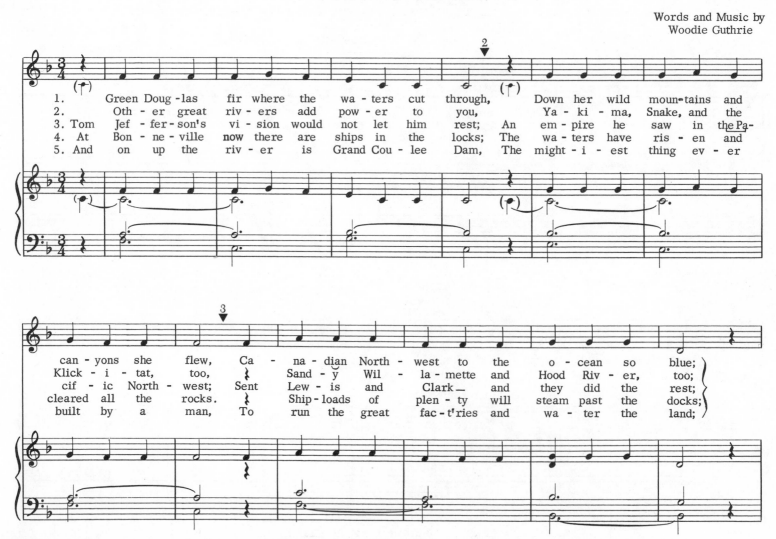

1. Green Doug-las fir where the wa-ters cut through, Down her wild moun-tains and
2. Oth-er great riv-ers add pow-er to you, Ya-ki-ma, Snake, and the
3. Tom Jef-fer-son's vi-sion would not let him rest; An em-pire he saw in the Pa-
4. At Bon-ne-ville now there are ships in the locks; The wa-ters have ris-en and
5. And on up the riv-er is Grand Cou-lee Dam, The might-i-est thing ev-er

can-yons she flew, Ca-na-dian North-west to the o-cean so blue;
Klick-i-tat, too, Sand-y Wil-la-mette and Hood Riv-er, too;
cif-ic North-west; Sent Lew-is and Clark and they did the rest;
cleared all the rocks. Ship-loads of plen-ty will steam past the docks;
built by a man, To run the great fac-t'ries and wa-ter the land;

6. Peace of the River

Music by Viola Wood
Words by Glendora Gosling

Peace I ask of thee, O riv - er, Peace, peace, peace. When I learn to live se - rene - ly,

Cares will cease. From the hills I gath - er cour-age, Vi - sion of the day to be, Strength to lead and faith to

fol - low, All are giv-en un-to me. Peace I ask of thee, O riv - er, Peace, peace, peace.

8. God of Our Fathers

Music by George W. Warren
Words by Daniel C. Roberts

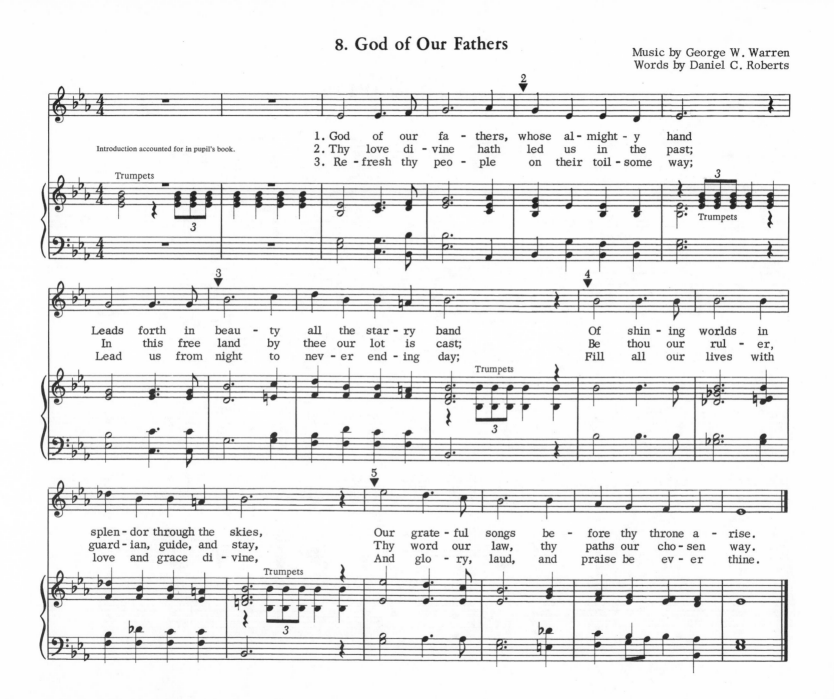

Introduction accounted for in pupil's book.

1. God of our fa - thers, whose al - might - y hand
2. Thy love di - vine hath led us in the past;
3. Re - fresh thy peo - ple on their toil - some way;

Leads forth in beau - ty all the star - ry band Of shin - ing worlds in
In this free land by thee our lot is cast; Be thou our rul - er,
Lead us from night to nev - er end - ing day; Fill all our lives with

splen - dor through the skies, Our grate - ful songs be - fore thy throne a - rise.
guard - ian, guide, and stay, Thy word our law, thy paths our cho - sen way.
love and grace di - vine, And glo - ry, laud, and praise be ev - er thine.

10. You're a Grand Old Flag

Words and Music by
George M. Cohan

Arranged by Kurt Miller

Introduction not accounted for in pupil's book.

You're a grand old flag, You're a high-fly-ing flag; And for-ev-er in peace may you wave; _____ You're the em-blem of the land I love, The home of the free and the

216

brave._____ Ev - ery heart beats true un - der

red, white, and blue, Where there's nev - er a boast or

brag;_____ But should auld ac - quaint - ance be for -

got, Keep your eye on the grand old flag._____

12. Swinging Along

Girl Scout Song

Swing - ing a - long the o - pen road. Swing - ing a - long un -der

(Melody)

Swing a - long _____ the o - pen road un - der sky that's

sky that's clear. Swing - ing a - long the o - pen road,

clear. Swing a - long _____ the o - pen road in the

14. Streets of Laredo

Cowboy Song

1. As I _____ walked out in the streets of La - re - do, As
2. "I see by your out - fit that you are a cow - boy," These
3. "Get six jol - ly cow - boys to car - ry my cof - fin, Get
4. "Oh, beat the drum slow - ly and play the fife low - ly,

I _____ walked out in La - re - do one day, I
words he did say as I bold - ly walked by; "Come
six pur - ty maid - ens to sing me a song; Take
Play the dead march as you car-ry me a - long; Put

220

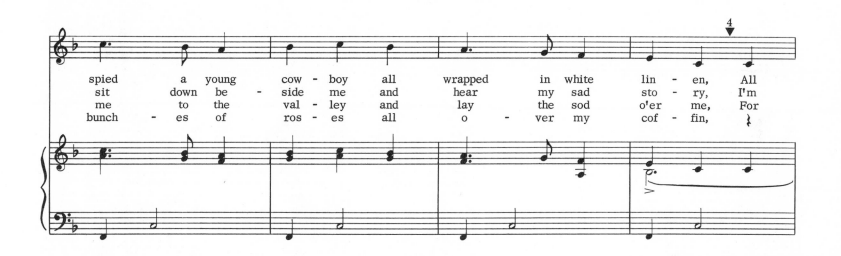

4

spied   a   young   cow - boy   all   wrapped   in   white   lin - en,   All
sit   down   be - side   me   and   hear   my   sad   sto - ry,   I'm
me   to   the   val - ley   and   lay   the   sod   o'er   me,   For
bunch - es   of   ros - es   all   o - ver   my   cof - fin,

wrapped   in   white   lin - en   and   cold   as   the   clay.
shot   in   the   breast   and   I   know   I   must   die."
I'm   a   young   cow - boy   and   know   I've   done   wrong."
Ros - es   to   dead - en   the   clods   as   they   fall."

15. These Things Shall Be

Music by Thomas Williams
Words by John A. Symonds

222

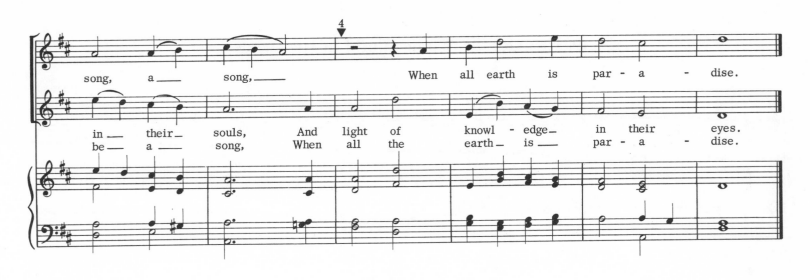

song, a ___ song, ___ When all earth is par - a - dise.

in ___ their ___ souls, And light of knowl - edge ___ in their eyes.
be ___ a ___ song, When all the earth ___ is ___ par - a - dise.

17. A Hundred Years Ago

American Windlass Song

1. A hun - dred years is a ver - y long time, Oh, yes, oh! A
2. A hun - dred years have ___ passed and gone, Oh, yes, oh! A
3. A hun - dred years will ___ come ___ once more, Oh, yes, oh! A

hun - dred years is a ver - y long time, A hun - dred years a - go.
hun - dred years have ___ passed ___ and gone, A hun - dred years a - go.
hun - dred years will ___ come ___ once more, A hun - dred years a - go.

19. He's Got the Whole World in His Hands

Spiritual

1. He's got the whole world __ in his hands, __ He's got the whole world __ in his hands, __ He's got the whole world __ in his hands, __ He's got the whole world in his hands. _____

2. He's got the wind and rain __ in his hands, __ He's got the wind and rain __ in his hands, __ He's got the whole world in his hands. _____

3. He's got both you and me __ in his hands, __ He's got both you and me __ in his hands, __ He's got the whole world in his hands. _____

20. The Peddler

Ukrainian Folk Song
Words by Margaret Lowrey

1. Look down the street, see the ped - dler come, With his heav - y pack up - on his back;
2. "Tell me, now tell me, my fair - est maid, Will you buy some lace to help my trade?"

He is tired and his shoul - ders ache, But he must move on for mon - ey's sake.
"Please, good man, you need not in - sist, For such love - ly lace I can't re - sist."

Refrain

Hai - da, hai - da, hai - da, hai - da,— Hai - da, hai - da, hai - da, da.

22. Tum Balalyka

Jewish Folk Song
Words by Ruth Robbins

(Boys) 1. Maid - en, maid - en, tell ___ me true, What can
(Girls) 2. Sil - ly lad, the an - swer true; A stone can

grow with - out ___ the dew? What ___ can burn for
grow with - out ___ the dew. Love ___ can burn for

years ___ and years? What ___ can cry and shed ___ no tears?
years ___ and years; A heart ___ can cry and shed ___ no tears.

226

227

30. Let Us Break Bread Together

Spiritual
Arranged by
William S. Haynie

228

34. Shule Aroon

Irish Folk Song

1. I would I were on yon-der hill, 'Tis there I'd sit_ and cry_ my fill, And_ ev - er-y_ tear_ would
2. I'll sell my rock, I'll sell my reel, I'll sell my on-ly_ spin-ning wheel, To_ buy_ for my love_ a _
3. I wish, I wish, I wish in vain, I wish I had my_ heart a-gain, And_ vain-ly_ think I'd
4. But now my love has gone to France, To try his for-tune to _ ad-vance; If he e'er comes back 'tis _

turn_ a _ mill,
sword of_ steel,
not_ com-plain,
but_ a_ chance,

Iss guh day_thoo a-voor-neen_ slawn.

Refrain

Shule, _ shule, _ shule a - roon! _

On-ly death can ease my woe, Since the lad of my heart from me did go, Iss guh day_thoo a-voor-neen slawn.

230

36. The Minstrel Boy

Irish Air
Words by Thomas Moore

1. The min - strel boy__ to the war is gone, In the ranks of death __ you'll find him; His
2. The min - strel fell __ but the foe - man's chain Could not bring his proud __ soul un - der: The

fa - ther's sword he has gird - ed on, And his wild harp slung __ be - hind him.
harp he loved__ ne'er__ spoke a - gain, For he tore its chords __ a - sun - der. And

"Land of song," said the war - rior bard, "Though all the world be - tray __ thee, One
said, "No chains shall__ sul - ly thee, Thou soul of love and brav - ery Thy

sword at least__ thy__ rights shall guard, One__ faith - ful harp __ shall praise thee."
songs were made__ for the proud and free, They shall nev - er sound __ in slav - ery."

38. Cockles and Mussels

Irish Folk Song

Liltingly

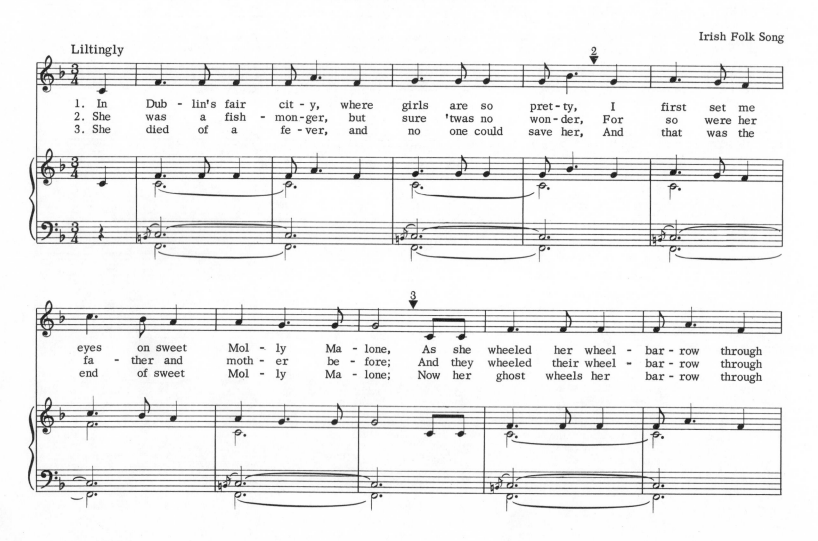

1. In Dub – lin's fair cit – y, where girls are so pret – ty, I first set me
2. She was a fish – mon – ger, but sure 'twas no won – der, For so were her
3. She died of a fe – ver, and no one could save her, And so that was the

eyes on sweet Mol – ly Ma – lone, As she wheeled her wheel – bar – row through
fa – ther and moth – er be – fore; And they wheeled their wheel – bar – row through
end of sweet Mol – ly Ma – lone; Now her ghost wheels her bar – row through

streets broad and nar-row,)
streets broad and nar-row,} Cry-ing, "Cock-les and mus-sels, a - live, a-live oh!"
streets broad and nar-row,)

5
Refrain

A - live, a-live oh!_ A - live, a-live oh!_ Cry-ing "Cock-les and mus-sels, a - live, a-live oh!"

live oh! live oh! "Cock-les, ___ mus - sels,_ live, live, oh!"

40. Turn Ye to Me

Scottish Folk Song
Words by John Wilson

Cold is the storm-wind that ruf-fles his breast, But warm are the
Hushed be thy moan-ing, lone bird of the sea, Thy home on the

down-y plumes lin-ing his nest, Cold blows the storm____ there,
rock is a shel-ter to thee; Thy home is the an-gry wave,

soft falls the snow____ there, Ho - ro, Mhai - ri dhu, Turn ye ——— to me.
mine but the lone-ly grave, Ho - ro, Mhai - ri dhu, Turn ye ——— to me.

42. Comin' Thro' the Rye

Old Scottish Air
Traditional adaptation
of a poem by Robert Burns

Ped.

236

43. Come O'er the Stream, Charlie

Scottish Folk Song
Words by James Hogg

Refrain

Come o'er the stream, Char-lie, dear Char-lie, brave Char-lie, Come o'er the stream, Char-lie, and
And though you be wea-ry, we'll make your heart cheer-y, And wel-come our Char-lie and

Fine **Verse**

dine with Mac - Lean; 1. We'll bring down the red deer, we'll bring down the black steer, The
his loy-al train. 2. If aught will in-vite you, or more will de-light you, 'Tis

lamb from the brack-en and doe from the glen; The salt sea we'll har-ry and
read-y, a troop of our bold High-land men Shall range on the heath-er, with

D. C. al Fine

bring to our Char-lie The cream from the both-y and curd from the pen.
bon-net and feath-er, Strong arms and broad clay-mores, three hun-dred and ten.

44. Migildi Magildi

Welsh Folk Song
Arranged by Kurt Miller
Words by Jack Dobbs

Introduction not accounted for in pupil's book.

Ho boys, to-geth-er we'll sing, with a mi-gil-di hi now now,

We'll sing you

What a fine and pleas-ant sight,
What a fine and pleas-ant race,
What a fine and pleas-ant sound,
Mi - gil - di ma - gil - di hi now now, For the warm-est bright-est place;
In the smith - y warm and bright;
When the songs and tales go round;

hi now ho now, Mi - gil - di ma - gil - di hi now now, Hi now ho now,

238

46. Greensleeves

Old English Folk Song

1. A - las! my love,_ you do me wrong,_ To cast me off _ dis - cour - teous - ly; For
2. Ah, Green-sleeves, now_ fare well, a - dieu,_ To God I pray_ to pros - per thee, For

I have loved _ you, oh, so long,_ De - light - ing in _ your com - pa - ny.
I am still _ thy sweet - heart true;_ Come once_ a - gain _ to meet _ me.

Green - sleeves_ was all my joy, ___ And oh, Green - sleeves_ was my de - light,

Green - sleeves, my heart of gold, ___ And all ___ for La - dy Green - sleeves.

50. Now Is the Month of Maying

Music by Thomas Morley

1. Now   is   the month of   May - ing, When   mer - ry lads   are   play - ing,} Fa   la
2. The   Spring, clad all   in   glad - ness, Doth   laugh   at win - ter's   sad - ness,} Fa   la

1. Now   is   the month of   May - ing, When   mer - ry lads   are   play - ing,} Fa   la
2. The   Spring, clad all   in   glad - ness, Doth   laugh   at win - ter's   sad - ness,} Fa   la

la   la   la   la   la   la   la,   Fa   la   la   la   la   la   la.

la   la   la   la   la   la   la,   Fa   la   la   la   la   la   la.

(1.) Each   with his bon - ny   lass,   A – danc - ing on   the   grass.
(2.) And   to the bag - pipes' sound   The nymphs tread out the   ground.

(1.) Each   with his bon - ny   lass,   A – danc - ing on   the   grass.
(2.) And   to the bag - pipes' sound   The nymphs tread out the   ground.

Fa la

Fa la la

la   la   la,   Fa la la la la la la   la   la la la   la.

la   la   Fa la   la la la,   Fa la   la   la   la   la   la.

56. A New Year Carol

Music by Benjamin Britten
Words Anonymous

245

64. Ma bella bimba

Italian Folk Song
Arranged by Kurt Miller
Words Adapted

Introduction not accounted for in pupil's book.

Ma co - me bal - li, bel - la

Ma co - me

bim - ba, bel - la bim - ba, bel - la bim - ba, Ma co - me bal - li, bel - la

bel - la bim - ba, Ma co - me

bim - ba, bel - la bim - ba, bal - li ben! Bel - la bim - ba,
bel - la ben! Guar - da che pas - sa
See how the pret - ty girl
Bel - la bim - ba

la vil - la - nel - la, Bel - la bim - ba sa ben bal - lar! Ma
la vil - la - nel - la, A - gi - le e snel - la sa ben bal - lar! Ma
danc - es so gai - ly, Bel - la bim - ba whirl - ing a - round!
danc - es so gai - ly, Dressed in a pret - ty gown, whirl - ing a - round!

72. Du, du liegst mir im Herzen

German Folk Song
Arranged by Mary Val Marsh

In Waltz rhythm

Du, du liegst mir im Her - zen, Du,
du liegst mir im Sinn, Du, du machst mir viel
Schmer - zen, Weisst nicht, wie gut ich dir bin;

249

74. Jesu, Joy of Man's Desiring

Melody by Johann Schop
Arranged by Johann Sebastian Bach

Je - su, joy of man's de - sir - ing,
Drawn by Thee, our soul's as - pir - ing,

Ho - ly wis - dom, love most bright,
Soar to un - cre - a - ted light.

75. My Heart Ever Faithful

Lively

Johann Sebastian Bach

Introduction not accounted for in pupil's book.

My heart ___ ev-er faith - ful, Sing prais - es, be joy - ful, Sing

prais - es, be joy - ful, ___ Our Fa - ther is here. My heart ___ ev-er faith - ful, Sing

prais - es, be joy - ful, Sing prais - es, be joy - ful,— Our Fa - ther is here.

(original Key: D-flat major)

78. The Trout

Music by Franz Schubert
English Words by Elizabeth Fiske

Allegretto

Introduction accounted for in pupil's book.

1. An a - gile trout shot glanc - ing A - cross the crys-tal__ stream; His
   fish - er - man came strid - ing, And cast a line near - by; He

an - tics were en - tranc - ing, I watched him__ in a dream. So
saw the small trout glid - ing, And cold joy— lit his eye. "Stay

nim - ble and__ so__ charm - ing This small fish was__ at__ play; Who
still with - out - a__ quiv - er, My trout, be - neath your stone; Make

The man is set on slaugh - ter; he knows a trick, And fast he churns up mud - dy wa - - ter, And makes a luck-y cast. The fish, de-ceived, was

257

81. My Homeland

German Folk Melody
Arranged by Johannes Brahms
English Words by Franz Wilhelm

With gentle motion

1. In my home - land   I   long   to be,   Friends   there a - wait   me.} O my
2. Though in dis - tance   I'm   far   a - way,   I'll   re - turn   some   day.}

home - land, my home - land, My home - land so fair!

(This interlude is not accounted for in the Pupil's Book.)

86. Evening Prayer

90. The Herdsman

German-Swiss Folk Song
Arranged by Kurt Miller

Introduction not accounted for in pupil's book.

1. Hol - la, Hol - li, sings all day
2. Hol - la, Hol - li, climb moun - tains

(Melody)

1. The herds - man is mer - ry, he sings all day
2. The cows keep Hans bus - y as they climb moun - tains

(Zither effect)

92. Le premier mois d'l'année

Traditional French Folk Song

1. Le pre-mier mois d'l'an-née, que donn' rai-j' à ma mi - e? Le pre-mier mois d'l'an-

née, que donn' rai-j' à ma mi - e? Un - e per-dri - o - le qui

va, qui vient, qui vo - le. Un - e per-dri - o - le qui vo - le dans le bois. ___

2. Le deux - ième mois d'l'an - née, que donn' rai-j' à ma mi - e? Le

deux - ième mois d'l'an - née, que donn' rai-j' à ma mi - e?

Deux tour - te - rel - les, Un - e per - dri - o - le qui va, qui vient, qui

vo - le. Un - e per - dri - o - le qui vo - le dans le bois.

96. Czech Riding Song

Czechoslovakian Folk Song
Words by Martha C. Ramsey

With spirit

1. Came a-rid - ing on a day,
2. Oft he asked in man - ner bold,
3. Now my heart I'd give to you,

Zum - ta-dy - ja - dy - ja;

A
Could

suit - or jaun - ty, bold and gay,
How could I my heart with-hold?
I be sure your own were true,

Zum - ta-dy - ja - dy - ja, *Hey!*

106. In Summer the Sunshine Is Brightest

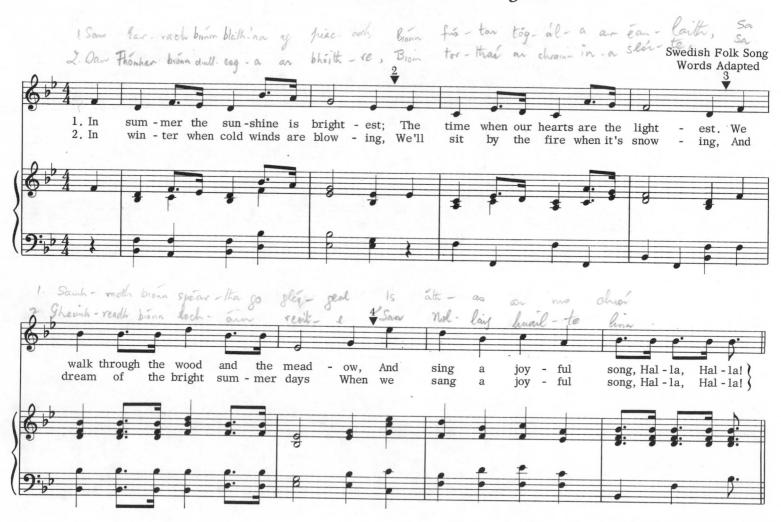

Swedish Folk Song
Words Adapted

1. In sum-mer the sun-shine is bright-est; The time when our hearts are the light - est. We
2. In win-ter when cold winds are blow - ing, We'll sit by the fire when it's snow - ing, And

walk through the wood and the mead - ow, And sing a joy - ful song, Hal - la, Hal - la!
dream of the bright sum - mer days When we sang a joy - ful song, Hal - la, Hal - la!

O come a - long and join our song; The day is bright, our hearts are light. When win - ter's

done and fun's be - gun, Our life is gay, you'll hear us say, "In sum - mer the sun - shine is

bright - est, So sing a joy - ful song, Hal - la, Hal - la!

109. I Came Home Late One Evening

Norwegian Folk Melody
Words Adapted

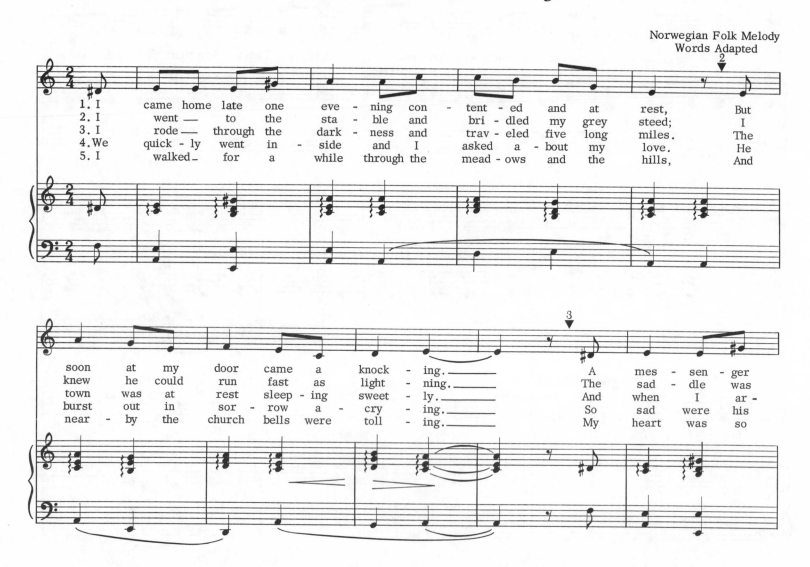

1. I came home late one eve - ning con - tent - ed and at rest, But
2. I went — to the sta - ble and bri - dled my grey steed; I
3. I rode — through the dark - ness and trav - eled five long miles. The
4. We quick - ly went in - side and I asked a - bout my love. He
5. I walked — for a while through the mead - ows and the hills, And

soon at my door came a knock - ing. A mes - sen - ger
knew he could run fast as light - ning. The sad - dle was
town was at rest sleep - ing sweet - ly. And when I ar -
burst out in sor - row a - cry - ing. So sad were his
near - by the church bells were toll - ing. My heart was so

stood, and he said, "Go to your love,
sil - ver, the reins were made of gold,
rived at the house of my love,
words, that I thought my heart would break
sad, that I could not bear to stay;

Ride quick - ly now to her
And in the pale moon they shone
Her broth - er was wait - ing to
to hear that my loved one was
I knew far a - way I'd be

dwell - ing."
bright - ly.
meet - me.
dy - ing.
go - ing.

O my love, my on - ly love, my dear one.

117. Far in the Mountains

Finnish Folk Song
Words Adapted

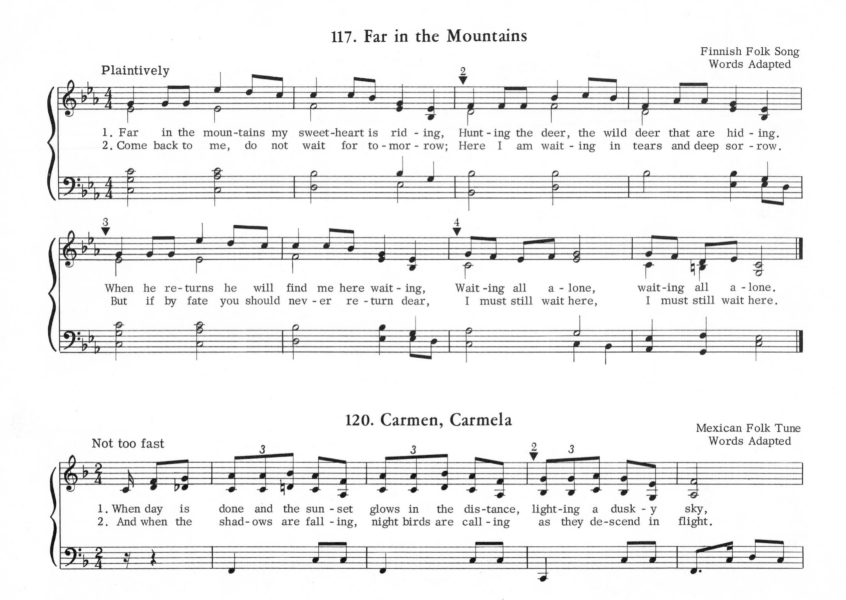

1. Far in the moun-tains my sweet-heart is rid - ing, Hunt-ing the deer, the wild deer that are hid - ing.
2. Come back to me, do not wait for to-mor - row; Here I am wait-ing in tears and deep sor - row.

When he re-turns he will find me here wait - ing, Wait-ing all a - lone, wait-ing all a - lone.
But if by fate you should nev - er re - turn dear, I must still wait here, I must still wait here.

120. Carmen, Carmela

Mexican Folk Tune
Words Adapted

1. When day is done and the sun - set glows in the dis-tance, light-ing a dusk - y sky,
2. And when the shad-ows are fall - ing, night birds are call - ing as they de-scend in flight.

272

I wan-der back to the val-ley where my Car-me-la waits for my joy-ful cry.
The stars are glim-mer-ing bright-ly, clouds drift-ing light-ly, soft-ly we say "good night."

Car-men, Car-me-la, my gold-en sun-beam, You ban-ish sor-row

with one sweet smile. May all good for-tune a-wait your

plea-sure, My gold-en trea-sure, Car-me-la, mine.

121. La Vidalita

South American Cowboy Song
Arranged by Kurt Miller
Words Adapted by Kurt Miller

1. Ev - ery day I ride, cross - ing prai - ries wide,
2. Night with star - ry light, at the camp - fire bright,

Ah,_____ La,

1. Ev - ery day I ride, cross - ing prai - ries wide,
2. Night with star - ry light, at the camp - fire bright,

La Vi - da - li - ta,

(Melody)

La Vi - da - li - ta.

(1.) Cat - tle mill - ing 'round, dust clouds hide the ground,
(2.) Noth - ing stirs the air, peace is ev - ery - where,

sí!

(1.) Cat - tle mill - ing 'round, dust clouds hide the ground,
(2.) Noth - ing stirs the air, peace is ev - ery - where,

Ah, _____ La, La Vi - da - li - ta. La Vi - da - li - ta.

La Vi - da - li - ta, sí! sí!

122. Me gustan todas

Spanish-South American Folk Song
Words Adapted

Me gus - tan to - das, me gus - tan to - das, me gus - tan to - das en ge - ne - ral. Pero e - sa ru - bia, pero e - sa ru - bia, pero e - sa ru - bia me gus - ta más.

No - so -tros an -da -mos siem -pre, y den - tro la luz del sol, sus

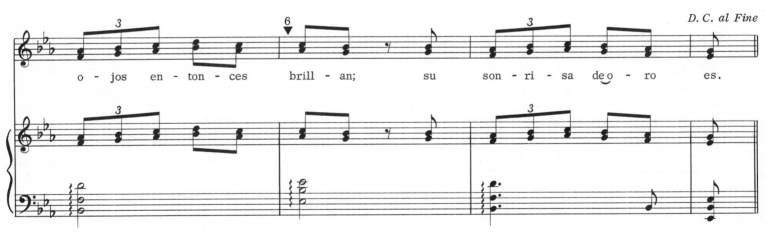

D. C. al Fine

o - jos en -ton -ces brill -an; su son -ri -sa de o - ro es.

124. Río, Río

Chilean Folk Song
Words Adapted

1. O fast flow-ing rí - o, rí - o, ___ Swirl-ing on to the sea; ___ O fast flow-ing rí - o,
2. O fast flow-ing rí - o, rí - o, ___ Swirl-ing on to the sea; ___ O fast flow-ing rí - o,

rí - o, ___ Swirl-ing on to the sea; ___ In the black-ness of your chan-nel, ___ In the
rí - o, ___ Swirl-ing on to the sea; ___ Tears of sor-row in your wa-ters, Joy-ous

white - ness _ of your foam, _____ O what se - crets, what ad - ven - tures, If your sto - ry _ we could know.
whis - pers _ deep be - low, _____

Refrain

Rí - o, rí - o, _ rí - o, rí - o, _ with your tales you _ o - ver - flow. _____ O what

se - crets, _ what ad - ven - tures, _ If your sto - ry _ we could know. _____

128. Water Come A Me Eye

Jamaican Folk Song
Words Adapted

Moderately slow

1. Ev - ery time I think of Li - za   Wa-ter come a me eye.
2. Don't know why you went a - way, __   Wa-ter come a me eye.
3. Time go slow when love is past, __   Wa-ter come a me eye.
4. Lis - ten 'cause I'm call - in' you, __   Wa-ter come a me eye.

Ev - ery time I think of Li - za   Wa-ter come_ a me eye.
When you com - in' home to stay?__   Wa-ter come_ a me eye.
When you come back, time go fast, __   Wa-ter come_ a me eye.
And my heart is call - in' too, __   Wa-ter come_ a me eye.

Refrain

Come back, Li - za, come back, girl, Wa - ter come_ a me eye.

5

Come back, Li - za, come back girl, Wa - ter come_ a me eye.

130. Hosanna

Jamaican Folk Song

Moderately fast

1. Ho - san-na, me build a house, oh,_ Ho - san-na, me build a house, oh,_ Ho - san-na, me build a
2. Ho - san-na, me build a house, oh,_ Ho - san-na, me build a house, oh,_ Ho - san-na, me build a

house, oh,_ I built it on the sand - y ground. Me house built on a sand - y ground,
house, oh,_ I built it on the sol - id ground. Me house built on a sol - id ground,

It will fall you see. Me house built with the sand all 'round, It will fall you see.
It will stand you see. Me house built on a sol - id ground, It will stand you see.

283

134. Los gallos cantan

Castilian Popular Song
Words Adapted

Los ga-llos can-tan al dí-a que di-rá us-ted._____ Los ___ A-
The roost-ers sing ev-ery morn-ing; I hear them call._____ The ___ Their

nun-cian-do el nue-vo dí-a a-sí ha de ser._____ A- ___ No te duer-mas, vi-da
song be-gins a new day, And so you must wake._____ Their ___ Don't you sleep now, O my

mí-a, no te duer-mas mi a-do-ra-da que vie-ne lle-na de vi-da la ma-dru-
true love, Don't you sleep now; it is morn-ing._ The sun-light greets you, my love, each dawn of the

ga - da_____ que vie-ne lle-na de vi-da la ma-dru-ga - da.
new _____ day. _ The sun-light greets you, my love, each dawn of the new _____ day.

144. The Purple Bamboo

Chinese Folk Song

1. See I bring to you pur-ple bam-boo shoot, Now 'twill make a love-ly flute;
2. You must try and grow like the bam-boo tall, Then those part-ing lips so small

But those lips so small Can-not play at all On a love-ly gold-en flute.
Soon will play the flute Made from bam-boo shoot; Sil-v'ry tunes will gent-ly fall.

Refrain
Ee -tee - tee, Soon will come the hap-py day. day. My son the flute will play.

147. Dune of Tosa

Japanese Folk Song

Introduction not accounted for in pupil's book.

To - sa no Su - na - ya - ma na a -

a ya - e Ko - me na - ra yo -

sfz

sfz

148. Si Pilemon

Philippine Folk Song
Words Adapted

O Pi - le - mon, _____ catch-ing fish was his __ tar - get. _____

O Pi - le - mon, O Pi - le - mon, _____ catch-ing fish was his __ tar - get. _____

(Melody)

__ He caught a fish _____ that he sold, O Pi - le - mon, _____

__ He caught a ti - ny lit - tle fish _____ that he sold at the mar - ket, _____

But not much mon — ey _____ for the fish was too small. _____

But not much mon-ey did they pay, _____ for the fish was too small. _____

What they gave him was a pen — ny, noth — ing ____ at all. _____

What they gave him was a pen-ny; That day he had not an - y good things to eat at all. _____

150. Mystic Lights

Philippine Folk Song
Words by Beth Landis

Here be-neath the sky I stand en - chant - ed; _____ Gar - den high a-

bove with stars im - plant - ed, _____ Mys - tic lights, how fair you

are! _____ Splen - dor shin - ing from a - far,

Mir - ror in the sky, the earth pro- tect - ing,_____ Beau- ty and friends who

dwell here with me re - flect - ing,_____ Ra - diant jew - els in the

heav'n a - bove, You are the eyes of life and love!_____

154. Suliram

Indonesian Folk Song

Su - li - ram, su - li - ram, ram, ram, Su - li - ram

yang __ ma - nis, ____ A - du - hai in - dung __ se o - rang, __

Bi - djak la sa - na di pan - dang ma - nis. La su - li - nis.

1.

2. *Fine*

155. Arirang

Korean Folk Song
Words Adapted

1. A - ri - rang,_ A - ri - rang,_ A - ri - rang,_ A - ri - rang,_ A - ri - rang,_
2. A - ri - rang,_ A - ri - rang,_ A - ri - rang,_ A - ri - rang,_ A - ri - rang,_

A - ri - rang,_ A - ri - rang fair. Through the pass_ I
A - ri - rang,_ A - ri - rang fair. Here I wait for you,

watch you _ go _ there._ A - ri - rang,_ A - ri - rang,_ A - ri - rang fair.
wait, wait_ and_ stare._ A - ri - rang,_ A - ri - rang,_ A - ri - rang fair.

164. Beautiful Dreamer

Words and Music by
Stephen Foster

Introduction not accounted for in pupil's book.

1. Beau-ti-ful dream — er,   wake un-to me,
2. Beau-ti-ful dream — er,   out on the sea

Star-light and dew-drops are wait-ing for
Mer-maids are chant-ing   the wild lo-re-

thee; _____
lei; _____

Sounds of the rude world heard in the day,
O - ver the stream - let va - pors are borne,

Lulled by the moon-light have all passed a - way. _____
Wait- ing to fade at the bright com-ing morn. _____

Beau-ti - ful dream - er,
Beau-ti - ful dream - er,

queen of my song,
beam on my heart,

List while I woo thee with soft mel - o - dy;
E'en as the morn on the stream-let and sea;

Gone are the cares   of   life's bus-y throng,⎫
Then will all clouds   of   sor-row de-part, ⎬

Beau-ti-ful dream-er, a-wake un-to

me! _____   Beau-ti-ful dream-er, a-wake un-to   me!

(This instrumental passage is not accounted for in the Pupil's Book.)

297

167. Shalom Alëḥem

Jewish Folk Song

Hë-vë-nu sha - lom a-lë-ḥem, Hë-vë-nu sha - lom a-lë-ḥem, Hë-vë-nu

sha - lom a-lë-ḥem, Hë-vë-nu sha - lom, sha - lom, sha-lom a - lë-ḥem.

168. Ev'ry Night When the Sun Goes In

Southern Folk Song
Arranged by William S. Haynie

Ev - 'ry night when the sun goes in,
Love, don't weep nor— mourn for me,

night _____ when the sun goes in, _____ I hang down my
weep _____ nor— mourn for me, _____ I'm go - ing a -

Hang my head and mourn - ful cry.
Goin' a - way to Mar - ble - town.

head _____ and mourn - ful cry. _____ 2. True love, don't
way _____ to Mar - ble - town. _____

300

170. Cindy

Southern Banjo Tune
Arranged by Kurt Miller
Traditional Words

(Girls) I went to see my, went to see my pret-ty Cin-dy gal, I

(Boys) I went to see my, went to see my pret-ty Cin-dy gal, oh, yes, I

have no nick-el; have no dime; I have no

wish I had a nick-el, I wish I had a dime, I wish I had a

girl to love me all the time. Get a-long home._____ Get a-long

pret - ty girl to love me all the time. Please won't you go now, Cin - dy, get on home?

home._____ Get a-long home._____ I'll mar-ry you some - day.

Go now, Cin - dy, get on home! Go now, Cin - dy, get on home, I'll mar-ry you some - day.

Home, _____ I'll mar-ry you some-day. _____ I'll

Cin - dy; Get a - long home, Cin - dy, Cin - dy, I'll mar-ry you some-day. _____ I'll

mar-ry you, I'll mar-ry you, I'll mar-ry you some-day, _____ Cin-dy?

mar-ry you, I'll mar-ry you, I'll mar-ry you some-day, now won't you go a-way, Cin-dy?

176. Green Grow the Laurels

American Folk Song

1. oo _____
2. Green _____ grow the lau - rels Wet with dew, _____
oo _____

(Melody)

1. I once had a sweet-heart but now I have none. He's gone and left me; I live all a - lone. I
2. Oh, green grow the lau - rels all wet with the dew, Sad from the time that I part - ed from you. The

oo _____ you'll prove true, _____ Change to red, white, and blue.
Hope

live all a - lone and con - tent - ed I'll be, For he loves an - oth - er one bet - ter than me.
next time I see you I hope you'll prove true, And change the green lau - rels to red, white, and blue.

180. Thumbelina

Words and Music by
Frank Loesser
Arranged by William Stickles

1. Though you're no big-ger than my thumb,_____ than my thumb,_____ than my thumb,_____ Sweet
you're no big-ger than my toe,_____ than my toe,_____ than my toe,_____ Sweet

Thum - be - li - na, don't be glum._____ Now, now, now! Ah, ah, ah! Come, come, come!
Thum - be - li - na, keep that glow,_____ And you'll grow, and you'll grow, and you'll grow!

When your heart is full of love, you're nine feet tall, you're nine feet tall. _____ 2. Though

nine feet tall, you're nine feet tall. _____

308

182. The Inch Worm

Words and Music by
Frank Loesser

Two and two are four, four and four are eight; That's all you have on your busi - ness - like mind. Two and two are four,

four and four are eight; How can you be so blind? _____

Refrain

Two and two are four, Four and four are eight, Eight and eight are six - teen,

Inch - worm, inch - worm, mea - sur - ing the mar - i - golds, You and your a - rith - me - tic, you'll

184. Wonderful Copenhagen

Words and Music by
Frank Loesser
Arranged by William Stickles

Won - der - ful, won - der - ful Co - pen - ha - gen, friend - ly old

girl of a town, _____

With her har - bor light, that she wears at night,

Like a gold - en, gold - en crown._____ Oh, won - der-ful, won - der-ful

Co - pen - ha - gen, salt - y old queen of the sea,_____ Once I

sailed a - way, but I'm home to - day, Sing - ing Co - pen - ha - gen.

won - der-ful, won - der-ful Co - pen - ha - gen for me._____

191. Thanksgiving Hymn

Netherlands Folk Song
Arranged by Edward Kremser
Words Translated by Theodore Baker

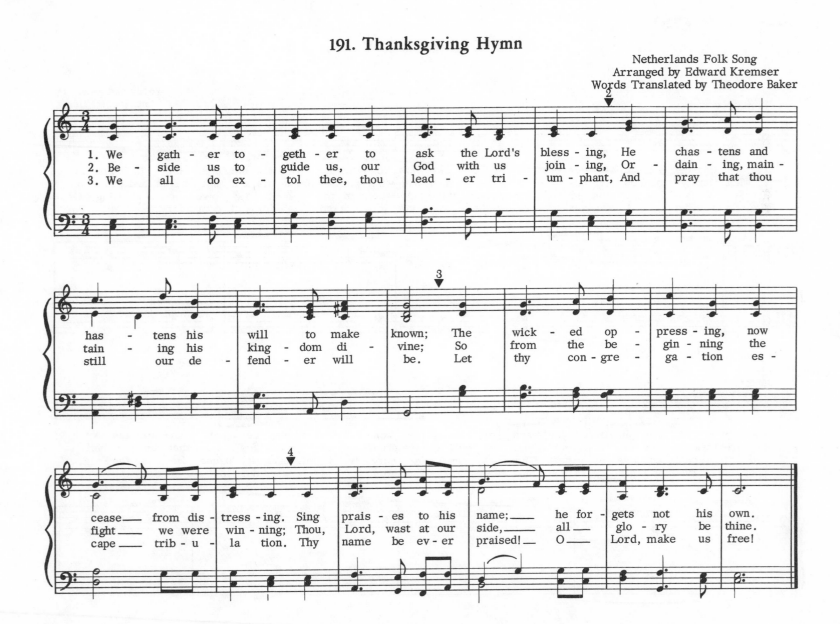

1. We gath - er to - geth - er to ask the Lord's bless - ing, He chas - tens and hastens his will to make known; The wick - ed op - press - ing, now cease from dis - tress - ing. Sing prais - es to his name; he for - gets not his own.

2. Be - side us to guide us, our God with us join - ing, Or - dain - ing, main - tain - ing his king - dom di - vine; So from the be - gin - ning the fight we were win - ning; Thou, Lord, wast at our side, all glo - ry be thine.

3. We all do ex - tol thee, thou lead - er tri - um - phant, And pray that thou still our de - fend - er will be. Let thy con - gre - ga - tion es - cape trib - u - la - tion. Thy name be ev - er praised! O Lord, make us free!

194. I Wonder as I Wander

Words and Music by
John Jacob Niles

Tenderly

1. I won-der as I wan-der out un-der the sky How Je - sus our Sav - ior did come for to die For
2. When Mar- y birthed Je -sus 'twas in a cow's stall, With wise men and farm- ers and shep-herds and all, But
3. If Je - sus had want-ed for an- y wee thing, A star in the sky or a bird on the wing, Or
4. I won-der as I wan-der out un-der the sky How Je - sus our Sav - ior did come for to die For

poor on' - ry peo-ple like you and like I. I won - der as I wan-der out un-der the sky.
high from God's heav - en a star's light did fall, And the prom-ise of a - ges it then did re-call.
all of God's an-gels in heav - en to sing, He sure-ly could have it, 'cause He was the King.
poor on' - ry peo-ple like you and like I. I won - der as I wan-der out un-der the sky.

316

195. Infant Jesus, King of Glory

Polish Carol
Words Adapted

Gently

1. In - fant Je - sus, King of glo - ry, Sleep-ing in a cat - tle stall. Moth - er
2. In - fant Je - sus, King of glo - ry, We pro - claim thy ho - ly birth. We have

Mar - y there be - side thee, Watch-ing o'er the king of all. Shep-herds
come to tell the sto - ry Of glad tid - ings, peace on earth. Come and

heard the an-gels sing — ing, Sing-ing car — ols bright and gay;—⎫ Christ the
join in hap — py sing — ing, Has-ten now with — out de — lay;—⎭

Lord is born to - day, Christ the Lord is born to-day.

softer

softer

196. The First Noel

Traditional English Carol

1. The first No - el, the an - gel did say, Was to cer - tain poor
2. They look - ed up and saw a star Shin-ing in the

shep -herds in fields as they lay; In fields where they lay
east, be - yond them far, And to the the earth it

keep - ing their sheep, On a cold win - ter's night— that was — so deep.
gave— great light, And— so it con - tin - ued both day — and night.

5 Refrain

No - el,— No - el, No - el,— No - el, — Born is the King— of Is - ra - el.

(Melody)

No - el,— No - el, No - el, No - el, Born is the King— of Is - ra - el.

200. Il est né

French Carol

Il est né, le di - vin en - fant! Jou - ez, haut-bois, ré - son - nez, mu - set - tes!

Il est né, le di - vin en - fant! Chan - tons tous son a - vè - ne - ment!

De - puis plus de qua - tre mille ans, Nous le pro - met-taient les pro - phè - tes,

De - puis plus de qua - tre mille ans, Nous at - ten - dions cet heu - reux temps.

202. Pat-A-Pan

French Carol
Arranged by Kurt Miller
Words Adapted by Kurt Miller

Introduction accounted for in pupil's book.

Pat-a-pat-a-pan, _____ Tu-re-lu-re-ley, _____

— Fife and drum to-geth-er play on this joy-ous hol-i-day.

323

ley;

play;   Fife and   drum to - geth - er   play on this joy - ous   hol — i — day.

Pat - a - pat - a - pan. _____

324

204. Haleluyoh

Jewish Folk Song

Ha - le - lu - yoh, ha - le - lu - yoh, Ha - le - lu av - dey A - do - noi, _____ Ha - le - lu - yoh,

ha - le - lu - yoh, Ha - le - lu es shem A - do - noi. _____ Ha - le - lu - yoh, ___ ha - le - lu - yoh,

Ha - le - lu - yoh, ha - le - lu - yoh, ___ Ha - le - lu - yoh, ___ ha - le - lu - yoh, Ha - le - lu - yoh, ha - le - lu - yoh.

207. Music in the Air

Words and Music by
George Root

There's mu - sic in the air, ___ When the in - fant morn is nigh. And faint its blush is

seen ___ On the bright and laugh - ing sky. Man - y a harp's ec - stat - ic sound Thrills us with a

joy pro - found, While we list en - chant - ed there To the mu - sic in the air.

326

208. The American Hymn

Words and Music by
Matthias Keller

1. Speed our Re - pub -lic, O Fa - ther on high, Lead us in path - ways of
2. Rise up, proud ea - gle, rise up to the clouds, Spread thy broad wing o'er this

jus - tice and right. Rul - ers as well as the ruled, one and all,
fair west - ern world! Fling from thy beak our dear ban - ner of old,

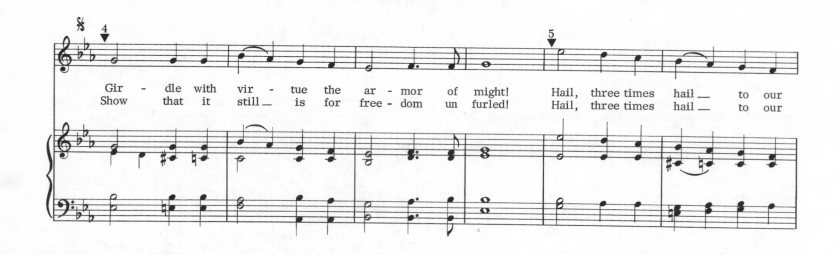

Gir - dle with vir - tue the ar - mor of might! Hail, three times hail __ to our
Show that it still __ is for free - dom un furled! Hail, three times hail __ to our

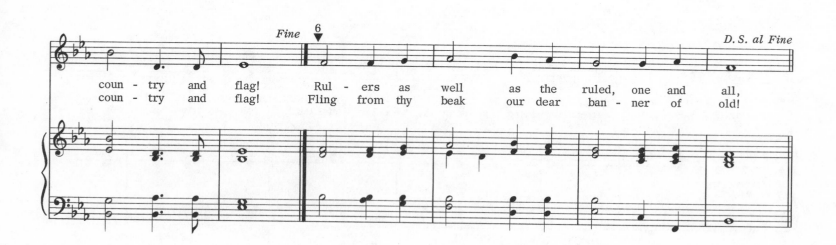

coun - try and flag! Rul - ers as well as the ruled, one and all,
coun - try and flag! Fling from thy beak our dear ban - ner of old!

Fine

D. S. al Fine

328

GLOSSARY OF MUSICAL TERMS USED IN THIS BOOK

A Cappella   Choral singing without instrumental accompaniment.

Accidentals   Chromatic alterations of single tones within a measure.

Aria   An elaborate solo song, with instrumental accompaniment, in cantatas, oratorios, and operas.

Arpeggio   A term referring to the notes of a chord sounded one after another rather than simultaneously.

Ballad   A narrative song in which all the verses are sung to the same melody.

Cantata   A composite vocal form consisting of recitatives, arias, and choruses based on a narrative text.

Chant   (1) A repetitive pattern sung as a vocal accompaniment below the main melody. (2) See Plainsong.

Chorale   Hymn tunes of the German Protestant Church, first introduced by Martin Luther during the Reformation.

Climax   The point within a musical line or composition, which serves as the highest point of intensity.

Consonance   A term used to describe a combination of tones, within a specific sequence of tones, which results in an effect of repose.

Contrary motion   The movement of two voice parts in opposite directions.

Counterpoint   A weaving together of two or more melodies to form a musical texture which is significant both horizontally and vertically.

Descant   A countermelody usually played or sung above the main melody of a song.

Dissonance   In contrast to consonance, a term used to describe a combination of tones that create a feeling of tension and demand to be resolved.

Drone bass   A tone, or tones, usually in the lower voice, which are sustained against changing harmonies in the upper voices.

Dynamics   The expressive markings used to indicate the degree of force or intensity of sound. The most common are *pianissimo (pp):* very soft; *piano (p):* soft; *mezzo piano (mp):* moderately soft; *mezzo forte (mf):* moderately loud; *forte (f):* loud; *fortissimo (ff):* very loud; *crescendo:* increase in loudness; *decrescendo* or *diminuendo:* decrease in loudness.

Fugue   A contrapuntal style of composition based on the development of a short melody, or theme, which is stated at the beginning by a single voice and imitated in each of the other voices in close succession.

Home tone   The first step of a scale on which a song or composition is based; the tone for which the scale is named.

Homophony   Music in which lower voices move with and harmonically support the main melody.

Imitation   The repetition by one voice of a theme previously set forth by another, as in a round or canon.

Interval   The distance in pitch between two tones.

Legato   A smooth, almost imperceptible connection between successive tones.

Madrigal   A polyphonic secular song of the sixteenth century usually employing from four to six voice parts performed by small groups.

Mode   A scalewise arrangement of the tones that may form the basic tonal material of a composition; specifically refers to the medieval church modes.

Modulation   The harmonic process of changing from one key to another during the course of a composition.

Motive   The shortest recognizable unit of notes of a musical theme or subject.

Opus   Work, composition.

Ornamentation   The embellishment of a main melody by the addition of decorative melodic figures such as trills, tremolos, appoggiaturas, etc.

Parallel motion   The consistent movement of two or more voice parts in the same direction, at the same interval from one another.

Passing tone   A nonharmonic tone that is sounded in passing from one chord to another.

Period   A term used to describe two phrases which together form a natural division of the melody.

Plainsong   Unaccompanied single-line melody which is modal, rhythmically free, and which uses a free prose rhythm.

Polyphony   Music in which two or more independent voice parts sound simultaneously, each maintaining its own distinctive melodic line.

Recitative   A vocal style in which the music is designed to imitate the rhythms and natural inflections of speech.

Sequence   Successive repetitions of a melodic (or harmonic) pattern at a higher or lower pitch.

Syncopation   A temporary displacement of the regular rhythmic pulse.

Tempo   Rate of speed. Terms used in this book are: *rallentando molto (rall. molto):* very slow; *poco ritardando (poco rit.):* gradually slower.

Tonality   Feeling for a key center.

Tone poem   An orchestral composition based on extra-musical ideas, poetic or descriptive.

Transposition   The writing or performing of a composition in a key other than the original.

CLASSIFIED INDEX OF MUSIC AND POETRY

American Folk Songs and Spirituals

Cindy, 170
Ev'ry Night When the Sun Goes In, 168
Go Tell It on the Mountain, 198
Green Grow the Laurels, 176
He's Got the Whole World in His Hands, 19
Hundred Years Ago, A, 17
Jacob's Ladder, 166
Johnny Has Gone for a Soldier, 3
Let Us Break Bread Together, 30
Streets of Laredo, 14
Talkin' Blues, 31

Christmas Carols from Other Grades (words only)

Deck the Halls, 200
Here We Come A-Wassailing, 200
Joy to the World, 199
O Come, All Ye Faithful, 199

Composed Songs

All Hail, Fridolin (J. Sibelius), 114
American Hymn, The (M. Keller), 208
Beautiful Dreamer (S. Foster), 164
Come, Follow Me (J. Hilton), 53
Evening Prayer (E. Humperdinck), 86
Farewell, Beloved Homeland (B. Bartok), 99
God of Our Fathers (G. Warren), 8
Home Road, The (J. A. Carpenter), 2
I Wonder as I Wander (J. J. Niles), 194
Inch Worm, The (F. Loesser), 182
Jesu, Joy of Man's Desiring (J. Schop—J. S. Bach), 74
Lullaby of the Sea (A. Frackenpohl), 159
Music in the Air (G. Root), 207
My Heart Ever Faithful (J. S. Bach), 75

My Homeland (J. Brahms), 81
My Little Bird, Where Do You Fly? (C. Nielsen), 112
New Year Carol, A (B. Britten), 56
Night Piece, The (A. Frackenpohl), 158
Now Is the Month of Maying (T. Morley), 50
Old Abram Brown (B. Britten), 55
Peace of the River (V. Wood), 6
Play on Notes (M. Babbitt), 188
Roll On, Columbia (W. Guthrie), 4
Tallis' Canon (T. Tallis), 47
These Things Shall Be (T. Williams), 15
Thumbelina (F. Loesser), 180
Trout, The (F. Schubert), 78
When V and I Together Meet (H. Purcell), 54
Wonderful Copenhagen (F. Loesser), 184
You're a Grand Old Flag (G. M. Cohan), 10

Dances and Singing Games

Blacksmith's Dance, 84
Calypso Game, 132
Greensleeves, 46
Kalvelis, 24
Merry Minstrels, 52
Tanko Bushi, 152
Totur, 116

Folk Songs from Other Countries

AUSTRIA
Glockenjodler (German), 91

BRAZIL
In Bahía, 126

CHILE
Río, Río, 124

CHINA
Purple Bamboo, The, 144

CZECHOSLOVAKIA
Czech Riding Song, 96

ENGLAND
Christmas Is Coming, 197
Greensleeves, 46
Merry Minstrels, 52

FINLAND
Far in the Mountains, 117

FRANCE
Il est né (French), 200
Pat-A-Pan, 202
Plowing Song, 94
Premier mois d'l'année, Le (French and English), 92

GERMANY
Du, du liegst mir im Herzen (German), 72
Lieb Nachtigall (German), 205
Spinn, spinn, meine liebe Tochter (German), 70

HUNGARY
Hungarian Round, 97

ICELAND
Icelandic Prayer, 108

INDONESIA
Suliram (Indonesian), 154

IRELAND
Cockles and Mussels, 38
Minstrel Boy, The, 36
Shule Aroon, 34

ISRAEL
Haleluyoh (Hebrew), 204
Shalom Alëhem (Hebrew), 167
Tum Balalyka, 22

ITALY
Buon giorno (Italian), 66
Ma bella bimba (Italian and English), 64

JAMAICA
Hosanna, 130

Water Come A Me Eye, 128

JAPAN
Dune of Tosa (Japanese), 147

KOREA
Arirang, 155

MEXICO
Carmen, Carmela (Spanish and English), 120

NETHERLANDS
Thanksgiving Hymn, 191

NIGERIA
Saturday Night, 27

NORWAY
I Came Home Late One Evening, 109

PHILIPPINES
Mystic Lights, 150
Si Pilemon, 148

POLAND
Infant Jesus, King of Glory, 195

SCOTLAND
Come O'er the Stream, Charlie, 43
Comin' Thro' the Rye, 42
Turn Ye to Me, 40

SPAIN
Gallos cantan, Los (Spanish and English), 134
Me gustan todas (Spanish), 122
Ríu, Ríu, Chíu, 206
Tarara, La (Spanish), 133

SWEDEN
In Summer the Sunshine Is Brightest, 106
Summer Magic, 107

SWITZERLAND
Herdsman, The, 90

UKRAINE
Peddler, The, 20

CLASSIFIED INDEX OF MUSICAL SKILLS

ALPHABETICAL INDEX OF MUSIC AND POETRY

ABCDEFGHIJ- ST -743210/6987